Praise for *A River Tril*

"W. D. Wetherell is a good fisherman, a better .... , able companion who has a deep feeling for the natural world in which his quarry swim."

—*Chicago Tribune*

"Wetherell writes about fishing with an angler's love for the sport and a novelist's eye for detail."

—John Gierach, author of *All Fisherman Are Liars*

"Wetherell defends the plain pleasures of his sport and the environmental purity to sustain it, as well as what he, a novelist, calls 'the wild upland province of words.' He moves naturally from the beauty of a Copper Run trout to Beauty itself . . . He has a naturalist's eye, glorying in the things mankind has not yet sullied, grieving for those we have."

—*New York Times*

"Wetherell has better than any writer I know caught the character of Eastern fly-fishing: the energetic personalities of its seasons, geographies, politics natural and unnatural, and inhabitants both civilized and wild. These books have been provided us courtesy of an artist unwilling to concede that there is a distinction to be made between what is said and the manner of its saying."

—John Engels, winner of the Pulitzer Prize for poetry

"*Vermont River* is one of those rare instances when fly-fishing writing overflows its banks and spreads freely into the fields of literature."

—John Merwin, founder of *Fly Rod & Reel* and author of *Stillwater Trout*

"These are bold little gleeful books by a writer I've admired for years that should endear themselves to everybody who likes streams and woods and country as well as simply to other fishermen, who will find them both astute and

—Edw
the Country of the Blind

"Immensely readable books by a young fisherman-writer equally obsessed by the twin pursuits of the elusive trout and the elusive word. I both love and envy them."

—Robert Traver, author of *Trout Magic*

"Wetherell understands the currents that flow through a fly-fisher's soul and he taps into them with rare wit and grace. One of the most talented voices to be heard in angling literature in a long while. I found myself wishing for at least one page more, or one chapter more, and one book more. So will you."

—Steve Raymond, author of *Trout Quintet*

"Delightful books that impart the soul of the river the angler, and the surrounding countryside."

—Ted Giddings, journalist

"This is my idea of what fishing books should be—and too seldom are. Like fly fishing itself, the books soothe the soul and answer more than a few questions all of us have asked of a day, a river, or a trout."

—Gene Hill, former columnist for *Field & Stream*

"Deeply felt yet resolutely unsentimental, consistently generous yet unflinching in its allegiances, Wetherell's is a voice of sanity and sense for our increasingly virtual age. Reading him is like coming home."

—Mark Slouka, author of *Nobody's Son* and recipient of a Guggenheim Fellowship

"Literary gems."

—Paul Marriner, author of *Atlantic Salmon: A Fly Fishing Primer*

"Wetherell is the ideal armchair companion—an elegant writer, a fastidious, observant angler, a charming streamside companion."

—J. Z. Grover, writer for *In-Fisherman*

A River Trilogy

A River Trilogy

A Fly-Fishing Life

W. D. WETHERELL

Skyhorse Publishing

Skyhorse Publishing books may be purchased in bulk at special discounts for sales promotion, corporate gifts, fund-raising, or educational purposes. Special editions can also be created to specifications. For details, contact the Special Sales Department, Skyhorse Publishing, 307 West 36th Street, 11th Floor, New York, NY 10018 or info@skyhorsepublishing.com.

Skyhorse® and Skyhorse Publishing® are registered trademarks of Skyhorse Publishing, Inc.®, a Delaware corporation.

Visit our website at www.skyhorsepublishing.com.

Vermont River originally published by Nick Lyons Books, 1984
Upland Stream originally published by Little, Brown & Company, 1991
One River More originally published by the Lyons Press, 1998

10 9 8 7 6 5 4 3 2 1

Library of Congress Cataloging-in-Publication Data is available on file.

Cover design by Tom Lau
Cover painting credit: *The Rapids, Hudson River, Adirondacks* (1894) by Winslow Homer

Print ISBN: 978-1-5107-2824-0
Ebook ISBN: 978-1-5107-2825-7

Printed in the United States of America

For Celeste, Erin, and Matthew

Contents

A Word at the Start

My books on fly fishing—"Celebrations," I like to call them—are now back in print, published together in one volume as I'd always intended. Thirty years have gone by since the first of the trio, *Vermont River*, came out, so I'd like to briefly explain how I came to write of rivers and fishing, then go on to talk about how the books have fared over the years, and how I view things now.

In 1981, I published my first novel, *Souvenirs*. It fared as most first novels do, or at least first earnestly-imagined, ambitiously-written, philosophical/experimental ones do. Respectful reviews, friends and relatives being kind, a publisher unwilling to do any promotion, the buzz surrounding its publication lasting all of ten minutes—and then nothing but remainders.

Bruised, battered, but in no way ready to quit, I cast about for my next project. I had fallen in love with fly-fishing as a teenager, thanks to my parents buying a summer house on a bassy Connecticut lake. This led me to fly-fishing, and then—a passionate reader as a kid—to the literature fly-fishing boasts of, the "fishing in print." Don Quixote fell in love with chivalry by reading romances about it; I fell in love with trout fishing by reading romances (for that's what most fishing books are) about it—and for many years my passion, like Quixote's, went largely unrequited.

1

My twenties were a wretched decade—and at least part of the reason was that, stuck in New York, I hardly fished at all. It was only when I met Celeste and we moved to northern New England that I at last began to fish as much as I wanted to. My love (well, two loves; Celeste and I were married now) was at long last requited—and the miracle of this gave me lots to write about.

I told my agent—a sophisticated West Sider who thought Siberia began just north of 86th Street—that I was interested in writing a book about fly fishing. "Fine," she said, lifting her lovely aristocratic nose. "But I am no longer your agent."

"Fine," I said back to her. "But I am writing it anyway."

It's a fool's errand now, but back in 1983 it was just barely possible to have a book considered by a publisher by sending it "over the transom" without anyone at the house ever having heard of you. The odds were long—your manuscript, if read at all, was pulled from the aptly named "slush pile"—but no worse than buying a lottery ticket, and all it cost you was postage.

I wrote a first chapter, sent it to Nick Lyons Books in New York, and why I picked them was because I knew Nick's name. I'd been a fan of his writing for a long time—he was one of those fly-fishing essayists I found in my teens. His *Fishing Widows* became one of my favorite books; here was a writer who, like me, was stuck in cement most of the time, but, on his treasured moments stolen on a trout stream, came alive both as a writer and as a man. His writing was (and is) witty, learned, lyrical, sensitive, street-smart and river-smart; he had a column on the back page of *Fly Fisherman* magazine, and, like thousands of flyfishers across the country, I read each one eagerly as it came out.

(How good is Nick's writing? Our summer house was broken into one winter, though the only things stolen was a Heddon fly rod I loved and my treasured copy of *Fishing Widows*. A thief of unusual discrimination!)

I wrote that first chapter, scratched my head for a title, came up with *Vermont River* (important, not to have an "s" on the end), typed it across the top of the page, and sent it to Nick in New York, with a letter briefly explaining who I was and what I was up to.

I can't remember if it came via a phone call or letter, but after a month went by I was surprised and pleased to find Nick loved it. "Make it brilliant!" he wrote across the bottom of the contract, and, armed with his enthusiasm, I did my best to comply.

Nick remained my editor for the next two Celebrations: *Upland Stream* and *One River More*. Anyone who follows fly fishing won't be surprised at this, Nick having godfathered into print more fishing literature than any editor before him, and, almost certainly, any editor that will come after. The secret of his success, from a writer's point of view, is simple: he does something no other editor seems to have time for now. He appreciates you. He's on your side. He cheers you on. "You're really writing well," he'll say—and while this doesn't sound particularly profound, only a writer used to the neglect that comes with publishing with the big boys will understand how important these rarely-uttered, morale-boosting words can be.

Vermont River was my homage to the fishing writers I loved as a boy. And Thoreau—I can't forget Thoreau, even though he was a perch and pickerel fisherman, not a fly fisher. Reading him at fourteen literally changed my life. If I could blend lyricism with preciseness, include some humor, find words that once in a miraculous while mirrored the beauty of what I was describing, then at least an infinitesimal increment in the debt I owed him would finally be paid.

The reaction when the book was published? It was the same as when I went on to publish *Upland Stream* and *One River More*, or even now when one of my essays appears. Readers who know me only through novels are surprised to learn I write about fishing; readers who know me only through fishing are surprised to learn I write novels.

To me, it's not the serious-unserious division some think. If you write contemporary fiction you have to deal with many hard and tragic things, and it's a relief to turn to writing of happier matters—a joy to write lyrically, wearing your heart on your sleeve.

And while fly fishing may not be one of the world's most important subjects, it is one of the most important nonimportant subjects, so when I write of rivers I never feel like I'm slumming.

You have to hide much of your meaning when writing fiction; it's part of the art to let the reader discover this on their own. Writing essays can be relaxing, even liberating in comparison—you have permission to flat out say what's on your mind. But not too relaxing—it's the first rule I made myself. If I was going to write nonfiction, not only about fly fishing but about travel and opera and soccer and family life and any other subject that caught my interest, I wasn't going to condescend to it, but give it the same attention and respect I gave my fiction.

There were several of us making the same discovery at about the same time, the mid 1980s and 1990s. Baby Boomers who were crazy nuts about fly fishing, and realized that a fishing essay could be about a lot more than fly fishing. We'd pay attention to the form—there was usually at least one trout caught somewhere in our twenty pages—but we'd take it in bold new directions, widen its focus, so instead of just writing about trout streams, bourbon, and male bonding, those staples of earlier fishing writers, we'd talk about politics and ethics and love and lust and family and culture, and—though me, not so much—drugs, sex, and rock and roll. Fly-fishing literature's New Wave—though none of us knew each other or fished together or frequented the same bars, and it was never an organized movement.

Reviewers picked up on this. One, writing in the *New York Times*, opined that I was only pretending to make my essays be about fishing, when they were really about so much more. Yes, good point, Mr. Reviewer sir. But in response I'd offer this: My essays that aren't really about fishing contain an awful lot of fishing.

All three books brought me new friends. People called and asked me to go fishing. Readers sent me gifts in the mail: hand-tied flies, homemade fly boxes, poems they had written about their own favorite rivers, fresh-baked cookies. Two of my oldest friendships began that way, with people telling me how much they loved *Vermont River*, and this happy fringe benefit continued with *Upland Stream* and *One River More*.

I think an important reason for the books' success is this: they are books written by a young man. Not age-wise (I was up in my thirties when *Vermont River* appeared, fifty when *One River More* came out), but in spirit. This is particularly true with *Vermont River*, where there's an undercurrent of boyish glee running throughout. I was high when writing it—high from finally having at long last against all odds achieved the most ardently longed for of my dreams. I was living in the country, fishing as much as I wanted to, writing seven days a week . . . and, most miraculously of all, I was married to the woman I loved, this after a decade in which I thought, for reasons I could never make sense of, I was sentenced to a life of solitude.

For Celeste, the dedication read. Thirty-two years later they're still my favorite words in the book.

One of the most surprising reactions the book elicited was praise from men and women who didn't fish. "Dear Mr. Wetherell," their letters often began. "I've never read a book on fishing before let alone ever caught a fish, but something made me pick your book up and much to my amazement I read every word."

No response pleases me more. And my guess is that, if these readers don't fish, they have a similar passion. Gardening, hiking, birding, banjo playing, woodworking, cooking. They know what it's like to build your life around an avocation, and how, if you do, you can find a world of interest, solace, and delight in something that, to workaholics without interests, seems slightly loony. We speak the same language, so it's no wonder they respond. They know a passion when they see one.

And there are no fishing theories or innovations or discoveries cluttering up these pages. I sometimes wish there were—wish I had invented a new fly or a revolutionary casting technique—but the only thing I've ever contributed to the art of angling is a change in vocabulary.

"I've caught five fish," I used to say, when I got home from a trip. But then I realized caught hardly does the experience justice. What about the fish I saw rising and couldn't fool? The fish lost while playing them? The fish glimpsed in the shallows before I scared them away? The fish my friend caught and netted? The fish—and here comes my favorite new fishing word— encountered.

A simple enough change, and my friends, to keep me happy, all use the word now, finding it a much more accurate term when it comes to describing what kind of day it's been. I've have mornings on the water where I've caught five fish and been bored; I've had mornings on the water where I've caught nothing, but encountered dozens—and it's those days I remember with the most delight. Then, too, it's a change in terminology that helps the fish, taking the pressure off catching them and switching it to experiencing them. Missed that strike? Don't let it bother you, pardner. You encountered him, right?

So, if after reading this you're in the mood to do me a favor, switch the words yourself. Don't catch fish anymore; encounter them.

When authors reread books they've written in the past they find themes and passages they would emphasize and themes and passages they would de-emphasize, and this is a natural part of my reaction to having these back in print: wishing I had done certain things differently.

The last chapter of *Upland Stream* is called "Why Fish." I put Geography as the first reason—something of a surprise then, and something (though I still love to explore) I would now rank second or third. What should be number one is Water, or rather,

Watery Beauty, since this more than anything is the reason I fish.

I love everything connected with water . . . love to drink it, love to swim in it, love to skim pebbles across it, love to dip my toes in, love watching surf, love watching whitecaps, love baths, love showers, love the way watery surfaces reflect light or pull it in, with a thousand different variations I never get tired of witnessing. And while, like an art lover strolling through a gallery, I could indulge myself in much of this merely by sitting down near a river and staring, it wouldn't be the same.

Fishing—having a mission; asking the natural world specific questions; getting out in it under all kinds of circumstances; making it the background for a quest—serves as the entre into a world of astonishing beauty and richness, bringing it alive in a way no passive connoisseur could experience. Rivers are beautiful without my standing in the middle of one, but the only reason I ever stand in the middle of one is to cast to a rising fish.

(I loved, as a kid, the half-rhyme of Walter with water. "Cool clear Wal-ter," my friends would sing, and even now a letter will occasionally arrive with the "l" left out, so it's addressed to Water Wetherell.)

I'd list another reason just under it: Things Happen. I'm one of those novelists who leads a quiet, solitary life; I've learned over the years that this is what my work requires. There are days, particularly in winter, when I don't talk to another human being other than my wife, and, if she's working late, not even her; the only time I go outside is for short snowshoe hikes through our meadow or hit-and-run raids on the post office.

I make up for this in fishing season. Things happen when I fish that don't necessarily involve fish; I get at the world and the world gets at me.

I find an abandoned kayak in a river backwater, tow it to shore, wonder who's it is, find a hand-lettered "Missing" sign at our general store, call the number, have a delighted young boy thank me profusely—he was in serious hot water for letting that kayak get away . . . A woman scuba diver, working at pulling milfoil from the bottom of a Vermont lake, comes back to shore for her lunch break, walks right over to where I'm stringing up my rod, smiles beautifully, points to the back of her wetsuit. "Can you unzip me?" she asks . . . A hot air balloon, in silence, skims the water inches behind my canoe . . . Flowers, waterlogged roses dropped by mourners on a lake as a memorial where a young teacher was brutally murdered, touch the sides of my boat—touch me . . . An osprey strafes up a trout, struggles skyward with it, shifts it around in its talons; an eagle, gliding down from the pines, patiently follows it until it lets go . . . A Jewish fishing guide born in Casablanca, sharing lunch with me on the banks of a Quebec salmon river, confides in me his worries about his wife . . . A dam starts releasing water long before its scheduled to, sending down a wall of water that knocks me over, rolls me around, strips my rod away, almost drowns me.

Things happen.

There's a subject I would spend more time on if I was writing these books now: fishing ethics. I may have given myself a pass on this in the trilogy, reasoning that since I feel such goodwill toward fish then surely they will understand, bear me no ill will, if I hook them in the lip and tug them toward me; surely the reader will understand, too, that ethically speaking, I'm one of the good guys.

That's what I used to think. Now, I'm not so sure. Our relationship with animals has come under a lot of scrutiny in our new century, and this includes reassessing such "blood sports" as fishing. We flyfishers think that practicing catch-and-release absolves us from moral blame, but animal rights activists think catch-and-release is particularly cruel. Killing a fish for food they grudgingly accept; playing it just for fun they can't accept, and in some European countries releasing a trout back into the water is now against the law.

I could be flippant on this . . . Surely Mr. Trout, if asked, would prefer to be caught and released rather than eaten. . . but it's a serious enough argument that I wish I had the room here to go into it with the attention it deserves.

I would end up admitting a lot of what activists are telling us, but, in the end, defend fly fishing with all my power, at least if practiced ethically, by men and women who bring to the river great humility and respect. As another writer once pointed out, ninety seconds spent with a small hook in its lip, when compared to the countless hazards of a trout's life, is far from the worst challenge it will face.

Then, too, what is hard on an individual fish is good for the species. Trout, bass, stripers, and the other "game" fish. Their deciding to look beautiful and fight hard, in evolutionary terms, was a very shrewd move, since it's convinced man to do everything we can to protect their environment. Nowadays, an animal needs political clout in order to thrive—needs a fan club, a constituency, lobbyists. Those fish that don't have this . . . lowly squawfish, various suckers, tiny darters . . . lead a perilous life, environmentally speaking, and never having to worry about a Royal Wulff in their lip is probably scant consolation.

(If anything, trout have succeeded too well politically. Out in the Rockies, the native cutthroat, let alone those squawfish, is taking it on the chin because of fishery policies favoring invasive browns from Germany and rainbows from the Pacific, who, from the fly-fisher's point of view, are sexier and more desirable.)

If pressed, I would admit that I may well give fish pain when I play them on a fly rod; certainly, they have better things to do than be pulled toward my net. I treat them as gently as I can; I do everything in my power to insure they will be released unharmed (this means, among things, no photos); I work for their environment; I write about them, with, I hope, the kind of sensitivity they deserve.

Is this enough to redeem the potential cruelty? For me, it is enough. For others, it may not be. But the argument, in my own heart, is far from over, and I'll be puzzling over these things until the day I die.

But these moral qualms pale when compared to a much larger issue: climate change. If it's as bad as scientists think it will be—and already is—then it's not just trout that are threatened; the two of us will be fighting for space on whatever spaceship goes flying out to try another planet.

I'm puzzled when people question whether climate change is really happening, since the evidence here in northern New England is everywhere you look. It's happening all right, and at breathtaking speed. Some of the trout streams described in these books are now too warm to support trout. Mayfly hatches begin earlier every season and last longer into autumn. Smallmouth bass spawn ten days earlier than they did when we first moved here. Blackbirds return to our hedgerow earlier and earlier every spring. Our blueberries ripen on the Fourth of July now, not on Bastille Day like ten years ago. The flowers in our window boxes bloom to mid-November. Celeste—the acid proof!—swims in our local pond beginning in June, when in years past it was too cold for her until July; I swim outdoors until mid-October, and last year fifteen of us plunged in on Christmas morning.

Warming is real, and for any writer who celebrates the natural world, this means it's hard to look our subject matter in the eye without feeling tremendous guilt and shame I'm not immune to this; I'm happy I wrote these books while I still could. If I wrote them today, the tone would be darker.

I began fly fishing when I was fourteen; I'm now sixty-nine. Do the math and you'll see why this trilogy is subtitled "A Fly-Fishing Life."

And I still fish as ardently as ever, though not quite so hard. The young man in me—stubborn to let go—still shakes with excitement when I approach a new river or lake. God, I love fishing! And when I calm down enough to string my line through the guides, wade out to the first pool and start casting, I always pause just long enough to remember how lucky I am to have pursued this sport, this art, for so many years, played with so many trout, explored such beautiful water.

Do I ever feel guilty about this, that my fishing time could better have been spent doing what we're supposed to do in a capitalist system, making money? I do not feel guilty. If I'm ever tempted in that direction, then I think of all the other things I could have devoted this ardency to—selling high-risk mortgage bonds, making up fake news, writing advertisements, lying for a politician, cheating on Wall Street, wheeling and dealing on a golf course. No, I don't feel guilty at all.

And I've always liked that part of the sport, the anti-establishment aspect. Yes, fly-fishing has been trendy for a good thirty years now, the activity of choice for the young and well-heeled, but there are signs this is fading out now, and we lovers of quiet and solitude will reclaim our sport as an antidote to all the havoc the one-percenters have caused. And young men play video games now rather than enjoying the outdoors; we may well see a time in the near future when a flyfisher working a good stretch of river is an increasingly rare sight.

In the meantime, resist! If you spot flyfishers accoutered in $4,000 worth of gear, coached by a $500-a-day guide standing obsequiously at their elbow, sneak through the bushes and throw stones in their pool.

More and more of my fishing is for smallmouth bass. We have fair-to-middlin' trout fishing here, but an outstanding bass fishery, and going after them with bugs and poppers is an enormous amount of fun. No one fly fishes for them around here but me, and the bass boys in their high-powered boats tend to go elsewhere. After vowing to never write another book about fishing after *One River*

More, I went and wrote a book about this new passion, *Summer of the Bass*, motivated by a missionary zeal to rescue this wonderful fish, so typically American in all its virtues, from the tournament fishers, the hucksters, who have held it hostage for far too long.

And I now fish still waters more than I do rivers. This is a natural progression when you get older—wading a rocky river gets harder on the knees. But it's not just old-fart fishing; fishing lakes is how I learned as a teenager, so it's coming back to my roots. I'd like to write a book about a lake or pond someday (I have the title all picked out: *Still Waters Run Deep*), since, while right off the top of my head I can think of a dozen classic books about men and rivers, I can only think of one for a pond, the obvious one by Thoreau.

I've become fascinated by "gulper" fishing, which means that when it comes to the ponds and lakes around here, even the largest, I'm primarily interested in the top three inches. This is the zone where cruisers cruise, gulpers gulp, sippers sip—often rainbows, sometimes browns, occasionally brookies. They're feeding on subimagos of the mayfly that haven't escaped to the air, midge pupae hanging shrimp-like in the surface film, terrestrials that have crash-landed before reaching shore. Trout cruise along happily sipping these, their noses bulging the water like the snouts of submarines, which, after looking things over, prudently submerge.

Often their fins are visible—they cut through the surface like they're slicing and dicing the water into private soup bowls they can slurp from without using a spoon. If you do everything right, you can catch them, though it requires a fussy style of fishing that's not for everyone.

Tiny flies, gossamer leaders, careful stalking (no bow wave from your canoe), delicate casting, a precise way of striking if you do raise a fish—how easy it is to mess up at any stage of the process. No, it's not for everyone. Not for anyone? I often wonder about this. Around here, the lake country of central Vermont and New Hampshire, few flyfishers try still waters at all, and when they do it's deep with streamers or weighted nymphs. Out west, on Hebgen Lake, fishing for gulpers is a popular activity, and lake fishers in British Columbia love their chironmids, but in all the years I've fished for cruisers here, I've never seen another fly-fisher doing it, no matter that a lake at sunset will come alive with rising trout.

It involves great beauty, gulper fishing. I don't mean the beauty of the lake as a whole—intensely focused on the trout, I hardly have time to take in the larger picture—but the beauty of those top three inches. We hear the term "surface beauty," and react in negative terms—true beauty, we're told, runs deeper. But the surface of a lake, wonderfully ruffled by the noses of trout, is as deep a beauty as I know, even though it extends only millimeters downward. If human skin is where our inner world meets the outer world, then a lake's surface film is where the mystery of the water's depths interacts with the world we dwell in ourselves, so it's no wonder that it's a zone of fascination, thin as it is.

The thing about surface film is that it's filmy—it does thing with light that are magically distortive on one hand and startlingly clarifying on the other. That creatures live and feed in this film makes it even more interesting—it's an animated film, a cartoon of happy motion, with some pretty grotesque characters to boot. Matters of life and death are played out there—this isn't a film played just for laughs—and so the surface film is of all places on a lake the most visibly dramatic.

I'm gulping, too, when I fish these lakes. I'm trying to cram in as much beauty as I can, skimming the surface for it, nourished just like those trout.

But now I'm gushing, not gulping. Let me just add this before I get carried away entirely. One of the delights of this kind of fishing is that it extends the season well into autumn, so nowadays I'm fishing #24 gray midges on the surface almost to Thanksgiving.

And there's one autumnal phenomenon I look forward to with great anticipation. Leaves will blow off the trees along shore, vivid red and yellow ones, and, collecting on the lake's surface, wafting out toward the middle, go on to form very distinct floating isthmuses or islands or rafts of foliage, in a pattern that sometimes winds sinuously from side to side for hundreds of yards.

Trout love these rafts. Many of the leaves have insects riding them that soon end up in the water; the rafts, acting like breakwaters, also trap and concentrate what insects are hatching in the surface film. Trout will rise right in the middle of the leaves—your first impression is that they're grazing on foliage—and, while it's difficult because of the debris, you can throw a zebra midge to them and be reasonably assured of a take.

I spent a wonderful morning fishing for these on Lake Fairlee in Vermont last Halloween, in one of the thickest fogs I've ever been out in. After much canoeing back and forth, I finally located the raft out in the middle, paddled to the center where the leaves were thickest, and not only saw dozens of rising trout, but heard them, the bulges left by their noses disturbing the leaves just enough to make a faint but very distinct crinkle.

Crazy, fishing the foliage! If I wrote about it, honestly, you'd think I was lying. But as it's much fun fishing as I've ever had.

In the thirty years since writing the first of these books, I've been fortunate enough to sometimes combine fishing with traveling. These are not jet-setting expeditions underwritten by major sporting publications, but trips funded by putting spare dimes in a piggy bank and scrimping. A dozen times to Montana, once to British Columbia, twice to Scotland, once to Labrador, once to Slovenia, once—by the time you read this—to Iceland.

Great fun—but fishing local is still what I love best. Most of my trips are solitary, two or three hours built into the day's routine. I like to go fishing on impulse, especially when—writing here in my office—I look outside and realize conditions are perfect. I'm too busy to (fill in the blank) seems to be everyone's motto these days, but I enjoy bragging the opposite. When it comes to what I love in life I'm not too busy at all.

Celeste accompanies me when she can, though she doesn't fish. She sits in the bow and takes pictures, or grabs the oars and plays guide, or yank-starts the 1954 Evinrude outboard we bought last year for our vintage Grumman Sportboat, or finds some shade and cheers me on from shore.

My kids, grown up now, still enjoy coming out with me. Matt has become a strong caster; he loves rock-hopping brook trout streams, searching for natives. Erin has become a proficient bass angler, and has the pictures to prove it. I introduced them to fishing when they were young, but was careful—maybe too careful—not to force it on them, hoping it would eventually take hold on its own. It has, and I feel a certain smugness, that my strategy had such happy results.

My great fishing pal—my partner in adventures going back thirty-five years—remains Ray Chapin, the best fly-fisher I know. Ray read *Vermont River* when it first came out, and was brave enough, at a party at a mutual friend's, to come over and tell me so, though we'd never met before this. He was born in Vermont, an avid fisherman, but just getting started with fly fishing.

"Why don't we go try the Waits some afternoon?" I suggested, drawn by his eagerness—and we've been fishing together ever since, not just on the streams and lakes around here, but the White in Arkansas, the famous Yellowstone waters, the Penobscot in Maine, Kepimets Lake in Labrador, and, just this past spring, a long-overdue pilgrimage to the historical Catskill waters like the West Branch, the Beaverkill, and the Willowemoc.

He has a new canoe, Ray has. Last October we launched at the mouth of the White River in Vermont, floated down to its junction with the Connecticut, tied on some nymphs, and started casting. Further downstream we came upon a hunter walking his Labrador along the steep bank.

"Catch any?" he called out to us.

We shrugged—zilch. He shrugged back at us. It was clear from his expression that 1) he didn't think much of our fishing capabilities, and 2) he was a lot more bullish about the river's potential than we were.

"Surprising," he said. "This river is riddled with trout."

Riddled with trout. We laughed over that all the way down to our cornfield takeout. It would be a good epitaph someday, perfect for a headstone, at least for flyfishers who love their sport as much as we do. Or, better yet: riddled with rivers. He led a life riddled with rivers.

Vermont River

The perfect river does not exist.

It takes a second to write the phrase, twenty years to learn it. The lesson is drummed in every time a fisherman goes out. Plans are planned, hopes hoped, dreams dreamt, and subtly but surely the magic river of our desire begins to flow—a trickle at first, widening to embrace our fondest imaginings, deepening to hold our longed-for trout, eventually carving out a channel that can seem so real and attainable that it dooms all actual rivers to insignificance. No river can match the rivers of our imagination. We stock them with fourteen-inch trout that rise readily to the fly, grace them with abundant shade and gentle breezes, preserve them from harm. There are no dams in our imaginary rivers. No pollution, no highways, no debris. They run unsullied between immaculate banks, our own inviolable preserve.

The river in this book is not imaginary. Were it, I would make some of the pools deeper, put them further from the road, inhabit them with bigger browns and shyer brookies. As beautiful as they are, the trout rivers that flow into the Connecticut in Vermont are not wilderness streams, and the towns that border them have their poverty and trailers and junkyards like everywhere else. Yet the realization that the river is less than my ideal subtracts not one iota from my enjoyment. Perfect rivers being mythical, the fisherman must adjust as best he can, finding what pleasure there is in the reality of it, facing up to the river's blemishes, trying to right them when he can, not letting thoughts of sylvan streams just beyond the horizon torture him into false comparisons. "Here I will begin to mine," Thoreau said, knowing that truth was as attainable in the woods around Concord, Massachusetts, as it was in the cities of Europe or the mountains of Tibet. It is with this same determination that I have decided to write about what the river has come to mean to me.

Readers familiar with Vermont will have little trouble identifying my river. If I have left it nameless, it is not for protective secrecy but because to me it stands for the dozen New England rivers I have come to know in twenty years of sometimes hard, sometimes casual fly fishing. Indeed, so similar are their qualities that my river could well be the epitome of them all, could actually be part of the same overlapping flow, making it seem as though I have been slowly fishing up the rest of them toward it all along. Vermont's Battenkill or New Haven, Grand Lake Stream in Maine, Connecticut's Housatonic, the Quashnet of Cape Cod . . . this book might have been written about any one of them, and there is not a memory or observation in these pages that didn't have its germination on one of their banks.

This book covers a year on the Vermont river I love. Mostly it deals with fishing, sometimes with the absurd, humorous aspects of the sport. Little advice will be found here. I am a writer first, not a fisherman, and the insights I am after have little to do with catching more trout.

Fly fishing is a discipline that in sensitive hands can account for a special perspective, putting its practitioners by its very nature into a closer, more harmonious association with the river they fish. When the fly fisherman goes empty-handed to the river, merely to sit and watch, he notices half the incidents and events he would notice if he brought a rod, the concentration fly-fishing demands being the price of admission to the intimacy he's after. Novelists are aware of the mysterious process by which the hidden truth of a situation or character often comes unbidden at the typewriter, revealed only in the act of being written down. So too with fly-fishing: the truth of a river comes in fishing it. Merge the fisher and the writer, merge the river and the word.

The perfect river does not exist. My Vermont river does. Here then, its exploration.

1
The River in Winter

Having grown to love the river in the course of a season's fishing, I decided to revisit it in winter to see how it fared as snow and ice. It was a quick, unpremeditated decision; I went with a curious and fraternal feeling, as if to a seldom-seen friend, expecting it to be different but essentially unchanged. The river isn't long—seventeen miles if you iron out every bend, forty if you include the trout water on its two main branches. As closely as possible I would follow the length of it from its mouth at the Connecticut to its source back up in the mountains in the short daylight hours of one February day.

I left the house before dawn, in time to be caught in a snow squall that kept my speed down around twenty. There weren't any other cars out yet, and the only sign of life visible through the slanting flakes were the soft yellow lights from barns. In summer, I make the drive in half an hour, driving faster than I should, my mind caught between the writing I've just left and the fishing ahead of me, my nerves a turmoil of both. That morning, though, I was between novels, between trout seasons, and there were no ungrasped metaphors or streamside tactics to torment me. The quiet solitude of the road, the soft drape of flakes matched perfectly my own contentment.

The diner comes conveniently halfway on the trip. It's a welcome sight that time of morning, its warmth and light too tempting to pass up. A magazine had just given it an award for the best cup of coffee in the state, and this is what I ordered—a big, thick mug with cream. It was crowded: telephone repairmen, construction workers, lumbermen, drivers. Their low voices and laughs went well with the clatter of plates. Someone had put a quarter in the jukebox to play a song three times, and as I nursed my coffee, Juice Newton's voice repeated the same lilting phrase over and over: "Blame it on the queen of hearts."

Back outside, the snow had stopped. The highway here is pinched in by cliffs, and whatever dawn there was in the sky stayed hidden until I broke clear of them south of town. I crossed the river on the Main Street bridge, parked in a lot by the post office, and started down a snowy bank intending to walk the short distance to the river's mouth.

It was officially sunrise now, but directly east are the White Mountains and it's always a few extra minutes before the sun clears the peaks. Looking back toward town in the gray light, I could see the glacier-carved terraces down which the river falls in three abrupt steps: the steep upper terrace leading back from the dam into the valley; the flat, crowded plain of the town itself; the matching flood plain below town over which the river curves to a gentle intersection with the Connecticut.

Part of the lower terrace has been made into a golf course— the flag pins waved in the drifts like the lonely pennants of a polar expedition. A band of oaks marked the river bed, and without them it would have been difficult to determine where the stubble-dotted white of the cornfield on the opposite shore became the unblemished white of the river. It's at its widest here, lazy and almost delta-like. I climbed down the snow-matted sedge on the bank, intending to use the river as my path, but the ice cracked under me, and after a few tentative yards I retreated back to the trees. At least I could *see* where the river entered the Connecticut, and I decided that I was close enough to say I was there.

The sun was up now, and with it came various sounds, making it seem as if all the scrapings and bangings, whispers and skids that comprise a town's morning had been waiting for the sun's energy to give them voice. A dog barked. A horn beeped. The river, muted by ice as it spilled over the dam, made a sound like wind through foliated trees. Of all these sounds, though, the one I fastened onto was both the steadiest and most subtle: the sibilant, folding lap of water racing between banks.

Sure enough, there it was behind me, missed in my hurry to get to the mouth: an open stretch of river extending for a hundred yards or more below the dam. Walking toward it, my adrenaline started pumping; ludicrously, I found myself wishing I had brought my fly rod. I stared at the running water trying to memorize its color and texture, then hurried back up the cliff to town, anxious now to reach the part of the river I knew best.

I took the long way around to my car, walking beneath the tarnished Christmas decorations that—two months after Christmas—still overhung Main Street. The town was coming to life. By the falls, the carpenters restoring the 1847 mill sorted out their tools. A man with a Santa Claus belly unlocked the laundromat across the street, paused to spit toward the river. An old woman wheeled a shopping cart up the steep sidewalk. Above them by the library, the statue of a Spanish-American War admiral, town born, squinted warily toward the east with poised binoculars, as if expecting Cervera's Spanish fleet to come steaming up the Connecticut in battle formation. Just as the river is the epitome of Vermont rivers, the town could be the epitome of Vermont towns: battered, living half in the past, but with a sense of itself more fashionable places will never know. Close your eyes, then open them again. The plume of spray gushing over the dam, the slender stalactites on its fringe, the musty Victorian commercial buildings cheek by jowl with the simpler Colonial homes, the smell of wood smoke, the view of the mountains, the forty-eight stubborn stars on the flag before the American Legion's 150-year-old-hall—you could be nowhere else.

The alternate road out of town follows the river toward the mountains. There are a sawmill, a few old houses, then—just before the comparatively rich soil of the valley gives out—a last red farm, its back turned resolutely on the forest behind it. Beyond this is trout water, fifteen rushing yards from bank to bank, and as I drove along it one part of me tried to take in what I was actually seeing, while the other part raced back toward the summer and was caught up with swirling afternoon light and quick strikes and the feel of a trout trembling exhausted in my hand.

This is how it should be in winter. A river is a better metaphor than most, and half-frozen it becomes a blend of anticipation and recollection, flowing one moment toward the future, one moment toward the past. Proust, were he a trout fisher, might have summoned his remembrances in the Loire or some other French stream, finding its ripples and currents as evocative as the richest, most memory-laden of wines.

There is a cutoff by the first deep pool, and this is where I pulled over and got out. The previous May I had come here for the first time. Wading against the steep current to a smaller pool between an island and a cliff, I had caught a trout on my first cast—to a fisherman, never readier for miracles than on his initial try in new water, the most propitious of omens. The trout (admittedly, a small rainbow) went skipping across the surface as if to beach himself on the island, then changed his mind and headed straight for me as if to surrender. I am heretical in many angling habits, but none so much as in the landing of fish. By the time I've hooked a trout and controlled its first run, I begin to see things from its point of view, and after a few more minutes, have no particular desire to land it—in fact, I'm rooting for it to break off. (Once on Long Island's Connetquot, I fought a ten-pound brown—a world-class fish—for forty-five minutes, and was positively *relieved* when, in trying to beach him, he slithered out of my arms.) This first rainbow, though, came to me like a puppy on a leash, and when I twisted the Muddler out of his lip, he hovered by my leg in the current as if reluctant to leave.

I walked down to the river through the snow, half-expecting to see that same trout swim up to me, wagging its dorsal fin in recognition. But there was little chance of that. The pool where I caught him was now a jumbled mass of ice, resembling pictures I've seen of the Khumbu icefall on Everest. The entire channel on the far side of the island was frozen, and the only open water was the stronger current at my feet. The weather had turned dry after a stormy spell earlier in the month, and the river level had dropped dramatically, stranding the old ice. It was piled on the bank to a height of four or five feet, extending three or more yards back from the river, laying in glacier-like slabs and blocks, some square as tables, others all sharp edges and points. The plates nearest the river had debris embedded in their exposed edges: fallen leaves, sticks, even small logs. I stepped on one of the largest ice floes, and it immediately broke away downriver, carrying me with it like Little Eva, and I had to do some fancy boulder-hopping to get back to shore. Chastened, I climbed inland a few yards and paralleled the river upstream through the safer snow.

The banks get steeper here. Before long I was thirty feet above the river. Some of the trees had been marked with orange paint for cutting, but the blazes were old ones; the road crews had overlooked them, and I used their branches to brace myself from sliding down. At a point where the road curves right and climbs uphill is the most productive pool on the river: the Aquarium, a deep, lazy flow at the foot of a sharp rapid. In an afternoon's fishing I would catch upward of fifteen trout there without changing positions. Now, though I could peer right down into it, I saw no fish. The weak sunlight washed everything into an impenetrable gray.

Further upstream the banks level off, and I was able to cross an ice bridge over a small tributary and make my way to the water. The snow that covered the ice there had a puffy look to it, like the crust on a freshly baked pie. The river itself was half slush, half ice depending on where the sun hit it—ice dissolved into slush where it was brightest; slush crystallized into ice in the shade. In the middle, where the current was strongest, the water flowed against the ice with the gentle slapping sound of a sailboat on a downwind reach.

There was little color in that landscape, and when my eye happened to catch something reddish-orange on the opposite shore, the effect was that of a match flaring suddenly in the dark. Determined to get closer, I picked out a spot where the river was widest and thinnest and started to cross, risking hypothermia with every step. The dash of color turned out to be a Mickey Finn streamer embedded neatly in the branch of a willow, its monofilament tag blowing in the breeze. It had to be mine—I fished the Aquarium all season without seeing another flyfisherman—and getting down on my hands and knees to penetrate the tangle, I quickly found three more flies, all broken off within a foot of each other: a bushy Bivisible, a tattered Light Hendrickson, a rusty Muddler. In order to fish the far end of the pool, it's necessary to wade chest deep, putting even a high back cast perilously close to the branches. At a dollar or more a fly, it's an expensive place to fish. I searched through the trees some more without success, then stuck the four salvaged flies in the wool of my ski hat.

Back to the car, through a wind sharp enough to bring tears to my eyes. I poured a mugful of hot tea from the thermos and sipped it as I drove upriver. Above the Aquarium, the river flattens out for three miles, a broad, rocky stretch reminiscent of the Housatonic Meadows. The gentler grade had given the ice more leisure to do its work, and it was frozen solidly from bank to bank. Anticipation was becoming more urgent as I moved upriver; I resolved to come back to the flats during June when the insect hatches were at their peak—in June and at night, when the browns would be on the rise.

The South Branch meanders in here, but the dirt road that parallels it was too icy to chance on my bald, impoverished-novelist's tires, so I continued along the main river. My favorite stretch lay ahead, a series of pine-shaded riffles and pools that compose a landscape out of any fisherman's dreams. The moment I pulled over, I realized the beauty was still there—if anything, the winter had only enhanced it. The sun had come out. The water streamed past snow-covered ice islands, long, flat, and narrow, the mirror image of the smooth granite ledges on the bottom, making it seem as though the river had been turned over and dusted white. As I made my way along the banks, I subconciously began to fish—dropping a fly in the eddy at the ice's prow, letting it drift down the edge of the miniature berg to the pool below.

It was on this stretch in early October that I met Doctor McKenzie. I had been fishing hard all day with little to show for it except weather and foliage so perfectly autumnal that they seemed like a cliché. On the rocks near shore were some of those furry, orange-and-black caterpillars that Vermonters like to claim portend a heavy winter. Tying on an orange Wooly Worm to imitate them, I was rewarded with a solid strike in the pool below the falls—one of my rare browns. I was releasing him when I heard a car door slam back up on the road. Turning, I saw a leprechaun slide feet-first down the bank.

I say leprechaun in all the gentle, sparkling sense of the word.

Doctor McKenzie—for so he introduced himself—was eighty-three years old and about five feet high, a retired surgeon who had traveled all the way from British Columbia to photograph the beauty of New England in the fall. He had a camera and tripod. He asked me to stay in place until he could cross the river and set up his gear.

Now I must admit that I made a pretty picture that day. When fishing, I usually wear an old chamois shirt and battered jeans, stuffing my fly boxes into whatever pockets happen to be available. That day, though, I was dressed as immaculately as an Orvis model: close-fitting waders, fishing vest, swordfisherman's hat, the works. Add to that a backdrop of forest at its most vivid red and shimmering gold and you have a calendar shot just begging to be taken.

"I've been looking all day for this," Doctor McKenzie said, excited as a boy. "Beautiful! It's absolutely beautiful!"

I was flattered, of course, but worried, too. I simply didn't see how a man so old and frail-looking could cross through that current without being swept away. I picked out the spot where I would plunge in to rescue him before he went flying over the falls, but it wasn't necessary—he waded through the rapids as daintily and gracefully as a heron, setting his tripod up on the one dry rock left above the foam.

He was there forty minutes and more, snapping away as I cast, muttering to himself in delight, signaling me to move here and there as the light dictated. When he finished, I followed him back to the car and we talked. He must have assumed I was playing hooky, because he assured me several times that my face wouldn't be recognizable in the picture, that he only wanted me to complete his setting. When he left, he handed me his card. Later that night over dinner, I told the story to Celeste and dropped the card on the table. Celeste, retrieving it, wrote the good doctor without telling me, and on Christmas morning I opened a package to find the picture beautifully framed: me, the river, and the trees, as perfect a souvenir as that autumn day deserved.

Some of those same trees were fallen over now, their uppermost branches splayed across the water as if, tiring of winter, they had flung themselves there from desperation. I am tree lover enough to mourn their falling, but fisherman enough to wonder if the new eddies and currents formed around their trunks will create holding places for trout come spring. Before, I had always thought of the winter as a quiet time when the river slept, but in the course of that day I found that exactly the opposite is true. The pressure from the built-up ice, the constant change back and forth from liquid to solid to liquid, the runoff from the snow—it's in winter that the river is being shaped, its weaknesses tested. The life *in* the water may be relatively dormant, but the life *of* the water is never more active.

The forest pools give way to a miniature canyon here—a dark, shadowy place where I am never comfortable. At the head of it, I walked back on the ice, lured by a fresh pattern of tracks. Deer tracks first, their pattern disappearing into the half-frozen slush in midstream. Fox tracks paralleled them—neat rows that as they neared the edge suddenly became skid marks. I laughed, thinking of the fox slamming on the brakes to avoid a dunking. There were other, smaller tracks, too, patterns that went every which way, as if left by creatures who had met there to dance a complicated quadrille. All the tracks were centered in an area no bigger than a pool table, giving the effect of an African water-hole. I wondered why they preferred this spot and no other.

There was a subterranean gurgle beneath my feet. I knelt, brushed away the snow from the ice. Through it, I could see milky bubbles running back and forth like disoriented atoms, trying either to flee the ice altogether and join the current or find a roughness to which they could adhere. One after the other found a small edge; a few minutes more and they were all pressed together, waving back and forth with the lambent quality of flame.

I had been concentrating so much on the river that I'd lost track of the weather. The promise that was in the sun had been blotted out by clouds, and as I headed back to the car it began to snow. I'd have to hurry to reach the headwaters; reluctantly, I passed up the fork in the road that leads along the beautiful North Branch, and continued on the main stream, past what surely must be the smallest ski area in the state of Vermont, then a cemetery, its stark granite markers silhouetted against the snow like miniature Stonehenges, then a small farm. Most Vermont river valleys narrow and close in upon themselves as you approach the headwaters, but here the landscape opens and spreads apart, admitting wider vistas of light and sky. The knobby hills and open meadows reminded me of the highlands of Scotland, the lonely road that travels from Inverness to Ullapool.

Signs of life were infrequent. Snowmobile tracks across a deserted field. A tireless car drifted in snow. Billboards so faded and illegible that they've escaped Vermont's prohibition: Blue Seed Fee, Nana's Craft Shop, Maple Syrup 500 Feet. At a point where the river narrows, I saw the first people out enjoying it besides me: a group of schoolchildren using their recess to ice-skate on the overflow.

It was past three now, and I remembered I was hungry the same time as the general store appeared up ahead on the right. I know too many loquacious Vermonters to accept the laconic stereotype, but the clerk behind the counter made me think twice.

"Cold out," I said, blowing on my hands.

On cautious eyebrow half-raised. Yes.

"Have any coffee?"

The lips, already pencil thin, thinner. No.

"This snow supposed to last?"

He threw discretion to the wind and ventured to half-raise his eyebrow and tighten his lips at the same time, as if to say any damned fool knew that snowstorms in that part of the state *always* lasted.

He was right about that. When I went back outside with my Twinkies, snow covered the road and I had to drive it at a crawl, my wipers in a losing battle with the ice.

The river—brook trout water now—was further from the road here, only visible by the row of bare trees lining its bank. Another mile and it was obvious that this was as far as I was going today. As I pulled over to turn around, the snow slackened for a minute, letting the sun shine through the clouds. Ahead of me, I saw the twin mountains in the shadow of which the river has its source. The view was gone within seconds. The snow fell back into place with doubled intensity, giving the effect of a curtain that had been teasingly raised, then immediately dropped.

I needed to get to the river once more before going home. Taking a chance that the plows wouldn't be by for a while, I left my car on the side of the road and started through a field toward the trees. It was a part of the river I don't know well, and the seesaw I'd been riding between recollection and anticipation tipped decisively toward the future. The river is narrow here, dwindling toward its first springs and beaver ponds. Watching it, I promised myself I'd come back after black fly season and follow its windings to its source. It felt good to make a promise; it joined with the vow I'd made to teach Celeste to fly fish, the vow to pick some lazy summer day to float the length of the river in inner tubes, the vow to learn how to fish a nymph once and for all, my vow to catch more and bigger browns.

The ice extended bank to bank, and the only break in the monotony was a small hole a few yards downstream. In the disorienting gray, the blinding snow assumed a significance out of all proportion to its size, looming in my imagination like one of those black holes in space that, collapsing, take with it all matter in its reach, becoming pure essence. The hole below me was the essence of my Vermont river, and as I turned regretfully to go, something bright and silver rose toward the middle, and faster than I can write it down was gone.

A trick of ice? A surge of water? A trout?

Spring will tell.

2
Quadrangles

Every March, I go temporarily nuts over maps. Not just any maps. Oil company maps, *National Geographic* maps, maps tucked in guidebooks, street maps, atlases, and globes all leave me cold. Maps on placemats, maps on matchbooks, maps on ashtrays or cribbage boards I positively despise. No, the focus of my addiction is much more limited, but infinitely more detailed: the beautiful green and brown topographic maps of the United States Geological Survey.

The local hardware store stocks them, in a fine metal case where the sheets lie immaculate without folds. The complex but rewarding Camels Hump quadrangle of 1948; the state-straddling Mt. Cube of 1931; the modern, somewhat mundane East Corinth of 1973; the vintage, all but legendary East Barre of 1957, companion of some of my happiest map-browsing hours . . . Mr. Waite's chest contains them all. On rainy afternoons I'm apt to spend a good hour or more going through them, tracing contour intervals up mountains I've hiked, following trout streams to their obscurest tributary, spreading the maps out on the wooden floor to match them to their neighbors, not stopping until a gentle inquiry from Mr. Waite makes me replace them sheepishly in their bins.

Occasionally, I even buy one; at three dollars a fix, they are among the cheaper addictions. I have four maps spread on the carpet below me as I write, their corners weighted down with fly reels. It is too warm and muddy to go skiing, too cold yet for fishing, and I am neither fly-tier nor hobbyist. The maps fill a vacuum, use up time that hangs heavy in the long weeks before spring. But they are more than that, too, and my fascination with them is comprised of many elements—their beauty, their elaborate detail, the mysteries they offer, the discoveries they reveal.

Beauty first. Even as mere objects, topographic maps are attractive things, and even less-inspired efforts like the East Corinth quadrangle are of gallery quality. They even *feel* nice; the crisp, no-nonsense paper reeks of trustworthiness and good sense. In unrolling it, the edges will tug gratifyingly on your fingers, as if the paper has a life and will of its own.

Hung on a wall and seen from a distance, topographic maps resemble late Van Goghs, with swirls and coils, elaborate circles and extravagant loops. The contour lines in their convoluted twistings are as suggestive as ink blots, forming here a butterfly or amoeba, there a breaker or cloud. Color is everywhere. Blue streams curve across brown contour lines over green forests. Red roads bisect black boundary markers by aquamarine ponds near terra cotta cities, and all is centered perfectly in broad, even margins of white.

But as beautiful as the colors are, I think the deepest beauty topographic maps offer is more cerebral: here spread before you is a small, comprehensible portion of the earth, its hills and valleys lovingly traced, its man-made additions duly marked, its unceasing hurry for one moment checked.

Within these lines and symbols there is much to explore. But a word of caution is in order. If there is one hazard in being addicted to topographic maps, it is in the danger of being overwhelmed by their detail, not seeing the mountains for the contour lines. After years of puzzling over them, I've begun to understand some of the basic details; i.e., that a 15-minute quadrangle covers a square that is fifteen minutes of longitude by fifteen minutes of latitude, and that a 7.5-minute quadrangle covers a quarter of that area with correspondingly greater detail (but with less sweep and breadth of view). I also understand about contour intervals; if the contour interval is twenty feet, then any point on a contour line is twenty feet above or below any point on the neighboring contour line. Scale is just as easy; if it's 1:62500, then any unit such as an inch or centimeter on the map equals 62,500 of the same units on the ground. The magnetic declination diagram in the margin shows how far magnetic north differs from true north—nothing tricky there. I know about bench marks, too, having tripped over one while fishing once, and given a good ruler, I can handle mileage scales tolerably well.

Some things, however, are mysterious. Grid ticks, for instance. Are they yardage markers in football or a new species of insect pest? On the East Corinth quadrangle are several small patches that are comprised of green polka dots. What could they possibly mean? Could there still be corners of Vermont that are terra incognita, polka dots being the government's way of saying they have no idea what's there?

After wondering about these and other equally arcane symbols, I finally sent to the US Geological Survey in Virginia for a folder describing topographic maps in detail. Grid ticks turn out to be "a network of uniformly spaced parallel lines intersecting at right angles," useful for engineers and their ilk. Green polka dots turn out to represent an orchard—in Vermont, an apple orchard more than likely. Three wavy lines in a river means rapids or falls. A straight line with crewcut hair growing out of it means a wooded marsh.

Some of the more interesting symbols aren't likely to be found on Vermont quadrangles. Green polka dots that are more tightly bunched than those for an orchard depict vineyards. A sinking ship represents an exposed wreck. A pretty green floral design means a mangrove swamp. A box with little curls in it means a lava field; a little triangle, oil wells. My favorite is a small black circle with a crescent on the top. The meaning? "A mosque or Sheikh's tomb."

There is a lesson in all this, and it is a simple one. If topographic maps are the most precise of precision instruments, then they are also the most suggestive, and an active imagination can find hours of pleasure in poring over them in wonder.

Take the quadrangle unfolded before me now, the one that maps the upper reaches of my favorite trout river. It's probably as close as you can come to a typical fifteen-minute swatch of

Vermont, including as it does two or three mountains, a score of hills, a whole network of unimproved dirt roads, idiosyncratic boundaries, several small hill towns, two or three "notches," at least one "hollow," and enough cemeteries hidden away in the forest to hint at how many human lives ran out there in the century before. The place names are a joy to say aloud: Michigan Hill, Duplissey Hill, Lyme Emery Hill, Pike Hill, Hurricane Ridge, Mount Pleasant; Riders Corner, Riddle Pond, Foster Notch, Hart Hollow, Goose Green . . . each one suggesting a story, each one a monument to a time when every feature of the Vermont terrain was familiar enough to some caring soul to be called by name.

A legend on the bottom of the map says that it was "compiled in part from aerial photographs taken in 1938," and as I look at it, I picture a yellow biplane circling the ridges, a camera mounted on its wing, the plane soaring on the updrafts on a Vermont summer day. For it is an aerial, bird's-eye view that topographic maps provide—run your eyes quickly from top to bottom and the effect is as dizzying as flight. And nothing short of flight gives you such a quick appreciation of terrain. The two symmetrical mountains between which the river has its source, the ones that always look to me like twins? Sure enough, there they are on the map, both topping out at exactly 3,166 feet, proof to the eye. That steep ridge above the pool in the river where I caught that big rainbow trout last June, the ridge beyond which I could never see? There it is, the contour lines pressed together like isobars, and beyond it is a plateau in the middle of which is a swamp. That tiny stream that comes into the main river over a miniature falls? I trace it back into the hills, find its source in a small pond a mile and a half above the river, vow to fish up to it come May.

There are houses back in the hills, tiny black squares that form the human dimension in the crosshatches and grids. Beside some of them are the white squares that represent barns; when they are connected barns, the white and black squares are joined. I imagine my way up to the most remote of them, my finger running west out of the small hill town that straddles the river (the homes, the church, the school are all depicted, the last with a little flag), tracing my way past the small cemetery, passing one or two lonely houses strung along the high open meadows beyond town, then entering the woods as the road turns to dirt. I can picture the ruts in that road, picture the humpbacked middle, the way that steep ridge pinches it in toward the stream. The house, by my ruler, is a mile further—not a house really, but a cabin, sharing a small clearing with a fallen-down barn, nest to owls. That nameless hill behind the house (elevation 2418) must catch a lot of the sun—night comes early in the late summer and fall. Looks like that swamp at its base must breed clouds of mosquitoes. Then, too, the nearest house is three miles—lonely place for a wife and kids. No wonder the barn is fallen down and abandoned. No wonder the town never votes to improve the road. No wonder it's lost now, lost except for this lonely black square on a forty-year-old map.

These journeys to polka dotted fields and abandoned hill farms I may never actually make, but there are other trips that I will start upon and topographic maps will be an inestimable aid when I do. This is the year I've promised myself that I'll follow my favorite river to its source, much the way Speke and Burton traced the Nile. Fishing the headwaters, it's hard to know which of numerous branches that form the main stream *is* the main stream. On the map, all is clear. The ultimate winding of the river departs from the highway opposite a small cemetery (elevation 1827), parallels a dirt road that shortly ends (good place to leave the car), and climbs through fairly gentle terrain for the first two miles, giving me time—once I start hiking—to limber up my legs. The contour lines gradually start closing up into arrowhead-shaped wedges—there may be falls here, forcing me to detour further from the bank in order to make any progress. After about half a mile, the contour lines flatten out, the mountains open up a bit, and with most of the climb behind me, it will be a fine spot to eat my lunch. Another hour should do it. The stream will become smaller and smaller, smaller than my stride, and I will cross it many times before I come to the spring in the ground that must be the river's highest source, smack on the crosshatched boundary lines of two Vermont counties.

Staring at the map, I can imagine the sound of that stream, feel the ache in my calfs as I climb, smell the breeze as it comes down off the mountains. But it is April now, the temperature climbs tentatively toward fifty, and as suddenly as my map-scanning passion came on, it is gone. Vicarious trips no longer suffice, blue lines make poor substitutes for streams, and stuffing the topographic maps in an old bookcase, I grab my fly rod and rush outside.

3
April Fourteenth

T he water, like the sky, had a scoured look to it. The dead reeds that lined the banks lay perfectly flat, as though a wire brush had been run through them a hundred times preparatory to spring—ninety-eight, ninety-nine, one hundred, smoothing them into a part, their tips all trending in the same direction. Above them, the sagging branches of uprooted trees touched the water, and where they touched the water their bark was burnished gold. Out in the current—the current which for its hard green brilliance might have been the coruscating agent itself—the rocks were as polished as gems. There was nothing extraneous in the landscape. It was stripped down to its elements—water and sky—the debris of winter washed away in one great torrent of brightness.

I went into it at the long stretch above the pine canyon, the part of the river I love most. The state of Vermont allowed me to fish beginning at 12:01 a.m. on Saturday, April 9, but I had chosen to start the trout season at my own convenience—at 8:01 a.m. on Thursday, April 14. Even later than that, as it turned out. For the season began this year, not when I got up in the morning, the adrenaline racing me through breakfast; not when I loaded my rods in the car and drove the thirty minutes of highway; not even when I first stepped into the current and began to cast. No, the season began at 8:05 or thereabouts, the moment when after picking my way gingerly around several huge and dangerous ledges, I found myself twenty yards out in midstream with the full weight of the river on my thighs.

Of all the sensations associated with fly fishing, this is the one linked most closely to spring. For if spring is energy—the light that lures crocuses from the soil, the warmth that birds track north—then this is energy made manifest, the pushing, rushing current breaking against your legs as you cast. Implicit in it are the fifteen miles of river upstream, all the tributaries to the river, all the tributaries to the tributaries, the trickles, runs, pools, drips and springs that comprise a watershed—all this is at your back, pressing your waders until the fabric clutches at your legs, pushing your feet out from their hard-won stance, supporting you when you lean against it, shivering you, even through lined pants and long underwear, with its chill. For all the current knows, you are part of the river itself, to be sprung against and pried at like any other rock or branch that gets in its way.

Current is the continuous note of a flyfisherman's day. All the casting, all the probing for trout, the tactics, are merely embellishments to that throb. And like any deeply felt sensation, it carries with it its own echo, so that even now, writing four days after I fished, I can feel the power of the river on my legs, a vague and very satisfactory hum.

The feel of it all—the sense of once again uniting muscles and nerves in harmonious, graceful ways—is one element of an April start. The other is more cerebral, depending as it does on the thread of memory that links the fisherman standing in the river to the boy who *dreamed* of standing in the river. Part of you is that boy, and the sensitivity to realize this is never sharper than on opening day when the dream is renewed with the most ceremony and deliberation.

I caught this thread several times that morning. The first was when I stopped in town to buy some flies. They lay in trays on the counter, bushy Marabou Streamers, slim Gray Ghosts, nymphs as hard and spare as stones. I picked through them with the same sense of anticipation I felt as a boy of fourteen buying lures to throw at bass on the Connecticut lake where I grew up.

It only lasted a few minutes. By the time I paid for them and went back outside to the car, my mind was back in the present, worrying how high the river would be. But the same thing happened again when I put together my fly rod at the river's edge; my hands shook just as they shook when I walked down to Candlewood Lake on opening day twenty years before. I went with the feeling this time, deliberately pro-longed the link, until by the time I waded out to the middle of the river and began to cast, I was in some sense standing aside from myself, looking at this tall fisherman waist-deep in a Vermont river with the eyes of the boy who wished for nothing so much as to be one day standing in a Vermont river casting for trout.

The fulfillment of a childhood dream is fishing's deepest reward. I think of an eighty-year-old I met one fall on the Battenkill (an eighty-year-old, by the way, with three fat trout in his creel)—how he talked constantly of next season's opening day, even though the season wasn't yet ended. "If I'm still around, that is," he added cautiously when he mentioned his plans. Opening day, youth, one more chance—these were all clearly linked in his phrase, and I felt tender toward him, and marveled that childhood's excitement and need could persist so long.

Thus, April 14.

"Here I am," I thought as I stood there casting. "Here I *am!*"

The fourteen-year-old in me would have had me catch a trout—a big four-pounder, bright with spring—but the part of me that's thirty-four knew better, and I worked through the reach without really expecting to find any fish. The water was clear enough, but too high, fast, and cold; the trout were still in a state of suspended animation, hungover from winter, in no mood to chase my fly. On the theory that cold water deserves a cold lure, I was fishing a Polar Bear Muddler, but on my third cast I snapped it off on a branch, and the rest of my flies seemed too summery to have much of a chance. I drifted a bucktail through the last pool, then climbed up onto the bank to warm myself in the sun.

There were some homemade doughnuts in my vest, compliments of Celeste. I ate them while I watched the river. On the opposite bank a flock of goldfinch assembled in a great congregation, darting from tree to tree in their swerving loops, chattering excitedly away. They're a common enough bird in

Vermont, but I never seem to see them, and I welcomed the chance. I was wondering where these particular ones had spent the winter when I noticed something out of the corner of my eye in the river—a log, I thought at first. But when I turned my head to look, it wasn't a log that I saw shooting past, but a kayak—a kayak and a life jacket and a helmet. By the time I realized there was a man in the center of all this, it was gone.

Three more came after that, spaced at intervals of about a minute. Judging by the way they threaded the rapids, they were all experts; there was an abrupt ledge above the canyon, but they steered right for it, as if this were exactly the sort of challenge they were seeking. Paddles windmilled back and forth as they fought to keep the kayaks from swinging broadside to the current . . . a moment of suspense as their bows shot over the ledge . . . then they were gone down the canyon, trailing behind them the sound of their triumphant laughs.

Motion, color, dash. The kayaks made me feel sluggish and land-bound, and I decided it was time to get back into the river. Not the main river. If I was going to catch a trout that day, it would have to be on one of the tributaries—the river itself was simply too high. I had talked to a man down in Woodstock earlier in the week who had caught his limit on one of the small feeders to the White. Nymphs, he said. Weighted and brown.

I drove the three miles to the junction pool, crossed the river on the new bridge, and started up the road that runs back along the South Branch. About a mile up, I pulled over and parked. I could hear the stream before I could see it; the bank is overgrown here, and I had to pick my way along it before I found an easy way down to the water.

The South Branch is much less pastoral than the main river, steeper and more mountain-like. Even so, I was counting on less water—during spring runoff, the higher tributaries usually clear first. What I hadn't counted on, though, was that the valley had retained more of winter, and there was still ice along both banks of the stream.

It was too late to back out. I crossed one of the ice slabs, and made it to a rock below a likely looking pool. Casting quickly, I laid a Hare's-Ear nymph on the spot where the current fanned apart, and let it bounce down the middle of the pool toward my stance.

No response. I cast again, this time shading it a bit more to the left. No response. The right side now, a slower drift. No response. I abruptly switched directions, cast for distance, let the nymph swing across the current in pocket water above a downed tree. No response. I let the nymph drift below me, let it hang there like a worm.

I spent an hour or more fishing all the water within reach. Only once did the nymph stop its drift, but when I tightened, it was on a submerged branch, not a fish, and I broke off the fly. Since fishing was hopeless, I decided to hike upstream, prospecting for likely pools I could fish later in the month. But even this modest intention came to naught. Above this stretch the ice on the banks became thicker, the blowdowns more frequent, and by the time I gave up climbing and headed back to the car, I was sweating from effort.

I took the rod apart and was pulling off my waders when a pickup drove past, going far too fast for that narrow road. A hundred yards above me, it squealed to a stop, went into reverse, went fishtailing across the road and stopped six inches from my knees.

A man my own age got out, grinning from ear to ear.

"How's the fishing?"

I told him. As he listened, he kept nodding up and down, as if he were taking great delight in what I was saying. He had the lean, ascetic look of a marathon runner, but rather than jogging clothes, he wore battered work pants and a thin cotton shirt.

"You don't see many fly fishermen on this river," he said, once I finished.

I shrugged.

"I'm a fly fisherman," he said, with the slightly defensive air of someone who doesn't expect you to believe him.

And so we talked. He was out of work—the lumber industry, the housing slump—and was trying to cheer himself up by thinking about all the time it would give him to fish; "for dinner," he said, laughing. He was new to fly fishing, and I answered his questions as best I could. Yes, nymphs were probably best this time of year. No, I hadn't read Schwiebert's later article on stonefly imitations. Yes, it was a beautiful river. More than beautiful.

"Big browns down there," he said, tilting his head. "I'm going to fish at night this year. You ever fish much at night?"

He asked me what I did, and I told him. He listened to me complain about the book business for a while; I listened to him complain about logging, and that settled, we got back to the fishing again.

All the while we talked, I was bothered by something in my tone—a note of condescension and weary patience. Where did it come from? He was my age, after all, and there I was talking to him like that eighty-year-old on the Battenkill had once talked to me; it was all I could do not to call him "Sonny." I think it must have been the difference in ages between our dreams. Mine was established and mature; his was brand-new, resembling in its enthusiasm and rough edges my excitement at fourteen. No wonder I sounded so all-knowing and wise. The latest theories, the latest tackle—once upon a time I had been full of these myself.

"Hey, I've got to go," he said, for the fourth time in ten minutes. "See you on the river, right?"

"Look for me."

"Hope you sell more books."

"Thanks. Good luck with the job!"

I had been intending to quit for the day, but our talk left me feeling the dream again in all its original intensity, and I couldn't bear the thought of leaving. I ended up fishing the entire afternoon. There's no need to go into details. It was the stretch above the Aquarium, but for once there were no fish there, and I wouldn't have caught any if there were. I cast quickly and badly, changed flies much too often, slapped the line against branches, rocks and logs, twisted the leader into knots, waded into spots where I had no business being, and in short made every mistake a flyfisherman can possibly make. I was aghast at my behavior, of course, but deemed it necessary; after a winter cooped up indoors, my impatience was as high as the river, and like the current, must have its way.

Four hours in water a little above freezing works wonders. By the time I climbed out onto the banks in the soft light of dusk, I felt as scoured as the river itself, rid of all the staleness that was in me, washed of my impatience and ready—once more— to begin.

4
My Brilliant Career

It occurs to me that, at least on paper, I qualify as an expert on fishing. I could list my stories, which have appeared regularly in America's most prestigious fishing magazine, my time as an editor at another fishing publication, my career demonstrating fly rods for a famous tackle company in Vermont. To the nonfisherman, these accomplishments may seem as nothing, but to the flyfisher, it is roughly like saying that W. D. Wetherell is Ernest Hemingway, A. J. McClane and Charles Orvis all wrapped up into one.

This is troubling. Not because I have anything against these men, but because I distrust experts in general and fishing experts in particular. (This is not necessarily uncommon; I once met a man who had developed a bitter grudge against Jason Lucas, the old *Sports Afield* columnist, and vowed to drown him should he ever appear on the same lake.) Am I an expert myself then? One of those smug, insufferably knowledgeable bores who inhabit with pollsters and developers the lowest terrace in my personal modern-day inferno? Let us examine the evidence in more detail.

My short stories. They have indeed appeared in America's best fishing magazine (I'm entitled to call it that, having worked three years on the worst), but any fisherman trying to garner tips on landing more fish from them would probably be more likely to give up fishing altogether. One concerns a man who fishes for bass "in order to free them from the mortal terror in which they swim" and ends up succumbing one night to the same terror himself; one deals with a trout fisherman undergoing a mid-life crisis in a Manhattan bar; the third is about a man who goes to Maine to spread his dead brother's ashes on his favorite lake, and in doing so, absent-mindedly destroys his reputation at the fishing camp where he had gone for years. Whatever their value, these are not your usual me-and-Dad-fishing-for-old-Mossback-in-the-lake-no-one-knew-about-except-us-and-those-times-sob-are-now-gone-sob-forever stories. If I try to come up with an influence that was behind me as I wrote, it would be Kafka—Kafka as a flyfisherman in a long black coat, casting shyly in some Prague trickle, fishing for the absurd the way other men fish for trout.

This, of course, is a long way from A. J. McClane.

Harder to explain are the three years I spent as an editor at a New York magazine I'll call *Angling International*. In tackiness, *Angling International* was akin to some girlie magazines, the cheaper kind that look as if they're printed in Peru. Rather than bosoms and rear ends, *A.I.* featured shots of enormous, repulsive-looking bass, only we weren't allowed to call them bass, they were always "Hawgs!" with an exclamation point. Alliteration was very important in all our titles. *Hooked on Hawgs!*, *Horsing for Hawgs!* and *Hip Hip for Hawgs!* were typical. The circulation was claimed to be upwards of 100,000, but we at the magazine never had a hint that anyone actually read it, and it was the considered opinion of most of us that the publisher ran it as a tax dodge.

Like a lot of sad involvements, mine began with an ad in the *New York Times:* "Editor wanted who enjoys fishing." I had just graduated from college with a degree in philosophy, a passable roll cast and not much else. Wes, *Angling International*'s managing editor, was intelligent enough to accept the essential absurdity of the magazine, and in keeping with this understanding, was quirky enough to hire me, sight unseen, as assistant editor.

Wes himself did most of the work. It was my job to copy-edit the stories, proofread, write a column on new products and do some research. One of my first assignments involved an article on fishing in New Zealand. All the prices mentioned were in New Zealand dollars, and I was to convert them into their US equivalents, the easier for our readers to plan their trip. Unfortunately, I used the wrong formula, dividing where I should have multiplied or vice versa, the result being that all the prices were converted into half the New Zealand amount when they should have been double, thereby making New Zealand appear the cheapest destination in the world. It was printed that way; I remember vividly the sad yet forgiving look on Wes's face when he learned of my error. Such mistakes were an inevitable accompaniment to his life, and even if they were someone else's fault, he naturally assumed they were his own.

We had another assistant editor, a blonde woman in her thirties who could neither fish, write nor spell. Joan was incapable of saying a sentence that didn't contain the word "hah" in it, and she would emit it with a honking, nasal intonation, like a goose. Depending on her mood, "hah" could be invitational, interrogative, denunciatory, decorative or prayerful—sometimes a mixture of all five. To this day, I'm not sure what she did at the magazine, but it must have been something.

We had some famous bylines in the magazine, fishing experts I had read and admired as a boy. As bad as it was, *A.I.* paid on time, and this attracted a lot of people who had to wait for their checks at the glossier publications. I was looking forward to working with these writers, and hoped that my involvement with them would lead to fishing invitations, free trips and gear.

Imagine my disappointment, then, to learn that some of these experts were for all intents and purposes illiterate, their careers having been established by rigged photographs and a great deal of cronyism of the old-boy-network variety. These weren't just bad writers, they couldn't write *at all;* much of my time was spent finding their subjects and predicates and linking them in some sort of reasonable order. It was a depressing task. It was 1974, the year of Watergate, and working on these ineffable manuscripts caused in me the same kind of disillusionment that other people were feeling toward politicians.

But like Wes, I gradually came to accept the essential ludicrousness of it all, and even began to enjoy it. Of all the *Angling*

International absurdities, Wes himself was by far the most interesting. He looked like a fisherman—his eyes had a distant focus
to them, as if they had spent hours studying rivers for the hatch;
his body was slender and wiry, like so many good casters—and
he was originally from Montana. But if the truth be known,
Wes—editor of a large fishing magazine, writer of a superb column of angling advice read by thousands—did not fish.

What he did was sit in his office waving a fly rod around
while he watched the elevated trains roll by. I rarely saw him
do anything else. Occasionally, he would talk on the phone to
one of our writers; occasionally, he would wander off to the art
department and wave his fly rod around in there, but this was
the limit of his small world. I would come back from weekend
fishing trips full of stories, and he would listen to these with
a look of haughty condescension on his face, as if to say that
these amateurish junkets of mine were all very fine, but to a
man who knew the Yellowstone . . . Well, someday he would
explain.

It was a comfortable life, but then the day finally came when
he was invited to go fishing out west by a famous fish and game
organization. His face was white as he put down the phone. I
think he realized that after five safe and lazy years, his bluff had
been called.

There were too many past refusals on his part, too many
last-minute cancellations for him to back out of it. He was gone
three days. When I came to work the morning of the fourth
day, he was at his usual place in the office, whisking the fly rod
around with his left hand—his left hand because his right one
was in a cast.

I never asked him about it and he never explained. From that
day on, though, his column began to take on a bitter, mordant

quality, and our receptionist had strict orders to screen all calls, making sure he was never asked to go fishing again.

This brings us to the third and seemingly most unshakable pillar of my expertise—my time on the staff of a famous tackle company in Vermont. I may as well admit right at the start that I have occasionally taken advantage of this experience to assert myself in the subtle one-upmanship flyfishermen sometimes indulge in. For instance, I'il meet someone on the river who drops references to his trips to Labrador, his new Garrison rod, his good friend Lee Wulff.

"That's interesting," I'll say, stifling a yawn. "Reminds me of my time working at."

"Your time working at where?" he'll say in disbelief.

"My time working at."

"You worked at?" Disbelief now turning to awe.

"Yeah, for a while. Is that a rise over there?"

Now saying you worked at is roughly like saying you were in the Yankee outfield when Maris and Mantle were in their prime. And I did work there once, the summer I was nineteen.

It came about like this. I had bought enough flies through the mail to be on the company's mailing list; reading their newsletter one day, I saw an ad for a flyfisherman to work in their store for the May to October season. They had started a fishing school that year, and the regular salesmen would be teaching, creating the opening. I immediately sat down and wrote a long letter listing my fly-fishing credentials, making half of it up (most of my fly fishing at this time being strictly vicarious). About a week after mailing it, I received a call from the company's manager asking me to come to Vermont for an interview.

I took the bus from New York. During the interview, I kept stealing peeks at all the beautiful gear displayed on the walls: bamboo fly rods, canoes, waders . . . this soon could be mine! As nervous as I was, I managed to stay fairly calm under the manager's polite questions ("I see in your letter that you once caught an eight-pound rainbow on a #22 Adams. Tell me about that."). An hour later, when I walked back through the snow to the bus stop, I had the job.

The position began in May. I spent the intervening two months practicing my casting, studying every fishing book I could find, memorizing the diameter of 4X tippets, and in general trying to assimilate enough information to hide my lack of experience. I drove up to Vermont the day before I was scheduled to go to work. Needing to find a place to stay, I stopped first at the store. The manager introduced me to the other salesmen; like *Angling International*, the company was fond of alliteration, and everyone had a nickname that started with the same letter as his surname: Sip Simmers, Pete Peters, Rap Roberts and so on. Thus, I was introduced not by my first name (which, alliterative as it was, wasn't quite alliterative enough), but as "Weth Wetherell."

None of the salesmen seemed particularly interested in anyone called Weth Wetherell, and they quickly resumed their interrupted discussion. It was all about "The 'Kill"—the Battenkill River, which was right down the road. One of the men had caught ten brown trout in the space of an hour using a Yellow Muddler. Another man had caught eleven on a Strawberry Blonde. The third man had fished all day without catching anything. It was a pattern I saw repeated several times the following day; it was considered okay to brag about catching ten or more trout, okay to admit you had caught none, but somehow amateurish to admit anything between one and nine.

I found a temporary room at a house in town, and went to bed early, ready for the big day. I arrived an hour before the store opened: as before, no one seemed particularly interested in talking to me. When the manager arrived, he issued me the same kind of khaki fishing shirt that everyone else was wearing, and explained what my duties would be.

These were: (1) to help keep the stock in order; (2) to see that the trout in the casting pond were fed each day; and (3) to help customers when they came in, and especially people interested in fly rods.

This is what the company was all about—the expensive, exquisitely crafted bamboo rods that lined one wall of the shop. Should a customer want to try one out, we were to drop everything and go outside to the casting pond with him, spending as much time as it took to make the sale.

Fine. The manager patted me on the back and disappeared. Not much happened for the first hour or so. I rearranged some fly boxes, dusted off a display case, tried to strike up a conversation with Sip and Rap. About eleven, a man came in dressed in a fishing vest. I asked if I could help him, but he shook me off and went right to the book display. Rap mentioned his name to me—he was a famous fishing writer, one I had read as a boy. He had a pencil and pad with him. As it turned out, this is how he did his research, cribbing from other people's books, which he was too cheap to buy.

At noon, I went outside to feed the trout. They were expecting someone—they crowded one side of the pond, and when I tossed the fish chow to them, they exploded through the water like sharks. I asked the manager if they had a poaching problem with the unfenced pond being so close to the highway.

"You kidding?" he said, pointing to where the huge fish were tearing apart the surface. "Kids in town are *scared* of them."

Feeding the trout proved to be the high point of the day. At lunchtime, the salesmen sat on benches at one end of the pond swapping stories, but I wasn't invited to join them, so I ate alone in my car. I was beginning to feel a little sorry for myself—the job was not turning out to be what I had imagined. Nothing happened during the afternoon to improve things. Customers did start to trickle in, but they were the worst kind of pompous, name-dropping snobs, and I remember being puzzled at the humorless way they went about selecting their equipment. It was a type I was to get to know better in the years to come—the affluent, middle-aged American male, as joyless in his play as he was in his work—but at the time, they were new to me.

The worst of them was a tall man with a complexion the color of rust. He was going salmon fishing on the Miramachi, and wanted a "fly rod that wouldn't embarrass" him. I knew nothing about salmon fishing except that you needed a heavy rod, so I grabbed from the case the longest, thickest one I could find, mounted a reel on the bottom and led him outside to the pond.

Here was my chance. I would sell him this $300 fly rod, sell him a $100 reel and $20 line to go with it, and win the grudging respect of the other salesmen and my first commission besides.

"Nice rod," I said casually, threading the line through the guides. "One of our least embarrassing models."

I suggested that he try a few casts. They weren't very successful, partly because his cast technique was weak, but mostly because I had mounted it with a line that was far too light.

"Feels floppy," he said, frowning.

"I think it needs more forearm," I suggested.

Now the first rule in helping someone with a rod was *never in any way criticize his casting*. The man's face immediately reddened.

"I think I'd rather have someone else," he said.

I ignored him. "Here, I'll show you how."

I picked up the rod. Working out some line, I started false-casting toward the pond. Everything went fine until I had about fifty feet out, when between one moment and the next my carefully constructed dream fell apart. The line, alighting on the pond, was enough to suggest a fish-chow pellet to the still-hungry trout. One of them made a rise toward the tip of my leader. Instinctively striking back at him, the line whistled past my head toward the customer's. He ducked—I yanked on the line and sent it flailing back again toward the pond, only now it was completely out of control. I had one more chance, but I blew it; the line, undulating back again over my head, coiled itself around one of the benches near the parking lot. Before I could stop myself, I had started my forward cast again, and the moment the line tightened, the rod shattered apart in my hands.

For a moment, all was silence.

"Jesus," the man said.

Even at nineteen, I was writer enough to recognize an exit line when I heard one. Without saying a word, without telling anyone where I was going, I took off my fishing shirt, placed it carefully by the pond, and voluntarily ended my brilliant career.

5
Symphony

The 21st now, and seventeen of these days have seen rain, most of it torrential. Just when it became insupportable—just when the rain and dampness became permanent in our souls—we had a change. It began to snow.

Welcome to May in Vermont.

My bus-driving friend Ken Baker put it best. We were following a snowplow down toward Hanover, watching the unutterably depressing sight of flowers disappearing under a heavy outwash of white.

"Well," Ken said, lapsing into the thick Yankee accent he saves for his wriest profundities, "was a pretty good winter until spring got here."

Ayuh. But while I can come to terms with mudholes, leaky roofs, and smothered tulips, I've had a harder time adjusting to what the rain has done to my river. It's unfishable, of course—so high and muddy and wide it reminds me of old black-and-white newsreels I've seen of the Mississippi in flood. And though my intellect registers that I have absolutely no business wading it, my instincts are programmed to May, and I gravitate toward its banks with all the free will of a withered daffodil caught up in its current.

I was a fisherman who—before drowning—badly needed a nudge. As it turned out, I got two, and both were gentler than I had any right to expect.

The first nudge was quite literal. I was casting in the rain above the longest of the river's bridges, the new steel one they put in last July. It's a thoughtful place to fish. On the left bank are the ruins of a century-old stone bridge the ice had long since washed out; on the right are the twisted beams of a more recent span, an arthritic victim of old age. I like the continuity there—fords are where the fates of rivers and man are longest entwined, and it's nice to be faced with reminders of their coexistence.

The sogginess having entered my brain, it was half an hour before I realized that by far the driest place to fish was underneath the bridge. I waded down through water that was up to my chest. By casting sidearm, I was able to fish the pool below the supports. Except for the pressure of the current on my back and the vibrations of lumber trucks ten inches above my head, it was like fishing indoors.

I was changing to a bigger streamer when I felt something slam into my waders above my hips—a log, as it turned out. We wrestled each other for a while, me trying to keep my balance, the log squirming like a little boy caught beneath my arm, spitting bark. I yanked on one of its branches and it pranced away downstream and vanished into foam.

"The trees are starting to go," my intellect said. It was very clear on that point. My instinct, though, still insisted on May.

"Three more casts," it said blindly. My intellect—scared witless now—said nothing.

I took a tentative step below the bridge. By leaning backward in the current as if I were hiking out on a sailboat, I somehow managed to keep my feet. It wasn't easy. The pounding water left me with something resembling vertigo. I felt I was teetering on the edge of a subway platform as the Seventh Avenue local roared by, in constant danger of being sucked in.

I was well past my three-cast limit when I became aware of a man in a yellow slicker watching me from beneath a pine tree on the bank.

"Water pretty cold, eh?" he said, displaying an even better Yankee twang than Ken's.

"Naw," I said. "Water's always nice in May."

But there was no fooling him. As he ducked around the pine tree his slicker opened far enough to reveal the uniform of a Vermont game warden.

"How's the fishing, sir?" he said, going to work.

"It stinks." I twisted around a bit so he could see the license pinned to my hat.

"Little rainy for fishing," he suggested. "Fact of it is, the river goes up another inch, highway department's going to close this bridge here. Won't be any getting east until it goes back down."

West of me were sixteen miles of flooded river, waterlogged trees that were beginning to tumble, dirt roads with no bottom, a car that started temperamentally in the rain. East of me was a warm pub with good Bourbon, my fiancée, a clean, well-lighted home. Getting out of that turgid water was the easiest decision of my life.

I talked with the warden as I packed my gear. He had been driving along the river intending to warn all the fishermen he met about the flood, but I was the only one he had found. Actually, he admitted with something like awe, I was the only fisherman he had seen in the last three days.

"Dedicated," he said, laughing.

"Stubborn," I said, putting him right.

As it turned out, the bridge held—the threatened flood never came. Still, there was enough rain throughout the rest of the week to make me consider all the alternatives to going back to that swollen river. The first was not to fish at all . . . Immediately rejected. Drastic measures were called for, but not that drastic. The second alternative was to head south for a drier Cape Cod and the "salter" streams I had fallen in love with when I lived there in the early '80s . . . Considered, then finally put aside. As beautiful as they are, those rivers formed a separate chapter in my life, and it would have been impossible to fish them without a heavy sense of *déjà vu*. The third was to fish a favorite trout pond in the New Hampshire mountains across the Connecticut. Attempted, then given up. Constantly bailing a leaky canoe has never been my idea of fun, and if any trout were rising while I was there, their circles were indistinguishable from those left by the rain.

So it was the river after all. There was a deeper reason for going back. This was the year I was devoting to the river alone, and I needed to stay in touch with it through all its moods, cranky as well as calm. As hard as its trout were to catch, the river itself—the sense of it—was even harder, and May was too soon to quit trying. There were occasional afternoons when the sun came out long enough to show what we were missing, and I would put away my writing and race the steaming shadows north. My fishing diary shows two rain-free hours on the 9th; three hours on the 12th; a whole afternoon on the 18th. As rare as the sun was, its effect on my face was galvanizing—I felt as if I had been switched onto solar, and the charge of energy was enough to last me through the inevitable change back to rain.

There was little chance of catching trout—the water was as high and thick as gravy in an overfilled tureen. But not catching trout is important, too. It opens up the fly fisherman to other moods and impressions, widens his focus from the small crescent of river swept by his fly. Troutless, we begin seeking alternate treasures to take home. Some might begin sketching or taking pictures of the river's scenery; some might use the time to reconnoiter parts of the river they don't already know. One woman I know picks up rocks along the river's edge, searching for fossilized nymphs; another goes into the woods in search of edible plants.

Me, I did none of these things. I opened up my ears and listened.

It would have been hard not to. A great deal of the river's energy was being expended in sound, and all my casts, all my journeys from stance to precarious stance, all my meditations, were backed by this roaring, rushing sweep. The aural power was intense—I felt as if I were in the middle of an amplifier, part of a circuit required for the sound's transmission. Overhanging branches strummed a whisking sound on the water racing beneath their tips; rocks clattered against each other like cymbals; boulders established a backwash of sound that was pitched to a slower, heavier rhythm than the current's main theme, a throb as ponderous and regular as surf.

The river had to raise its voice to get my attention. Like most flyfishermen, the sound of moving water has always been a pleasant accompaniment to my day—an *accompaniment*, little more than background noise, though of the loveliest kind. It had never occurred to me to try to analyze it. Sound's part in stalking fish, after all, is largely negative: we try to avoid making any. As a positive force, sound seldom enters our consideration. Fly fishing is primarily a visual sport—the finning trout and quick rise come to us through our eyes. Touch plays a part—there's the feel of the bottom as we wade, the pull on our line as a trout takes hold. Give up his sight or his sensation of touch, and the flyfisherman would be seriously handicapped; give up his hearing, and his skill would be reduced not at all.

Trout are partly to blame for sound's unimportance. They emit no beeping noises that help us locate them; they neither whistle, squawk, rattle nor hiss. A bubbly, splashing sound as they feed is the best they can do. Their dumbness is a curse and blessing both. It makes it harder for us to find them, but easier to fight them once we do. Would flyfishermen still enjoy catching trout if the fish could groan? "I hooked a noisy rainbow in fast water," we might say. "He ran out a hundred yards of line, screamed at the top of his voice, then took to the air . . ." No, somehow I don't think we would.

Between the trout's silence and the flyfisherman's unreliance on his ears, sound has not received the attention from fishing writers that it deserves. Like surf and wind, a river's rush is one of the elemental voices in which nature has chosen to speak. But the writers who are best at describing a river do it primarily in visual terms; we can see Haig-Brown's Campbell or Grey's Rogue, we can often feel them, but can we ever hear them?

Describing sound is not easy. The vocabulary of inanimate noise is limited. Things ring, pop, click, buzz, bang, creak, hum, clang, sizzle, squeak, and not much else. These are landbound, static words—they lack the dynamic flow liquid sound requires. Simile helps a bit; for instance, there's a small rapid below the Aquarium that makes a steady, sprinkly kind of sound, like the fountain on the terrace of Lincoln Center when it's turned on full blast. But while it is almost impossible to write about sound without such similes, they stand in the way. If we can only refer to a sound by relating it to other sounds, we sacrifice preciseness, put our words one or two steps beyond the sensations they're meant to describe.

A race of fishermen could easily invent a vocabulary to get around this. Take a sound that every fly fisherman knows well: water falling over a weir or small dam. It's a drumming, happy kind of sound, at least in English. In our angling vocabulary we could avoid all images of drums and happiness by giving it a precise name: *umshoo*. "I was fishing by the dam, listening to the river *umshoo* we could say, and fly fishermen everywhere would know what we meant. Water dropping over two or more weirs in succession would make a sound with one beat or more: *umshooeen*. Water running beneath an undercut bank would make a soft *squahish* noise . . . and so on.

Until such a language is adopted, fishing writers must rely on the similes on hand. Luckily, there is one vocabulary that is devoted pure and simply to describing variations in sound, and it fits a river quite well: the vocabulary of music.

A river's sound is nothing if not symphonic—one beautiful whole composed of scarcely less beautiful parts, each of which can be distinguished within the overmastering rhythm. The light, percussive effect of pebble hitting pebble; the reedy drone of sand washing away from a bar; the brassy fanfare of spray against granite . . . they weave their way in and out of the steadier, cello-like continuo of the river's motion. A river bed is a sounding board over which water strums the earth, shaking molecules against other molecules until a wave is formed which—reaching a certain frequency—reacts pleasantly on our ears. This scale established, the symphony begins.

A drop of water falls from a branch high upstream with a soft plucking kind of noise . . . solo at first, then joined by another drop further back toward the branch's stem, then another, then a fourth, until finally the pluckings become simultaneous, and the first liquid chord of the river is created—a high treble rill of sound as the merged raindrops sparkle down a grooved rock into the stream. The rain-formed current pushes a drowned branch against a boulder, then lets it spring back; pushes it, then lets it spring back, establishing a soft metronomic click from which the entire river takes its beat.

The character of the music is evident right from the start. The White River, for instance, is romantic even in its tributaries—a broad sweep of sound that suggests Smetena's *Moldau*. The Battenkill, running in a narrower channel, is more classical, a river composed by a Mozart or Haydn, with pure tones and an effortless harmonic impulse that carries you along.

My river in its upper reaches is unmistakably baroque. It begins far from the road in a quiet wood where silence is so absolute it seems not the mere absence of noise but a creative force waiting to be tapped. The instrumentation that gathers it is the simplest—there are those raindrops forming into rills, the baby tributaries with their high, brittle bounce, the miniature falls whose notes are as clear and distinct as a harpsichord's. With no heavy rapids to drown out their sound, the soloists retain their distinctness as the process goes on; close your eyes and you can still find the percolating drops of rain within the metallic, more ornamental notes of the falls. I listen to a Bach cantata by following one instrument or voice as it winds its way through the entirety of the piece, using it as a guide through the beautiful intricacy of sound, and I find myself listening to the upper stretches of my river in the same way.

Upstream, the sound is channeled into definite boundaries. Walk fifty yards from the banks, and the music is indistinguishable from the wind's. Below the first substantial tributaries, the sound widens and darkens—waterfalls add their bass notes and rapids pitch everything to a speedier tempo. Culverts give a hollow sound to the river; the supports of the highway bridges make a steely, atonal kind of noise that is out of sync with the river's lilt, giving the effect of an Ives forcing notes onto something by Schubert.

There's a rapid below the last bridge that makes a sound very much like human song—a delicate soprano voice struggling to be heard over the orchestration. The first time I fished there, I swore someone was calling my name from the bank. I turned to see who it was, but there was no one—the sound was coming from the rapid itself, as if there were a maiden entombed beneath the flow. How to account for it? Is there an underwater rock whose configuration mimics the human larynx? Is the rapid's pitch that of speech? Or is there a maiden entombed there after all, an Indian princess scorned by an early settler who took her life over the falls? Standing there listening to that unearthly whisper, it's easy to understand how myths begin.

Below this rapid, it's harder to separate the river's sounds into parts. I wade out to the rapid's edge to listen more attentively, but it's too close—there is a roar of white noise in which all kinds of boomings, skitterings, raps, and gurgles lay concealed.

You have to go along with the sweep. With a river as with a symphony there comes a time when you have to stop trying to analyze it and let yourself be swept along in its sensuous beauty. By the time the South Branch comes in, the river's sound is at fullest amplitude, the various riffles, rapids, chutes, and falls joining into one churning vibrato that becomes its own echo. A jet of water beats apart the muting bark of a log; a poorly balanced boulder rumbles sideways in the current, groaning Fs; a rapid sets up a sizzling noise as it drops shatter apart into spray; white, downpressing water drums furiously toward the bottom, then boils up again further downstream . . . all the river's effects are in chorus now, *allegro* now, then *presto,* joining together for one magnificent finale as the river gathers itself for that last percussive leap over the dam, a showy display of sound that is felt more than heard.

The invisible conductor of things brings his baton down, the last note fades away. The river makes a random, shuffling kind of noise in its last hundred yards to the Connecticut, like that of an orchestra's members going their own ways after the concert reaches its end. The river's undetectable currents finally merge. The flow out of silence into silence returns.

6
Take a Writer Fishing

I dreamt one night that I was fishing with Joseph Conrad. We were on the open stretch of the river above the first bridge. I was casting a dry fly toward a shallow spot that couldn't possibly have held a trout; Conrad was shaking his head in disapproval, muttering something in Polish that I couldn't understand. He was fishing with a handline, hauling it in over his shoulder as if it were an anchor rope, really straining—his fine beard was drenched in sweat. I would have liked to help him, but was too shy. More than anything, I wanted him to approve of the river and love it as much as I did.

Too soon, he faded into Bob Cousy. But so vivid was his image that when I woke up that morning, I went to the library to determine whether there's any record of his having fished. Had I put him on that trout stream by myself, or was there some half-remembered reference to the sport buried away in *Nostromo?*

I suppose I'm to blame. None of the novels or stories contain fishing scenes, and there's no mention of any interest in his autobiographical writings. In the course of his maritime career he must have known men who fished hard for their living, and fishing for fun must have smacked to him of affectation.

Searching through Conrad, remembering the dream, I began trying to list all the great writers who are known to have been dedicated fishermen. It's a remarkably short list, and I'm not sure why. Is it because great writers are too intellectual to take any interest in something so earthy as fishing? I don't think so—fly fishing has always attracted a brainy sort, and among its practitioners are a great number of scientists, engineers, artists, and teachers. Is it because writers bear too complicated a burden of worry and concern to enjoy fishing's basic premise? This might be closer to it. Like any other human activity, fishing has its share of ironies, and perhaps the act of trying to fool a trout into thinking a piece of feather and steel is a mayfly is too fundamentally absurd for a great mind to endure . . . partly this, and partly that writers with their torments know too well what it's like to have a barbed hook in their throat, and have no wish to inflict the same torture on another harmless soul.

Let's go down the list. Hemingway is first, if for no other reason than that his love for fishing was the most self-advertised. The popular conception of Hemingway as a fisherman revolves around his days fishing off Cuba and the Keys on his beloved *Pilar,* with the kind of epic, day-long encounters with marlin that formed the basis of *The Old Man and the Sea.* While this kind of big-fish fishing, with its competitiveness, its emphasis on sheer physical power and machismo, obviously meant a lot to Hemingway and revealed much that was fundamental in his character, it doesn't present him in a particularly attractive light. Would it have been fun to be on the *Pilar* with him fishing the "great blue stream" of the Gulf? For a while, perhaps, then something of a bore. Arnold Gingrich, his friend and sometime publisher, claimed that "Ernest was a meat fisherman . . . intensely competitive about his fishing, and a very poor sport." This seems like an accurate appraisal; it's fun to catch a big fish, but not if your manhood is being measured by how fast you reel him in.

It's the younger, not-yet-legendary Hemingway—the Hemingway who fished grasshoppers for trout—who's the appealing one. The golden moments of his boyhood revolved around his trips to the lakes and streams of the Upper Peninsula of Michigan, the locale of his "Big Two-Hearted River." In this, and in his early journalism for the *Toronto Star,* there's a boyish sincerity and brightness that gives way to pontification twenty years later when he's writing about big game. Included in his early journalism are accounts of streams he'd visited in Canada and Europe, illuminated by the typically compact Hemingway style. Here's a man who can sum up the enchantments of a trout river in one beautiful phrase: "A pool whose moselle-colored water sweeps into a dark swirl and expanse that is blue-brown with depth and fifty feet across." Here's a man who has an eye for other things than trout, and can include in an account of a Swiss fishing trip meditations on barmaids in station buffets, Napoleon's army in the St. Bernard pass, and the latest news in a trout-stained *Daily Mail.* This Hemingway—the young man who hiked across the Black Forest in the '20s with a rucksack and a fly rod and not much else—is the one with whom I would have liked to fish.

Thoreau's another writer it would be fun going out on the river with, though you'd have to be prepared for some trouble. I don't mean dealing with his reserved personality (Sophia Hawthorne said that taking his hand was like taking the hand of an elm), but with his ambivalence toward fishing. Did he love it or hate it?

Read his account of night-fishing on Walden, and you'd swear no one ever loved the sport more. He tells of returning late to the pond from the village and spending the dark hours of midnight fishing from a boat, "communicating by a long flaxed line with mysterious nocturnal fishes . . . now and then feeling a slight vibration along it, indicative of some life probing about its extremity, of dull uncertain blundering purpose there, and slow to make up its mind."

Thoreau, for all his talk of simplicity, was too complicated a man to leave it at that. As much as he enjoyed fishing (we have that famous image of Thoreau playing the flute in his boat, charming the perch gathered about the bow), he was convinced that he *shouldn't*—that fishing, like hunting, was an important but essentially immature response to nature and its wonders, a pursuit for "embryo" man and not those attuned to the "higher laws." He puts down the fishermen who come to Walden thus: "They might go there a thousand times before the sediment of fishing would sink to the bottom and leave their purpose pure." He's equally hard on himself: "I have found repeatedly, of late years, that I cannot fish without falling a little in self-respect. I have tried it again and again. I have skill at it . . . but always when I have done I feel it would have been better if I had not fished . . . with every year I am less a fisherman . . . at present, I am no fisherman at all."

There's no apology at all in that other great nineteenth-century nature writer, John Burroughs. While Thoreau was at

Walden deciding whether or not to fish, Burroughs was out on the *Neversink*, celebrating trout fishing with some of his happiest prose. "Trout streams coursed through every valley my boyhood knew," he writes in his essay, "Speckled Trout." He describes trips to the *Delaware, Rondout, Beaverkill,* and *Esopus*— trips in which it was nothing for each fisherman to take a hundred trout.

Burroughs had more insight into the sport than Thoreau. He claims he'd seen more of woods and nature in "threading my native streams for trout," than he would have in any other way. Fishing "pitches one in the right key" to accept nature; the fisherman "is a kind of vagrant that nothing fears . . . all his approaches are gentle and indirect." With this attitude, fly selection is no problem: "When you bait your hook with your heart, the fish always bite!" And later: "A certain quality of youth is indispensable to the successful angler, a certain unworldliness and readiness to invest yourself in an enterprise that doesn't pay in the current coin."

Washington Irving fished some of those same Catskill streams. One of the essays in his *Sketch Book,* "The Angler," is a self-deprecatory account of his flirtation with trout. Reading Izaak Walton has left him "stark mad [about fishing] as was ever Don Quixote from reading books of chivalry." Thus intoxicated, he ventures out on an upstate stream with all the necessary accouterments ("perplexed with half a hundred pockets") and begins to cast.

The results are meager. "For my part, I was always a bungler at all kinds of sports that require either patience or adroitness . . . I hooked myself instead of a fish, tangled my line in every tree, lost my bait, broke my rod and gave up the attempt in despair." Poor Irving! How we can sympathize with him!

Nothing daunted, he ends the day reading his beloved Walton under the shade of a gentle oak. "There is certainly something in angling," he concludes, "if we could forget, which anglers are apt to do, the cruelties and tortures inflicted on worms and insects, that tends to produce a gentleness of spirit and a pure serenity of mind."

Irving's contemporaries were less fond of the sport. His friend Sir Walter Scott described himself as "No fisher, but a well-wisher to the game." He must have known a little about the subject; there's a scene in *Redgauntlet* where Darsie Latimer dismisses Charles Cotton's writings as not being applicable to Highlands streams, then goes on to spin his version of the familiar barefoot-boy-out-fishing-sophisticated-angler story. Scott's dismissal of Cotton is echoed in Lord Byron's put-down of Walton: "The quaint, old, cruel coxcomb in his gullet; should have a hook, and a small trout to pull it." Tennyson's poetry includes an occasional reference to fishing—apparently he shared with Burroughs and Irving the opinion that it was good for the soul to engage in something so absolutely *uneconomic*. "Lusty trout to him were script and share; and babbling waters more than cent for cent." To find the real angling poet you have to move ahead forty years to Yeats. It's funny about him. There's no mention of any fishing trips in his autobiography, and yet he wrote some of the finest poetry on the subject extant. There's "The Fisherman": "Although I can see him still,/The freckled man who goes,/To a grey place on a hill,/In grey Connemara clothes,/At dawn to cast his flies"; and "The song of Wandering Aengus": "Because a fire was in my head . . . I dropped the berry in a stream, and caught a little silver trout."

Reading Yeats, you come to the conclusion that what he really loved was the sound of the word *trout* and the pastoral, innocent image it conveyed. To him, trout were like fairies in the Irish hills—something you thought well of without actually wishing to catch. In all the fishing in print has there ever been a more magical line than the one from "The Stolen Child"? "We seek for slumbering trout, and whispering in their ears,/Give them unquiet dreams."

If Yeats is the epitome of the mystical fisherman, then Chekhov is the personification of the earthy one. No great writer ever loved fishing more. Nina, speaking of the writer Trigorin in *The Seagull,* could easily have been describing Chekhov himself. "And is it not wonderful that a famous writer, the darling of the public, mentioned daily in the papers . . . should spend his whole day fishing and be delighted because he has caught two chub."

Chekhov would have been a good man to fish with—caring nothing for orthodoxy, whether in literature or fishing, and with that rare ability to forget he's a great man. Fishing was a welcome diversion from the cares of literature and medicine; the moment he bought his country estate at Melikhovo in 1892, he began stocking his ponds with tench imported from Moscow in glass jars. Trigorin, the bemused writer stumbling about other people's lives carrying a notebook and a fishing rod, is in some part Chekhov's wry laugh at himself. (I once saw a performance of *The Seagull* in which Trigorin—a man fishing a farm pond for chub—carried the kind of huge saltwater rod Zane Grey might have used, thereby making ludicrous what was otherwise a fine production.)

Chekhov's real fishing masterpiece is a lesser-known story called "Fish." It bears the simplest of plots. Berasim, a peasant, is working by the river preparing a bathing shed when he grabs a huge fish that's hiding under some willow roots. Other peasants come over and offer their advice on how to land him

("But why do you keep poking with your hand?" cries the hunchback Lubim, shivering as though in a fever. "You blockhead! Hold him, hold him, or else he'll get away, the anathema! Hold him, I tell you!"); the matter isn't resolved until the master himself, Andrey Andreitch, hears the commotion and joins the fun.

"A famous eel-pout," mutters Yefim, scratching under his shoulder blades. "I'll be bound it weighs ten pounds."

"Mm . . . yes," the master assents. "The liver is fairly swollen! It seems to stand out! Aach!"

The fish makes a sudden, unexpected upward movement with its tail and the fishermen hear a loud splash . . . they all put out their hands, but it is too late; they have seen the last of the eel-pout.

It's all there—the simple excitement of it, the suspense, the climax and immediate anticlimax. Chekhov has always been regarded as the writer's writer, and based on the insights he shows in this story, he was the fisherman's fisherman as well.

T. H. White was another writer who had an uncanny insight into fish and fishing. We have that masterful scene in *The Sword in the Stone* where the Wart, the young King Arthur, is transformed into a tench by Merlin so he may swim about the castle moat and complete his education among the fish, nearly being swallowed by a pike in the process. White had a great natural affinity with animals, birds, and fish; nature was a balm for the torments of his inner life, offering him the companionship he could never find with another human. White—with his falconer's patience—would have been a methodical fisherman and a learned one; he and Chekhov could have taught each other a lot.

With White, the list nears its end. (It could be extended by including contemporary fiction writers like William Humphrey,

Caroline Gordon, Norman Maclean, Richard Brautigan, and Tom McGuane, people who have written about fishing in imaginative and original ways.) Looking back on the writers mentioned, several names stick out by their absence—writers whose silence on fishing is in some ways a surprise.

Take Melville, for instance. Here's a man who in *Moby-Dick* gave us what is arguably the best "fishing" story ever written (Melville, remember, insisted that the whale was a *fish),* and yet there are only three or four vague references to fishing in his entire output, and they're all less than memorable. Take this poem from *Mardi:* "Fish, fish, we are fish with red gills/Naught disturbs us, our blood is zero/We are buoyant because of our bags/Being many, each fish is a hero . . ." Which is a long way from Yeats. But it's easy to understand why Melville wasn't a fisherman. To anyone who had clung to the sides of a whale boat on a Nantucket sleigh ride, catching ten-inch Berkshire trout must have seemed pretty tame.

Dickens is another novelist you might have expected to write about fishing, if for no other reason than he seems to have written about everything else. There are no anglers among his characters, not even among the sporting Pickwickians. Dickens does, however, hold an honorary place in the angling hall of fame. The Dolly Varden trout is named after the irrepressible Dolly Varden of *Barnaby Rudge,* "the very impersonation of good-humour and blooming beauty . . . giddy, flirtatious and coquettish."

Robert Frost should by rights be an angler. Of all the greats so far mentioned, he's the only one who might have known the rivers I love, and I regret there's no record in his poetry of any involvement. Ernest Poole, the novelist who was Frost's Franconia Notch neighbor, mentions in a reminiscence that Frost liked to go fishing in the spring, but these expeditions left no trace in his work. In his collected poems there is only one reference to fishing; it comes in "The Mountain" where the local farmer, in explaining his relationship to the mountain that rises behind his farm, says "I've been on the sides,/Deer-hunting and trout-fishing . . ." And that's it for Robert Frost. There are no hymns to New Hampshire trout streams, no recollections of fishing trips in the Green Mountains—his Hyla Brooks are always fish-less. Like Conrad, he knew too well the hard work that went into wresting a living from nature to spare much attention to people who went to the woods for sport.

And what about William Faulkner? Why didn't he leave us a fishing equivalent of "The Bear"? He lived in a region where fishing was a way of life, and he must have listened to his share of fishing stories during his spell of purgatory at the local post office. Mississippi is bass country—the stories would have been of monster largemouths caught on frogs. And while these were the kind of oral legends Faulkner thrived on, he never got around to writing as lovingly about fishing as he did about hunting.

There is one account of Faulkner's interest in fishing, and it's a poignant and moving one. After his death in 1962, his neighbors in Oxford put their recollections of the man they called Bill into a book. Among the contributions is one by J. Aubrey Seay in which he describes meeting Faulkner by a lake four days before the great writer's death. Seay was going fishing, and he asked Faulkner if he would like to come along. Faulkner politely declined—he wasn't feeling up to it—but he asked if he could sit and watch them fish through binoculars.

I've thought of that scene often lately—the great man bundled up against the death that was around the corner, staring out over the lake's surface with an old pair of binoculars, trying one last time to watch and learn. I think of Seay casting for bass from the bow of that boat across the lake—how fishermen can never know when they're posing for someone who might just possibly make them eternal. I picture myself on the river under that doomed, all-seeing gaze, and it makes me cast a little more carefully, doing everything in slow-motion so that Bill Faulkner—his hands trembling on the binoculars—can get it right.

7
June Sixteenth

I teeter between two illusions when fishing. The first is apt to come on dark afternoons in early May when the river is so rain-swollen and muddy that even to think of casting into it seems an act of maddest optimism. No insects brighten the surface, no fry scoot from beneath my feet, and no trout intercept my streamer on its dull and hopeless course downstream. At these times I'm apt to conclude that acid rain, pesticides, and hazardous waste have finished their poisonous work, leaving the river utterly fishless, devoid of life in any form.

My second illusion is the direct opposite. It consists of the absolutely unshakable belief that there are fish in the river after all, and not only *in* the river, but that the very river itself is *composed* of fish, and that what normally would be taken for rushing water is in truth the speckled, iridescent backs of countless thousands of trout, rainbows and browns combining like hydrogen and oxygen in an elemental bonding. For a fly fisherman, this is a happier illusion. It makes fishing a much simpler chore, the taking of even a large trout being about as difficult as the act of dipping your hand in the water to drink.

I indulged in this second illusion once for fifteen-sixteenths of a perfect June day. The river, after being near flood stage for over a month, had settled into its proper springtime banks. The sogginess in the air was gone, swept out by a northwest wind that managed to combine the sharp clarity of fall with the lush promise of summer. The farms along the river had roses growing in the marge of their fields. Baby lambs tripped over wildflowers; cows pranced as exuberantly as colts. Ten-year-olds, newly released from school, marched single-file through the meadows above the junction pool with butterfly nets, hunting for who knows what adventures in the tall and waving grass.

Me, I was fastened to a trout. It was the shady, narrow stretch above the cemetery, a part of the river I had never fished seriously before. As usual when searching new water, I had on a Muddler—a fly whose effectiveness and versatility make it a fine tool for probing. In confirmation of this, the fly was attached to the lip of a ten-inch rainbow who was bouncing out of the water below me as joyously and airily as spray. After a fishless month, I badly needed to feel him in my hand, and beached him more carefully than his size required. I held him in the current for several minutes before releasing him, partly to let him recover his strength, partly to re-establish my connection with the pulse of the river's life.

I had four more trout in the next eight casts—five if you count the miniature brookie I caught when I changed positions and let the line drag unattended behind me. Sometimes a river will come exactly into place with all its components—proper hatches at the proper times, perfect blendings of light and shade, optimum water level and temperature—and the fish will feed freely all day, as if compelled by the classic setting to do their part.

This is the kind of perfection I was wading through. By eleven, I had gone for the cycle—at least one rainbow, one brookie, and one brown. It's not an uncommon feat on the river; the bright, native brookies tend to inhabit the upper stretches, but I have caught the paler stocked ones as far downstream as the dam, and the rainbows turn up everywhere. Brook trout are the natives here, of course, but in this part of the river there is a rootlessness about them that makes them seem like interlopers. I catch them in the riffles mostly, spots that are probably their second or third choice after the rainbow- and brown-usurped pools. It's a pathetic story, this—a hundred years ago, the river was entirely theirs. The human analogy would be the sons of farmers you see milling about the bars in New England towns, perpetual renters, their fathers' land gone to condominiums and malls.

There is a bit of this in the rainbows, too, as abundant and strong as they are. They're flashy and intelligent, these western transplants, but a bit much so for these quiet Vermont hills. When they zip across the river toward the west on the end of a line, I always imagine that they're trying, however forlornly, to get home.

It is the brown trout that seems most comfortable here. Why this should be so, I'm not sure, but I sense it every time I catch one. The brookies dash about in a semidisoriented way; the rainbows go airborne, but the German browns pull with the knowledge and power of successful imperialists. Just before noon, I took a fourteen-incher—on the river, my best brown by far—and he fought with what can only be described as a supercilious air, running downstream with enough hurry to let me know he was annoyed but not enough to betray any anxiety. When I beached him, it wasn't because he submitted, but because he was bored, and he swam off after his release with the offended air of gentry compelled to argue with tradesmen over the price of beef.

And so it went. I caught fish on whatever fly I tried—a yellow Marabou, a Gold-Ribbed Hare's Ear, Matukas in three different shades. The only thing that seemed to matter was the direction they were fished; on a slow drift diagonally across the current, I could count on a trout every third or fourth cast. There came to seem an inevitability to it after a while. The line uncoiled and landed across the river; the fly surfed for a moment on the lip of the current's edge; the main, heavier current caught the belly of the line and pulled it under; the fly swung in a long arc downstream; the line, just as it tightened straight below me, tightened again, harder this time, as a trout took hold.

The catching became a pattern, a consistency that seemed part of the warp and weave of the day itself. This unfolding, scalloped arc of the fly-line as it gradually swung downstream . . . it was hard not to believe that this was precisely the dynamic geometrical line that nature had picked to align itself on during that particular June day, and my success with the trout was because—recognizing the grain—I had aligned myself with it, too.

Number nine, number ten, number eleven. With each one, I came to like this new stretch of river more and more. Vermont rivers, with their infinite variation on the basic riffle-boulder-pool theme, have the ability to suggest a great variety of other, more distant trout waters. The hundred yards or so I was fishing is particularly rich in these suggestions. Below me was a gravel bar that could have been right out of the steelhead/salmon rivers that run down from the Olympics in Washington. Behind me, the river narrowed enough for the willows in either side to touch tops and form a tunnel, reminding me of forest brook-trout water in Maine. The pool I was fishing now had the sandy bottom you can find on the streams of Cape Cod, and the rapid beyond it was as steep and tumultuous as any mountain brook in Colorado.

With a nice rainbow, I was up to a dozen, and it seemed like a good time for lunch. I climbed out of the river below the cemetery and walked over to the grass near its edge, sitting down only when I found a spot where the shade had my face, the sun my legs. Celeste had packed some sandwiches. I had been carrying a beer around in my wader pocket, and it was still satisfyingly cold.

Now it is hard to be near a cemetery sipping beer without doing some serious reflecting. What I mainly wondered about was whether anyone had ever written a treatise explaining why so many good fishing spots seem to be near cemeteries. I can think of half a dozen places off hand, and that's only in Vermont.

Is it because people avoid the area around a cemetery, thus ensuring that the pools there are underfished? Is it because our eighteenth-century ancestors had a lovely eye for terrain, and always picked out meadows to bury their dead, meadows that would be situated above placid, easy stretches of river? Is it because cemeteries with their calm, thoughtful air make the fisherman calm and thoughtful, too, thereby instilling the perfect attitude for taking trout? Or is it none of these things, but a mystic something that establishes communion between the ghosts of trout and fishers past with trout and fishers present?

I opened the gate to the cemetery to take a closer look. It's rectangular in shape, about an acre in area, with a gentle slope uphill from the river. Three sides are bordered by stone walls, the fourth by a strange Victorian version of a wire fence. With the sun at its highest, there was enough shade for all the graves—shadows cast by oaks that were saplings when the last burial there took place.

None of the headstones are dated past 1880—most are from a time far earlier. Roughly half are the same four-foot height, simple and unadorned, but here and there one rises above the others where a family had indulged in some morbid one-up-manship. (Seeing them, one can picture the conflict in the eighteenth-century Puritan mind between the need to show that dear departed whoever was no better than anyone else and the belief that he or she *was* in fact better, and thus deserved a *slightly* higher headstone.) The only truly extravagant one features a scowling man in what's apparently meant to be a toga, towering above his headstone with one finger gravely raised to heaven like the Commendatore in *Don Giovanni*.

Efforts had been made to keep the cemetery neat, but the grass hadn't been cut in weeks and several of the headstones had tipped over. There was yellow lichen growing in the inscriptions—it was only by kneeling down and squinting that I could make out the words.

There are some real patriarchs buried in that little grove. Phineas S. Cobb, for example, who died February 27, 1832, aged seventy-four; a Revolutionary War veteran who would have been eighteen in 1776, old enough to be with Johnny Stark's men down at Bennington. Not far from him lies Susannah Thompson, who died September 20, 1859, aged ninety-three—a life span that took her from the time Vermont was an unexplored wilderness to the eve of the Civil War.

Some of the headstones are tragic reminders of a time when parents routinely outlived most of their children. Thus, "Freeman J. Claflin, Died Dec. 24, 1831, Aged 1 Year 7 Months 21 Days," or below it, "William W. Claflin, Died Nov. 25, 1831, Aged 20 Days." Picture that hideous winter in the Grant home. The baby dead first, just when the trauma of birth was over and he had begun to be dear to them all, then the other boy, down with perhaps the same flux or cough that had taken the baby, dead Christmas Eve.

Some of the headstones have poetry that is still legible, including Esther Loop, who in 1852 was addressed as follows: "Thus Like the Sun, slow Wheeling to the Wave;/She sank in Glory to her welcome Grave." Others are unintentionally funny. The last headstone I read marked the final resting place of a Wealthy A. Flint and her husband, Worcester T. One can picture the charming old fellow, a character out of Dickens as played by W. C. Fields.

When I returned to the fishing, it was with the feeling that I knew a little more about the river and the valley and my place in it. The sun had gotten around the trees now, and there was a sheen on the water that seemed as liquid and real as a second, higher river superimposed over the first. I caught my thirteenth trout of the day on my first cast, and within half an hour was up to fifteen.

Flyfishermen insist that it is quality, not quantity they are after, but even so most of us go around with a figure in our head that represents our own personal high. Mine is fifteen trout caught and released—tied several times, but never broken. I've come to think of it as a psychological barrier, a limit beyond which sport veers toward greed. The truth is that by the time I've caught even ten trout, I'm sated, and any further catching seems repetitive and dull. Even worse: at ten, a fisherman can pat himself on the back, pride himself on his skill; at fifteen, it's easy to believe that skill has no part in it at all, and that even Wealthy A. Flint herself, dead these ninety years, could catch her limit.

Still, it was too nice an afternoon to quit—I saw no harm in raising my record one more notch to sixteen. About twenty yards upstream, the river divided itself around a small island; the channel closest to the bank spilled over a large, flat rock into a pool the size of a card table. There was a trout there and a good one—I could make out his back beneath the competing swirls of sunlight.

By crossing to the lower end of the island, I could drop a fly over him without any problem. Once hooked, he would speed down the pool into the main current where I would have room to control his runs. Checking off number sixteen in my head, I tied on a nymph.

So far, so good. What I've forgotten to mention, though, is what I had forgotten to take into account: a water-smoothed log jutting obliquely out of the water in the pool's center, as sharp and menacing as a tank trap. There was no way around it. I could wade upstream and fish from above, but the river shallowed out before the pool, and there wouldn't be room to get the necessary swing in my drift before the fly grounded on the island. Even if I did hook him from above, his first run would inevitably carry him around the log, dooming my leader.

I started thinking. Maybe not a nymph after all—maybe a small Hendrickson dry. But no—there weren't any Hendricksons hatching. Perhaps a Quill Gordon instead. A Quill Gordon, or maybe an Adams.

I ended up using all three. My first cast brought a rise, but a halfhearted one, and when I struck at his shadow, the fly snapped back into my face.

Fine. A little more determined now, I went to the Muddler—for the trout, the kiss of death.

"Sixteen, you're mine," I said to myself, working the fly out so it would drop a little shy of the log.

If I listed all the flies I left sticking out of that wretched log in the next hour, you would have a complete inventory of my fly boxes; if I described all the different positions I cast from, you would be bored. The upshot, of course, was that I didn't catch that fish. No more rises, not even a quiver of interest as the occasional fly bumped his nose. By the time I gave up trying for him, the other fish had stopped taking, too. In the shreds and patches of my illusion, it seemed as if the trout-composed water had evaporated into dusk.

I was mad for a while, damned mad, but reflecting on it now, I realize that this last uncatchable trout was the most important fish of the day. The balloon of my pride had been expanding all afternoon, and the trout had been the gentle agent of its puncture. My sated, smug feeling was gone, replaced by the puzzled yet hopeful attitude a flyfisherman should never lose.

Next time, I would deliberately cast a small Bivisible *across* the log, letting it swing down like a pendulum left to right, teasing him, until . . .

Next time, I vowed as I climbed out of the river. Next time, trout. Next time!

Which—when you stop to think about it—is the nicest gift a fish can give.

8
Dusk into Dark

The past is often compared to the twilight, but what about comparing the twilight to the past? It has that remoteness to it. In July, when the sky at nine is three faint shades from the most delicate orange, it has that remoteness. It has the finished quality of the past, the sense that nothing essential can any longer be added or removed. The moving hand, having writ, moves on; the sun, having warmed the day and glorified its last few seconds, moves on. The past's serenity is reproduced in its setting. Watching it, the hurry in us dissolves, vanishing into a spacious sense of well-being and completeness that mirrors the dusk's calm. Anxiety can't touch it. It is the only moment in the world's long day that demands a single response: peace.

And so I fish it, staying as close as I can to its edge.

Edge. It's difficult to pin down. Put simply, it's the dividing line between dusk and dark, the light remaining between the moment the sun disappears beneath the horizon and the moment when it is finally night. The first limit, of course, is charted and fixed. In Vermont, summer sunsets are around nine, though fragments of blue and white may persist in the sky for another hour. This makes the other limit of the edge, the dark, much harder to determine. Is it when the soft pink is gone over the western hills? Is it when the flyfisherman can no longer see his fly riding on the river's surface? When he can no longer see his line?

This last is closer to it. There comes a moment when casting begins to lose its measured rhythm and the flyfisherman senses he is beginning to lose control. The fly shoots back dangerously close to his forehead; the leader, lost in half-light, refuses to uncoil. Hooks become un-threadable. Rocks once safely dormant spring to life—malevolent rocks that reach out a gritty edge to trip us. There is a hurry in our fishing that is all the more dramatic for its contrast to the preceding minutes of calm. One moment the flyfisherman is the picture of civilized grace; the next, he's a caveman caught in the nether world far from fire. This loss of control—this sensation of entering another realm where our power is dramatically reduced—is the essence of night and its only true boundary.

Put it at 9:40 or 9:45. The half-hour that comes before is my favorite time to fish in the summer. I have a redhead's sensitivity to the sun, and the intense light of July afternoons makes me as prickly and shy as a vampire. Fly fishing at night is something I'm ambivalent about at best. It is dusk when I am most comfortable, the brief period when enough sun is gone to cool the river, but enough is left to light it.

It can be a magic time. The haze of daylight is gone, liberating a coolness that was latent in the earth all along. Our sense of hearing becomes more acute as the power of our eyes declines, and sounds that were merged into undifferentiated background noise become separate and distinct. A church bell in the distant village chimes the hour. Firecrackers left over from the Fourth pop harmlessly over the hills. Birds sing with the enthusiasm and purity they had at sunrise; a whippoorwill starts up in that always vague, undetectable locale that is the bird's domain.

Casts become like brush strokes. This cast upstream toward the center of the willow-draped pool is a quick stroke of red, spun downstream toward you with a last decorative splash of pink; this cast quartering toward the far bank, a stroke of purplish-black that bleeds into sky.

Is it the shortness of twilight that gives it such richness? I remember flying out to Colorado once—how for an hour or more the plane kept pace with the sunset, and the horizon retained the same underlining of orange. It was dusk, but not real dusk; without fading it carried no regret, no ending, and lost half its beauty for that reason.

I wonder if trout are saddened by it. It's a facetious question, but I wonder all the same. Does the gradual blackening of the water above their lies make them think back on their days as fingerlings, regret mating partners they've lost track of, make them sense their mortality? Dusk must be a great disturbance for them, faced as they are with a dramatic change in the elemental lighting through which they swim. If trout were ever prone to introspection, surely this would be the time.

If there is a caddis hatch on, they're probably too busy feeding to think about anything at all. In a pool like the Aquarium, they will be everywhere, splashing the water apart as if to fan it back to light. Their hurry can be contagious. Instead of contemplating the sunset smoking his pipe, the fisherman is casting toward the rises in a frantic, beat-the-clock sort of way. It's the hatch you want to keep pace with, the insects' urgency, and a trout actually caught at dusk can seem like an interruption.

The interesting fish are the ones that lead you *over* the edge. I was fishing the stretch below Jonathan Sharp's dairy farm—the stretch with the Sphinx-sized boulders—and about fifteen minutes after the sun disappeared, hooked a good trout. At first, the fight went all my way. I tightened on him quickly, managed to hold my rod high enough to keep the line disentangled from the boulders, and had no trouble chasing after him along the bank. If anything, I was too casual about it. Between one moment and the next, dusk was into dark and the equation had drastically changed. The trout could see exactly where he was going, whereas I had begun to stumble. It was no contest—the trout's night senses were better evolved than mine, and on his next run past the bank, he twirled the line around a boulder and broke free.

He had taken me into night and left me there—blind, lost, and angry. I had absolutely no idea what to do next.

It's strange about fishing at night. Not too long ago, I would have told you that it was my favorite time to be out on the water, but this was when I was fishing lakes for bass. There are all kinds of lights and landmarks on a lake, and the reassuring presence of the boat acts as an axis on which you can orient your senses.

This is not the case when fishing a river. You're on your feet *in* the river, and there's never any telling what the next step will bring. Landmarks are few. On narrow stretches, the trees form a dome, blotting out the stars. Even if you're on a section of the river you know intimately, the dark has a way of distorting features until your very knowledge works against you. Ah, a big flat rock. Then surely I must be above the junction pool. But how could I have gone that far? I must have gone by it. Perhaps there are other flat rocks?

The mind becomes snarled.

I have been fishing at night all month, and I still can't master it. There are world-class rock climbers who can never go to the Himalayas because something in their physiology can't take altitude. Is it the same with fly fishermen? Are there some whose senses don't have that night adaptability, that mysterious blend of touch, sight, and hearing that only comes into play when light is gone?

Deeper yet. Is fly fishing all wrong at night, a misplaced conceit? If we use the fly rod as a means of becoming more intimately involved with the river, then perhaps it is. Intimacy does not lie in flailing the water with badly timed casts, nor is it found in stumbling blindly over rocks. The problems night-fishing presents are those of navigation, not presentation, and the less bother your tackle is, the more you can concentrate on this fundamental task. A worm on a bent pin would be best. Against the mystery of night, anything else is ostentation.

Consider the problems. Here I am again in that meadow below Jonathan Sharp's night-grazing cows. It is ten o'clock on a perfect Vermont summer night. I would like very much to enter the river, but I can see no way down the steep and slippery bank (a flashlight is cheating; if you fish at night, fish *in* night).

Even if I find a path, I have no idea where the pools are that hold trout. Should I locate one, I will have trouble fishing it, since the absence of a clear horizon makes me mistime my casts. Even if I straighten these out, I still have no idea what fly to use. Dry flies are useless if you can't see them; I've read about hooking trout by sound, but it's clearly impossible—there are too many other slurps, trickles, and plops around to distinguish a quiet sip. I could fish a sunk fly, but not without hang-ups; I've lost over forty flies this month—in tree limbs, earlobes, and bat wings. But what difference does it all make? If I hook a fish, I'll have no way of following his fight and he'll break off anyway . . . Here I remain in the meadow beneath Jonathan Sharp's night-grazing cows.

I'm sure there are answers to all these dilemmas—the hell of it is, I can't find them. I've consulted my library of fishing books, but without much luck. Fishing for trout after dark was illegal in most states until fairly recently, and there is no tradition of night-fishing lore to draw upon—no Gordon to seek advice from, no Bergman. The only book I found that had much to say about the subject was Lawrence Roller's *Taking Larger Trout*. Don't use conventional flies, he says; lull the fish into a false sense of security, and keep your fly in the water at all times. "In all night operations for trout, the emphasis is on constant casting, quiet movement, and slow fishing."

Okay, Mr. Roller. But doesn't constant casting contradict slow fishing? And exactly how am I going to lull the fish into a false sense of security? If anything is real and unshakable in my river at night, it's the trout's security—there's nothing false about it.

Out of ten nights' fishing this month, I've caught only one trout. I was wading through the moonlight above the pine canyon last week. I had stopped to examine something there in the water (it was a branch, but I thought at first it was the skeleton of a dead trout), when my line suddenly tightened. This is it! I thought. Night-fishing's balleyhooed reward—the monster brown that feeds only at dark. But alas, it wasn't he. It was a four-inch brookie, the smallest trout I've taken all year.

I'm staying out late again tonight. As discouraging as the process has been, there have been aspects of it that I've enjoyed. The light of the moon on the water, the way the current ripples it into overspreading little waves, the scalloped Vs that resemble a child's drawing of gulls, only in silver; the flickering yellow beams of kerosene lights on farmhouse porches through the trees; the quick, illuminating arc of a headlight thrown across the river as a car negotiates a bankside curve; the distant haze of stars; the new mysteries night brings to familiar water . . . all these things will continue to lure me out, and in the course of the summer I may begin to catch a sense of what night-fishing is all about.

Until that time, dark will always be a limit—my favorite time on the water will continue to be dusk. Not day, not night, but the peaceful edge of beauty in between.

9
A Trout for Celeste

For me, fly fishing and fly fishing alone have always been synonymous. Out of the several hundred times I've gone trout fishing in the last ten years, I can only think of two occasions when someone went with me, and these were both very recently. Being alone has become as much a part of my fishing as the river's current—a constant push of solitude, sometimes destructive, sometimes soothing, but always there.

Solitude has always seemed to me an enormous force. At various times I have cursed it, longed for it, used it, feared it, lost it, and found it again. What I have never done, though, is understand it. Thus, it's difficult for me to account for the strange gaps solitude has created in what's otherwise been a reasonably gregarious life. I write fiction for a living, yet I've never met another novelist; I like opera, yet know no opera fans. So too with fly fishing. Having loved it as much as I have, having pursued it with such attention, you'd think I would have enjoyed many rich friendships based on a mutual love of the sport, garnered many fine memories and anecdotes about my friends. I have none of these, and envy those who do. A friendship made on a trout stream must be a precious thing, almost as precious as solitude itself.

As solitude itself. I put it that way deliberately, because it's an accurate description of the way I once felt. Right from the start the memories that meant most to me in fly fishing were those of being alone with the river and the fish. I can remember a September day on Cape Cod's Quashnet when I fished upstream into a setting sun—how the river seemed the sun's emanation, a narrow path leading into the secret heart of things, wide enough for one traveler alone. I remember an April afternoon on the Battenkill when the river was so high I had no business being in it, and how as I fought to stay upright, fish suddenly began rising on all sides, so freely and willingly that it seemed I was being initiated into their presence, made—in recognition of my daring—an honorary trout. Closer to home, I can think of dozens of times when I uncased my rod along the river feeling the kind of bitterness about my writing that verges on tears, then returned after an hour alone feeling calm and whole again, ready to work no matter what the cost. . . . All these things solitude has given.

It would be wrong not to total up the debit side as well. Not having anyone to go fishing with has probably made me less adventurous than a good flyfisherman should be; there are remote trout ponds I've had to pass up because they require too much hard bushwhacking to do alone, distant rivers that require too much driving. Then, too, my fishing education has proceeded more slowly than it would have if I'd had a fly-fishing friend to learn from, my store of experience to draw upon when selecting a fly reduced by at least half. I would dearly love to watch a good nymph fisherman in action, for instance; I've tried to teach myself how to do it, but without someone to study, it's been frustratingly hard.

Two serious demerits. But I think what I have lost most by my solitude is the companionship of another memory and perspective, someone to recall for me events and scenes that have long since slipped away. We're all aware of the marvelous moments that can come between friends who haven't seen each other for a long time—how your friend will mention an incident that you had completely forgotten, making you smile in discovery and delight, as if recovering a lost, precious jewel you only at that moment realized you owned. I remember that sunset on the Quashnet and that hatch on the Battenkill, but there are other events of those days that are beyond my recall, and it would mean much to me to have someone else who had shared them—a keeper of one-half the memory who had reflected on and preserved a portion of an experience that can at times seem too beautiful and vast for one imagination to hold.

Solitude, in other words, came to seem an enchanted castle half-deliberately created, to be longed for at some times, escaped from at others. The problem with erecting castles, though, is that they can become too real to be lightly given up, their ramparts too thick to be conquered by even the warmest of affections. *Wanting* to fish alone is one thing, but *having* to fish alone is something else, and I had begun to wonder whether I had crossed the line. With a decade's solitude at my back, had it become so precious to me that I couldn't relinquish it? Not be able to go fishing with anyone else without foaming at the mouth, throwing rocks at their fish and in general acting like an unsociable hermit? Exactly how high had those castle walls become?

Not too high, thank God. The ramparts have come tumbling down and the heroine who bid them fall is as intelligent and beautiful a princess as any fairy tale ever boasted. How Celeste entered my life is outside this essay's bounds, but what is important is the total unexpectedness of it. I was thirty when we met, at the age when friends start referring to you as a confirmed bachelor.

"I am waiting for the perfect woman," I would say, in response to their teasing. "She will emerge out of the woods one morning equipped with a backpack, a fly rod, a tape deck with Jussi Bjoerling on it, a Newfoundland puppy, and a well-thumbed copy of Melville's *Pierre*."

Celeste came unencumbered with any of these things, but what she does possess is infinitely more dear—a complete willingness to blend her enthusiasms with mine. We shared fishing right from the start. It wasn't fly fishing, not yet, but the kind of random trolling I used to do with my Dad. We'd drive over to one of the big Vermont lakes and rent a boat, cruise in big loops along the shoreline, talk about every subject imagination can hold. There were muskrats to play tag with, beaver and seagulls and geese. Celeste, being French, has determined notions about what a good picnic lunch should include, and we had some real feasts as we drifted lazily there in the sun.

Celeste hooked her first fish on Lake Champlain in May. It was probably a bass, and I say probably because I was so excited for her that I nearly fell out of the boat in my anxiety to reach the engine and shut it off. Celeste was just as excited as I was—there was a lot of yelling, a lot of wild balancing to keep the boat from tipping over, then a moment of sudden and utter dejection when we realized the fish was gone.

No matter. A hundred yards up the shore she had another bite. Through a superhuman effort of self-control, I managed to stay where I was in the bow, and she landed it herself: a fine smallmouth bass of almost two pounds. As I write, I can look up at the wall and see their picture—the bass looking sleek and strong; Celeste holding him with a big grin on her face, the same irresistible grin I've seen in photos of her taken when she was five.

She followed up this first success with a landlocked salmon on Lake Willoughby. Once again I nearly managed to blow it for her. We were trolling, and I kept insisting that she let out more line. Celeste, trusting my advice, let out line even when I didn't tell her to, until her Dardevle was a good 150 yards behind our boat.

"Hey, there's a salmon!" I yelled, pointing toward the far side of the lake. It was jumping, and I couldn't understand why.

"My rod!" Celeste screamed.

The tip was bouncing wildly up and down. Still, I couldn't see the connection—the salmon was simply too far away to be hers.

Celeste's naiveté won her the fish. She began cranking the reel as if the salmon *was* hers, and to my complete amazement it was. After a ten-minute struggle, she had him alongside the boat, just in time for me to realize I had left the landing net back in the car. I grabbed the salmon as firmly as I could by the tail . . . For a moment I had him in my hands . . . He gave a convulsive twist and was gone.

Celeste looked at me with an expression that managed to combine suspicion, hope, anger, and trust.

"You got him!" I said, putting the best light on it I could.

"But I wanted to hold him!"

"Well, we were going to let him go anyway. But as long as we touch him, it counts."

"I can tell people I caught a salmon?"

"Sure. As long as one of us touches him, like I said."

Which is a pretty liberal interpretation of landing a fish. We've adopted it as a rule now; flexibility in logic makes fishing with Celeste a joy.

Having shared these things with Celeste, the next step was to bring her to the river I loved. I was fishing it three and four times a week, coming back at night with all kinds of stories. It was funny about these. I talked like she knew the river as well as I did; we shared so many other things, I felt as if by a natural osmosis she should have absorbed my knowledge of the river, too, even though I had never taken her there.

My stories all ended the same way. "Someday you'll have to come with me."

"Okay."

And we left it at that. For a while, it was a satisfactory compromise—Celeste was sharing some of my fishing, but I was left with my precious solitude. The river was still my secret place— not *for* me as much as *in* me, and Celeste sensed it too well to intrude.

I'm not sure when the turning point came. As our relationship deepened, I began looking at the river in a different way. Before, I had always taken in its beauty as something to be hoarded, used in some future translation—a book perhaps, or simply a memory. Now, though, I was trying to see the river through her eyes, imagine what her response would be to its multivarious forms. A trout finning easily in an eddy below a rock; a heron gliding in for a landing on a quiet pool; a coil of silver water swirling over sand—these were my secrets, and between one cast and the next I wanted more than anything to share these secrets with her.

"Someday you'll have to come with me," I said one night, describing the heron.

"Okay."

"How about tomorrow afternoon?"

Celeste looked at me carefully. "Okay," she said.

That easily can a decade's habit disappear. I won't describe every moment of our day. I didn't foam at the mouth, or throw rocks at the fish or feel violated. We fished the pine canyon, then the Aquarium, then the South Branch—having waited so long to share the river with her, I wanted to cram as much into our afternoon as possible, and I raced her madly from pool to pool.

In one of the last I caught a trout for her—a rainbow who took my bucktail near the surface and put on a melodramatic display, with extravagant leap after extravagant leap, as if he were showing off for her just as much as I was. How macho we both were! There is nothing more satisfying to the male ego than catching a trout for the woman you love, and when I beached it, I laid it at her feet like a knight at a tournament, waiting for her decision.

"Let's keep it," she said in delight. Then, seeing its beauty: "No, let's put it back."

I handed her the rod after that, and showed her the first steps in casting a fly. She made all the beginner's mistakes—whipped the rod back and forth too fast, tilted it sideways at the wrong angle to the water—but beneath the awkwardness was a rhythm and grace that promised great things for the future. I called out advice at first, but that was tactless, and after a while I was content to sit there on the bank and watch her puzzle things out for herself.

We stayed until late in the afternoon, started to leave, then decided to stay a little while more. There was a sunset to share with her—cooling shadows and the evening hatch. . .

We shared the fishing now, and we shared the river, but there was a third, missing step in the equation: Celeste still hadn't caught a trout.

It wasn't any trout she wanted. Listening to my stories, examining the pictures in my books, she decided her first trout should—no, *must*—be a brook trout.

"What's wrong with a brown?" I said.

"Brook trout are prettier. They're like maple leaves."

"Maple leaves?"

"They're part of Vermont."

Now there are at least four streams within five minutes of us that contain brook trout, and it would probably have taken a half-hour of lazy effort to fulfill her goal. There was a problem, though: our wedding. It used up all our free time for a month.

True, we were going out west for our honeymoon, but that naturally meant a cutthroat or rainbow for her first trout, not a brookie.

We flew to Seattle and rented a car. The Olympics were first. We spent so much time hiking, climbing, and beachcombing that fishing had to take a back seat, which in a strange kind of way was all right with me. I found the rivers so beautiful that I was half afraid to go near them, fearing that once under their spell I could never leave. We did fish the Skokimish for an afternoon, and then later the Quinault, but only briefly, and without catching anything. The day before we were due to fly back home we were in Mt. Rainier, and we decided to have one last try.

It was an eerie time to be there. A cloud had settled on top of the mountain, and everything above four thousand feet was draped in fog. At Paradise, the parking lot was filled with bewildered tourists groping around trying to find the lodge, only a few yards away. A ranger had been dispatched to help everyone. We asked about the fishing, and he recommended hiking into Mystic Lake—there were plenty of trout there, some running to size.

I pointed at the map. "What about this Snow Lake?" It was on the trail beyond Mystic, higher and more remote.

"It's pretty," the ranger agreed, "but it's sterile. There are no fish in there at all."

Mystic Lake it was then. Driving at a crawl, we finally located the trailhead. It was good weather for hypothermia—damp, in the low fifties—and I suddenly had this great desire to end our trip with a celebratory glass of Bourbon back in the Paradise bar. Celeste, though, already had her climbing boots on, and was starting resolutely up the trail.

The mist grew thicker the higher we climbed. There were wildflowers along the trail, but it was all we could do to make them out. According to our map, Mystic Lake was a mile and a half uphill, but we walked much further than that without spotting it, and the pond we finally came to had a sign that read Snow Lake.

The ranger was right about its beauty. All we could see of it in the mist was the outlet—a jumble of water-burnished logs under which the lake funneled itself into a stream—yet it was enough to suggest the wild, remote beauty of the whole, just as the glories of a string quartet may lie implicit in its first brief phrase.

We balanced our way out to the thickest of the logs, and sat down to eat lunch. A few hikers came by. Seeing our rods, they told us what we already knew: the lake was completely fishless. We decided to wait for a while to see if the fog would lift enough for pictures, then head back down to Mystic to fish.

In the meantime, strange things were happening. Something flew past my head and I swatted at it, without really sensing what it was. A moment later, a second something drifted by. I was ready for the third: a big brown mayfly, newly hatched.

Without saying anything to Celeste, I scrambled across the logs to get a closer look at the water above the logjam. Out there in the mist, so faint and fragmentary I thought I was hallucinating, were rings. Ripples against a rock, I assumed; but no—they were breaking across the surface at irregular intervals.

Curiouser and curiouser.

"Know something?" I said, turning around.

Celeste looked up from the map. "What?"

"There are trout in this lake."

She didn't believe me. Still, once she saw me casting, she came over and started fishing, too, more to humor me than anything else.

"There aren't any trout in this lake," she grumbled, only "lake" became a two-syllable word—lake as the first syllable, a scream of delight as the second.

"I've got one!"

A fish had plucked her fly off the surface just before it drifted into the logjam, hooking itself. It was a bad place to play one, and Celeste in her excitement stripped in line too fast, but it was exactly the right tactic—once into the logs, her leader would have been doomed.

Snow Lake never heard such happy shouts. Celeste had the fish dancing by our log now. Using my hat as a landing net, I knelt down and scooped him up, pressing him to my chest so he wouldn't squirm away. It wasn't until we reached the safety of shore that we dared to look at him.

"What kind is it?" Celeste asked.

I kissed her. I couldn't stop laughing.

"What kind!" she demanded.

"Celeste, you have just caught yourself a dyed-in-the-wool, authentic, bona fide . . . brook trout!"

Three Vermonters and there we were, two and a half thousand miles from home. They must have been stocked there, I explained—probably some program that was started with all kinds of hope, then abandoned for lack of funds. It was a long way to go to catch our neighborhood trout, but no matter—Celeste had her fish story now, and the adventure of it sealed our sharing.

"Take our picture!"

And I did, and as I focused the lens, the fog lifted, and behind her I saw the snowbanks and glacier and cliffs that framed the pond, revealing themselves only now when the moment was perfect. I held the camera steady until the beauty of the water and the woman and the trout came together, then—the moment captured—I crossed over the logs and took my wife by her hand.

10
The One That Got Away

Wariness is among the prime Vermont virtues, but it is not among mine. I have not had to cope with the maddening swings of New England weather for an entire lifetime, I have never tried to pry a living from its soil, and my formative years were not spent among a people whose first, instinctive reaction when faced with any dilemma or choice is to do nothing.

Still, wariness is a quality I could use a little more of, particularly during August's low water. Take yesterday, for example. I had every intention of making a lazy day of it. Breakfast at the diner, a leisurely drive to the river, then some unhurried casting for some unhurried trout.

It was all a trick, of course. By lulling myself into a relaxed mood, I was hoping to surmount my usual abruptness, the better to catch trout that were bound to be as wary and uncoaxable in the summer sunlight as the oldest farmer in these hills.

I got out of bed as cautiously as though the fish could see me; I shaved and showered as quietly as I could. Breakfast was slowly and deliberately chewed, coffee daintily sipped—if I was going to spook any trout today, it wouldn't be in the diner. I drove the few remaining miles to the river more slowly than usual, and even went so far as to stop when I passed the farm with the hand-lettered sign: GOOD JUNK CHEAP!

Now, I am not a tag-sale freak, though I'm related to people who are (the date of our wedding had to be changed because there was a tag sale on the common outside the church on the same day, and we seriously wondered whether half the guests, given the choice between second-hand junk and a wedding, might not choose the junk). I will stop, however, if I see some books; for the past couple of years, I've been on the lookout for those two gentle classics of Vermont fishing, Frederick Van de Water's *In Defense of Worms,* and Murray Hoyt's *The Fish in My Life.*

There was a dilapidated Ping-Pong table on one side of the yard; sugaring barrels and old crocks on the other. In between were card tables and boxes piled high with stuff—muffin pans, headless dolls, old milk bottles, the works. Behind the wobbliest table stood a woman in her fifties who seemed as battered and used as any of her goods. Before her was a sign that read NO REASONABLE OFFER REFUSED, but there was a suspicious, hard-looking quality in her expression that let you know she had very strict notions about what that word "reasonable" meant.

As usual, the books were all romances, and I had turned to leave when I noticed something jutting out from the bottom of the midden heap on the Ping-Pong table. I'm still not sure what caught my eye first—the soft brown fabric of the cloth sleeve or the bright silver ferrule exposed above it.

Slowly, doing nothing to betray my interest, I worked my way across the yard, being careful to examine all the miscellaneous junk that intervened. The stuff on the table was high enough to block the woman's view; kneeling, I peeled the sleeve down far enough to see that it contained a bamboo fly rod, and a good one. The inscription near the butt was worn off, and only one letter was legible, the letter L. L, I decided, as in Leonard.

Eureka. Still, I wasn't going to blow it now. With a tremendous force of will, I left the rod where it was and made a circuit of the other tables, doing my best to seem disinterested and bored. Five minutes went by. When I turned to go back to the rod, a man with a complexion like cheap corduroy was waving it back and forth in his hands.

Where had he come from? I looked back toward the driveway. A purple Lincoln Continental with Jersey plates was parked there with its motor running, three kids crammed in the back. I cursed myself, then went back over to the crocks to await developments.

The man wiggled the rod back and forth for a while, bent it, whipped it about some more, then with a "why not?" kind of shrug, took it over to the woman.

"Four dollars," she said.

I could have strangled her. A Leonard in that kind of shape (and I was convinced in my frustration that it *was* a Leonard) is easily worth a thousand. There was still hope, though. Judging by his pained look when he took out his wallet, the man had no idea what a bargain he was getting.

I intercepted him before he reached the car.

"I'll give you ten for that," I said abruptly.

It was a mistake. Vermonters may be wary, but New Jersey-
ites are paranoid, and I had awoken all his suspicions.

"Naw, it's for the kid," he said.

"Make that twenty."

By way of answering, he slammed the car door and locked
all the buttons. His boy had the rod now. I could see him in the
back seat as the car disappeared, whacking the tip section over
his sisters' heads.

11
August Twenty-third

The river was half its May width. What had been an even, bank-to-bank current was now broken up into separate flows, with scattered rapids that were as small and dainty as the water-falls in Japanese gardens. Two feet of water had been sliced off the river's top, exposing a lumpy cross-section of boulders and rocks.

Places that were chest-deep in June were now only knee-deep, and there were shoal areas to the outside of the pools where the water barely wet my toes.

After all the fitful striving of early season, the river seemed settled and at rest. The heavy current that had hidden so much of its life was gone, and the shallows that were left were as interesting as tidal pools on a saltwater beach. Tiny hellgrammites, graceful water spiders, minnows and miniature trout—they were all there among the rocks, scurrying under the crevices to avoid the monstrous intrusion of my hand.

A day for lazy distraction. A day, that is, for letting life pass dreamily downstream.

I fished in my bathing suit, not my waders—a bathing suit, sneakers and a long-billed swordfisherman's hat that kept the sun from my face. I carried only a few flies: gaudy Royal Coachmans in fan-wing and Wulff ties (against all the rules, but I've found them to be effective low-water patterns), a few Light Cahills and an assortment of terrestrials. These last are dry flies designed to imitate landbound insects that tumble into the river. Letort Hoppers, Cinnamon Ants, McMurrays . . . There's nothing very complicated about them, ants and grasshoppers not being among your more esoteric insects.

I was using a twenty-year-old fly rod that is already something of a relic. Back in 1963 when I first started fly fishing, ultralight tackle was all the rage. Bankrolled by my grandfather's Christmas present, I ordered Abercrombie and Fitch's "Banty" fly rod—a four-foot bauble that weighs only an ounce, complete with a special "Banty" fly line and a Hardy Flyweight reel. I remember my delight when the package arrived from New York; seconds after opening it, I was false-casting over the bushes on our snow-covered suburban lawn.

Long graphite rods are the fashion nowadays, and I suppose I elicit some chuckles when I trot out my "Banty," but the truth is I like it, and its miniaturization of the whole fishing process suits perfectly my summertime mood.

I've noticed this before about tackle—how you can fit it to the kind of attitude you happen to wake up with. On days when I'm feeling irritated, not to be trifled with, I'm apt to go out with my nine-foot Browning, a brute of a rod that throws an incredible amount of line and lets me feel like I'm dominating the river, beating it into submission. Other days, feeling lazy, I take along an ancient Heddon that handles an equal amount of line, but is much easier on the arm, and lets me roll cast without doing much wading. On my last trip to Britain, I bought a light, seven-foot Hardy; using it, I have to get more involved with the river, wade more carefully—it's the kind of rod you feel you should be fishing with on tiptoes, and I save it for my artsier moods. Those infrequent days when I wake up feeling well-balanced, I take along my eight-foot Vince Cummings—when it comes to attitude, as neutral a rod as you can find.

The Banty requires a lot of arm work if you're going to get out any line, and it was half an hour before my casts started unrolling. The Wulff landed with all the delicacy of an anchor, but the trout must have been amused by it, and I immediately began to have strikes. Strikes, not fish. I had assumed the trout would be in a sluggish mood to match the water, but they all seemed jet-propelled, and the fly was in and out of their mouths before I could hook them.

Just as catching fish will make a flyfisherman quicker to react, not catching fish dulls his senses, leads him into temptations he would otherwise avoid. I was just above the Aquarium, in the shallow, even stretch before the falls. There's lots of shade here, and the trout will drop back from the sunny stretch above it to cool off. With the reduced current, drag was less of a problem than in spring, and I was getting rises on some very long drifts.

I let the fly drop near some overhanging shrubbery near the bank, and was stripping in line when I noticed something drifting toward me about six inches below the surface. It was a rose—a red rose broken off at its stem, floating perfectly upright downstream, as magically as in a fairy tale.

It was as nice a conflict as a person could be offered, but a conflict all the same. What should I do? Reach down and pluck the rose from the water before it vanished downstream, or continue stripping in the line, thereby being ready for a strike?

My bride of three weeks liked roses. I dropped my left hand from the line and stuck it underwater to intercept the flower; at the same moment, not ten feet away, a fish clobbered my drifting fly. I struck back at him, but he was already gone, and in my haste I dropped the rose and it vanished downstream over the falls.

No fish. No rose. There was a message there somewhere, but I'll be damned if I could figure out what it was. It seemed like a good time to break for lunch.

There was a sandbar along the opposite bank. After finishing my sandwich, I stretched out in the shade with my eyes closed, enjoying the sounds and smells of the summer day. These seemed to come in pairs. There was the rich, heavy smell of newly cut hay with the clanking sound of a tractor; the steady buzz of insects with the sweet aroma of honeysuckle.

I may have dozed for a while. When I woke up, it was to the voices of two young boys engaged in a furious argument. Shading my eyes in the glare, I made them out a hundred yards upstream, bumping down the river in inner tubes.

I say bumping, because that's exactly what they were doing. There wasn't enough water to float the tubes. They would get a little headway in the rapids above the pools, then come to an ignominious stop on the rocks below. Stranded, they stood up in the center of the tubes and waddled over to the bank, yelling at each other all the while.

One of them was bleeding from a cut on his knee; the other's bathing suit was ripped along the side. They acted glad to see an adult.

"We're floating the river in inner tubes," the redheaded one said.

"So I see."

"There's not enough water," his friend added.

"We should have gone last week like I said!" the redhead yelled.

"Come off of it!"

"You come off of it!"

It seemed like a good time to intervene.

"Those are pretty unusual tubes," I said. "What's this for over here?"

They had customized them, adding extra strips of rubber to act as bumpers, lashing orange bike pennants to the sides so they could find each other if they became separated. An extra tube had been attached to the redhead's for supplies, but it had hit a sharp rock and sunk. They had started up by the North Branch at 8:30 in the morning, and at this rate, they figured they'd make it to the Connecticut in October.

I helped them relaunch their tubes.

"Watch out for the dam," I said, pushing them out.

They looked at each other. "Uh, what dam?" the redhead said.

I told them. They didn't seem impressed.

"No sweat!"

They were bouncing down through the Aquarium now, spinning around as if on snow saucers, and in between their continued arguing, I heard their whoops of joy.

They took a lot of life with them when they left. It was midafternoon, and the hazy sun was pressing down with all its weight. The farmer had left off haying—even the insects seemed muzzled. I tried a few casts, but it was too hot to fish. My rod hidden in the grass, I was getting ready to dive in for a swim when my second visitor of the afternoon arrived: a solitary duck the like of which I had never seen.

He came floating down the river as awkwardly as the boys. I think he was a mallard, though I'm not sure; he had a mallard's neck, but his feathers were as multicolored and scruffy as a Manhattan pigeon's, and he swam with the grace of a turkey.

We immediately became friends. I'm a sucker for open personalities, and this was a duck that held nothing back. He swam right up to me looking for a handout, and when he saw I had nothing for him, decided to stick with me anyhow. I was wading downstream toward a deeper swimming hole, and he tagged along at my heels.

All was fine for the first ten yards, then he fell behind. The low water confused him. He managed all right in depths over eight inches, but when it got shallower than that, he would bump into partly submerged rocks and be unsure whether to swim over them or climb them—at every rock his webbed feet slithered back and forth in indecision. He was embarrassed—he kept rearing back in his best threat posture, his wings beating furiously as he tried to bluff each boulder from his path.

He kept me company while I swam. Occasionally, he would wander off a bit, duck his head underwater and come up with weeds. He worked these furiously through his beak, then spit them out with distaste, like a kid eating spinach. Was he fishing? I was trying to remember if ducks ate fish, when with a quickness I wouldn't have credited him with, he ducked his head again and came up with a minnow.

I never saw anyone take a fish with such commotion and pride. Fish was wiggling around in its beak, duck was going through contortions to keep him there; fish was limp, duck was struggling to climb up onto the bank with him; fish was swallowed, duck was stretching his wings in the threat posture again, quacking in triumph.

"Way to go, duck," I said, saluting him.

Praise is what that duck was after all along. Getting it, he headed downstream in the same direction as the rose and the boys and the day, bumping from rock to rock like a pinball, battered but proud.

12
Really Good Stuff

T he good stuff—the really good stuff—is in the back beneath the grinning fox. The rest of the store has at least five incarnations. Go in the door on the right and it's a typical Vermont gift shop, with maple fudge, wooden tomahawks, and postcards. Go in the middle door, the one that sets the bell jangling, and it's a typical Vermont drugstore, with liniments for aching muscles, syrups for scratchy throats, and balms for softening the udders of cows.

It's at the edges of Sanborn's where things start to get interesting. You're out of the new part of the store now (new as in 1870 something), into the older wing where the floorboards sag beneath your feet and you have to duck to get out of the way of the antique clothing—the flapper dresses, capes, and evening gowns—that hang suspended from the ceiling, their sleeves wafting gently as if swayed by invisible arms.

The wine is there to the right on three long shelves. It's a democratic assemblage, amusing in its lack of pretension, but with a . . . how shall we say it? . . . *mongrel* breeding: a few Moselles for class, a token Liebfraumilch, a cloudy looking White Mountain white, maple wine bottled in Vermont, a few of the pop Italian brands and whatever other curiosities Mr. Sanborn happens to enjoy. You can either spring for a bottle now and take a chance you'll have enough for flies, or wait until you buy the flies and get the cheaper vintage with what's left.

A ramp leads to the back. The battered thirty-five-cent paperbacks are on either side; browsing through them is like leafing through the best-seller lists of the last thirty years. *A Generation of Vipers, Travels with Charley, Advise and Consent, Anatomy of a Murder, Growing Up Absurd, Peyton Place, The Godfather, Jaws.* Past them, the real bookshelves begin, with over a thousand old volumes. The section on Vermont is beneath the moosehead, the one that drools papier-mache; included are *27th Vermont Agricultural Report 1907, University of Vermont Service Records 1917–18, History of Athens, VT, Ancient Craft Masonry in Vermont, The Autobiography of Calvin Coolidge,* and—even better—*Grace Coolidge and Her Era.*

If you follow the town histories down into Massachusetts, then cross over to the shelf on war books, then follow the fiction past the cookbooks, you're into good stuff, but not the really good stuff: spinning rods hanging from their tips, bait buckets stacked haphazardly in the corner, lures taped by cellophane to the walls. These are bass lures; is there anything more typically

American in proud illiteracy and cartoon rhythm than their names? River Runt, Bugeye, Cop-e-cat, Flutter chuck, Hawg Frawg, Krocodile, Lusox, Sputterbug, Kweet Special, Augertail, Bopper Popper . . . they're all here, with a flash and energy that are as aural as sound.

Between the bass lures and the really good stuff is a wood stove, a big Defiant. It's seldom on. Propped against its cold side are some old paintings, the kind that itinerant artists would toss off in the 1850s, workmanlike imitations of the Hudson River school, landscapes featuring valleys, castles and clouds. Never mind their holes. For ten dollars, they're atmospheric bargains to hang on old walls.

You're in the remotest corner of the store now, into the really good stuff at last—the flies, nets, fly rods, and reels. The stuffed fox hangs from the ceiling over the fly-tying supplies; he's mounted with one paw lifted in a pose that manages to be bloodthirsty and delicate at the same time, and as you browse through the fly trays, you wonder whether he's snarling at you or smiling.

Ah, the fly trays. They're a glorious mess. The Bivisibles are mixed in with the streamers, the terrestrials are combined with the nymphs, and the midges are God knows where. It takes a good half hour to find what you're looking for. At the bottom of one tray is a snelled bass fly with a huge yellow wing, the kind Doctor Henshall might have used; at the bottom of another is a Parmacheene Belle, or some other antique.

About the time you make your selection, Mr. Sanborn will appear. He looks like a moody Santa Claus, with a belly that spills over his belt, a snow-white beard, and an introspective frown. He's wearing wool pants and a checkered shirt—it makes him look like Santa all right, but a Santa who runs a trap line on the side.

"Help you there?"

Unless you're a local, Mr. Sanborn won't recognize you, no matter how many times you've been in his store. He'll recommend some flies, then fill you in on his fishing. This won't be on the river (he last fished it in the 1940s, and according to him it's been going downhill ever since), but on the nearby lakes. Downriggers with Golden Demons in ten feet of water, he says. Ten trout last night, twelve the night before.

"You fish them like I tell you, see what happens. Jigger it right back to you soon as they bite. Ayuh, that's fishing."

His voice is deep, comforting. You can dig away at the flies while he talks. You can wonder whether the fox is happy or sad, puzzle out what kind of wine you should buy, and make a mental note to find out, someday, exactly what *Grace Coolidge and Her Era* is all about.

I'm lucky to have Sanborn's so close. A good tackle shop can complement a good river, act as prelude to its delights. Ordering tackle through the mail is a sterile pleasure in comparison; what the flyfisherman needs are fly trays to paw through, reels to click experimentally, rods to wiggle appraisingly in his hand. Just as the rivers I've fished seem to link themselves in my memory into one long river, the tackle shops I've known seem to merge into one gigantic store, a cornucopia of impressions departmentalized by the years.

Bob's Bait comes first, fragrant with the smell of coffee-ground-bedded worms. It wasn't far from the lake where I learned to fish, and we would stop there for shiners on our way to the boat. As tackle shops go, it was small—maybe ten by five at the most. Roughly two-thirds of that space was taken up by galvanized tanks for the bait; into the rest was crammed an incredible assortment of rods, reels, and lures. An acquisitive twelve, I couldn't go into the store without drooling—I never wanted anything as much as I did those cleverly displayed lures.

Bob himself was an impassive man with a martyred expression; whenever I tried to tell him about the fish I had caught on his bait, he grunted and turned away, leaving me close to tears. I couldn't imagine anyone selling such marvelous stuff being less than marvelous himself, and it was a great disappointment to learn that Bob was totally pedestrian, with very little interest in fishing, and even less interest in humoring enthusiastic boys. Looking back, I suppose his feet hurt or something—that's the only expression I ever saw on his face.

I had been buying lures at Bob's with increasing reluctance when a competitor opened up closer to town. The Angler's Pool was everything Bob's Bait was not, with immaculate display cases trimmed with cherry, fly tackle arranged in spacious rows and a friendly and knowledgeable owner. Franz had come originally from Germany, and his accent added just the right amount of exoticism to his gear. He loved to talk fishing. I would show up in the morning when no customers were around (I found out later that no customers were *ever* around), and he would take me out back to his stockroom to show me the latest order that had come in.

Poor Franz! He was a collector, not a shopkeeper, and his love for fine tackle soon did him in. Flyfishermen with the money for good equipment were scarce in that town; by the end of the summer, he was out of business—the shop was turned into a beautician's. As a parting gift, Franz gave me a dozen of his best Light Cahills.

Bob, of course, continued to prosper, scowl and all. It was an early lesson in economics: when it came to tackle shops, good guys, or at least good flyfishermen, did not finish first.

The Angler's Pool had initiated me into the pleasures of classy tackle shops. Casting about for a replacement, I went right to the source: Abercrombie and Fitch.

Poor A & F! Like Franz's, its New York store was having trouble staying in business, faced as it was with competition from the cut-rate sporting goods stores like Herman's, and the mail-order houses like Bean's. The outdoors was being democratized in the '60s, and Abercrombie and Fitch's eliteness seemed too fuddy-duddy to endure. I suppose the market for $200 croquet sets and elephant-hide footrests was never a very big one to begin with, even at the best of times.

Though its glories were fading when I knew it, there was still enough glitter left to impress a fourteen-year-old boy. I would take the train into the city, walk crosstown from Penn Station to Madison Avenue. There were bookstores along the way, record stores, too, but I sailed past them like Ulysses past the Sirens, saving my three or four dollars of spending money until I got to Abercrombie and Fitch itself.

It always seemed to be raining when I got there; the store was in its autumnal phase, and everything in it had a patina of venerability and age. Walking through the door into the ground-level floor was like walking into the British Museum—the accessories displayed there seemed the spoils of Empire—and it was hard to remember that everything was for sale. You never noticed the cash registers. Were they even there?

I took the elevator right to the fishing tackle on the eighth floor. They were great elevators. They'd be filled with stuffy-looking businessmen on their lunch hours; I loved their baldness, their quaint tweed, the authoritative way they reached out and pushed the button on the floor of their choice.

I stepped out onto the eighth floor with the excitement with which other kids must have entered Disneyland. There was some really good stuff there! Over in the left-hand corner by the elevator bank was a gold-plated fighting chair, the kind Hemingway must have used for marlin, and jutting out from it was a tuna rod with two tips—*two* tips, branching apart from the butt to form a Y. To the right of it, the fly tackle began—I remember how beautifully brown the bamboo rods were, how afraid I was to touch them. The flies were in long flat wooden trays, displayed as delicately as butterflies. Beyond them were the bass lures, at double the price of Bob's. Along the wall were glass display cases with the reels—I remember a miniature bait-casting reel that shone in the fluorescent light like an emerald. Scattered about the counter's top were Wheatley fly boxes and streamer wallets lined with wool. Further to the right was a bookcase, with books by people like Edward R. Hewitt and George M. L. LaBranche, authors whose ghosts probably still shopped there once the regular customers were gone.

All of the sales clerks looked like Herbert Hoover. I don't think any of them ever deigned to wait on me. They acted like they worked there merely as a genteel means of killing time between fishing trips—asking one of them for help was like breaking the silence in the reading room of Mycroft Holmes's private club.

I never dared do that. I would walk around for a while try-ing to find something my three dollars would buy, then—since the A & F elevators seemed only to ascend and never descend—sadly take the stairs down to the street. Three dollars went a long way in those days, but only at Nedick's.

I shouldn't have laughed at the sales clerks. Before long, I was working as one myself—at Macy's, the biggest store in the world. It was 1969. I was dropping out of college with a certain degree of regularity, trying to find the time to write. Macy's seemed like a reasonable stopgap. In those days, the shoe clerks all wanted to be tap dancers, the lingerie women dreamed of being Carol Chan-ning, and the luggage department had more poets than Columbia.

They put me in sporting goods; as far as I know, I was the first would-be novelist they'd had. The rest of the group was varied enough. Gus the Greek was thirty-four and aggressively single; he was a storehouse of information on singles bars, '50s rock singers, and bluefishing. Tom O'Brien was a former All-Ireland drum major who had brought his strut with him to America; it was hard to know where the blarney left off and the truth began—he was too small to have played international rugby for Ireland, but you had to listen to his stories or he'd get mad. Jim was a recently returned Vietnam veteran—none of us probed his silences too hard. Bob Stern, our boss, was smooth-talking and ambitious, but took a boyish delight in breaking store rules, and was something of a hero to us for that reason.

In those days, sporting goods was in what was called the "Outdoor Shop." It was a separate wing from the main store, and the floorwalkers pretty much left us alone. The rest of the clerks got twenty minutes for their breaks—we all took forty. Our lunch hours were apt to start around eleven and end shortly before three. Times when business was slow, we'd go down to the stock room and start up games of wiffle ball or hockey; Gus once broke a window with a slap shot and set off all the alarms.

I was the resident intellectual. Bob Stern would keep me busy forging letters from customers to Macy's president raving about how courteous and helpful the clerks in sporting goods were; Tom O'Brien had me draft letters to Queen Elizabeth denouncing British policy in Ulster. I was paid for these in fishing tackle.

It worked this way. Management was always putting pressure on Stern to get rid of his unsold inventory by putting it on sale. These were unadvertised sales; he'd mark things down and put them out on a table. It soon occurred to us that no one at Macy's cared how little these items sold for—the important thing was to get rid of them. We all had our favorite sport. What we started to do was deliberately order things we wanted, hold them for a while in the stock room, then without telling anyone, put them up for sale at outrageous prices and buy them ourselves.

There were some great bargains. Gus got a brand-new AMF bowling ball for eighty-five cents; Jim got a Shakespeare hunting bow for a quarter. Our consciences didn't bother us very much; after all, these sales were available to the public, too—available, that is, if they could get into the store before the ten o'clock opening.

I did quite well for myself. There was an Italian spinning reel marked down from $59.99 to ninety-nine cents; a Garcia fly rod that went for a quarter; Cortland fly lines for ten cents; Rapala plugs at five for a nickel. By the time Stern got transferred and the scam came to an end, I had enough fishing tackle to last the next twenty years.

In a way, the cheap gear at Macy's was too much of a good thing. It ruined tackle shops for me, at least temporarily. Having bought so much for so little, I couldn't bear paying full retail for a rod or reel. There were other tackle shops in the next few years, but none with sufficient charisma to recreate that former allure.

It was 1976 before I found another one worthy enough to add to my collection. I was spending the autumn in London, and on rainy afternoons would take the tube to St. James Park and cross over to Hardy's on Pall Mall.

Hardy's, of course, was the snobbiest fishing store in the world. When it came to disdain, the clerks made Abercrombie and Fitch's look like Kiwanians. This gave them a certain historical charm—with all the changes in the world, it was nice to find a place where you could still be patronized as a rude colonial. For a long time, I was tempted to buy one of their Northumbrian jackets. It's a waxed game coat, the kind you can't buy in the States, but at sixty pounds it was too far out of reach. Still, I enjoyed trying them on. A clerk gave me his understated sales pitch the first time, but after that they began to recognize me, and I was left to browse in peace.

British tackle shops are five or six times more interesting than American ones. They understand about shops in Britain—there are no malls, and the people that wait on you have a broad knowledge of their sport. Hardy's aside, I've found them quick to ask about American fishing, and generous in their advice. I visited two tiny shops in Chester last year. One was devoted to fly fishing, one to coarse fishing. In the first, I had a delightful conversation with the owner about trout; in the second, I listened for an hour to a monologue on roach. It was a fine afternoon.

Now when I go to Europe I make it a habit to stop at any tackle shop I can find. You get a lot of instant camaraderie that way; you can also find some really good stuff. The best souvenir I've ever bought came from a small tackle shop in Paris on the Seine: a twelve-foot-long metal pole, the kind those eternal Parisian fishermen use on the quays. The best fly boxes I've ever seen come from a shop on the Zentralstrasse in Berne; the Swiss have a way with miniaturization and these boxes are spaciously compact.

It's a long journey from Bob's Bait in Connecticut to Hardy's of Pall Mall. From Hardy's to Sanborn's of Vermont is in a sense an even longer trip, for my attitude toward tackle shops has evolved over the years. I no longer want the predictable rows of mass-produced rods and ray gun-looking reels, but shop instead for the unexpected and offbeat. I have a Vermont river that is varied, full of wonder. The shop that goes with it must be the same.

Sanborn's. Liniment, udder softener, antique clothing, wine, books, and flies. My kind of store at last.

13
A Home by the River

There's a piece of land for sale on the river, six acres of meadow, pine and oak rising gently from the south bank. Through the middle runs a stream no bigger than a person's stride, a stream bridged by weathered planks that creak as they sag. An old woods road runs up to the open field at the hill's crest. There are wild blackberries growing along the edges of this road, blueberries further up in the sun. A spring on top provides water. The view east is of hills and farms and the sunrise.

I walked up to it yesterday in the middle of a summer rain. The small, hand-lettered For Sale sign had been nailed to a tree on the far side of the river since May, and though I had been tempted several times, it was only now that I had gotten around to crossing over.

It's good land. If you poke around abandoned hill farms as much as I do, you come to have a sense of whether the land you're walking on was once cherished or once cursed. Shadows that never disappear, even in winter; ground that is rockier than most Vermont ground; stone walls that seem hastily thrown together, as if hurled there by the farmer in his frustration at tilling such soil . . . these are all tokens of land that has been detested, to be avoided no matter how cheaply it may be had. No sunlight for those solar panels you plan so hopefully to install; no soil for the tomatoes your wife wants to plant; a well that dries up every June—land that broke people in the 1780s can break people in the 1980s, in subtle, persistent ways.

My parcel (and how ready I was to call it mine!) had traces of a gentle hand. Someone had taken pains in cutting the road, looping it in gradual curves that understood the contours of the hill. In clearing the meadow, they had spared many of the trees—some of the oaks I was walking under were probably as old as any in Vermont. The stone wall that ran along the western boundary was skillfully arranged, not merely dumped; someone had matched flat rock to flat rock, round one to round one, and it was a masterpiece of its kind. The land, having once been loved, could be loved again.

I found a stump to sit on under a hemlock that held back some of the rain. Our house, I quickly decided, should go in the center of the meadow facing the river. The oaks would provide shade in the summer, but by fall their leaves would be gone and there would be sunlight to warm the bay window in our study. I could write there. We could have a library on the side, with built-in shelves for our books, cedar cabinets for our rods. The bedroom would be upstairs where the last sound we'd hear at night would be the voice of the river. A guest room would go nicely above the garage. A guest room with a large picture window facing east so all our friends could enjoy the view we had come to love.

There would be fishing, of course—fishing that required no advance planning or long drive, but came as easily as a whim on a warm summer's night. The water there is not the best trout water on the river, but its broad and easy air would wear well over the years. There are no deep pools or fast runs. You get the feeling there are only small trout there, not monsters, and it frees you from the burden of catching them. It would be a fine stretch of river on which to teach a child to fish.

I dreamed, in short, of a home that would be worthy of the river that ran by it. There are dozens of homes in this valley; many are weathered farmhouses that blend into their setting as only New England homes can, yet they all turn their backs on the river, and not a single one has been built deliberately to enjoy it.

Wondering about this, I began thinking not only of the land I was walking on and the home my dreams erected, but of the valley and its future. Was it wrong in the 1980s to put all your love into a piece of unspoiled earth? Wrong to think that the work and worry and hope that went into it would ever be requited by anything except pollution and development and noise? More to the point: did anyone cherish this river besides me? Even to pose the question like that was an egotistical conceit, but I was considering the river's future now, adding up its allies, and it was a question worth asking.

The farmers cherish it in their sober, undemonstrative way. I hear them speak sadly whenever a good piece of farmland is gone back to trees or sold to summer people, and the river is why their own land continues productive when all the hill farms have been abandoned. You can catch them staring off toward it in their rare respites from work; after a lifetime of toil, it must come to seem a brotherly presence in the year's slow turn.

Anyone else beside them? Do the fishermen who come here cherish it? I don't think so, not as they should. The people from town fish it in spring and at no other time, and I've followed enough of them through the pools to know they are the ones dumping bottles and cans. The flyfishermen I meet are almost inevitably out-of-staters, and though they may value the river for its productivity, their interest is of necessity only brief and intermittent.

The river is not famous. There are no summer resorts along its banks, no major ski areas or tourist attractions. Sometimes I think that it is this very obscurity that saves the river, makes it worth loving. Other times, I know I'm wrong, realize that the only thing that will save the valley from the development that will one day come isn't neglect, but the concerted efforts of people who love it as I do, people whom I fear are simply not there. Conservationists have banded together to save portions of the Beaverkill and the wild sections of the St. John, but what of all the smaller, more obscure rivers in between? How many of these vanish with hardly a whimper, undefended and unloved?

Vermonters are easy marks for developers. Their insistence on being able to do what they please with their land makes them reject zoning out-of-hand; their distrust of anything abstract makes them suspicious of regional planning and imposed controls. Times are bad here now—there are people in this valley who live in cold trailers throughout the winter. In the face of their poverty, meeting their eyes, it would be hard to argue against the construction of a new highway or large factory, yet either would doom them just as surely as it would doom the river. Development brings in skilled workers from Massachusetts with whom they can't compete; better highways bring in commuters with money, drive up the land to prices young families can't afford.

The trend has already started. The six acres I was walking across would have sold for two or three thousand dollars as recently as five years ago, but with the condos and second homes inching closer, it was probably priced at eleven thousand or twelve. I wondered if we could afford that with a house. I began to think of mortgage payments, insurance, building permits, taxes. I thought of those things, then I thought of the income the kind of fiction worth writing brings in. My dream house, so easily created, just as easily disappeared.

If it weren't for reality, none of us would have any problems. Still, it costs nothing to dream, and it's a time-honored way of spending a rainy afternoon. I walked slowly back down the road from the meadow, doing my best to rid my thoughts of the future and concentrate on the here and now. The rain, so gentle at first, had changed just as gradually as my mood, and fell now with a cool and determined hardness, rattling the trees as loudly as hail.

The wind, switching directions, blew from the north. There was the smell of damply packed earth, the sound of a distant chain saw. A leaf fell ahead of me on the road, then a second, then a third, and as easily and gracefully as that it was fall.

In a hurry now, I turned my collar against the rain and climbed down through another man's land to my car.

14
A Year of September

The best day of the year to go fishing is the first day of school. Leaving early, you drive past children waiting by the road for the bus—newly clothed, sneakers white, immaculate; skin scrubbed as shiny as pot bottoms, hair glossy as palominos', obediently banged, ponytailed, shagged, whatevered; book bags slack, empty, like deflated balloons; pencils stiletto sharpened, pens bursting blue; voices raised, biceps pinched, races run, footballs tossed; children, that is, with their lightly worn burden of crabby teacher, bossy coach, unrepentant bully, unrequited love, pickled

beets, algebra, condemned to spend this fairest of September days
locked indoors, regretting summer, hatching plots, humming revolutionary song ("Mine eyes have seen the glory of the burning
of the school"), wishing more than anything to be outside. You
pass all these, and you head on toward the river to play with trout,
unscrubbed, unshaven, nonimmaculate but free.

In the valleys that run west from the Connecticut, there is a direct
correlation between wealth and no trespassing signs. In the more
affluent valleys they are everywhere, so thick it makes it seem as if
the owners of the land are trying to lock the rivers away in boxes,
each slat of which is another sign: VIOLATORS WILL BE PROSECUTED
TO THE FULL EXTENT OF THE LAW!

Travel up to the poorer valleys that begin north of the White
River and you will see few such signs. The Vermonters who live
there are still too close to the old days to make much sense out of
the kind of miserliness that puts limits on the land's enjoyment.
On the river, I can think of only one no trespassing sign, but
it's in a vital spot, and it involved me in three seconds of moral
dilemma.

Below the elementary school is a powerful chute I had never
fished before. On my third cast with a yellow Marabou, I hooked
a rainbow who immediately tore off downstream, right through
the middle of a deep pool.

I couldn't coax him back in the current, nor could I follow
him downstream through the pool—it was well over my head.
My only recourse was to take to shore and follow him along the
bank. I had started . . . I had gone about five yards . . . when

I ran smack into a big NO TRESPASSING sign and a rusty strand of barbed wire.

I hesitated, both because I was surprised, and because that black print was so intimidating. No Experience Allowed This Side of Me, the sign seemed to say—No Enjoyment, No Wonder, No Curiosity, No Joy. I thought about it for a second, then I thought about Woody Guthrie's "This Land is Your Land, This Land is My Land," and the last verse, the one they don't sing in the easy-listening versions or teach the kids in school.

> As I was walking that dusty highway,
> I saw a sign said Private Property,
> But on the other side, the sign said nothing,
> That side was made for you and me!

And stepping over that barbed wire, I went in pursuit of my trout.

The leaves have been slow to turn this year. I drove to the river on the tenth expecting to see those early reds and yellows that lead the way into autumn, but everything remained stubbornly green. The only colors I found were on dead maple leaves lying along the banks. There was a yellowish-red flush to their scalloped edges, a deeper red where the veins came together near the stem.

Where had they come from? Further upstream where it was higher and wilder, solidly fall? Spontaneously generated from the crispness in the air? There weren't any bare trees around and their presence was mystifying. They seemed plotted—arranged.

They overlay each other on the rocks like decoys set in sunshine to lure the other leaves down.

September means morning fog in Vermont. If you were flying in a glider across the mountains you could look down and see tributary fog in narrow white seams, each of which hides a valley. The seams gain amplitude as they flow east, joining snowier bands, merging finally with the great fog river that is the Connecticut.

These rivers are lifeless from the air, but were your vision somehow to penetrate the white, you might see a flyfisherman at the very bottom—a giant fisherman, his size exaggerated by the magnifying quality fog has. He's casting slowly, blowing on his hands to keep them warm. In summer, the fog hides the sun's heat and is welcomed; in fall, the fog hides the sun's heat and is endured.

Fog is expectation. Something momentous is going to be revealed—you feel it the moment you enter the river. It adds an intenseness to the fishing that can seem almost unbearable. You are in the midst of a secret, *part* of that secret, unable to decipher it from the center. Fog will halo a man, throw a penumbra round his shoulders, but it's a shining that can only be detected from outside.

Morning fog. When it lifted this morning, the sun streamed in on my back like a jet of hot air. Turning, I saw a huge rock that was the last bit of river the fog hid, a glacial wanderer that had come to a stop in the middle of a broad pool. It gradually emerged—the broad tawny base, the narrowing, prow-shaped middle, and then on the very top, the secret. A blue heron, as immobile as the rock itself, watching me with a knowing and patience that were prehistoric, sculpted of the same timelessness as the fog.

There are trade-offs to be made in fishing a river. One may be full of huge trout, but be impossible to wade; another is wadeable, but too crowded to enjoy. Each trout stream carries with it these contradictions, and it's up to the fisherman to reconcile them as best he can.

Take my river, for instance. The wading is a pleasure—the bottom is firm and comfortably rocky, and there's enough room so the trees don't imperil your casts. The valley is beautiful, fishing pressure is light, and trout are abundant in three varieties. Big trout, however, are scarce. The three- and four-pounders are down in the White River or over in the Lamoille, and to take anything over fourteen inches is cause for celebration.

All the more reason, then, to rue the trout I missed yesterday morning. I was chest-deep in the Aquarium, casting upstream with a grasshopper imitation. Earlier in the season I couldn't have stood there without being tumbled over by the current, but the pressure had eased with autumn and my stance was secure. I had missed a teasing rise over on the left bank; there's a rock a yard out and a trout lying behind it can get first crack at anything drifting over the falls.

I cast again, this time aiming it so the line draped itself over the rock. It's a trick that's worked before; when the line tightens and pulls the fly onto the eddy below the rock you get a vital second of drag-free drift.

Perfect. The grasshopper, landing on the rock, crawled over its downstream edge and hopped into the water. Immediately, a trout was on it—the river fell away as if in the vacuum of a depth charge, and in the gap where water had been appeared a monstrous back. I struck as hard as I could, but tightened on nothing—the fish and its promise were already irretrievable, a moment in the past.

Stripping the line in, I examined my fly. The hook was intact and sharp, but its hackles were flattened, as if it had been scared out of its wits by the trout's ferocity.

A big one, then—a once-in-a-season trout. In missing him, I felt like I had missed some connection with the river itself—had lost a chance to learn something important about its capacities, and the huge swirl with the question mark in the middle tormented me the rest of the day.

I went up to Maurice Page's this afternoon. His shop is on the North Branch, a hundred yards above its confluence with the main river. It's a rickety affair of red boards that contract and expand with the seasons. In the warm September sunshine, the cracks in the walls were fully open, as if the entire shop were inhaling one last time before winter.

COOPER, the sign near the loading platform reads. Above it is another sign, this one hand-lettered: "If I'm not here, honk three times. If I'm still not here, honk some more." Beyond it is a notice warning people that they enter the shop at their own risk. In order to read the faded print you have to enter the shop anyway, so it seems stupid to leave.

There was a big wooden tub on the platform, the kind farmers use to water their cows. Next to it were some boards that Maurice hadn't gotten around to cutting. Closer to the edge were footstools, birdhouses, and printer's trays, the kind of things Maurice keeps in sight in case any stray tourists happen by.

An important October birthday was coming up, and I had my eye on one of his chests. Maurice sells them unpainted, for a fair price. Even better, a portion of his personality comes with them, and a blanket chest made by Maurice Page is a lively, solid thing, part of a Vermont that is vanishing.

I was looking one over when Maurice came out. "You don't want it," he said, shaking his head. He opened the lid, then banged it in disgust. "See there? Top don't fit. I messed that one. I've got something better inside. Watch your step now."

Pine is everywhere in the shop—in the corners, on the lathes, in the air. Sawdust and shavings are September smells, sweeter than incense, more honest than perfume, and every leathery inch of Maurice comes bathed in its glow.

"There's your chest," he said, slapping its side. "Course you want, I could make it bigger. Here, come up here."

Deeper and deeper, up the stairs. There's the old water-power transformer near the top, dusty now that the dam is gone (1924 was the date it went out, but Maurice talks about the catastrophe as if it happened yesterday). Among the scraps and leftovers in the loft is a pine board that measures fourteen inches across, and Maurice decides it is just what I need for my chest. We agree on the dimensions—

Maurice hands me the tape measure and lets me do most of the measuring myself.

Maurice is a Vermonter who likes to talk. It's next to impossible to describe the texture of it; in it are weaved strands of laconic understatement, subtle teasing, old-fashioned courtliness, rhetorical interrogation, free association and whatever elocutionary devices Maurice happens to be in the mood for. As he talks, the light from the windows catches the stubble of his beard with the effect of a thousand sequins, making him twinkle.

"Yep, lived here all my life up to now," he'll say if you're a stranger. "Born in that house right there across the road seventy-five years ago." Then, if you're a woman: "You come up here in winter, I'll take you for a ride in my snow machine, don't forget now."

We talked for a while. A documentary had recently been made of another cooper up in Barnet, and I asked Maurice if he had seen it.

"Wasn't that a marvel? That Ben, he's a wizard. Aren't too many of those fellas left still use water power. Me, I flick a switch, on it goes."

He reached behind him. Instantly, the pulleys, gears and belts that line his shop clanked into action. He waited until the shop was really shaking, then shut it off.

"Nope, don't pay me now," he said when he saw my wallet. "I might not finish it, and then what happens? I don't want to be in debt to you, do I?"

We settled upon a pick-up date. I turned the car around in the cutoff and was circling past the shop when he flagged me down.

"Here's a wooden spoon," he said, jabbing it in the open window. "Good for porridge. Give it to your mom."

There's a short story by V. S. Pritchett about a businessman who's good at falling down. Whenever he's at a loss for words, bored, embarrassed, or surprised, down he goes. It's his only talent. He knows a dozen ways to do it; when the story ends, he's showing off his latest tumble to his aghast business associates at an important meeting.

It's a character I can relate to. I've had some classic falls of my own this month, half of them caused by impatience, half by my dislike for waders. I've been fishing in jeans and sneakers since summer, and the cold water has finally caught up with me. I clanked from pool to pool like a wind-up monster with rusty gears, an angling Frankenstein.

There's a good lie near the cemetery that can only be covered by casting from a rock in midstream. I was halfway up it when I slipped. As falls go, it was only fair—say an 8.5 in difficulty, a 7.5 in execution. Still, it was enough to drench me and I had to hurry back to the car for a dry set of clothes.

My waders are the cheapest kind you can get, slippery, ill-fitting, and porous. Wading wet, though, was out of the question, so I tugged them on. What I gained in warmth, I lost in traction, and later in the afternoon I took another spill, this one much more spectacular than the first.

I was back in the Aquarium, stalking the big trout I had missed earlier in the month. We'd had the usual heavy rain around the equinox, and the water was higher than it had been the previous time—high enough to increase the force on my legs and feet. About a foot to my left was a nice flat boulder that would allow me to get above the worst of the pressure. I shuffled over to it and gingerly stepped onto its middle.

False-casting about twenty yards of line out, I dropped a big Spuddler a foot above the rock where the trout had struck. As the fly landed, I shifted position slightly, just enough so that the tread under my weight-bearing foot slid from the security of gritty granite to the peril of slippery moss.

It was a backwards somersault this time, a fall I had never

pulled off before, not even in school. What was remarkable about it was its slow-motion quality—I had enough time and horizon left at the apogee to see a huge boil beneath the fly. Upside down, I yanked back with my rod hand, but there was no rod there—it was flying through the air behind me with the arc and thrust of a javelin.

"I must prepare myself for this," I thought, but before I could, I was splashing in the water, already past the icy shock of entry. I grabbed for my sunglasses, but the current had them on the bottom, scurrying over the rocks like a plastic crab. I started to chase after them, but the river was in my waders, and the weight tumbled me over so that I was floating face-up. My wallet, buoyed free of my pocket, bubbled dollar bills past my chest; my fly box, sprung from my vest, bobbed like the coffin of the *Pequod*.

There was no use fighting it. I gave myself up to my klutziness and let the current push me over to a sandbar—a lump now, a sack of wet nothingness to be stripped clean and flung disdainfully on the shore. Somewhere in my passage from vertical to horizontal to vertical again I managed to bump heads with a rock, resulting in a concussion that laid me up for three days, giving me plenty of time to puzzle out the moral of all this.

Never underestimate the capacity of a river to humiliate you, and always wear felt-bottomed soles.

Autumn is leaf-peeping time in Vermont, and after a few sudden stops you learn not to tailgate out-of-state cars. Of all the unofficial seasons here (mud season and black-fly season are the two others), foliage season is by far the silliest. While flatlanders are peeping at the leaves, natives are peeping at the peepers, and peeping-atrocity stories are numerous.

I have two this year. I was driving over a hill on I-91 this morning when I came upon a station wagon with New York plates parked right in the middle of the northbound lane—*in* the lane, not on its edge. A man in a safari suit was sitting on the opened tailgate studying the view with his binoculars; a willowy blonde sat on the hood absorbed in a sketchbook. I honked at them—they waved pleasantly as I swerved past.

The second happened on the river. I was on my knees trying to revive a small brookie before letting him go when I heard someone beeping a horn up by my car. Tourists had been stopping all morning to take pictures of me against the trees, and I assumed it was someone wanting me to pose. I swam the trout back and forth until he was able to manage on his own, then waded over to the road.

Ohio plates, a carful of peepers. The man who was driving stuck his head out the window—it had a red and mushy look, like stewed tomatoes.

"Where's this desert thing at?" he demanded.

I have this strange capacity to understand illogical questions. Most people would have looked at the man in incomprehension; I understood right away which desert he was after.

"You mean the Desert of Maine?" I said, referring to a popular tourist spot.

"Yeah, that desert thing, Where's it at, pal?"

"You take this road over to New Hampshire, then turn left on Route 10 up to 302. It's right down that about 180 miles."

"Thanks, pal."

Off they went.

And just for the record, the foliage peaked this year at precisely 3:38 p.m. on Thursday, September 29. I was there when it happened. I was fishing by the elementary school, and had stopped to stare in awe at the trees. There were dark storm clouds overhead, the wind would be stripping most of the leaves off by dusk, but for now the black sky framed perfectly the bittersweet reds and yellows, giving them a color so vibrant and urgent that their radiation was a tug on the heart.

As I watched, something remarkable happened. The sun found a hole in the cloud just large enough for one crepuscular ray to leap through. It slanted obliquely toward earth, catching a gold tree on the bank and casting its radiance onto the surface of the river, spinning it gold. My fly rode on its shimmer for the space of a yard—for that one fleeting moment I was fishing a golden fly for golden trout on a golden river. Then the cloud clamped shut around the sun, and the peak was passed.

I heard voices up on the bank. A boy and girl, each about eight, were kicking through the leaves piled against the trees. Every few yards they stooped to pick one up and put it in a plastic bag they jointly carried.

They waved, and came over to watch me. As it turned out, the leaves were for their oldest sister, in college out west. She was homesick for Vermont's autumn, she had written; they were collecting a bagful of the yellowest yellows and the reddest reds to send her to cheer her up.

"Here's one for you," the girl said, handing me a maple leaf.

"Thanks, I'll keep it on my desk this winter. It will remind me of September."

The boy saw his chance.

"September," he said, spreading his arms apart as if to embrace the smells, the colors, and light, "is my best favorite year."

15
Fathers and Sons

Between the years 1961 and 1966, I was the most obnoxious teenager to fish with in all of New England, and if you don't believe me, ask my Dad. Vain, overzealous, opinionated, dictatorial, insufferable, fierce—any combination of negative adjectives would aptly describe the tall redhead I can see in my mind's eye casting from the bow of the battered, fifteen-foot runabout, and it was my poor father, casting patiently from the stern, who took their brunt.

Fishing fathers, fishing sons. The literature on the subject is immense, and invariably follows the same pattern. Wise, experienced, pipe-smoking father (Big Bill) teaches eager, barefooted, gum-chewing son (Little Bill) the tenets of good sportsmanship, the better to tame the youngster's fish-killing propensities. ("It's a noble brown, Little Bill. Let us raise our hats to him and give him his freedom!") Teaching a son to fly fish has become a sacred duty, a rite of passage, a cliché.

And, of course, a very difficult chore. It's not easy to instill tradition in a teenager whose every instinct is to smash tradition. I saw a father and son on the river who perfectly illustrated the problem. Both were dressed in the same wader-fishing-vest-Tyrolian hat combination; both fished with expensive rods. I could see the father teaching the son how to roll cast—the son was nodding, albeit grimly. There were trout rising in the next pool, and the father went to investigate. Left alone, the son started whipping the water in front of him with his rod—actually whipping it, as if punishing the river for some infraction . . . No, not an easy chore at all.

In our family, it was backwards. I was the one who taught my father how to fish, damned near killing him in the process. Naturally, I harbor a lot of guilt about this. The memory of how I treated him goes with me each time I fish the river, descending like a sudden black cloud on an otherwise perfect day. One taste of the madeleine was enough to recreate for Proust the chaotic emotions of youth, and so it is with me. One snarled leader, one sloppy cast, and I am fifteen years old again, slapping the side of our boat in impatience, giving my father hell.

Life puts a statute of limitations on the apologies that are due between a father and son, a few quick years after which they will remain permanently unspoken. Here then, before that limit expires, is mine.

It started the summer I was thirteen. My parents had owned the lake house for a year, and in that time I had become totally dedicated to fishing. My long-standing passions for baseball, basketball, cocker spaniels, and West Point were as nothing compared to it; I read every book on the subject I could get my hands on, subscribed to three different fishing magazines, spent every allowance dollar on lures and flies. It was an enthusiasm with all the force of puberty behind it—whatever I was sublimating, I was sublimating in a big way.

It wasn't long before I considered myself an expert roughly on a par with Lee Wulff. This had nothing to do with catching fish; indeed, it was only about once in every six weeks of casting that I managed to find a trout or bass suicidal enough to take my lure. Teenagers being teenagers, my lack of success only made me more rigid in my theories. I fished where the books said to fish whether I caught anything or not, and sneered at those who caught fish where they weren't supposed to be. In short, I became a fishing snob—a snob who combined an inquisitor's detestation for heresy with a Schweitzer's missionary zeal. Casting about for a disciple to mold in my own image, I found my dad.

Dad had fished a bit before. Friends from the office would charter a party boat out of Freeport on Long Island and he would go with them, returning at the end of the day heroically sunburned and unshaved, reeking of flounder. For a time when I was small, we owned a boat of our own with friends of my parents—a leaky wooden cabin cruiser called the *Betty Wayna* in honor of the wives. It was over the *Betty Wayna's* side that I caught my first fish. Dad asked me to hold his line for a second while he went for a beer; taking it, I immediately caught a bright and wiggly porgy, a fish I suspect was already securely hooked when Dad handed me the rod.

As much as he may have enjoyed fishing before I got my hands on him, Dad's enthusiasm was limited by one important fact: he was legally blind. It had happened gradually after the war—why, the doctors couldn't say. Having two young children to support, he had tried to ignore it as long as he could. Driving to work one day, he realized he couldn't see the crossing guards outside an elementary school, and that was it—he never drove a car again. Through a tremendous effort I can only guess at, aided all the way by my mother, he used the blurred remnant of sight that was left to him to continue his career, and succeeded even more importantly at ridding himself of self-pity and despair.

This battle won, his eyesight became the source of some famous mix-ups, slapstick routines that no one laughed over as much as Dad himself. Most of these occurred at our summer house, and were of such a dramatic and sudden character that they remain etched in our family's memory as a series of tableaux, each with title. There was, for instance, The Time Dad Walked Right Off The End Of The Dock In His Business Suit; The Time Dad Threw Out Mom's Bag Of Jewelry Thinking It Was Garbage; or, most memorably, The Time Dad Snuck Up On His Friend Charlie Beaudrie Floating In An Inner Tube And Dumped Him Over, Only It Wasn't Charlie Beaudrie, It Was A Stranger.

The manmade lake where all this took place was a typical New England resort lake, with summer homes, marinas, and camps along one shore, trees, rocks, trout, and bass along the other. It was still possible in those years to meet old-timers who remembered the valley before the lake had been created, but they were dying out fast, and the traditions of that corner of New England were going with them. It was still country in 1963, but the corner had been turned, and in the years we lived there it steadily became more suburban.

Most of our fishing was done at night, after dinner. We'd walk down to the dock together, me weighted down with three rods, a huge tackle box, and a lantern; Dad with the landing net and the simple spin-casting rig that was all his eyesight could handle. During the day the lake was blighted with water-skiers and speedboats, but at night it was calm and deserted enough for me to pretend I was in Maine.

"We'll go over to the island," I'd say, nodding sagely (I'd been reading Louise Dickinson Rich's *We Took to the Woods* that summer, and I thought of myself as Gerrish the Guide). "If we don't get lunkers there, we'll head down to the big rock, fish the drop-off. I'll steer. You sit in the back and keep quiet so we don't scare lunkers."

There was no question of Dad's authority in every other aspect of my life, but when it came to fishing, he abdicated all responsibility.

"I think I'll try a popper," Dad would say when we coasted to a stop. He loved catching bluegills.

"No poppers," I'd say, frowning. "We're after bass tonight. We're big-fish fishermen."

Dad would take this all in. "Big-fish fishermen, huh? Okay. Tie on something good."

I had to tie on all Dad's lures, untangle his line, point him in the right direction to cast. I wanted to be patient with him, knew I had to be patient, and yet was never patient enough, and would end up getting more and more irritated with him as the night wore on. "You're casting too close to shore. Cast further out."

Dad probably couldn't *see* the shore. He'd nod though, and start casting in a different direction.

It would be quiet after that. If the moon were out, our Jitterbugs would glide across the milky beams as gracefully as swans.

Occasionally, the wake would reach us from night-cruising boats further out—easy swells that gently rocked us, then draped themselves across the rocks near shore. It was peaceful, but frightening. I had a friend whose father had explained the facts of life to him when fishing one night, and I was afraid that Dad would choose the same time and place for his explanation.

"You're not making your plug gurgle enough," I'd say, hoping to keep the conversation strictly on fishing. "Make it gurgle more." He'd reel a little faster.

"There's too much moonlight out," I complained. "Fish don't bite in moonlight."

"Last week you said moonlight was good."

"Not above seventy degrees. What's that?"

"What's what?"

"You have a bite! Hook him!"

Dad, who could see neither the plug nor the commotion behind it, would raise his rod tip so gently and timidly that it would infuriate me. "Sock it to him! Pump him in!"

"What is it?" Dad would say, peering over the side.

"It's gone! Why didn't you reel harder?"

Dad would smile as broadly as if he had caught it. "It was a keeper."

"You lost him," I'd say accusingly. "You lost a bass."

There was no way Dad could win. If he lost the fish, I was furious at him; if he landed it, I was jealous. Luckily for both of us, the fish were few and far between. We'd try every lure in my tackle box, run from one end of the lake to the other, and invariably return empty-handed. It would be ten or eleven by the time we quit. The few simple tasks that Dad could do without help were important to him, so I would wait on the end of the dock while he buttoned the rain-cover over the boat, staring up at the stars—the stars that he couldn't see. We would walk back along the dark road to our house, Dad's shoulder jostling mine as he tripped and caught himself, the lantern swinging circles of light back and forth before our shoes. Holly, our golden retriever, would have the scent of us now and be barking in delight. My mother would be reading by the fireplace, ready with her inevitable question.

"Catch anything?"

"It was a moral victory," I'd say. "Dad had a bite."

And Dad would tell her about it, laughing gently over how excited I had become.

I continued insufferable for the next five summers. Dad would no sooner catch up with my latest theory than I would switch it, insist that night-fishing was for amateurs, demand we go out at dawn, use spinners rather than plugs. I started fly-casting when I was fifteen, and my clumsy efforts imperiled his head, yet he continued fishing from the stern as patiently as before, marveling at my new skill. He even went so far as to buy his own fly rod at Macy's—alone, without my advice. The salesman sold him the wrong kind of line and the wrong kind of reel, and I don't think Dad ever took it out of its case.

By the time I was sixteen I was starting to catch more fish. Plastic worms fished slow were my latest tactic, and for a change I had one that worked. I tried getting Dad to use them, too, but his eyesight wasn't good enough for him to see the line peeling off the spool when a bass took, and he never acquired the knack of sensing a strike with his rod. Still, he took as much pleasure in my fish as if he had caught them himself, and would tell all our friends about my accomplishments, making me nearly burst from pride. His unselfishness was gradually softening my ferocity; I began to need the look of delighted surprise that swept over his face on those rare occasions when he caught a good fish.

In the meantime, Dad's store of misadventures was steadily increasing. There was The Time Dad Hooked An Immense Trout, Only It Wasn't A Trout, It Was A Cris-Craft; The Time Dad, Fishing Without A License, Struck Up A Conversation With The Game Warden; and The Night The Boat Sank.

This last was especially traumatic. We were fishing again at night, and had anchored along the western, uninhabited shore. My Uncle Buzz had come along with us. I had just reeled in the first fish—a catfish, the only one I've ever caught, a mustachioed, portentous creature that we fastened onto a stringer attached to the boat's side.

It was an omen, but we weren't sure of what. We continued casting, listening as usual to one of Uncle Buzz's war stories.

"We had catfish like that in New Guinea. These crackers from Alabama would catch them on doughballs. I remember this other time over in New Caledonia this sergeant, name of Runnels . . ."

I wasn't listening. There was water sloshing around the bottom of the boat, and I had stood up on the seat to keep my brand-new moccasins dry. Now, though, the water was lapping over my feet again, and I was annoyed. Annoyed, not scared. I took off my moccasins and continued casting.

Ignorance is bliss. The boat had been at the marina earlier in the week being repaired for engine trouble. The mechanic had neglected to replug the drain hole in the stern—a hole we didn't even know existed. Planing at full speed, the hole was above the water line, but the moment we stopped, the boat settled, allowing the water to flow in. A frogman boring a hole in the bottom couldn't have sabotaged us any better.

Buzz was too busy telling war stories to notice anything was wrong. Dad, of course, couldn't see. That left me. The water was up to my shins now, and I was beginning to realize that something important was happening. I had just finished reading Walter Lord's *A Night to Remember* about the *Titanic* disaster, and I was very concerned not to do anything that would cause panic.

"Uh," I said, as casually as I could, "we're sinking."

The water was up to our knees and rising fast. Uncle Buzz hopped into the stern to see what was wrong, which was precisely what he shouldn't have done, since the added weight made us sink faster. I fought my way through the water to the steering wheel, intending to get us closer to shore before we went under. Dad, though, had always had this phobia about ramming our propeller on an underwater rock, and he yelled for me to cut the engine. We were about fifty yards from shore now, and the bow was rising slowly in the air as the stern sank.

Remembering how many people had been pulled under by the *Titanic's* suction, I climbed onto the side with the intention of jumping clear. I was on the point of leaping . . . I was up to three in my count . . . when the water suddenly came to me, and I felt the side drop away beneath my feet.

Dad and Uncle Buzz had been deposited in the water, too; all we could see of the boat was the descending bow light. When it met the water, its heat sent up a ghostly kind of steam.

"Are you okay?" Dad shouted.

"I'm okay!" I shouted back. "Are you okay?"

The seat cushions had floated loose. I found one for Dad, then swam back to get one for myself.

"Wait for me, guys!" Uncle Buzz, remembering his Boy Scout training, had grabbed the boat's life ring, and was swimming with it toward shore. What Buzz had forgotten, though, was that the ring was still attached by a line to the boat's side. In effect, he was trying to tow the sunk boat with him, huffing and puffing from the strain.

We disentangled him. I saw my tackle box floating in the moonlight, and made a start for it, but I was too worried about Dad's eyesight to leave him. We formed a little convoy and started paddling toward shore. I yelled "Don't panic!" so much that Dad probably thought I *was* panicking, and he kept talking to me in the kind of soothing, reassuring tone he used with babies.

"Here we go now. Everything's perfectly fine. How you doing? We'll just keep swimming now, nice and easy . . ."

Reaching shore, we argued over what to do next. It was too far to walk home, and there was no trail through the woods. Water and pickerel grass streamed off our clothes—we were shivering in the cold. We decided we would have to call for help.

"Let's not panic!" I kept saying.

"Right," Dad said. "We don't want to scare your mother."

We called for help as apologetically as anyone ever called for help.

"Help!" we yelled in unison. "We're all right, but we need some help!"

Nothing. We tried again.

"We'd like some help over here, please!"

Dad and Buzz soon got tired of shouting. I continued alone, with stranger and stranger variations.

"S.O.S! Please acknowledge. S.O.S!"

After about an hour of calling, a passing cabin cruiser heard us. We were back on our dock a few minutes after that. As meek as they were, our yells had woken up half the community, and there was a small crowd waiting for us when we arrived. Some of the women had blankets. One of the teenagers, no doubt having read the same *Titanic* book I had, offered me a cigarette. I took it—to this day, it's the only one I've ever smoked. It was great being a survivor.

Though I didn't realize it at the time, The Night the Boat Sank marked the turning point in our fishing relationship. Besides my moccasins, I'd lost a beautiful bait-casting outfit, a fly rod, and a tackle box containing roughly a hundred lures. Losing all this chastened my pride, and I was never quite so dogmatic and pompous about fishing again. Then, too, it hadn't been me who had stayed calmest during the sinking, for all my fantasies about being a guide, nor had it been Buzz, despite his war stories. The true hero had been Dad.

By the time the boat was dredged up and repaired, the summer was over. The following year I was working, getting to the lake less and less. Dad would try to go fishing without me, but with little success. I would tie big loops of monofilament on his lures so he could thread his line through them rather than the small eyelets, but I think he used to confine himself to the spinner my mother would tie on before he left; if it broke, he would quit and go home. The times we did go fishing together, I was much gentler with him, realizing at last that the talk and the being there in the twilight were what counted, not the fish we didn't catch. The last few years before they sold the summer house, he had his granddaughter to go fishing with. They would cast off the dock for sunfish, and he would pull the same hold-my-line-while-I-go-over-here trick with her that he had used with me in those far-off days on the *Betty Wayna*.

Dad doesn't fish much now. I still call him whenever I catch a big one on the river, and he is as delighted over it as if he had caught it himself—no, *more* delighted. And this is the lesson he taught me, taught me slowly and subtly all those summers in the boat when I cast and pontificated, cast and fumed. Catching fish is a joy, but what is even better is having someone you love catch one, when the delight is doubled. This is the true lesson to be taught a fishing son, more important than any theory regarding fish or fly, and I hope that one day I may pass it on to a son as patiently and unselfishly as my father passed it on to me.

Dad came to Vermont for our wedding in July. I took him fishing on the river. He got his line tangled. I told him where to cast, and got mad at him when he reeled in too slow. "Catch anything?" my mother asked when we got back to the lodge. We hadn't. It was the best fishing trip of the year.

16
October Nineteenth

It's hard to know when to give up on something. A hope, a dream, a friendship, a love. Each of these has a natural life of its own—they are apt to begin in obscurity and flow in ways unpredictable to man. Only their endings sometime enter the realm of our control, and in exchange for this concluding power we are handed a delicate risk. Say goodbye too soon and you risk missing the fruition, severing the feeling before its last echoing chord—the bittersweet afterglow—fades away. Say goodbye too late and emotion that seemed more concentrated and intense than the purest essence can become diluted and stale, losing the enchantment it once had over us, losing by this transformation its accurate place in our memory.

So it is with rivers. The beginning of a trout season is ritualistic and well-defined; the middle takes on a natural rhythm that is closely tied to the river's life, offering the angler participation but not control. It is the ending of a trout season, the yearly severing of his connection to the river, that the fly fisherman must choose for himself. Many states allow fishing until the end of October, but usually the sport is over well before that, and the moment the fly fisherman quits for the year depends on factors more instinctual than any fixed date.

I fished too late last year. The leaves were off the trees, the water was high and discolored, and the trout were as sluggish as carp. Every quality that attracts me to fishing—the hope of it, the mystery, the quick swirling life—was gone, replaced by a cold rushing blankness on which nothing could imprint. What was worse, the blankness stayed with me for the next few months with the tenacity of remorse, blocking my earlier memories of the river with this last wintry impression. It had been a good year, a year full of exploration and delight, but there were those stale, cold afternoons tacked on the end. I had been greedy, pushed the river two or three weeks too far. For a writer, a person trained in endings, the mistake was inexcusable.

Fly fishing, after all, is an attempt to make connection with the life of a river. If that life is gone, the attempt becomes absurd. Howard Walden, in his classic *Upstream and Down*, dismisses autumn fishing as "an evocation of ghosts, a second childhood of the trout season, more like a haunting recollection than a living experience. It is a ghoulish disinterring of something better left buried."

It can certainly be that; fish too late, the ghoulies get you. But there is an equal, opposite risk in giving up on a river too soon. A fisherman subscribing to Walden's dictum would have the trout season end with the last small hatch in late summer, thereby cutting himself off from a month and more of fine weather, and trout that still rise willingly to a fly. On my river, quitting too early would mean losing out on some of the year's best days, cloudless, exhilarating afternoons that I would give anything to have back come December. A trout season is an accumulation of puzzles, some of which can still be solved in the fishing's last few days. Quit too early on these and the answers may not be offered again. It doesn't matter if trout are scarce. A fly-fishing season begins in unfulfilled expectation sharpened by optimism; it should end in unfulfilled expectation softened by acceptance.

Vermont's autumn trout season is controversial from a conservation point of view—there are spawning brookies and browns to protect—but there is a fundamental rightness about it in one respect: October is the quintessential Vermont month, and it is a fit and proper feeling to be wading one of its rivers with red leaves at your back. I am not a hunter—my means of assimilating the outdoors is a fly rod, and I want to be able to wield it as far into the autumn as new impressions endure.

"One last time," I said to myself that morning as I got into the car. It was the nineteenth now, we had had our first hard frosts, and on the summit ridges of the White Mountains east of us I could see faint tracings of snow. Goodbyes were on my mind. I drew out all the rituals of my fishing day as far as they would go—the scrambled eggs and cranberry muffins at the diner, the stop at Sanborn's for new leaders, the drive upstream along the river, the donning of my waders, the careful preparation of line and fly. "One last time," I said, and it transformed even the most banal of my routines into bittersweet farewells.

I began further upstream than I usually go; on this last day I was anxious to have the river where it was comprehensible and small. That it wasn't the fishiest spot on the river didn't bother me. What I wanted was the view of the village across the fields, the white church steeple rising over the elms, the Holsteins grazing by the overgrown stone walls—the milkmaid, the arbor, and the meadow.

It was a trout that brought me back to the fishing. I had on a wet fly, the first I had used all year, and a small brook trout had grabbed it as it dangled downstream. I hadn't been concentrating; the sudden tug on the line affected me exactly like a sudden tug on the sleeve—it was as if the trout were mad at me for not doing my part.

I turned my attention back to the river. It was easy to total up all the things that were gone. The leaves, for one. There were great gaps in the foliage, whole trees that were already bare. A New England autumn can be so colorfully full that you forget the curtains of red are supported by a framework of limbs, and their reappearance—stark and straggly—is always something of a shock. The new abundance of light affects you the same way. In summer, the sun on the river comes in shafts, glimmers and reflections; in mid-October, it's everywhere, hidden by no leaves, merged with high white clouds into a sky that seems freshly painted. Had there even been a sky in July? There was no boundary to this October light, and it seemed to well up from the river's bottom just as exuberantly as it poured down from the sun.

There was still a lot of foliage to admire, most of it in the river. I caught my share. On every third or fourth cast, my fly would snare a maple leaf the current was sweeping downstream. Some leaves were real monsters, with pendulous edges and thick fatty stems; others were little fry, miniature leaves that could have fit on a stamp. As I pulled them in, my line tightened and they skittered across the river's surface like miniature kites trying one last time to become airborne.

The insects were gone. The big hatches of spring end by mid-July, but there is a great deal of lesser activity right through the first few frosts. The long decline in their numbers is never final—I have seen insects dancing over the river's surface on warm days in December—but early October seems to mark a turning point in their domination. Until then, there is at least one variety of insect whose predictable appearance makes it worth imitating; after that, the river seems as devoid of bugs as it does fish. Nothing swarms over by the far bank, no clouds hover an inch above the river, and nothing plops from the tree limbs into the eddies to be inhaled instantly.

The autumnal insect in Vermont is the wooly caterpillar— the thick orange and black beastie whose "fur" is supposed to be an infallible guide to the upcoming winter's severity. (It's a superstition I don't take much stock in; their fur is always thick, and predicting a long winter in New England is not exactly going out on a limb.) You see these caterpillars trying to inch their way across the roads this time of year. I've caught lots of October trout on orange and black Wolly Worms fished just below the surface, so at least a few of them must find their way into the river.

And speaking of flies, by October there are great gaps in all my fly boxes, springs and clips that hold nothing, making it seem as if the flies had died off in the cold or migrated with the real insects they copied. I go through an extravagant quantity of flies in the course of a season, and if I didn't limit myself somehow, I'd quickly go broke. Because of that—because I need a reason to use those experimental flies I couldn't resist last spring—I declare a moratorium on all fly buying as of September first. After that date, I use what's in my box, and buy no replacements until the following year. It works fine for a while—I almost always have enough Wulffs and Muddlers to get me through September. By October, though, most of these have been left in trees or trout, and I'm fishing with the chaff. Bushy monstrosities I tied as a kid, snelled wet flies I found at a flea market, saltwater flies from my days on the Cape—they're all trotted out now, and occasionally a trout will take one from sheer astonishment.

Halfway through the morning I snapped off the wet fly on which I'd caught the brookie. For lack of anything better, I switched to a Daniel Webster. It's a "salter" fly—a green and red bucktail designed for sea-run browns—so I wasn't surprised that I didn't catch anything with it.

I contemplated my alternatives. There was a Honey Blonde in a size suited for tarpon; some battered Light Hendricksons, and half a dozen other creations the names of which I had forgotten.

There was one more possibility. In the course of a season's shufflings and unpackings, flies drop out of their boxes and get caught all over the car—in the mat of the trunk, the floor carpets, and upholstery. I decided to go back and see what I could glean.

I had waded downstream at a pretty good clip, and it was a long walk to the car. By the time I got there, a hot cup of something was sounding pretty good. I pulled my waders off and got behind the wheel, debating which way to head. A mile east was a general store, but it was a filthy, depressing place. I decided to take a chance and head upriver.

I didn't go very far. About a mile up the road and hanging over it was a banner riddled with holes: OLD HOME DAYS OCT. 18–19. Beyond it was a green arrow pointing to the left; on an impulse, I joined a line of pick-ups and jeeps heading in that direction.

An old farmer with a cane pointed me to a parking spot on a straw-covered field. He was very businesslike. When I tried to take a spot nearer the front, he poked his cane at the car like it was a recalcitrant cow, forcing me back.

The fairground was simply a four-acre field, half of which had been turned into a rough soccer field for the elementary-school team. It was set on a small plateau above the trees, and the temperature in the wind must have been five degrees colder than it had been back in the valley.

It wasn't hard to find the coffee. Boy Scout Troop 82, the "Cobra" troop, was selling it by the abandoned "Dunk A Dummy" booth, and that's where most of the fairgoers were huddled. Warmed, a few of them broke away to watch the soccer game; the local team was being trounced by a bigger squad, but the cheers were good-natured for both sides. Vermont schools often lack the boys to make up an eleven-man team, so girls play, too, and the ones I saw were doing just fine—there was a small, shifty redhead who had a murderous shot from right wing.

The rest of the fair was just getting started. An auctioneer who could have been Robert Frost's brother was unloading junk for the charity auction—some old skis, broken televisions, sleds, and shovels. Further up the hill was the tag sale, the vendors sitting on lawn chairs before their merchandise, wrapped in blankets. Behind them was the horseshoe pitching. Though it was still early, a dozen or so games were already in progress, and the clank of shoe hitting stake was the metronomic sound that underlay everything—the distant cheers, the tape-recorded music, the wind.

I found some shelter in a dugout along the first-base side of a diamond that Abner Doubleday might have played on; there was an old-fashioned dirt cutout between the pitcher's mound and home plate, and rickety stands straight out of an 1880s mezzotint. It was a good vantage point. There in right field a crew was setting up the carnival rides and food concessions, testing the neon. Try a Jaffle! one sign urged. None of the fairgoers seemed interested. They were selling ices, taffy, and soda; the rides were summertime rides, too, and it all seemed out of place in the wind.

For the carnival, this stop was the end of the line. The larger towns booked for summer, then the medium-sized ones, then the small ones, and then finally—on the last open date before winter—the hill villages like this one, 500 or fewer souls trying to pretend it was still summer.

But it didn't matter, of course. It was all good-natured, the take was for charity, and everyone seemed to be having a good time. Two members of the 4-H club found me in the dugout and sold me a raffle ticket. The word was out after that, and I had to turn down chances offered by the quilt club, the snowmobile club, and the Masons. A reporter from the local paper came up to me next. Yes, I was having a good time, I said into his tape recorder. Yes, I thought things were done just fine.

We talked for a while after that. He was upset about his assignment—he would have much preferred to be down at

Dartmouth for the football game. Still, it was kind of nice with the kids and the leaves and all. His daughter was a Rainbow Girl and if I wanted to buy a chance on a new woodstove, he'd send her over.

I stayed long enough for another cup of Boy Scout coffee, then started back to the river. I was still ambivalent about fishing. The morning hadn't been very productive, and I was worried about pushing the river too hard again, prolonging the season past the point of reasonable expectation and reward.

But I couldn't quit, not yet. When I was a boy, we would drive back to the city from our weekend home on Sunday afternoons; in following the lake, I would see men going out in boats to fish, fly rods sticking out from the stern, their parkas puckered tight around their chins. I would envy them, wanting nothing so much as to be out there, too, in the October wind. To be able to do what appeared to me the very epitome of freedom, and autumn afternoons have generated the same yearning ever since.

"One more time," I said, for the second time that day. I went into the river three miles upstream of the stretch I had fished in the morning. I was getting up into the headwaters now—the water was six or seven feet wide at the most. The falls, rapids, and pools were all miniaturized, and I fished downstream expecting nothing bigger than miniature trout.

I had on a tattered white nymph I had found in my box under some Irresistibles. In this kind of water, tactics aren't complicated—do what's necessary to keep the fly in place, and the rest is up to the trout. Thus, I concentrated on letting the nymph dangle worm-like in the deep spots, and did my best to avoid the leaves.

There was nothing for the first hundred yards. The pools deepened slightly as I moved downstream, until I came to the deepest of the stretch: a slow, hemlock-shaded glide between

matching boulders. I fished the far side of the left boulder without a rise. I fished the far side of the right boulder—nothing
there, either. There remained one possibility. Letting line out
slowly, I swam the nymph in the dark channel between boulders,
and—so perfect was the spot—hooked the fish in my imagination a moment before the real trout took hold.

One of the delights of hooking a fish on a nymph is that
for the first few seconds you gain no impression of its size. The
current had tightened the line enough to set the hook, but the
trout's first movement was upstream toward me, and I had to
reel in fast in order to get to the point where I could feel him.
It was this moment—the instant when the line came taut and I
sensed his weight and power, sensed, that is, a life beyond my
expectation—that was the best of the fight.

The rest was interesting enough. A trout that size in such
narrow water could easily have broken free, at least in a big-river
style of fight. But by some accommodation I couldn't penetrate,
the fish geared his struggle to the miniaturized stream, and confined his runs to short, flashing darts between rocks. As usual, I
was fishing a 6X leader—the merest gossamer—so I didn't dare
force him. I waded from rock to rock, flushing him with my
wader boot, gaining eight or nine inches of line before he made
it to the next rock in our progression.

Space was on my side. The water was getting shallower as
the river widened, and each rock gave the trout less protection.
After ten more minutes of tag, I urged him gently toward shore,
and he was tired enough to go along. The rocks gave way to wet
stones that eased his transition from water to land; I nudged him
onto the sand, and he lay there gasping in the mingled surprise
and fear with which the first prehistoric fish must have flopped
from the sea.

A rainbow and a good one—fifteen inches, with a thick, streamlined flank and a brightness fresh as the sky. For that part of the river, a very big fish indeed.

I looked around for a rock large enough to kill him. It's a tradition with me; I release all but three or four of the trout I catch each year, but the last one is to be taken home, cleaned, cooked, and eaten, thereby reminding me of exactly where in the food chain I stand. (I have an anthropologist friend who refers to my fishing as "hunting and gathering," and at some basic, instinctual level she is right.) I had the rock in my hand—I had picked out the spot on his head where I would hit him—when for a reason that wasn't immediately evident, I changed my mind.

I took the trout with both hands and brought him back to the water. Kneeling, I swam him into the current, moving his tail back and forth until he had revived sufficiently to hold his place in my loosely cupped hands. We retraced the path of our fight in stages; I held him behind each rock in turn, letting him adjust to the increased pressures before moving him on. It was ten minutes before he was strong enough to release. I started him off with an encouraging shove, and this time there was no flank-turning, sideways retreat back to my hands—he swam off powerfully toward the depths of the pool.

It wasn't until I saw him swim away that I found my reason for releasing him. Winter was coming, and I wanted to be able to sit at my desk and picture him there in his dark pool, enduring the snow and ice as patiently as I did, waiting for spring with the same kind of certainty and hope, my emissary to May.

Winter. It was in the river now—the light was washed from it, the warmth and life. I had my reel off and my rod unjointed before I reached the bank.

A good season. It was time to get out.

17
A Tracer of Streams

One could do worse than be a tracer of streams. Following a river to its source through every winding, battling flood, drought, and disease, a Livingston in moral fervor, a Burton in intelligence, opening up to human imagination a country spacious enough for a million dreams, pinning down its origins on a map heretofore blank, sharing the journey in a book more adventurous than any

Odyssey—they have always been epic tasks, fit for the Lewises and Clarks of the world, the Stanleys and the Spekes.

To those who only know it in its navigable reaches, a great river's source is among the most unimaginable of things, an Ultima Thule we can never picture, so small and obscure is that first irreversible impulse that gives it life. The Hudson is the river that flows past the skyscrapers of Manhattan a thousand yards wide, but it is also that portion of the small waterfall high in the Adirondacks which, splashing on a convex rock, follows the right-hand grooves south.

To follow great rivers to their source was my boyhood dream. I pictured myself a mountain climber dipping my hands in the Andes brook that was the Amazon, letting the water flow off my face before continuing its run down to the sweltering jungle, coming home through great peril to write the book of my adventures. As dreams go, it wasn't a bad one; as time went on, it was less abandoned than transformed. At fourteen, I made the acquaintance of the great writers, men like Tolstoy and Conrad, and realized that they were following streams to their source as well—streams of character, history, and fate, on journeys every bit as difficult as the greatest explorer's. It was this kind of trip I eventually embarked on, starting off into the jungle with a rusty machete, a wobbly compass, rebellious bearers, and no guides, but with all the hope in the world.

And yet there turned out to be a river in it after all—the river of this book. It is no Missouri or Nile, not even a Hudson, but a gentle trout river flowing from modest mountains in the small state where I live. I went to it first partly as a relief from the expeditionary labor of writing—the tracing of various threads through novels and stories—but in time, the river began to seem a thread worth writing about on its own, linking as it did not only the separate, sunlit afternoons when I fished it, but the memories of fishing that lay scattered across my life without locus. In writing about the river through the seasons, I had been trying to trace it to its source just as surely as if I were hiking along its banks, map in hand. The river at dusk, the river in August, the river in fall—these were all windings that had to be explored if I was to reach the elusive spring that was its beauty's source.

At the same time I was following the river in a figurative sense, I was following it in a literal one. The fishing season's impulse was upstream—each afternoon seemed a bit above the one that preceded it, until by October I was fishing the river where it was only a few yards wide. Below me the river was familiar through a hundred trips, but upstream the water was always new, and I waded through it with increasing delight.

I had made the resolution to hike to the river's source as I stood by its banks in a February snowstorm, but the time had never seemed propitious. Spring meant black flies, mosquitoes, and mud; summer brought heat, and September had been crowded with too much fishing. Beyond these reasons was my own insistence on doing things in the right order. I wanted to find the spring or pond that was the river's source only when the rest of it was thoroughly explored, saving that final expedition as the cap on all my experiences. The moment would come when striking out for the headwaters would seem as natural and unpremeditated as fishing a slightly higher pool, and I trusted my instincts enough to wait.

I went the same October afternoon I released the big rainbow. It was on an impulse—it wasn't until I was in the car driving west that I understood what had prompted me. As curious as I was to find the source, I had been waiting until the fishing was over for the year so I could walk the river's banks without feeling compelled to wonder about its trout. In fly fishing, each pool and rapid becomes momentarily the entire world, curiosity is localized, and the rest of the river may as well not exist—we fish in fragments of space just as we do fragments of time. Fishing was the medium that had taught me most about the river, but now, in trying to grasp a larger section, it would only be in the way.

The road stayed by the river at first. There's a small hill town where the valley starts to narrow. I had thought of it as having the neat, rectangular perfection of a village on a model train layout, but that was in summer, and without the camouflage of leaves, the homes looked battered and exposed. Beyond its outskirts, I came to the summit of the river's main valley. At the top, the road joins another road that crosses it like a **T,** changing the trend from vaguely east-west to vaguely north-south. The river's channel was less obvious than before, but I knew from studying the map that it was still somewhere off to my right. A few miles after turning, I crossed it on a highway bridge. It wasn't parallel to the road anymore, but at a right angle to it, racing down through a dark tunnel of spruce. I was tempted to park my car there and follow it through the woods, but then decided to see if I could pick it up again further upstream.

It was a different country I was driving through, an open, lonely tableland that had more of Montana in it than Vermont. For some unknown reason, I had expected the river to become more like itself as it neared the top, and the transformation from pastoral, meadowed valley to rugged, timbered plateau took me by surprise. Signs of man were few. There was a fallen-down, roofless barn with the words "Barn Dance!" scrawled across it in mocking red paint; a cemetery whose headstones just barely cleared the weeds; a bullet-scarred road sign announcing a change in counties. Other than that, nothing—just two quiet mountains with cloud shadows laying across their synclines like heavy wool blankets.

The river started somewhere high in the folds of those slopes. I drove the highway to the top of the height of land, looking for a road or trail that would branch off in the right direction. I went too far—over the summit of the plateau, down into the beginnings of a separate watershed. Turning around, I came upon a dirt road that looked promisingly obscure. It was worth a try—in Vermont, dirt roads head toward water with the sure instinct of thirsty cattle let loose on a Texas plain. There were too many ruts and washouts to drive it. Leaving the car on the edge of the pavement, I got out and started to walk.

I went about a mile before I picked up the river. The road ran toward the mountains' base through a meadow-like expanse of second-growth timber, spiky larch on the verge of turning amber, and gnarled apple trees that had survived every cutting. Every now and then I would see a bullet casing in the leaves by the edge of the road, gleaming like golden chips dropped by hunters so they could retrace their way. But for once there were no bottle or beer cans to go with them, no roaring power saws, no harsh reminders of the land's misuse.

There was a stream where the road first dipped, but it was too small to be the river proper, so I kept walking. About ten minutes later, I came to the main stream, or at least its bed. It was five feet wide here, nearly empty. It hadn't rained in several weeks, and there was even less water in the center of the rocks than there was in the tributary. Still, it was obviously my river—I walked upstream just far enough to make sure its course aimed for the sag in the mountains where the map said it began.

There wasn't time to follow it now. It had been a successful reconnaissance, and in the morning I would be back.

Or so I thought. At dawn, the drumming of rain on the roof made the thought of bushwacking through the woods less appealing than it had seemed the night before; my exploratory impulse firmly under control, I turned over and went back to sleep. The rain continued for three days, then business interfered, so it wasn't until the end of the month that I was able to get back: Halloween, as it turned out—a fit day for mad enterprises of every kind.

I parked at the same place I had on my first trip, and hiked the dirt road to the river beneath the first blue sky in days. The rain had changed the equation. Instead of a dehydrated trickle, I found a racing mountain torrent that in places was over its banks. This was both good and bad. Good in that it seemed more recognizably my river; bad because I no longer had a dry staircase of rocks to climb to the top. I went through my pack to make sure I had a compass, tied my climbing shoes tighter for good luck, then—taking a deep breath—started off into the woods.

It was easy going at first. There was a deer trail parallel to the banks, and little of the underbrush I had been afraid would slow me down. The river was only a few feet wide here, but the pools were deep, and the rapids strong enough to cover the obvious fords. I hiked an hour before the volume of water appreciably slackened; after that, I could count on finding a place to cross every few yards.

Without leaves to block it, the sun was surprisingly warm, and it wasn't long before I peeled off my sweater. Like most Vermont hillsides, this one had once been farmed—there was the inevitable stone wall buried in forest detritus, the telltale apple trees lost amid maple, the barely discernible cellar holes choked with vines. With the leaves gone, the birch stood out with more flair than they had earlier in the fall; their white was more frequent the higher you looked, making it seem as if they were marching in formation up the slopes. It's an effect I enjoy. For all the talk of foliage, Vermont only seems itself—its gritty, unadorned, spare self—when October's extended shrug is over and the leaves are finally renounced.

It was only during breaks that I was able to give the scenery the attention it deserved. The rest of the time I walked with my eyes down, concentrating on the terrain one or two steps ahead. Most of the hiking I had done lately was in the White Mountain trails over in New Hampshire, and it was much easier; the trails were well-marked and graded, and—at least on the easier ones—you could stroll along without worrying what your feet were up to. Here, every step had to be selected with care. Flat boulders turned out to wobble when stepped on; firm-looking logs had a trick of disintegrating. Twist an ankle in the Whites and another hiker would eventually come along and help you; twist an ankle on these rocks, and it would mean a very cold, lonely night to contemplate my mistake. I was going slow to start with, and after getting a foot wet when a boulder used as a bridge unexpectedly rolled sideways, I went even slower. I began to worry that I might not have time to reach the source after all.

I had crossed the river thirteen times, and was preparing to cross it a fourteenth when I realized that the bank I was following flattened out up ahead into a clearing. This was a change in the established pattern. Always before, the bank would remain level for several hundred yards, then dramatically steepen as the river began to curve, forcing me to cross over to the other bank in order to make any progress. I was zigzagging, walking more sideways than uphill.

This time, I decided to continue on until I came to the clearing. A deer yard, I assumed, but no—rather than closing in a circle, it shaped itself into a funnel pointing upstream. It was an old logging road, one of those providential passageways you often come on in New England just when the bushwhacking turns ridiculous. It was unquestionably the oldest, bushiest, most obscure logging road I had ever encountered, but I was thankful for it just the same—it speeded up my pace by several m.p.h. It took the path of least resistance up the valley, sometimes hugging the river, sometimes crossing it, sometimes running away from it up the ridge. Times it ran away, I stuck to the river; after following it so long, it had become like one of those nature walks for the blind you see in the national parks, a rope guiding me through the forest which I dared not let go. Sticking to the river meant scrambling over granite ledges, climbing blowdowns and hopping rocks, but it was worth it—more than anything, I needed to stay in touch with that bright, racing ribbon to which I felt increasingly tied. A hundred yards of hard going and the logging trail would rejoin the stream, easing my way.

I crossed the river three more times before taking a break. Each ford was a new challenge; picking a way across the river required the same kind of half-premeditated, half-instinctual route-finding climbers use in scaling a cliff, and the same kind of balance. The trick was in finding a bridge of stones that led slightly upstream, so that you were crossing from lower rocks onto higher ones, thereby keeping your inertia within reasonable bounds. Hop downstream and the tendency was to keep going head-over-heels; hop upstream and gravity acted like a pair of cushioning arms. The best kinds of fords were where the rocks were flat, but far enough apart so you didn't take them for granted; the trickiest were the ones where the banks were closest together, tempting you into a jump. At the less obvious fords, I tried making bridges out of whatever log was handy, but this was time-consuming, and by continuing upstream I could usually find a place where the crossing was easier.

The scale of the river was changing the further up it I hiked. I no longer made diminishing comparisons to the broad stretches where I fished, but began taking it on its own; if anything, its sound and light filled that narrow valley more completely than it did further downstream. The lower water shared the landscape with farms, highways, and towns, but here near the source the river was everything—the dominant fact—and it seemed to paradoxically widen in my imagination the narrower it became, until finally there was nothing else in my senses but that bouncing, impetuous flow.

I stopped for lunch on a small island around which the river divided itself in mossy, inch-deep riffles. A family of grouse had beaten me to the driest patch of leaves; hearing me, they burst away in five scattered directions. I opened my pack and took out an apple and some cheese. There was a log behind me that doubled as backrest and table. Thirsty, I drank right from the stream, cupping my hands under the tiny falls until the water bubbled off my wrists. The water had the flavor of transparency. Swallowing it, I wasn't aware of taste, but only idea: purity. Purity had a cool feel on the lips, and nourished a delicious sense of well-being. Purity ran down my skin and made me shiver. Purity made me drink again and again, as if from a well I wanted to prove was endless.

Sitting there, I had a chance to watch the river more carefully. The rain of the previous week had washed down thousands of small twigs, and the water was still deciding where to put them. Some of the thicker ones were already jammed into a miniature dam; as I watched, smaller twigs were swept into it and gently tucked by the current underneath the upstream edge, weaving the dam even thicker. With the river at its smallest, even a foot-long branch was a major impediment, and the banks were grooved with dry, alternate channels the water had explored and abandoned in its drive downhill.

My thoughts were following it now, gradually widening my focus from the small, hemlock-shaded island where I sat in the same way the river's banks gradually widened, admitting more and more. It was an aerial view I was aiming toward—a perspective from somewhere up above those trees. The river was a mountain brook running through a forest abandoned when the white men who settled it in the 1780s moved west a century later. The river was an upland stream moving past the hill towns of two hundred people that still clung to life in a remote valley of rural Vermont. The river was a medium-sized trout stream running through the Green Mountain foothills to a junction with the Connecticut. The river was one of hundreds flowing down the ocean side of the ancient Appalachian chain on the East Coast of the United States. The river was one of thousands lining the continent, one of millions creasing the earth—a microscopic gram of hydrogen and oxygen lost in an immensity of waterless stars. A grain of water in the universe, a thread of water on the planet, a small river in North America, a trout stream in the Appalachians, a mountain brook in Vermont, and that brought it all the way back down to me, sitting there against the damp husk of a long-dead oak, wondering where the hell in this immense scheme I fit.

And what about me? What was this insignificant scruffy atom of consciousness thinking about as it telescoped so glibly up to the stars and so precipitously back down again? I was thinking about the opening day of the trout season back in April—how conscious I had been of my boyhood dream of being able to fish a trout stream at will and the dream's fruition, the actual river itself, icy, powerful, and real. In between were long years in the city when the only rivers I knew were vicarious ones, just vivid enough to keep the dream alive and torment me by their ever more doubtful realization. The visits I made to real rivers only reminded me of what I was missing, and by my midtwenties, I was beginning to talk about trout fishing as something I *used* to do. A lover of streams, a good caster, a fan of trout, a reader of all the right books and where was I? Stuck in the city, bitterly wishing.

But the thing about dreams is that you never know. Herman Melville, an old man living forgotten in New York, had above his study desk the motto "Be true to the dreams of thy youth." I had another boyhood dream besides fishing: I wanted to write. Pursuing it took all my energy and courage for ten hard years. Slowly, taking three steps back for every advance, I managed to establish a career. With it came freedom; I was able to move to the country, and there in the hills above my home found the river, the second of my boyhood dreams, trailing along in this first dream's fulfillment. The beautiful mountains, a woman I loved . . . it was as if the dream of writing had been dreamt so intensely that it had established a force-field powerful enough to tug other dreams in its wake, a balm for the bitterness the yearning engendered.

And so I was thinking how lucky I was to be sitting there contemplating the overlapping valleys, metaphorical and real, the river connected. The other thing about dreams is their short-ness, but that was all right, too. I had my dream as few people ever had theirs, and though it should only last this one season, I was going to get it down on paper once and for all.

The wind was coming up now—I felt it on the back of my neck as the gentle pressure from a woman's hand. It was time to start hiking again. But there was one more thing I wanted to work through before leaving. It concerned a trout, a fourteen-inch brown trout that appears nowhere else in this book. I caught him on a Cinnamon Ant in the late afternoon of a late August day, and had been trying to put him out of my mind ever since. In playing him, I was never so aware of a trout's being—its strength and beauty, its single-minded impulse toward life, its perfect coexistence with water. I was torn between wanting him to break loose and wanting to have him in my hand before letting him go. As it turned out, he was gut-hooked, already bleeding from the gills by the time I beached him. I took a rock from the bank and quickly finished the job.

Happy and sad, happy and sad, the inevitable conjunction! I had felt the life of that trout so intensely because he was dying; the strange sympathy that links hunter and hunted had been in full force for those few moments we were connected, and I felt severed when his life dropped away. Even something as harmless as fishing comes down to it in the end: the bitter and the sweet, the pleasant memory tinged with sadness, the trout living and the trout dead.

With luck, I would know and love the river for many years to come. Never would I live it with the same intensity. My dream had reached its apogee with the hooking of that trout, and by the time I took the rock and killed him, another bit of boy in me was gone.

I shouldered my rucksack and started up the eastern bank. The sun had gotten around behind me while I was resting, and its lower edge was disappearing below the trees on the ridge. I walked faster now, taking fewer detours as the logging trail stayed closer to the stream. The climbing was less strenuous than before. After that first narrow valley, the terrain had flattened out into a gently sloping plateau. A steep climb around water-falls would have indicated the source was near; this easier grade meant the river was less hurried, its energy conserved, its source further off than I had thought.

Eventually, the logging trail trickled out, and I began bush-whacking through vines, brush, and trees, forcing my way rather than finding it. I resented even the slightest detour now—the river seemed the one life in the forest besides mine, and I hated to let it go. The stream bed was shallower, not as rocky and well-defined as it had been lower down; it wasn't cutting through the hillside as much as racing over it, and judging by the ferns and moss growing well to either side of its present course, it often slid a bit to the right or left, depending on its mood.

With the fading daylight, the increasing cold, my journey up the river was taking on the quality of a race. I tried to slow myself down, took frequent breathers, but there was nothing I could do about the adrenaline I felt pumping through me each time I stopped. As it had so many times before, the river itself forced me to adopt an easier pace. Two hours after I stopped for lunch, I came upon the first significant falls. They weren't high—four feet at the most—but in the reduced scale I was trav-eling through, they loomed as large as Niagara must have to those early voyageurs trying to work their way up the Great Lakes.

Above the falls was a surprise: three channels, each as full of water as the one I had been following. I felt like Lewis and Clark at the headwaters of the Missouri: disappointed that the main river didn't continue; curious as to which of the tributaries led furthest west.

There was nothing for it but to explore each in turn. The left fork—the one that ran perpendicularly west from the falls—looked promising, but soon petered out into a leaf-choked channel of mud. Retracing my way downstream, I started up the middle fork, the one that ran straightest into the falls. This time I hiked a strenuous half-mile before the water ran out. It was a pretty little brook, probably nonexistent when it didn't rain, and obviously not the main branch.

So it was the right-hand fork after all. The minute I started along it, I knew it was my river—there was a life and impetus to it the other two branches didn't have. And since I had been forced to explore each of them, the time lost was vital. It was obvious now that I wasn't going to reach the source, not today. The river was dwindling, but in an unhurried way, and the underbrush along both banks was getting harder to penetrate the higher I climbed. Even if I turned back now, it would be dark by the time I got below the island, and I would have to grope the rest of the way back to my car.

Still, it was hard to stop. The further up the river I traveled, the more private and secret it seemed. I felt I was approaching an answer that had long eluded me, at the stage where the solution was almost in sight, requiring no further decisions or agonized puzzling out, but only endurance . . . that it was there and there was nothing left to reaching it but sheer endurance. I would stop, turn my back on it, start downhill, then turn around and start climbing again, resolved to go just a little bit further.

The fourth stop was my last. There are mountain summits in the Himalayas that are sacred to the peoples living at their base; climbers, respecting this, stop a foot short of the summit, leaving that final temple of snow forever virgin. It was out of this same worshipful impulse that I turned back from the source. I would never know the river so well that I would lose my awe of its beauty, and it was right that its last few yards—its inviolable beginning—remained a mystery to me still.

I straddled the river, a leg on each side, then slowly bent down to dip my hands ceremoniously in the water, letting the pure, cold drops roll down my fingers back into the flow from which they came.

A few things more, the light growing fainter. A leaf brushing my neck on its way to the ground . . . a woodpecker rattling a tree in the distance behind me . . . the wind in the pines as it came down off the mountain . . . the sound of the river . . . a last quiet look . . . and all the rest is simply going home.

Upland Stream

January 16

I have this weakness as an essay writer: when I start out with the intention of writing an essay about, say, middle age, the subject has a way of swerving around toward fly fishing; when I sit down to write an essay about fly fishing, it hops tracks and ends up being about middle age. My solution in this book is to let these tendencies have their head, and my own purpose here at the start is to warn flyfishers and nonfishers that the swerves may not always go in the direction they would wish.

191

There's another thing to remember: I write fiction for a living—my job is to lie as persuasively as I can. Link this to the natural tendency of a fisherman to exaggerate and embellish and there may be a passage or two where even the most patient credulity is strained. Nevertheless, except for the parts where I very broadly wink, and a few protective pseudonyms, the events in this book are true, and the only liberty I've taken is to sometimes rearrange their chronology, the better to bring everything into the yearly focus on which the essays are framed. Here in rural New England the seasonal cycle is the adventure by which we all live, and a fisherman's slice of it is made richer by its fleeting and bittersweet briefness. I don't think I'm to be blamed for wanting to slow the clock down from time to time, stop the hands from moving faster, and even occasionally push them back.

Mid-January now—a good time to be thinking of streams and rivers and trout. A good time, too, to pay tribute to the man who got me started writing about fishing, the editor and essayist who has written and published more good fishing in print than anyone in the literature of our sport, Nick Lyons.

Twenty-three below zero last night by the thermometer on our porch, and yet there are barrel-sized openings in the ice, and from their centers the river draws its breath in frosty puffs, gearing up now for spring.

There can't be too many places in the world where it's possible to stand in all four seasons simultaneously and be uncomfortable in each. The hills above my home are one of them—the oddly beautiful, oddly tortured New Hampshire hills of granite and spruce, brook trout and beaver, bogwater and Frost. By late April the snow is almost gone there, though enough remains to trap, squeeze, and soak heavy boots. The leaves, last autumn's crop of them, lie in slick matted heaps on the forest floor, their red and gold blended into an amber in-betweenness with the treacherous texture of mud. The sun, with no shade on the trees, burns even faster than in July. The wind, the thawing vernal wind, slaps back and forth like a wet towel, adding a chill in your middle to go along with the chill in your toes. Add a few precocious blackflies, potholes of slush, and some fresh tangled blowdowns and you have a pretty thorough set of variations on one masochistic theme. Come spring and the start of the trout season I would be nowhere else.

It's Copper Run I'm talking about here, the small upland stream I've come to love in the course of five years' fishing. Never wider than ten feet, never deeper than four, it drains a small unspoiled corner of New England woods, leaching as it does so all the beauty to be found there, so that it becomes the liquid, flowing locus of the surrounding hills. Seldom visited, it's possible to walk along the banks the better part of a day without coming upon any human trace other than a rusty bolt or tinny water can dropped by a logger fifty years before. Not in every pool but enough to make it interesting there are trout— miniature brook trout that seem in their color and quickness to be essence of stream, spontaneously generated, living crystals of orange and black. To take even a single six-incher—for one short moment to be attached to something so vivid and alive—is reason enough to suffer the multiple discomforts of the April woods.

There are more mundane reasons, of course. The need once the weather warms to bolt from the prison a house can become. The need to justify the new graphite rod I treated myself to at Christmas. The need after a long winter's writing to be out and questing after something besides words. Around the third week in April these things reach their peak, and it only takes a gentle, triggerlike pressure—a surge of sunlight? geese returning? a southerly cast to the wind?—to make me shed the last of my inertia and make the five-mile migration that separates a Copper Run longed for and imagined from a Copper Run stood beside and real.

Last April's trip could stand for any. There was the busy rummaging in the closet for leaders and flies, the casual "Think I'll try a few casts up on the mountain" to a knowing Celeste, the raid on the refrigerator for nuts and oranges, the hydroplaning, swerving ride up our dirt road that in mud season passes for driving—the abrupt dead-end when the ruts became frozen and the joyride stopped.

The stopping point varies each year, but I'm usually left with an uphill walk of at least a mile. On this trip it was a little more than that; I made it to the frozen pond where the deep woods begin, parked on an icy pull-off, pushed my rod into a rucksack, and started off on foot. It had been a hard winter, and the earth in the middle of the road was still in the process of turning itself over, lined with the stiff petrified creases that are, I suppose, the earthy equivalents of groans. There by the marge the ground was softer, potted with moose prints. I've seen moose here in the past on their journeys from pond to pond—great lumbering browns wearing a look of perpetual bafflement, as if they can't quite figure out who or what they are or whether they should care.

At about the same time the hardwood starts giving way to spruce there comes a perceptible flattening as you emerge on the height of land. There's a bridge here, nothing more than a rude corduroy, and it's possible to walk right across it without realizing a trickle of water flows beneath. Leave the road—follow the trickle through the first tangled briars—and in less than twenty yards you come to the start of Copper Run proper at the towering Gateway Arch.

I call it this quite deliberately for the drama of the May evening I discovered it. Celeste was pregnant, and in the course of one of our evening walks for exercise we crossed the corduroy bridge on our way to a small pond whose star attraction, besides its wildness, was a resident loon. I had my rod with me, of course; I caught perch in the pond's shallows as Celeste readied our picnic and poured out our tea. After dinner, curious, I left her admiring the sunset while I walked back to the bridge and followed the trickle upstream to see if I couldn't find where it began.

It began in a beaver pond, as it turned out, and a big one; on the far shore, framed by the fingers of dying tree trunks, rose the gray bulk of Slide Mountain, emphasizing the vastness even more. There were insects hatching everywhere; between their rings, the wake left by the resident beaver, and a slight evening wind, the surface of the pond buzzed with as much activity as Lake Sunapee on a weekend afternoon. I managed to balance along the beaver dam to a place I could cast, but if there were trout in the pond they were occupied elsewhere and I soon gave up.

So back to the bridge then. Back to it—and then off into the woods downstream. I'm not sure what prompted me to do it; it was close to dark and the stream was more shreds and tatters than a definite flow. But the future has a magnetism all its own, and there in the twilight, in the mountain stillness, with the sensitivity toward omens even a vicarious pregnancy brings, I was more attuned to it than usual, and it would have taken a deliberate act of violence not to have given in to its pull.

"Just a little way," I told myself—the old indisputable justification. There by the bridge the bank was all briars, and it was hard enough to make any way. Since the future not only tugs us but shapes us into the correct posture to meet it, I was bowing my way (a low, reverential bow) through a particularly bad tangle when the watery tatters suddenly gathered themselves and changed from a pedestrian pewter to a rich, luminous copper; the effect was that of stepping into a sunset turned molten. At the same time, or perhaps a split second earlier, I noticed a darkening overhead, and looked up to see the branches of two white pines meet high above the stream, forming with their intersection a perfect proscenium or arch.

A Gateway Arch—the expression came to me the moment I saw it. It wasn't just the perfection of the framing, the changing color, but how both came embellished with a roll of drums—with a deepening and staccato-like increase in what had been until that moment nothing more than a vacant gurgling. Just past the arch, where color and sound were richest, was a small pool formed by the junction of two smaller streams—the outlets of the two ponds already mentioned. Waving my rod ahead of me like a Geiger counter—like the antenna of a probing ant—I shook my Muddler down into the pool's center, letting it sink toward the sharp rocks that lined its sides. Immediately there came a pull, and then a moment later a six-inch brook trout was splashing across my boots, sending up a little shiver of happiness toward my neck. I let him go, then tried another cast, this time a little farther downstream. Again, a six-inch trout, this one even deeper-bodied and more brilliantly speckled, with a soft coppery cast on his back that seemed the water's undertone.

I caught six trout in all that first evening, each a yard or so downstream of its predecessor. In the twilight, in my twilight mood, it was clear they were deliberately tugging me deeper into the woods, the better to ensnare me in their enchantment. After the sixth I broke away and waded back through the darkness toward the bridge. By the time I rejoined a worried Celeste (who knew my Hansel-like susceptibilities well enough), the experience had settled just far enough for me to realize I had stumbled upon what in flinty New England terms was a virtual Shangri-la.

Something of this surprise, something of this ceremonial quality is still present whenever I go back to Copper Run, and never more than on that first April trip after a long winter away. Again, I slip and slide my way from the bridge through those deceptively small riffles; again, I bow through the hoop of briars; again, the arch of pine forms overhead, and then, after a quick clumsy cast, my fly line is uncoiling down across the coppery water in floating N's and straightening in a tug—*two* tugs, the first as the Muddler swings tight in the current, the second as a trout takes hold with what can only be described as a hearty handshake of welcome. And just as the arch seems to beckon me each time, so too when I've passed under the branches it seems to seal me in. Back beyond the arch is noise and worry and confusion and doubt, but this side of it—stream side of it—there is nothing but that shiny, exuberant mix of rapid, riffle, and pool, and no requirement upon me but to align myself with its inspiration and let the current lead me down.

So into the water then—away from the snow and slush and bad footing and directly into it, frigid as it is. The banks along this first section are too steep and heavily forested to balance along, and there's no alternative except to wade. I'm dressed for it, of course. Woolen underwear, wool pants, silk liners, heavy socks. For shoes, I wear old suede boots from my rock-climbing days, with hard toes and heels that absorb all the bruises and enough insulation to hold the coldness at bay . . . at least in theory. In actuality, with the water in the forties, my toes lose their feeling about every fourth cast, and I have to climb my way out of the stream and stamp up and down on the nearest boulder for a good five minutes before the feeling is restored.

By the time I've fished through the first pool, if I'm lucky, I've caught my first six trout, perhaps even the same friendly sentinels that were there the evening I discovered it. By about the fourth one I begin to relax. Behind all the anticipation and excitement that lure me here each spring is a darker emotion: the nagging worry that something terrible will have happened and all of it will be gone. Copper Run, the dancing water, the iridescent trout—all gone. It always takes an hour of being immersed in it—of feeling those twin chills merge, the coldness of the water and the happy shivers transmitted by the trout—before my doubts finally vanish and I let myself wholeheartedly believe.

Below the entrance pool the banks taper together and the water drops between rocks in three distinct runs. They come together again at the bottom, then fan out across a broad shelf of granite into a second, slower pool. The water is darker-looking here, deeper, with large mossy boulders that absorb the sunlight rather than reflect it. A good place for trout, only there aren't any. I fish it each time to make sure, but never once have had even the suggestion of a nibble. Is it too exposed to otter and heron for a trout to be comfortable? Is there some hidden interplay of current that disturbs their equanimity? Or is it just that Copper Run trout are too cranky and original to place themselves in a place so obviously suited to their well-being? If nothing else it gives me something to think about, and lets me know the easy successes of the first pool won't be duplicated on the same lavish scale.

As pretty as it is, the first hundred yards of Copper Run are pretty much a warm-up for what comes next. The water spills from the fishless pool in one of those terracelike steps that are so characteristic . . . churns itself over a few times for good luck . . . then deepens to form a bowl that is so perfectly round and so tropically shaded it's impossible to look at it without thinking of Gauguin.

If Copper Run is essence of mountains, essence of woods, then this pool is essence of Copper Run. I've spent entire afternoons here trying to separate out all the strands that go into making it so perfect. The smell is one of them; besides the wet leaves, the thawing earth, there's a sharper, more acrid smell that is metallic and not at all unpleasant. The trace elements, I decided—gold and silver tinges scoured by water from rock.

A short way beyond the tropical pool a small tributary seeps in. I say *seep* quite deliberately—it's a damp, spongy wetness more than a definite flow, and it doesn't appear on any map. Copper Run itself *is* on the map, but only as a thin scrawl between contour lines, with only the most approximate relation to its actual course. It's too small to register properly; its improvisational, quicksilver meanderings are if anything anti-map. Were I the cartographer in charge of the New England hills I would acknowledge its chanciness, slap a Gothic *Terra Incognita* over the entire height of land, and let the curious and energetic go about discovering it on their own.

Which, in my stumbly fashion, was exactly what I was trying to do. The truth is that despite the visits of five years, I still had only the haziest notion of Copper Run's course. I knew where the water started: the combination of ponds there behind me on the ridge. I knew where, via a larger river, the water ended: an old mill town beside the Connecticut twenty miles farther south. But the things that happened in between—the twists of its channel, the dark woods it traversed, the possible waterfalls, its junction with larger streams—were for a long time as unknown to me as the headwaters of the Orinoco.

This was not due to any lack of curiosity on my part—quite the opposite. The water I came to seemed so rich in possibility that each yard deserved an afternoon of admiration to itself. My trips were of pilgrimage, not reconnaissance; each pool had to be sat beside, admired, and fished. What with revisiting the familiar pools and lingering over the new ones, about three new pools per visit was the fastest pace I could manage and still get home before dark. Add the fact that between bugs and low water I only visited Copper Run in spring and autumn—add a dozen tributaries that in their miniaturization and mystery were just as alluring—and you can see I had set myself a question mark the erasure of which was beginning to seem a lifetime's work.

That was my resolution for last year: to increase the tempo of my exploration, to force my pace downriver, to learn before spring ended where Copper Run came out. There would be less time spent exploring each pool, less time to fish, but a labyrinth has its own charms, and I was trying to focus back on it to reach some comprehensive understanding of the whole. I knew the spill where the water surged across a fallen hemlock, grooving the wood until its grain seemed to ripple; I knew the falls where the water washed sideways off a mica-flecked cliff; I knew the spots where the spray kicked high enough off the boulders to wet my face, the best fording places, the pools most likely to hold fish . . . and now it was time to thread these beads together in a necklace to marvel at, fasten, and share.

And if I was proceeding downstream in a pleasant geographical blur, I was proceeding in a pleasant historical blur as well. I knew little about the history of Copper Run, though there was little enough history to know. The stone walls that marked the limit of the early settlers' audacity—the stone walls that climb even Slide Mountain to heights awe-inspiring and tragic—end well below Copper Run. Even the surveyor's tape that dangles everywhere in the woods now, fluorescent and mocking, has only reached the fringes of this notch. Between these two limits—the patient, backbreaking husbandry of the past; the easy, land-grabbing mentality of the present—Copper Run sits like a lost world, removed for a good century and a half from the curse of events. The trees grew, then someone cut them, then they started growing again, and all along Copper Run danced its way south, oblivious to any imperatives but those of gravity.

Our exhaustive town history contains only one story from the height of land—the story of a woman who spent her life in the woods as her father's unpaid assistant in a small logging operation. The older people in town can remember seeing her drive a wagon full of logs past the common to the Connecticut—a straight-backed woman who teetered between proud dignity and shy wildness and never lingered long enough for folks to get to know her. I've seen her grave, the last one in a cemetery where everyone else had been buried seventy years before. It stands alone in one corner beneath some birch; in its simplicity, in its apartness, it could stand for all the solitary lives that have escaped history's record.

She died in 1957—more than thirty years now. In the decades since probably the only big thing to hit Copper Run have been the Vibram soles of my size-twelve boots, stirring apart the moss on rocks that are as old and untroubled as any on earth. Seen in those terms, I was an invasion—a whole new chapter in what so far had been, as far as man was concerned, a relatively blank book. This placed upon me a certain responsibility; it was up to me, in my short visits there, to conduct myself in a manner befitting an explorer—not an explorer hot for commerce, but an explorer out to record what he had found as faithfully as he could, the better to understand the hidden, threatened beauty of this one fragile place.

So what did I find there? What justified those afternoons along its banks that could have been more usefully spent writing short stories or splashing paint across the barn? What was the payoff for those icy immersions? All pretty stuff, but what—a skeptical Queen Isabella might ask—does this newfound land contain?

Pygmies. Bush pygmies eking out a precarious existence high in a forest remote from man. Copper Run trout, to complete my metaphor, are small, not stunted; independent, not docile; shy, but not so shy a properly placed bauble won't lure them from their haunts. Like mountain tribes, they are splendidly suited to their habitat, and have the happy knack of taking on its qualities—not only its coloration but its very element, so that catching a Copper Run brookie is like catching and holding a condensed length of spray.

And since it is pygmies we're talking about here, it's best to dispose of the size question right at the start. An average Copper Run brook trout is six inches in length; a good one, eight inches; a monster, nine. By the time you've adjusted to the miniature pools and miniature riffles, say fifty yards in, the scale has begun to right itself and you understand what a genius Einstein was when he spoke of relativity. In an eddy twelve inches deep, a six-inch trout takes up a not inconsiderable space; in a shadowy forest, its copper richness is not an inconsiderable source of light.

There's another thing to keep in mind: small is not necessarily easy. The trout come willingly enough to a fly, but they're quick, quicker than the current, and it takes near perfect timing to connect. Then too, for all their innocence, these fish are not gullible rubes; a trout that strikes and misses will not come again. Add to this the sheer difficulty of placing a fly on the water—the protective overlay of blowdown and branches, briars and boulders—and you have fishing that is as challenging in its small way as any other.

For the flyfisherman, this goes right to the heart of the problem: the chore of keeping your backcast free of the trees. After an hour and perhaps fifty collisions, it hardly seems like casting at all, but a particularly vexatious form of air traffic control; you spend more time looking back over your shoulder than you do looking in front, and any cast that manages to uncoil without hitting branches seems a pretty successful flight. Take a day of this, and you will be left with the illusion you haven't fished the water at all but the air, and your dreams that night are apt to be laced with hemlock-dwelling trout that mock you with their inaccessibility.

I've learned the hard way not to fight this, but to incorporate the obstacles as part of the challenge. Rather than bring a hundred flies along and moan each time one is broken off, I now bring only two—a Muddler and a backup, thereby assigning a definite limit to just how clumsy I can afford to be. I usually manage to snap off the first one by the third or fourth pool, but you'd be surprised at how long that last one stays on. I've climbed my share of Copper Run trees, plunged my hand deep into pools to work feather out of bark, and even occasionally twisted a hook from my earlobes, but never once have I headed home early for the lack of a fly.

The two-fly limit has another happy effect: it simplifies the process, and simplicity is what this kind of fishing is all about. All fishing, both sport and commercial, has about it something of a complicated hide-and-seek, but small-stream brook trout fishing—the fishing that fascinates me—retains the hide-and-seek quality in its most basic, childlike form. Mountain trout spend their lives hiding in an environment that is perfect for their concealment, and what I find so compelling and interesting in fishing for them is the trick of waving a fly across the water and thereby finding out exactly where they are. The fight, the actual landing—for fish this size, none of that counts. It's the first flash I'm after—the brief but exquisite pleasure that comes when a swirl of water swirls suddenly faster and a life from out of nowhere firmly tugs you, shouting "Here!"

In some pools the trout are just where they're supposed to be—the satisfaction is the smug one of knowing their hiding places so thoroughly. In other pools the hiding places are there, but not the trout—my smugness stands chastened. It's beyond these, in the unexplored water downstream, where the game becomes most interesting. That plinth-shaped rock in the current's fringe—there should be a trout right in front or right behind. Is there? A careful cast, the fly landing perfectly, the current sweeping it down . . . No. That log aslant the bank with the deep pocket along its head. There? Yes! and a good one, all splashing iridescence, to be brought quickly to my feet, defeathered, and urged gently home.

Once this simple curiosity is satisfied, there's room left for a whole complicated superstructure of conjecture and wonder. Why do Copper Run trout seem to migrate with the seasons and in a direction reverse to what you might anticipate, heading upstream when the water turns colder, downstream when it warms? What autumnal hint triggers their color change, when their copper deepens toward crimson and their spots take on a vivacity that makes even maple leaves seem dull? Why does their size seem to diminish the farther from the road you go? Why will they smash a dry fly and not rise, at least perceptibly, to a living insect? Why this, why that, and then suddenly I've raced through three new pools and some pretty connecting water, and my wondering has run away from me and I find a dry, sunny spot to climb out of the water and rest.

There are several of these resting places along the stream—flat, grassy terraces just big enough to admit my outstretched body, slanted so I can stare at the water while flat on my back. Removed from the iciness, plied with oranges, I am free to devote myself, for a few minutes anyway, to one of those vast metaphysical questions that only occasionally seem worth the asking. Why, if I am so enchanted with the sheer beauty of this stream, must I bring along a rod and reel in order to fully appreciate it? Why can't I just stroll down its banks in simple adoration? Why, when you come right down to it, fish?

There's a teasing, quicksilver-like quality to Copper Run—like any stream, the moment you try to grasp it, it's gone. And so, too, with any question posed on its banks; the best you can hope for is a partial, impressionistic answer that leaves in the air as much as it settles. Still, fishing for brook trout on a small mountain stream is about as simple and pure as the endeavor becomes, so that motives stand out with a clarity they lose in bigger, murkier waters.

Why fish? Leaving out on one side the obvious reasons like being outdoors and the healthy exercise, and leaving out on the other side the complicated reasons of blood lust and the ancestral promptings of our watery origins, I think I can begin to find the beginnings of an answer. It has to do with the exploring I mentioned earlier—that ritualistic, challenging version of hide-and-seek. Fly fishing is the only means I have to enter into the hidden life of a stream and in a remarkably literal way, so that if my cast has been a good one and my reflexes sharp, that life—through the energy of its fishy emissary—pulses up a taut leader through a taut line down a curved rod to my tensed arm . . . to my arm, and by the excitement of that conveyance to my heart. A fishless stream might be every bit as beautiful as Copper Run, but it's the fish that whet my curiosity, stocking it with a life I need to feel to understand.

Discovery, and the vicarious thrill that comes with having my surrogate self—my Muddler, Royal Wulff, or Cahill—go swimming off through a pocket of rapids, being at one and the same time an extension of my nervous system and an independent, unpredictable agent of free will. Like *Alvin*, the tethered submarine guided by cables through the *Titanic*'s wreck, the fly answers our commands and does our probing; in some mysterious, sympathetic way we *see* through our fly and understand the water better beneath it than we do the water we're actually standing in twenty yards upstream. That little back eddy near the alders, what's under it? Sweep the rod to the correct angle and our surrogate drifts over and checks it out. That granite reef sunk beneath the brightness? Shake some line loose and our surrogate plunges down.

Our nerves are transmitted to a tethered cell of tinsel and feather—that and the added, exhilarating bonus of knowing any second we may be jumped . . . that our surrogate selves are liable to be eaten. Anyone who compares fishing to hunting has got it backwards; it's the thrill of *being* hunted that gives fishing its charm. For the few seconds our lures swim beneath the surface we recapture the innocence—the dangerous, stimulating innocence—of the days when man walked the earth not as master but as prey. It was, it is, a dangerous thing to be a human, and we need to be reminded from time to time not only of our abstract mortality, but of a mortality that springs from ambush and clamps down.

Why fish? Notes toward the start of an answer, not the answer itself. In this resting place, beside a small ribbon of water on a fine April day, it's the best I can do.

I balance my way onto a rock in the center of the current and begin casting again. With the sun going down, the chill more penetrating, it's time to admit something I've tried to keep from my story as long as possible. The fact, the sad inescapable fact, that Copper Run is threatened, and by the time you read this its miniature perfection will almost certainly be gone.

This will come as no surprise. Here in the last decade of the twentieth century it has become a given that something beautiful is something threatened. A beautiful marriage, a beautiful custom, a beautiful place. We cannot admire any of these without hearing a meter in the background ticking off borrowed time. If that something is remote, fragile, and cherished, then it is doomed even more—there are garbage dumps on Mount Everest, for instance, and the Borneo rain forest is being ground into pulp. Our century has extracted its share of payment over the years, payments social, political, and environmental, but not yet the full amount. The day of reckoning is approaching, and before it, like a glacial moraine, comes the huge debris of extinction, this heavy, pervasive sense of doom.

We're a race of Cassandras now, not Pollyannas, and I have no wish to gloss over the facts. For the corner of New England woods I love the threat is quite simple on one hand, quite complex on the other. The remote notch Copper Run drains is owned by a paper company that is in the business of selling trees. The trees along Copper Run, the trees that entangle my backcasts and darken the riffles, are fast approaching a marketable size. All winter long, as I sit typing, trucks roll past my house loaded with logs. It is too much to expect that none of them will be from Copper Run. The vague uneasiness I experienced last April was not without reason; here spring is approaching again, and yet when I think of returning I feel not anticipation but only dread.

This is not the place for a lengthy discussion of the pros and cons of timber management. Timberland, at least for the time being, is land not being developed or macadamized, and in this part of the country the paper companies have traditionally allowed public access to the woods. Still, any organization whose sole raison d'etre is greed cannot be trusted to do anything except be true to that principle on any and all occasions.

As it turns out, I know the man who owns the company that owns Copper Run, at least by sight. He's in his fifties, balding, of average height and weight, fond of wearing the rumpled chinos and flannel blazer of the perpetual Ivy Leaguer. He doesn't appear particularly greedy; occasionally, I'll hear him joking with our postmistress when I go to pick up our mail. It's hard, looking at him, hearing him laugh, to connect his appearance with my happiness—to know at a word from him, at a tuition bill due for his son, some ready cash needed to float a new deal, a political contribution to be made, Copper Run and all its treasures could in the course of a day disappear . . . disappear, and that were I to protest, the whole weight of law and custom is there behind him to prevent any appeal.

And yet he looks perfectly harmless; he even drives a car smaller than mine. At night when I drive past his house all the lights are on in every room—every room, every light, no matter how late it is, and I feel a hollow spot in my stomach when I see this and know with a certainty beyond reason that Copper Run is doomed.

Taking the long view, I can reconcile myself to this, at least partially; cut forests eventually grow back. But it's another characteristic of our age that the threats come shotgun style, so that even if you dodge one projectile, there are enough left to cause serious damage. The threat of development, constant road building, the dangers posed by the warming of the atmosphere and acid rain . . . all these make cutting seem positively benign. Even my own walks along the banks must be included in the dangers; as careful as I am, as gently as I bring them to hand, there are trout that die when you hook them, and the loss of even three or four good fish a season, in an environment so fragile, is the equivalent of a major kill. Like Steinbeck's Lenny, that animal-loving fool, we can hug the things we cherish until they die.

But here's where the complexity enters in. Just as there is a real Copper Run faced with real, mortal dangers, so too there is an abstract Copper Run faced with dangers that are abstract but no less mortal. I refer to the relentless, vicious attack on the beautiful that is going on all around—an onslaught so widespread and successful the only conclusion to draw is that its goal

is the destruction of the very notion—the very *humane* notion—
of Beauty itself.

Like the environmental dangers mentioned above, you can
make your own list. The brutality and trivialization of popular
culture; the abominations posing as architecture; the not-so-co-
incidental fact that the richest society the world has ever known
is also its ugliest . . . all you have to do is look out the window.
And though on one hand a sterile glass box designed for the
entrapment of a thousand office workers in Indianapolis, Indiana, would seem to have very little to do with the fate of an
upland stream in the New Hampshire woods—the mindless,
flickering images these office workers watch with their children
on a glass screen when they go home even less—the connection
is a direct one, it being, when it comes to Beauty, one world
after all.

For if Beauty dies in the mass, how can it be expected to live
in the particular? How can I possibly describe to that caged-in,
image-drugged man sitting there in Indianapolis what a hemlock twig looks like spinning its way down a Copper Run riffle—how the reflected sunlight welling up from the bottom
enlarges it so the needles drift within their own delicate halo?
How can I explain how a Copper Run trout, held against the
palm in the moment before its release, will send a shiver through
you that for one fleeting second reconciles you to everything?
How to explain all my love for this? How?

A person who writes for a living deals in the raw material of
words. And, like rivers, mountains, and forests, words themselves
are under attack, so that even the means to describe the desecra-
tion are fast disappearing. The gobbledy-gook of advertising, the
doublespeak of bureaucracy (*beautification* for something made
uglier; *restoration* for something lost), the self-absorbed trendiness

that passes for literature; the sheer weight of illiteracy . . . again, the wretched list. Words like *lovely* and *fragrant* and *natural* have been inflated so far out of proportion they form a kind of linguistic freak show where words that were once suggestive of all kinds of richness now mean something grotesque. Emerson's "Every word was once a poem" becomes, in our century, "Every word was once for sale."

Again, the connection to Copper Run may seem a subtle one, but again it is simple and direct. For the devaluation of words makes for a devaluation of the things words describe and sets up a vicious circle from which there is no escape. With fewer words left to describe our Copper Runs, it becomes harder to justify saving them; as the Copper Runs vanish, the need for a language to describe them vanishes as well.

To a writer—to a dealer in raw materials—a polluted, unreliable source is the worst of calamities. But while the assault on words is every bit as depressing as the assault on the environment, at the bottom is to be found a strange kind of exhilaration, at least for those with the spirit to fight back. For perilous, degenerate times put a great responsibility on those who care for what's threatened, and endow their actions with a significance that is not just symbolic.

Here is where the link between these separate conservations becomes clearest—the conservation of Copper Run, the conservation of Beauty, the conservation of words. For just as the world has seen the wisdom of creating refuges that are as far as possible removed from the hand of man, the better to protect the lessons of untrammeled life, so too should writers seek to create a refuge of words where notions of Beauty and joy and solitude will endure in the very heart of a despoiled language, so that even if the worst happens and our methods of expression become as vacant as our method of living, there will still be books and stories and descriptions to go back to so we can see exactly what has been lost—so we can see these things and so there will remain a gene pool from which Beauty might flourish once again.

I spend my life writing fiction; among other things, it presupposes a certain ability of imagination. If I could, I would have no scruple in making Copper Run imaginary, giving it a make-believe course through make-believe woods protected by make-believe laws in a kingdom of my own design. But an imagination that seeks only escape is no imagination at all, and the best I can do . . . the best I can hope for in these twenty-odd pages of celebration and lament . . . is to state the dangers facing Copper Run as simply and directly as language can manage, and thereby protect, if not this wild upland province, at least this wild, upland province of words.

An ending, and yet not the end. For now it is April again, and I have gone back to Copper Run to find it only slightly changed. The trees are a little higher, a little thicker, but still uncut; the trout are smaller, but they seem just as plentiful; the water, while it may be more acidy, still vaults across the boulders in happy leapfrogs, and the sunlight still takes on that grainy, shaftlike quality as you go deeper into the woods. I retrace it pool for familiar pool, moving so slowly there's only time this first trip for a small portion of new water: a bright rapid surging between matching boulders overhung by a giant spruce.

Only one new step, but who knows? Maybe this will be the year I keep my resolution and follow Copper Run to its junction with the larger river to the south. It can't be far, and it's only my enchantment with what I've discovered that keeps me from pushing ahead at a faster rate.

Will I be disappointed to find an ending? I don't think so— well, only partially. For if the Copper Run I love is finite after all and joins a woods road or path I've already traveled, at least I'll have the solace of the pattern's completion. In the end, it's all we can ask of the unknown—that it leads us around at last to the familiar and sets us off on the trek once again.

May 12

*S*tarted *this morning* with four pages to go before the end of a story. Striking distance, so I went for it, holding out the prospect of an afternoon's fishing on the Waits to urge me along. A cool sunny day. Adrenaline weather.

With Celeste at nine months—with a baby due any moment—there are more preparations to be made than merely grabbing my rod and bolting out the door. The Protestant Work Ethic (branded a scarlet PWE on my soul) is sticky enough at the best of times, but add some incipient paternal angst and the guilt slows you down. Is the phone working? The obstetrician's number written down in plain sight? The extra car full of gas? The neighbors at home and alerted?

Celeste, who is managing just fine thank you, finally shoos me out the door. Call you every hour, I tell her . . . which turns out to be a lot harder than it sounds. Always before I had thought of the half-hour drive up to the river as a progression past a familiar, pastoral set of landmarks. The bridge over a Connecticut rolling gently in the sunlight; Gray's auction barn with its holding pens and pensive cows; Morey Mountain with its beetling cliffs; half a dozen farms, each field greener than its predecessor, each barn more eccentric in its windowing and sheds. Now, anxious, I see the drive strictly as a succession of phone booths, or rather a desert of them. I find one by an abandoned railroad station, quickly dial home—situation normal. There's a long stretch without any, so I pop into an antique store and beg the use of theirs—again, nothing at home has changed. A thirty-mile stretch of Vermont with only one pay phone? I'd never thought of the landscape in those terms. A bad country for spies, philanderers, and expectant dads.

One of the things I love about the Waits is how it comes into sight suddenly, the road making one fast left-to-right swerve. Voilà. It's high, but clear, the midstream rocks covered in clean purpled shadowings. Perfect shape for early May. Parking by the pool called the Aquarium, pulling on my waders, I formulate Wetherell's First Law of Fishing: *That the success or failure of a fishing trip is determined by the ease or lack thereof with which a fly line is threaded through the guides of one's rod.* For a change I do it smoothly, without missing a guide or having the line sag maddeningly back through the seven I'd already threaded. Add to that the ease with which I tie my first blood knot of the day and all the auguries are favorable.

As well they might be. I wade out into the middle of the current at the base of a broad pool; the water, catching my legs, finding my waist, gives me the same surge of togetherness that comes with donning a new pair of jeans. All spring I've been trying out a new act on the smaller streams:, a weighted nymph fished upstream with an indicator. Now, with the water level high, streamers not producing, I'm ready to open, as it were, on Broadway.

It's a weighted Hare's Ear I'm using, though from the look of it a hare's turd would be a better description. The indicator—a sticky fluorescent press-on of orange—goes around the leader eighteen inches up from the fly. The whole rig is cast clumsily upstream. The orange press-on bobs around a bit, aligns itself with the current, then starts downstream like a guide scouting out the river for the timid nymph. If the orange suddenly stops—if, better still, it suddenly dips below the surface—you strike hard with your rod and thereby hook, in textbook fashion, your nymph-feeding trout.

Which, to my amazement, is exactly what happens. Not only once, but seven times in a row. Cast, orange stop, *fish*. Cast, orange disappear, *fish*. What's odd about the whole process is that, unlike fishing with a dry fly or streamer, there's a built-in delay between the time you strike and the time the fish is felt—a fish that is, after all, swimming *toward* you in order to catch the nymph. Thus, it's hard to know who's more startled: me to find the trout is attached; the trout to find he *is* attached. The fight doesn't take long as a result—the trout all but raise their fins in surrender.

I twist the barbless hook out and off they swim, a new lesson stamped upon the miniaturized, solid-state computer chip of their brains.

It's a lot of fun. No, more than fun—exhilarating. To have a new method by which to explore my river, to probe riffles and currents where I've never been able to raise a fish before. Exhilarating! There's something in the enterprise reminiscent of fishing a bobber with worms for sunfish, and takes me back to those eleven-year-old days when all my longing, all my hope, was pinned on that little plastic bubble of red and white—on intensely wishing for the moment it would give a tremulous side-to-side quiver and abruptly sink.

Law Number Two. We fish for our childhoods.

I continue to catch fish all afternoon, though never so easily. More than fish. Those old stock cartoons of a fisherman pulling up a dilapidated shoe? I've never caught a shoe, never so much as a sneaker, but on one drift my nymph manages to snag the rubber lid of a mason jar, souvenir of some farm wife's autumn canning. At four it begins to rain, but I keep at it until trees, fields, stone walls, and sky are washed into the same gray intermingling.

It's been five hours since I called home. When I arrive there it's to the aftermath of mass hysteria. Cars parked on our grass, people running about, a man toting a camera. One suggestive touch: a baby carriage on our front porch complete with freshly plumped quilt! I rush inside, ready to apologize for not calling, ready to boil water or coach breathing exercises, my emotions a churn of guilt, anxiety, and pride.

But there is no baby, at least not one that's ours. Celeste is in the parlor talking excitedly with a friend from up the road who cradles their three-month-old on one knee. The scene outside is quickly explained. A moose—a young male—had wandered down through the village, stopping traffic, causing a mad rush for cameras. The moose, head tilted in bemusement, sauntered past the post office, then crossed the road and began eating the flowers in our neighbor's garden . . . or at least sniffed at them as if he would *like* to eat them.

Tulips. The old Unicorn in the Garden syndrome. Celeste, walking carefully, takes me over to show me the evidence of the trampled stems.

River of Rivers

It's a fish story that starts on dry land, the stretch of route that drops from Peru to Manchester like a gigantic slide. A water slide to be exact—it was May and raining hard. I was on my way to the Battenkill for my annual visit, and to pass the drive had slipped into the cassette player one of those rare inventions that helps justify our age: a tape-recorded book. In this case, it was the short stories of John Cheever, and not just any Cheever, but "The

Swimmer," in which suburbanite Neddy Merrill decides to swim the eight miles home from a cocktail party via neighborhood swimming pools.

"He seemed to see, with a cartographer's eye, that string of swimming pools, that quasi-subterranean stream that curled across the country. . . . When Lucinda asked him where he was going, he said he was going to swim home."

It's a classic story, read well by the reader, and if nothing else it made me slow down enough to fit the ending in before the snarl of Manchester traffic. By the time I was down to Arlington, the tape was over and the sun was out again, silvering the raindrops that clung to the guardrails and trees. My mind, so absorbed in Neddy Merrill's problem, only gradually switched focus to W. D. Wetherell's: Battenkill browns and what they would be in the mood for after a week's steady rain.

I parked near the store in West Arlington, and within minutes was up to my waist in cold water, false-casting an antique Honey Blonde toward a hemlock that tilted over the current like a finger pointing "Here!" It was good to be in the Battenkill again—good to see those deceptively lazy folds of water come sweeping past, making me think as they always do of an exquisitely fine silk being ceremoniously unrolled.

And it was good, or at least not that bad, not to catch trout right away. The Battenkill being the Battenkill, there were no suicidal trout waiting around to hurl themselves onto my hook, so after an hour without a bite, it was obviously time to forget my literary daydreaming and put some effort into the enterprise.

I switched to a Muddler, began paying more attention, and yet a part of me was still off in Neddy-Merrill-land, so that as the fishless casts began mounting up, I began concocting a Cheeverish fantasy of my own. What flashed before my waterlogged brain wasn't a chain of swimming pools (yuppies or no yuppies, there still aren't that many in Vermont), but a chain of trout streams. Would it be possible, I wondered, to travel all the way around Vermont, all the way up the Champlain Valley, across the Green Mountains, down the Connecticut, and never once leave a trout stream? To fish clockwise around the state and never touch dry land?

Two images immediately came to mind, the first superimposed over the second in a graphic overlay: the vivid sharpness of a Vermont state road map, with its twisty red highways and even twistier blue streams; the vaguer, hazier, but no less real map of memories I've garnered in fishing several dozen Vermont trout streams over the course of the past twenty years. On the matter-of-fact level where they met, it was clear that to fish one stream into the next and never leave water was impossible. You could come close, tantalizingly close, but eventually each river would end on a height of land separating it from the watershed in the adjacent valley. What *was* possible, though, was to drive around Vermont and never be more than a few miles from prime trout water, setting up the possibility of an around-the-state trip fishing each river in turn. As a stunt, you might be able to do it in two full days, three if you lingered a bit over the scenery. Thirty rivers in three days? It was a nice idea for a future expedition, say in the indeterminate future of postponed dreams and procrastinated projects I always refer to as next "autumn."

Back to the fishing. While my mind was busy computing mileage and routes, my Muddler was taking a leisurely swim downstream toward some alders overhanging the undercut bank. Forty feet upstream, still daydreaming, I stepped around a saucer-sized pool of sunlight, scaring up a good-sized brookie. I cursed, mad at my clumsiness, and was starting to strip in for my next cast when there was a heavy tug on my line in the direction of the vanished Muddler.

I struck immediately back, half expecting to find I'd hooked a canoe or at least a good-sized inner-tubist. But it was neither of those things. The water, heretofore so silky, splintered upward like a burst piece of metal, and through the hole where the river had been appeared the snout, the Muddler-festooned snout, of the largest trout I'd ever seen, dreamed, or read about—a once-in-a-lifetime trout, that is; a butter-flanked-hooked-jaw-monstrous-old-granddaddy Battenkill brown.

A *smart* Battenkill brown. The moment he felt the hook he set off in the direction of Sushan, stripping off thirty yards of line before the significance of what was happening to me fully sank in. I started off in pursuit, running through the shallows as fast as my waders permitted, every now and then staring down anxiously at the bare spots in my reel where the backing was disappearing fast. It was obvious now that the brown was trying to pull the old cross-the-border trick on me. I had no New York license, and once he made it around the tight bend that uncoils across the state line he would be safe.

Risking everything, I hauled back on the rod. The trout, startled, pranced across the water on its tail like a sailfish. My leader made the ominous pinging sound wire makes before it snaps, but—miraculously—it held. The brown raced upstream past me, giving me just enough of a glimpse to turn my legs to syrup. Fifteen pounds, I remember thinking. Fifteen pounds!

I ran upstream after him, retracing our route, getting into new water above the covered bridge, then making it into that classic tree-lined stretch that parallels 313. There were a lot of fishermen about, and they scurried to the banks to make way for us, calling out encouragement and advice. I felt pride and embarrassment both—the fish, after all, was playing *me.* "Give him line!" one fisherman shouted; I wasn't sure, but he seemed to be shouting this to the trout.

We were already up to the curve where the river approaches Route 7 and heads north. The soles of my wading shoes, thin already, were wearing out fast on the rocks and briars along shore. The trout showed no sign of weakening; if anything, the colder, faster water where the Roaring Branch comes in seemed to invigorate him, and he increased his speed to something phenomenal. Luckily, there was an old Grumman canoe lying abandoned on the shore. In a flash, I was into it, and, instead of chasing the trout along the shallows, let him tow me in comfort up the center of the main stream.

It was a wise move, at least at first. We were into that beautiful, unwadable stretch below Manchester suggestive of a river lazing its way through the château country in the south of France. It would have been sticky going without the canoe, and the extra drag on the trout—the sea-anchor effect—slowed him up by a full knot. Unfortunately, the river as we approached the Equinox Golf Course began to shallow out, forcing me to abandon the canoe again and start after him on foot.

Somewhere to the left was Orvis headquarters, and I had half a mind to tether my trout to a tree somewhere, rush off, and ask my friend Tom Rosenbauer for advice. Tom knows more about trout fishing than any ten men I know, and what's more he knows how to have fun while fishing, an even rarer quality. I was just deciding I'd have to manage without his help, when who did I see cheering me on from the riverbank but Tom himself! He was waving a pen at me, shouting something that sounded like "Make him talk! Make him talk!"

Tom might be able to make trout talk, but not me. I chased

mine upstream past the falls in Manchester Center (over which he leapt with salmonlike ease) to the cheers of shoppers in the street above. The trout, shied by the traffic noise, continued straight up the Battenkill through town. There was a moment when I thought he might veer off into the West Branch, try to force his way to the Mettawee back toward New York, but a subtle tug on my part kept him on the main river. I raced after him, tired now but feeling a lot more optimistic than I had since Arlington. It was clear that the trout would soon run out of water to thrash around in—that at the point where the Battenkill becomes a brook hardly deep enough to support a chub, the trout would beach himself on a sandbar and be mine.

Mine? It is to laugh. For it was here, where the Battenkill vanished, that the trout proved what a truly extraordinary creature he was. An ordinary trout would have surrendered at this point, turned belly up and finned toward my net. A brighter than average trout might have tried to make the leap into Emerald Lake, swim across it in a futile attempt to reach the headwaters of Otter Creek. What my trout did—what this fabulously huge, fabulously intelligent trout did—was make a flopping, jackknife motion with its middle, wiggle up onto the bank across some pine needles, then—my Muddler still attached to his lip—start cross country through the rain-soaked lowlands heading north.

I scarcely trust my memory here, so surprising was this shift in the trout's strategy. I've caught my share of fish over the years, but never one that did its fighting on dry land. Still, there was no use standing there feeling sorry for myself. I loosened the drag on my reel, hitched up my waders, and started after him. Rather than force his way through the raspberry bushes, he elected to follow the railroad tracks that parallel Route 7, flip-flopping from tie to tie. It was tough keeping him in sight, but after a mile of this he changed tactics again and squirmed through the puckerbrush over to north-flowing Otter Creek.

Fine, I decided. Otter Creek gave me roughly one hundred miles of water to play him in, and if worse came to worst I could land him in Lake Champlain. We were up to Danby now; as if reading my thoughts, the trout veered east into the first tributary we came to: the beautiful Big Branch, one of my favorite mountain streams. Besides its impressive gorge, an interesting stretch of Long Trail, its wild rainbow trout, it boasts one of the truly great assemblages of boulders ever deposited in one spot. It was through these that my trout was now porpoising, heading directly east past Mount Tabor into the heart of the Greens.

Fatigue-wise, this was the hardest part of the entire battle. Not only did I have to race upstream, I had to do it over boulders, so that it was more rock climbing than fishing. Somewhere along the way we passed the mouth of the Black Branch, where on a cool October day in 1971 I saw a man with forty-two dead brook trout laid out on a newspaper; the man was smirking proudly, waving hikers over to see, and in his lapel he wore the button of a prominent conservation organization.

I raced past the spot with a shudder, determined now to catch up with the trout once and for all. He went under the suspension bridge below the Long Trail, did a somersault in the next pool, then raced back downstream toward Otter Creek, forcing me to spin around like a clumsy matador, but giving me a good look at his totality. It was gargantuan—on the scale of the Big Branch boulders. His tail alone was three times bigger than any trout I'd ever hooked!

In some respects, our battles up to this point had been all preliminary; we had been feeling each other out, as it were, and now it was time to get down to some serious fish-playing. Unfortunately, I was currently in a poor spot to exert any pressure: downtown Rutland. Otter Creek being too deep and foul to wade there, I hitched a ride with a passing motorist, sticking my rod out the window and signaling with my free hand which way to turn. By this method, I was able to follow the trout past the State Street Bridge. Some school kids, on their lunch break, began tossing Hydrox cookies down at him, scaring him upstream. We followed, swerving recklessly to avoid oncoming cars. In a few minutes, free of the city, I hopped out, thanked the driver for his help, and began wading through the marshland along the river near Pittsford and the mouth of Furnace Brook.

I was hoping the brown would swerve off into this stream as he had the Big Branch—it's a pretty little river and has a starring role in Harold Blaisdell's fine book *The Philosophical Fisherman*. This trout, however, was not about to grant requests. After the briefest of forays into Furnace, he continued upstream, making similar short runs into the Neshobe in Brandon and the Middlebury ten miles farther north.

The New Haven was the next tributary after that—an excellent dry-fly stream and one I know well. Apparently, the trout thought highly of it, too, for the moment he got to its mouth he sped right up the middle, not stopping until he reached the open stretch behind the Dog Team Tavern. He chased his tail in ecstasy for a good ten minutes here, drunk on the smell of sweet rolls emanating from the restaurant's kitchen. The smell was a nostalgic one for me, too. As a freshman at Middlebury back in the sixties, I would hitch rides north to fish the New Haven, cutting class to do so, hitching a ride home again after a long, trout-filled afternoon.

There were lots of memories here, both of people and days. My friend Murray Hoyt, a fine writer and a gentle man; Murray, who loved the New Haven as much as I did, and when someone asked him how the fishing was, would take the single good trout he'd caught out from his creel, hold it up for admiration, put it back in, then pull it out again, repeating the performance three or four times. The willow-shaded pool near the cemetery below Bristol Flats where on a hot August afternoon of joy and crushing disappointment, I hooked and lost the biggest trout I'd ever seen prior to the one I fought now. The stretch above the swimming hole where in the years before development it was possible to take a dozen iridescent brook trout in as many casts. The tiny upland cemetery near West Lincoln where, one morning before sunrise during the height of the Vietnam War, I passed a burial in progress, with an honor guard of three uniformed soldiers, a flag-draped coffin, and nothing else—no mourners, no spectators, nothing to disturb the heart-wrenching poignancy of the scene.

It was at this point—racing after the trout where the river climbs the mountains toward Lincoln Gap—that it began to occur to me that the trout was familiar with an unusually large portion of the state. This was startling in its way. You expect a trout his size to have a map imprinted on his brain of every rock, current, and channel in his home river, but to have a map of Vermont imprinted there? It made me curious to see which route he would choose to cross the mountains: the New Haven south toward the headwaters of the White, or the woods overland toward the headwaters of the Mad.

The Mad. In one long plunging sweep he was out of the river, into the underbrush, up and over the old logging roads that crisscross the height of land. At Sugarbush, he took to the ski trail, sliding down on his belly like an exuberant otter to land with a magnificent splash in that big Mad River pool above Waitsfield. My arm at this point felt as if I'd just received six tetanus shots in a row, double strength; my waders, torn from sliding down the mountain after him, flapped indecently. Even so, a new determination had taken hold of me, and by the time we tumbled over the falls below Moretown, I had half convinced myself the trout was beginning to show signs of tiring.

Down the Mad we raced to the Winooski, upstream past the statehouse in Montpelier, up the Dog past those sylvan, gravel-bottomed pools that back the Norwich campus—the trout towing me now, so that I hydroplaned on my stomach back and forth past the startled picnickers, drenching them in spray. I shook the fly line up and down like the reins of a horse, trying to nudge him toward Roxbury and the headwaters of the Third Branch near the hatchery. But no—this trout had an itinerary of its own. Back down the Dog he rushed, up the East Branch of the Winooski through that fine rocky pool by the high school in Plainfield, then into the sandier, high-banked pools below Marshfield farther along. He paused to catch his breath here—I tethered the line to a willow, rushed into the Rainbow Café for some brioche and a Linzer torte—then off we went again heading due north.

Time blurs here. I'd been fighting the trout for the past five and a half hours, and the strong May sunlight was beginning to do odd things to my brain. Nevertheless, when I got home that night I was able to trace our route on a map with a felt-tip marker, and it makes for an interesting line. When the trout ran out of Winooski, he went overland to the chain of ponds near Woodbury, traversed them toward Hardwick and the Lamoille, followed the Lamoille downstream to the Wildbranch, followed the Wildbranch upstream to the headwaters of the Black at Eligo

Pond, sped north on the Black all the way to Lake Memphra-
magog in the heart of the Northeast Kingdom, swam across the
lake to the Clyde, headed up the Clyde south to Island Pond,
ran down the Nulhegan to the Connecticut, up and down Paul
Stream to cool off, up and down the Wells for a bit of sightseeing, up and down the Waits for more of the same, back down
the Connecticut to White River Junction, up the White to the
Tweed to Mendon Brook, and so across the main ridge of the
Greens back to Otter Creek heading south.

There's a book's worth of adventures in our two-hundred-
mile odyssey, but of all the memories several in particular stand
out. How the trout danced a cha-cha up the Clyde near Derby
Center. How depressed I became at the tires and innersprings
and bleach bottles tossed down the stream banks; how that was
nothing compared to the discouragement of seeing too many
For Sale signs by too many farms. How lovely the Wells turned
out to be, with deep undercut banks that rolled us out of earshot
of the century. How on the Waits—the lyric, fragile Waits, my
home river—I passed a teenager fishing the pool known as the
Aquarium; how during our brief talk he mentioned a man had
written a book about the Waits and I was able to tell him it was
me. How on the White I spotted my friend Terry Boone sipping
coffee on the bank behind Tozier's; how this conservationist
friend of all Vermont trout cupped his hand around his mouth
and yelled, "You're going to release that fish, right Wetherell?"
How my other fishing friends, Tom Ciardelli, Dick Ayers, Peter
DesMeules, and Ray Chapin, stood behind him, nodding their
heads in agreement. How below the hatchery in Bethel the
salmon parr clustered around my trout as though they had found
their long-lost mother. How as the fight continued on into the
early evening I began feeling as though I wasn't attached to a

fish at all, but a deer or bear—something too mammalian for comfort, so that as we raced down Otter Creek back toward the Battenkill, I began half rooting for him to escape. How I almost had him once on the Tweed—was able to lead him exhausted to the bank, when my clumsy boot poked him in the side and sent him tearing off again.

In Cheever's story, Neddy Merrill swims through so many swimming pools it's all he can do to pull himself from one to the next. "He had done what he wanted, he had swum the county, but he was so stupid with exhaustion that his triumph seemed vague." In a similar manner, I stumbled my way down the Battenkill to the spot where my Muddler had first disappeared back in what now seemed the remote past. Like Merrill, my mind swam in exhausted circles, so I no longer could tell hallucinated trout from actual ones, literal rivers from dream rivers, a Vermont of the imagination from a Vermont that was real.

There ahead of us in the middle of the river now appeared the largest logjam I'd ever seen before—one so huge, complex, and twisted it could only have been built by steroid-drunk beavers . . . and built in the course of a single afternoon. The trout, sensing its chance, made right for the middle, plunging toward the bottom where the branches were thickest. At first I was able to hold him—for an instant the leader ran free—then with a sickening sensation that was half victory, half defeat, I saw the line stretch, hold, stretch . . . stretch . . . and snap.

I don't remember much of my immediate feelings; I think I was too drained to think about much at all. I do remember looking down at my watch. Ten-thirty, it read. Ten-thirty **a.m.** The morning sun had risen enough to erase the silver from the tree limbs. I shook my head to clear it. Downstream in the riffle where the logjam had vanished, a twelve-inch brown rose to a floating mayfly—rose twice, knocking it down in a splashy second effort. I stripped my Muddler in and changed quickly to an Adams.

One river at a time, I told myself, working out line. One beautiful Vermont river at a time.

May 27

Needing some flies, needing a nice zinfandel to go with a picnic we were planning for Memorial Day, needing to have some film developed, needing most of all to spend a few minutes with a man I admire a great deal, I stopped Monday at Lee Chapman's store over in Vermont. I'd call it a general store, if it wasn't for the inspired specificity of the place: rare books marvelously arranged; flies just as marvelously disarranged; bag balm, cough syrup, and other patent medicines; antique gowns and lace doilies collected by his wife, Oddie; the wide selection of wines tended knowledgeably by his son Will. It's a store where you might buy just about anything you want, as long as the wanting stems from something curious, tender, and happy in the human spirit, not something venal, quick, and mean.

Perhaps it's only in retrospect, but something hollow—a vacuum, the actual empty feel of it—was present the moment I swung open the heavy screen door. Oddie and Will were standing by the counter near the old-fashioned cash register; what they said was said first by their expression.

"Lee died Saturday."

It was the jarring kind of news that can't come as a surprise. Lee had been in and out of the hospital down in Hanover for the past few years; his heart, just because it was so generous, was having trouble keeping up. Saturday night it had finally quit, but not without one last Chapman quip. A few moments before the end, Lee opened his eyes, looked around, saw his family sitting there, and staring right at them said, "My God, am I still here then?"

That was Leland Chapman—druggist, fast squad leader, air force officer, storekeeper, fisherman, hunter, fly-tyer, and friend to an amazing cross section of humanity, from the kids of the village to the movers and shakers of the larger world. I'd written about him in a little book, described him as a "moody Santa Claus" (it wasn't until I knew him better that I realized only the last two words applied), and after the book came out I was a bit apprehensive about how he would take it all. I needn't have been, of course. Lee was tickled pink by his inclusion, and to the shelves of liniment and typewriter ribbons and spinning reels was added several dozen copies of my book.

We talked about fishing a lot the last few years, planned on going out together, but it was one of those things—we never found the time. Now that it was too late I felt guilty and intrusive.

After the usual inadequate words—after finding out when the funeral would be—I was starting to leave, when Oddie took me gently by the arm.

"We'd like you to read something at the service," she said.

At first, I demurred. For all the respect I had for Lee, our time together consisted largely of turning through plastic fly boxes, searching for some elusive pattern he wanted me to try. But I was wrong to think this kind of friendship wasn't just as real as one developed over long years. Lee's life was full of such friendships, the friendship that comes in short intense bursts, and as representative of the hundreds of people who knew him this way, I was honored to have a part.

This was on Monday. Today, in brutally hot weather, they held the service in the white Congregational church that stands within casting distance of Lee's store. It was standing room only—the overflow sat out on the lawn. The numbers were matched by the variety. Farmers, leftover hippies, a contingent from the Masons, an honor guard of firemen and police, people in suits, summer folks from the lake, the flamboyantly artistic, the self-effacing and polite. As I stood there waiting to go in, I tried matching each person to the appropriate merchandise in Lee's store, wondering which were the fly-casters, which the book collectors, which the liniment users or connoisseurs of wine.

Lee's coffin was set in the middle of the church, covered with a flag. His family sat in the pews to the right. I slipped into one of the last spaces toward the back, and nervously read through my reading while waiting my turn. The minister did his part, but it wasn't until they came to the portion of the service where his neighbors and friends spoke that the proceedings seemed to have anything to do with Lee. They were funny stories mostly, tender and human. A woman read a poem she'd composed about

Lee's love of fishing, and when she finished the minister signaled me and up I went to the pulpit, sweating bullets.

What I read was by Robert Traver, a man whose love of life mirrors Lee's own. "Testament of a Fisherman," it's called. Oddie, coming up to me later, said it fit Lee to a T.

I fish because I love to; because I love the environs where trout are found, which are invariably beautiful, and hate the environs where trout are not found, which are invariably ugly; because of all the television commercials, cocktail parties and assorted social posturing I thus escape; because, in a world where most men seem to spend their lives doing things they hate, my fishing is at once an endless source of delight and an act of small rebellion; because trout do not lie or cheat and cannot be bought or bribed or impressed by power, but respond only to quietude and humility and endless patience; because I suspect that men are going along this way for the last time, and I for one don't want to waste the trip; because mercifully there are no telephones on trout waters; because only in the woods can I find solitude without loneliness; because bourbon out of an old tin cup always tastes better out there; because maybe one day I will catch a mermaid; and finally, not because I regard fishing as being so terribly important, but because I suspect that so many of the other concerns of men are equally unimportant—and not nearly so much fun.

Last Voyage
of the Bismarck

Buoyancy is a quality I have always admired, but always from afar. To be carried along on the choppy froth of things, bouncing, floating, skipping, held above the turbulence by an unquenchable welling up—these seem to me in my leadenness the happy pinnacles of joy. Swamped as I am by bothersome detail, weighted down by brooding, ballasted by doubts, it is all I can do to manage a rough treading water, let alone actually float. And though I have never had it tested, I suspect my specific gravity corresponds to that of granite. Solid, Wetherell undoubtedly is. Buoyant, Wetherell definitely is not.

I feel the lack most tangibly when I'm fishing. An awkward enough wader at knee depth, I become positively enshackled when I venture into waters above my waist. The wader fabric clings to me like one of those heavy rubber suits the pearl divers were wont to drown in; my wading shoes send up vibrations frighteningly similar to those produced by ball against chain. What makes it worse is my aspiration. Not content with the shallow, easily wadable stretches, I'm always reaching out for more—reaching so far that my right hand furiously false-casts a rod held aloft like a sinking Excalibur, while my feet—touching nothing—pedal back and forth like an inebriated duck's.

The ultimate futility of this struck me quite forcibly one morning several years ago when I was on Franklin Pond. As usual, I was up to my shoulders in ice-cold water, casting to brook trout that, as usual, rose a teasing yard from my best efforts. I went through double-hauls and triple-hauls and hauls for which no name exists, but they had no effect whatsoever except to chase the trout out even farther; I could cast forever and not catch a fish. And though the long-term solution was obvious, it penetrated my waterlogged brain very slowly, as if having to course the same slow evolutionary furrows up which it dawned on prehistoric man.

A boat. Of course. Something to float me out to where the fish were feeding. Eureka!

For a moment, I let the thought of it carry me away. As always, the effervescence of that first inspiration quickly sank into something heavier and dull: the writerly poverty in which

I dwelled. For if I was going to acquire a boat, it would have to be a modest one. No flashy runabout with gleaming outriggers, no cedar skiff with loving overlaps—these were unquestionably too dear. Nor did the "belly boat" have any appeal for me, that weird bastardization of waders, inner tubes, and fins that makes a fisherman resemble a cross between a hanging tenpin and one of the lumpier pea pods in *Invasion of the Body Snatchers*. No, what I needed was an actual craft of some kind, maneuverable, portable, lightweight, and cheap.

It was in the flash of that first dawning notion that the solution lay. For if I was aping prehistoric man in the similarity of our ends, so too could I ape him in the actual means. Man did not make his first leap from shore in a Ranger bass boat with dual Merc outboards, nor did he shove off in an Old Town ABS canoe. He made the first timid venturing on a raft made of hippo bladders, a glorified and bubbly balloon.

As it turned out, our local sporting goods store had three of the latest models. Inflatable rafts, two-, three-, and four-man versions, propped next to one another on the wall like siblings of steadily increasing plumpness and height. They weren't made of hippo insides, but plastic—plastic that had all the quality and thickness of a ninety-nine-cent beach ball. So although I'd had visions of myself coming home with the kind of durable Avon favored by Jacques Cousteau and amphibious commandos, it was apparent that I was going to have to settle for something considerably less grand.

I examined the rafts more carefully. For something so simple, there was an amazing proliferation of reading matter stenciled across the sides, with extravagant claims of weight-bearing capabilities contradicted by repeated cautions about life jackets. That the rafts were made in Taiwan didn't bother me: the Chinese were an ancient people, and hadn't they invented the junk? The price was reasonable, too, with the two-man model selling for the same price as a dozen bass bugs.

It was the two-man model I finally chose. With a weight-bearing capacity of four hundred pounds, it could carry Celeste and me with freeboard to spare. The coziness of the actual *sitting* room bothered me (I estimated its measurements at roughly three by five feet), but I let the box illustration override all my doubts. Pictured were *four* bikini-clad models riding the two-man model in what appeared to be not only comfort but also outright joy. Convinced, I went over to the shelves and pulled a box out from the bottom. The actual purchase, for something that was to become so lifelike and personal, seemed anticlimactic and crass. The see-through wrapping, the smell of newness, the exchange of cash. It smacked of buying a child.

I unswaddled it gently when I got home, worried lest any stray pin or splinters puncture it at birth. Spread across the carpet with the flat whiteness of pita bread, it was slow to inflate. (Indeed, the inability of any of a dozen pumps to inflate it in anything less than half an hour was the Achilles' heel of the whole enterprise; the slow *press press press* of foot against bellows was the monotonous cadence of its life.) Only gradually did it grow into a delightful roundness and buoyancy. And round and buoyant is how the raft looked when inflated, with the swelling billow of a magic carpet yearning to be airborne. The contrast between the loftiness of its ambition and the modesty of its means suggested the name. By the time I called Celeste into the room to marvel at what air had wrought, she was *Bismarck*, and *Bismarck* she remained.

Her maiden voyage came that very evening. There's a remote lake on the height of land behind our home that is so wild and lovely I hesitate to even whisper of its existence. Lightly visited and seldom fished, it harbors a fussy population of largemouth bass, some running to size. An old jeep trail runs up to it, but there are no launching ramps, and it would be a long, brutal portage for a canoe. Various rowboats and runabouts have been carted in over the years; their stoved-in wrecks dot the shallows like huge planters deliberately installed for the propagation of lilies.

It was, in short, the perfect place to let *Bismarck* do her stuff. At nine pounds, she was a delight to backpack, and in no time at all, Celeste and I were standing on a granite shelf that slopes into the lake, alternating steps on the air pump. Celeste *oohed* and *aahed* over the scenery; I *oohed* and *aahed* over *Bismarck*'s squat lines.

She looked good in the water. Alert, stable, round. Damn good. Even Celeste thought so.

"Why, she's pretty," she said. She rolled her jeans up to wade out to her, then suddenly hesitated. "Uh, how do we get in?"

As usual, she had gone right to the heart of the matter. For *Bismarck*, lovely as she was, was a maddening, ornery, downright impossible bitch to board. The very buoyancy I admired would make her shy away at the slightest ripple, so that approaching her required all the stealth and caution necessary in mounting an unbroken colt. By holding onto the side and bracing my feet against some rocks I was able to boost Celeste into the stern, followed quickly by our fly rods, picnic supper, and wine. By the time all was settled, there wasn't much room left for me.

Correction: no room at all.

"Goodbye!" Celeste yelled, reaching for the oars.

"No, wait a second," I said. "Can't you just . . . scrunch?"

Scrunch is what we did. Celeste tucked up her legs to make a space, I turned sideways and heaved myself up perpendicular to the inflated thwarts, then by judicious wiggling we managed to wedge me in. My first remark was the obvious one.

"It's a good thing we're married."

With our arms intertwined about fly rods, our legs jutting out around each other's chest, I suppose we must have looked like a pornographic carving on a temple devoted to piscine love. I reached for the oars and promptly stroked them into Celeste's chin; she, experiencing a cramp in her right leg, stretched it toward my throat, tipping off my hat. Our fly lines immediately became entangled; the overturned picnic basket leaked pickle brine down over our knees. *Bismarck*, feeling the breeze now, drifted out from shore.

"You sure this is the two-person model?" Celeste asked.

I thumped the lettering. "Here, read for yourself. Two people. Two intimate, acrobatic, contortionist dwarfs. And there," I said, pausing dramatically, "is our bass."

A school of them was tearing apart the lily pads on the far shore in pursuit of—what? Frogs? Shiners? Or was it just their own compacted joy in their bassness, the tremendous joy and lust for existence I sense whenever I have one on the end of my line? We rowed over to find out.

It was a long row. A very long row. *Bismarck*, filled to the gunwales, was not a happy sailor. Halfway there, I fell back in exhaustion. Celeste took over, and by the time we were actually in casting range, collected sweat had added another few inches to the bilge beneath our bottoms.

But that's the sad part of the story. Not another negative word will I inscribe beside *Bismarck*'s name, for once we got to the lily pads we caught bass aplenty, the largest weighing in at over four pounds. *Bismarck*'s good qualities were evident on every one: the stealth and silence of her approach; her low waterline, with its canny view into the bass's own plane; her stability; the ease with which a hooked fish slithered in over her side. By the time we left that night, *Bismarck* had more than justified her existence, and plastic though she was, I already felt that sentimental affinity that can make a boat the most precious and dearly loved of a man's things.

Though Celeste and I continued to play this funny twosie the rest of the summer, it was as a solo craft that *Bismarck* really came into her own. Alone, I nestled into her bottom as if into a soft and yielding waterbed, casting from a comfortably horizontal position, my neck pillowed by the air chamber in the stern. When I was alone, *Bismarck* became a delight to maneuver, responding so quickly to the oars that I often spun her around and around in mad circles just for fun. She rowed quickly and steadily, and seemed to skip under all but the strongest breezes with enough freeboard to keep me reasonably dry. Her lightness and airiness were constant sources of amazement. There were days when I had fish on that towed us halfway across the lake, so that I felt like Ishmael on a miniaturized Nantucket sleigh ride, my mouth dropping open in delight.

What impressed me even more was *Bismarck*'s sturdiness. I fished her hard that summer and autumn, then again the following spring, often taking her out five or six times a week. One of the smaller air chambers developed a leak, but the other three were enough to float her, and I began deliberately seeking out tougher water, to see what she could do. The wide Connecticut in a northwest chop, *Bismarck* bouncing along like a stubby tugboat; huge Newfound Lake, where powerboats threatened to swamp us with their wakes; remote trout ponds, where briars scratched the plastic but punctured her not. . . . We fished them all. There was even one magic afternoon when

I found some white water for her—the mouth of a trout stream that empties into the Connecticut. She did well, of course. I backed down the current stern first, and she went bouncing off the rocks like an exuberant pinball, impervious to harm. Confidence expanding, I took her to salt water and tried her out on a windy bay; I took her to a nearby lake in deep autumn when a capsize might have finished us both. *Bismarck* met every new challenge with aplomb.

And the two of us caught fish. Smallmouth that showered her bottom with spray; trout that scissored back and forth near her bow like escorting dolphins; a pike that threatened to puncture us; big walleyes that towed us farther than any bass. Viewed simply as a fishing tool, *Bismarck* proved herself many times over, and I was surprised never to encounter another fly-fisher so equipped. Occasionally, I would see sunburned, angry teenagers paddling along in similar craft near shore, but I never saw one being seriously fished, and most of the time I had to myself whatever body of water I was exploring.

Our partnership remained intact for three full seasons. I had originally thought of her as little more than a disposable boat, to be used several times then discarded like a tissue. Now, her durability proved, I began making the opposite mistake: thinking of her as something permanent and fixed. If I did picture her end, it was always in some cataclysmic happening that would send us both to the bottom in style: a spectacular collision with a spear-shaped rock; a pike big enough to disembowel us; a foot too heavy on the air pump, blowing her to smithereens. That she might die more slowly and subtly never occurred to me at all.

The truth is, she was dying—dying from neglect. By the time that fourth spring rolled around, I had forsaken her exuberant chanciness for the firmer rhythm of a canoe—a fifteen-foot

Old Town with a separate beauty all her own. *Bismarck* sailed less and less; for long months altogether, she remained in the backpack, her plastic folds stiffening from nonuse. Occasionally, I meant to take her out, but my back was always aching too much to carry her, or it was too windy, or . . . But why make a list? Excuses count for nothing, not in love affairs, not in boats. She was the apple of my eye, then one day she wasn't, and it's as simple and sad a story as that.

And yet we were to have one more day together after all. It was in May, a weekday afternoon when I felt weighed down with a leadenness that went beyond mere fatigue—as flat as one of those leftover leaves one finds on the forest floor. That I desperately needed a filling of water, sky, and trout was obvious. I started to pull the canoe out of the barn, then—motivated by a sudden, overpowering instinct—went back into the mudroom and grabbed the backpack instead.

Fifteen minutes later, I was hiking up the trail toward Franklin Pond, a bundled *Bismarck* perched high on my shoulders like an eager baby spotting out the terrain. The morning sun had given way to ominous yellow clouds, and I hiked faster than usual in order to stay warm.

The pond sits tight against the slope of the one legitimate mountain our town has. It's about five acres in extent, stocked occasionally by helicopter, and unfishable without some sort of raft. So miniature is it, so silver and round, that the usual analogy is to a gem, though I tend to see it as a bowl instead—a punch bowl cradling the liquefied granite essence of the surrounding hills. Trees reflect on its surface; a breeze will ripple the tops of the surrounding spruce, then drop to strum the water, so that the two waves are never quite synchronized, and the dual shimmers shimmer continuously. So pure is the water, so generous the reflection, that casting into its depths gives the sensation of casting into midair.

I unrolled *Bismarck* on the rough tent platform that is the only man-made structure on its shores. Again, I went through the old familiar ritual of making her waterborne. The slow accordion press of the air pump; the furious shutting off of valves; the precarious launching and more precarious boarding; the quick assembly of oars. It was good to return to something I loved and find it unchanged. Unchanged except, that is, in one important respect. As I stroked my way toward the far shore, feeling her generous and yielding tug, I realized with what can only be described as a sinking sensation that *Bismarck,* my neglected *Bismarck,* was sinking.

Slowly sinking. The long winter in the mudroom with its constant freezing and thawing had opened *Bismarck's* seams. Water seeped in through a dozen thin cracks—my butt was already numb from icy pond water collected in the stern. It was obvious that *Bismarck* was on her way out, and yet . . . well, it wouldn't happen immediately. The two air chambers that formed the hull were already empty, but a quick check showed that the largest chamber, the outer one, was still partially filled. With luck—if I handled her carefully—*Bismarck* had an hour's float left.

Risky, sure, but there was a compelling reason not to return to shore at once: the trout. Between one moment and the next, as if on an invisible maestro's dramatic cue, they had begun rising on all sides. I worked out some line and immediately caught four brookies in a row on a small Gray Wulff. The lower *Bismarck* sank, the easier it was to slide them over the side, until finally it was hard to determine where pond ended and boat began, and the trout bubbled around my stomach in perfect contentment as I twisted free the fly.

I don't remember how many trout I finally caught. The flies were hatching so fast on the water that the pond literally boiled. A hungry swallow flew down from the mountain, then another, then a third, until finally the air seemed just as thick with darting birds as it did with lazy insects. There were swallows everywhere, coming in squadrons, peeling off, strafing the surface, jetting away. It was a miracle I didn't snag one on my backcasts, but they seemed to be deliberately toying with the line, ducking under it like girls jumping rope. They were teasing me—inebriated with the same airy exuberance as the rising trout and the hatching flies.

Then it began to snow.

Huge snowflakes, falling faster than their size should warrant, tumbling down over the swallows and the flies and the trout until everything became jumbled together in a world where there were no separate planes or spheres of perspectives, but everything was one. Was I casting for flies or for trout or for swallows? Was I fishing water, snow, or sky? Man, trout, bug, or bird? It was dizzying, but I was sinking in it, and I began rowing *Bismarck* toward shore, not from self-preservation, but simply because I needed the ballast of the oars to keep my soul from flying away. As I neared shore, a brown shape glided beneath *Bismarck*'s hull in a rush of fluid and backward-flowing fur: a beaver, and it was too much for me, and I realized for the first time what those nineteenth-century writers meant when they wrote the word *swoon*.

I didn't, of course. I didn't turn into a swallow, and I didn't swoon, and, more importantly, I didn't sink. *Bismarck* and I reached shore together, though by now all that was left of her was a thin plastic pressure against my bottom, her last cradling gasp. She boosted me onto a flat rock within stepping distance of land, then made a final expiring sigh and sank away in bubbles. By the time I pulled her up on shore, her seams were open from bow to stern.

I folded her up more carefully than I ever had when she was whole, then started back down the trail to my car, zigzagging through snowflakes that spread apart into sun. My thoughts were inflated by the miracles I had just witnessed: I walked so fast and with such light-footed sureness that it was almost as if I had inherited *Bismarck*'s very air. I was . . . yes, there was no mistaking it now. I was buoyant. Buoyant at last.

Bismarck. June 14, 1982 to May 5, 1986.

She was a lot more than a toy.

June 18

Ｎew Hampshire's an embarrassing state to live in, God knows, what with the reactionary politics; the *Manchester Union Leader* and its gutter journalism; the "Live Free or Die" threat on the license plates (referring less to freedom than to the state's legendary cheapness); the reliance on liquor sales for much of the state's income; the depressing roll call of New Hampshire nonentities who have made it big in Washington, from Franklin Pierce to Sherman Adams to John Sununu; the fact that our most famous native son, Daniel Webster, spent the greater part of his life in Massachusetts; Emerson's jibe about how "the God who made New Hampshire taunted the lofty land with little men" . . . the fact that no one west of Vermont seems to have the slightest notion of where the place is.

There are all these things—and then there is Grafton Pond. It's typically New Hampshire in the best sense of the phrase. Granite shoreline shelving out into astonishingly clear water; banks shaggy with fir trees; a generous scattering of islands; the way the whole pond seems to lie not flat but on an inclined plane tilted toward the bald dome of Mount Cardigan eleven miles to the north . . . the whole set in a part of the state that's nestled off the tourist routes, scruffy, un-condominiumized, unspoiled.

I went over there this morning to get a good helping of its beauty and to check whether the bass were in close to shore. They weren't, but it hardly matters. Just to be out there on the sunny surface, my canoe fitting the water so perfectly it was as if we were propelled by the impression of her shadow, was reward enough for the long drive.

Even the blackflies seem to respect Grafton's beauty. They are there on shore when I arrive, all hot and bothered and happy to see me, but once I paddle out from the shady launch area they peel off me like gloom's bitter cloud. I dab on a layer of sunscreen over the Cutter's, pop one of Celeste's homemade brownies in my mouth, toss out some line, anchor my fly rod in the stern, then start west along the shoreline, threading my way through the shallows that separate the first big islands.

The Laurentian Shield must look like this, rocky, spruced, and scrubbed. Even the weeds; they don't lay flat and heavy but toss in the current like fields of wheat. Up on shore are old stone walls built by the farmers who lived here a century and a half ago; where they meet the water they keep right on going, and with the transparency being what it is, I can trace them a good fifty yards out from shore, the rocks growing smaller and less golden the deeper they plunge. Grafton Pond, for all its naturalness, is man-made, impounded to provide water for a distant town. What I'm drifting over are the remains of a vanished New England, the rural, self-sufficient life that pretty much disappeared seventy years ago with the paving of the first roads.

As I make the circuit of the pond, hopping from island to island to take advantage of their lee, it's hard not to think of those farmers and their backbreaking toil. Could any of them have guessed, at work on a hot day, loading the stone boat with heavy boulders, whipping up the ox, that the wall they so patiently constructed would one day be the shelter for bass? Would anyone believe it now? That the condos and marinas we cram so obscenely around our lakes will one day be the haunt of minnows, admiring their reflections in the cracked and algae-stained glass? I take reassurance from both notions. To go with all its beauty, Grafton has a bittersweet, haunted air; floating over these walls is like floating over a poem by Robert Frost.

There are lots of smallmouth in the pond, either out amid the rocks of the islands or in among the fallen trees toward shore. I've caught three-pounders here in the past, thick and sassy, but today the big ones seem to be sulking. The high barometer probably—so exhilarating to me, it depresses bass no end. All I manage is an occasional bluegill . . . not that there is anything wrong with that. Sunny, fat, and fierce, the bluegill is a noble fish, and I wouldn't mind having been one in a previous incarnation.

It's funny about the fishing. A year ago I would have tried every bug and streamer in my box, tormented every last inch of shoreline with casts, and—not catching much—let the poor results pretty much ruin my day. Today, though, catching fish seems almost beside the point, and I'm content to try a lazy cast now and then and put most of my effort into watching.

This is the year I'm devoting to puzzling out the fishing motive, so it's worth trying to decide what causes this new serenity. Is it the birth of our daughter? The fact that having now spawned (to stay in metaphor) I find my predatory urge much duller than before? Is that what all these hours spent chasing fish are about, a sublimated, ersatz sort of fathering? Does the fishing urge, like so much else, come down in the end to the sexual one?

Murky depths, too murky for a pond so clear. I paddle faster, drowning out the philosophical in some good honest sweat. While most of Grafton's islands lie clustered in a convoy near shore, there's one that sits alone by itself out in the middle, as if demonstrating to the others what real islandhood is all about. There in a cove on its near side is a splashing commotion, and I head over to see what's what.

It's a family of otters—five I can count. My canoe doesn't seem to bother them, though it's clear they're aware of it; they turn a synchronized somersault, then shift their shenanigans a few rods farther out into the pond. Seeing them at play is like watching an allegory by Edward Hicks, and gives me another boost of optimism. The otter shall frolic with the fisherman, the lion lie down with the lamb—on Grafton Pond anyway, on this one perfect June day.

Watching this, feeling the sun on my face, the spray kick off the bow and wet me, I realize something else that fatherhood has given me: the gift to see all this as *new*. My daughter is a month old—it will be years before we can bring her safely out in a canoe—and yet for me her perception is already the measure of the pond's beauty, and just in time, too, because my own abilities when it comes to perception are fast beginning to wane. As a boy and even into my thirties, I could stare enchanted at a perfect cloud or sunny waterscape for long minutes and be content. Now, thickened with life's trivialities, distracted by disappointment, hurried, my own senses perceptibly dulled, I find it harder to take such sheer undiluted pleasure in "mere" scenery. But here is the possibility of escaping all that and starting fresh. Not just in the fictional empathies that are such a large part of my life, but every day, in the most commonplace ways, by this vicarious, fatherly looking-out . . . to see as Erin sees.

I have them waiting at home, my wife, my daughter. Around five, after a long day's drifting, I begin to wonder what they're doing—how to put my gentle adventures into words and bring them back to my family intact.

Big (Smoky) Sky

As fiascos go, this was the worst—worse even than the time I landed in Ireland during the biggest snowstorm in forty years and sat eleven hours on a stranded train between an alcoholic priest from Boston, a homesick construction worker from Ohio, and a garrulous professor of Italian at Trinity College, Dublin; worse even than the time I went out to British Columbia for two weeks of mountain climbing and broke my arms falling over a six-inch-high fence my first day there. Worse because warned by both disasters I should have taken out an insurance policy against disappointment and thereby been armed.

In a sense, I had. I knew about the forest fires. All summer the papers in the East had been full of them, each new article revising upward the amount of Yellowstone acreage involved. On Labor Day, two days before I was due to leave, I spent the afternoon on the phone to Montana, calling park rangers and tackle-shop owners and game wardens trying to find out exactly how bad the problem was. All my contacts were very patient with me, took pains in describing the current situation, and were quick to suggest others I could call to learn about conditions in adjoining watersheds. Most of them agreed that (1) the fires were bad, particularly in Yellowstone; (2) the rivers were critically low from the summer's drought; (3) despite 1 and 2, the fishing, at least on headwater streams, was the best it had been in ten years.

Before most trips I find myself looking for excuses not to go. The inertia of a settled life, my history of disaster, the disturbing, impossible-to-erase remnants of the chronic homesickness I suffered as a child—these are all excuses for not putting any part of myself at risk. But this was no ordinary trip—it was to Montana, mecca of American fly fishing even when all the advertising promoting it as such is discounted, a land so vast filled with waters so brilliant it would expand my notion of riverine beauty in one overwhelming flash. And it was no ordinary time, either; I would be forty in a month, and it seemed right to treat myself to one last thirty-something adventure that would launch me exuberantly into middle age.

I had my plan all worked out. Starting at Bozeman, I would make a slow clockwise loop around the compass; fish the Gallatin upstream along Yellowstone Park's western boundary, spend a day or two on the upper Madison below Quake Lake, then head over to Dillon to fish Poindexter's Slough and the Beaverhead. The nice thing about this itinerary was that it kept me well in reach of Yellowstone; if the fires let up, if it started raining, I could make a fast raid into the park and try some of the famous water there (even the Firehole, which, given the circumstances, might have been an experience too literal to enjoy). If worse came to worst and the fires were still burning, I could make reservations on the spring creeks near Livingston and thus complete my circuit in style.

It was a good plan, at least in theory, and I full believed in it until I landed in Denver on the late afternoon of September 6. Flying cross-country, the atmosphere had been unusually clear, and I'd gotten a good view of the mustard-colored scars left across the prairies by the summer's brutal drought. It gave the impression—in its extent; in the lifeless way nothing stirred—of a land waiting for a match to be applied to its crusted, hemplike edge.

And then in Denver . . . in my frantic change of planes there; in the quick gulp of air I managed as I raced between terminals . . . the match was struck. Denver's air is always smoggy, but this was something far different that had settled in—an actual pall with an acrid bite. The moment the Bozeman flight was airborne we were immersed in thick, rolling clouds that were far darker and grainier than any I'd ever seen. My seatmate pointed toward them and shrugged; that it was smoke from the Yellowstone fires was too obvious to mention.

The landing in Bozeman was scary enough, God knows, what with the nonexistent visibility and the sensation of descending through a force far too mysterious and powerful for a 707 to handle. The air over the terminal was thick with smoke, and this time, in the carbon reek of it, I caught the cinnamon underline of burning vegetation. It was odd in its effect. All the adrenaline that was building up in me, all the nervous irritation that comes after a long day's flying, and yet after a few minutes on the ground I felt relaxed and strangely soothed.

What my heartbeat was responding to was the smell—the smell that took me back thirty years to the vanished autumn ritual of burning leaves in the suburban town where I grew up. The memory was ludicrously out of proportion to its source—a burning Yellowstone Park—and yet something of this narcotic, lulling nostalgia lingered on all week, to see me through my perils with, if not equanimity, at least a certain amount of perspective.

But all that was ahead of me. On the shuttle to pick up my car, the driver, a young man named Dave, was quick to rave about how good the fishing was, quick to offer me suggestions on rivers and flies.

"What about the fires?" I said, as we peered up at a stoplight, trying unsuccessfully to make out its color. "As bad as it looks?"

"Nah," he said. "Water doesn't burn."

He glanced up in the mirror to catch my reaction—it was obviously a joke he'd had a lot of fun with.

Then, as he was helping me unload my bags: "September fishing is the best of the year. Tie on a hopper, work the edges, stay out of Yellowstone, and you'll do fine."

I'd been in Montana twenty minutes and already learned one thing: people were either fatalistic about the fires or angry, and it paid to find out early in the conversation which type you were dealing with and gauge your remarks accordingly.

"So you don't think the government's to blame then for letting the fires burn?" I asked.

He shrugged like he had that first time. "Wood burns, Mr. Wetherell. Water doesn't."

Dave's terse optimism was just what I needed. When I went to bed that night at my Bozeman motel, I felt more confident than I had all day. True, the TV news was filled with scenes of a burning Yellowstone, complete with villages being evacuated, overcome fire fighters being borne off on stretchers, and the realistic sound of crackling flames (I could picture a producer back in New York shouting over a bad telephone connection: "Give me more crackle, Smithers! More crackle damn it!"). But still, I was convinced the fires would merely form a vivid backdrop to my fishing, add a little punch to the battle stories I was sure to bring home.

Still on eastern time, excited at the prospect of beginning my trip in earnest, I woke up before five. Packing quickly, I ferried my luggage down to the car. With the smoke, the darkness was total—even the mercury highway lights, those harsh ugly deterrents to night, barely dented the blackness. Conditions had obviously worsened overnight. The smoke had a smothering, heavy quality that made it difficult to breathe. Even worse, the wind was out of the south, hot and desiccating . . . bad news to those thousands of fire fighters who must even now have been heading back toward the fire lines for another day of futile effort.

"Water doesn't burn," I said, remembering Dave's upbeat assurance. I said it out loud and I said it twice.

I headed across the parking lot to the lobby to check out. As I did so, I passed a newspaper vending machine set against the motel's window. Automatically, as I have a thousand times in a dozen different cities, I reached into my pocket for a quarter, dropped it in the slot, reached down, blindly grabbed, tucked the paper under my arm, then went into the lobby to the desk.

There was no sign of the desk clerk. While I waited, I unfolded the paper to scan the headlines.

GOVERNOR BANS OUTDOOR RECREATION IN MONTANA.

Six words, fourteen syllables, thirty-eight letters, and together they spelled one of the worst five moments of my life. I read quickly on, praying there was some mistake, but fate had it spelled out for me right from that wretched opening line.

The governor of Montana, in response to the fires sweeping across the state, has closed all land, public and private, to any unnecessary usage, including camping, hiking, hunting, and fishing.

It would be impossible to describe my emotions upon reading this in anything less than four paragraphs. One to describe the sheer disbelief, the way I read and read again trying to end that sentence just one word earlier; another to describe the overpowering, physical sense of disappointment, the way it came over me like a giant's hand shoving me to my knees; a third to describe the vexation and anger, the quick computation of how much money I had poured into this trip, the real sacrifice my family had made to enable me to come; a final paragraph—once the others were written, shed, and done with—to describe the absurdity of it all, the melodramatic, overwritten irony of a man landing in the West to celebrate his fortieth birthday with a fishing trip on the first day in history—the first day ever!—that a Montana trout season was ever prematurely closed.

Only one paragraph—the irony, even after a year, is simply too great to be borne. After what seemed like hours, I put the newspaper back down on the desk. I spoke to the clerk in normal enough tones, paid my bill in cash, then walked back to my car, without the slightest idea what to do next.

But that's the good thing about turning forty—you have certain defenses. When you're up against the big things in life, be it fire, foolishness, or fate, the best thing to do is fight back with a heavy dose of the commonplace. Among all the surging emotions that had hold of me, I found a homelier one and latched onto it in gratitude: I was hungry, hungrier than I remembered having been in a long time, in urgent need of a decent breakfast.

I drove down the strip into town. The only place open that early was a pool hall/bar that probably never closed. It had that familiar college-town smell of urine and old beer, but at least the counter looked clean and there was a fresh pot of coffee perched on the end.

I ordered an omelet with pancakes on the side. The waitress, bored, went off with my order; the only other person in the place was an old man slouched alone on a stool like a model for Edward Hopper. The *Today* show was on the television above the grill; there were vivid pictures of the flames approaching Old Faithful, and more of that loud, morbid crackling.

Absurdity took full command now. With no one else to talk to, all but bursting with the need for sympathy and advice, I explained my predicament to the indifferent waitress and lifeless old man.

". . . all the way from New Hampshire," I said, concluding. "And now the fishing season is closed? How long is this going to last? Does that mean everywhere or just on state land?"

Both of them listened patiently enough, but all they could do for me was scratch their heads—the waitress metaphorically with a slow, sleepy frown; the old man literally, as if he had never come up against the like. Speechless, we turned toward the TV set and the glaring orange flames; surely someone would make an announcement and everything would be fixed.

After a third cup of coffee, I took my troubles out to the street. There were several possible courses of action, none of them good. I could fly back East on the next available plane; prudent from a financial point of view, but to cut and run before the situation fully sank in would increase the hallucinatory effect even past the point where it was now ("You went to Montana for a day? Just a day?"). I could head down to Idaho and try the fishing there; a possibility, though I had already changed plans so often before coming that I didn't have much heart for a third effort. I could hang around a few days and see what happened; a policy of default, but not a bad policy all the same.

The weather forecast was for rain moving in for the weekend—this was Tuesday. Five days until rain, a day or two before the bureaucratic treadmill reversed itself, and that would bring me up to eight days at the earliest before the fishing season reopened—and even that was only a possibility.

What to do?

One of the things I had brought west with me was a list of contacts and friends of friends to look up in the course of my trip. One of these ran a tackle store in Bozeman. Obviously, he was just the man to seek out for advice.

I pulled into the driveway just as he was unlocking the shop. To say it was a bad time to introduce myself is putting it mildly; if I was surprised and disappointed by the ban on fishing, the store owner—whose livelihood depended on the guiding he did in the fall—was shocked and irate.

"That goddamned gutless governor!" he screamed. "The frigging gutless son of a bitch!"

He would get his lawyer after him, that's what he would do. He would get all the guides and outfitters together and force the state to rescind the ban. The governor was just covering his ass, same as always. He had already closed the bow-hunting season because of the fires, and the hunters had let out such a cry that he was extending the ban to fishermen just so no one could say he was playing favorites. If he was serious about the fire danger, why not extend the ban to loggers and miners? They were still allowed in the woods, and they posed a hell of a lot more fire hazard than a fly-fisherman sitting in a drift boat or wading chest deep in a stream.

His anger—his perfectly justified anger—was awesome in its way; as the flames were to later, it dwarfed my own puny disappointment. Eventually, he mastered it long enough to give me some advice: go ahead and fish, at least for today. The rangers wouldn't be issuing summonses for a while, but just ordering everyone off the water. He sold me a one-day license, then sent me off toward Quake Lake the long way around via Ennis (thereby avoiding Route 191 along the Gallatin, where the fires were said to be bad). When I went out the door he was already screaming at someone in Helena over the phone.

As for me? At least I had a direction now, and an ersatz kind of hope that would do in lieu of the real thing. A few miles out from Bozeman the rangeland begins, and though the smoke kept it hidden behind a gray, gauzy veil, it still resembled the Montana landscape of my boyhood picturing.

The Madison comes into view quickly at the Route 84 bridge, and the sight of it—open, rock-studded, and strong— was sufficiently impressive. There were some fishermen wading the edges by a beached drift boat; clearly, they were either ignoring the prohibition or out too early to have learned it was in effect.

After a quick stop in Ennis (the tackle shops crowded with somber fly-fishermen seeking consolation), I drove to where the Madison leaves Quake Lake. Within minutes I was up to my waist in it, enjoying the cold, clear rush of the current, the interweaving side channels, the generous and willing trout. The Madison, I told myself. The goddamn Madison! In less than a half hour I had caught a dozen rainbows and browns on my old reliable Royal Wulff. In the instantaneous quality of it all, the way the trout seemed queued to welcome me, it was almost exactly the Montana fishing experience of which I had dreamed.

But not quite. There was something missing—there were no mountains in the background, not even hills. The smoke hid the views in every direction but west, and not just any smoke, but smoke with rough, ominous edges that suggested the flames weren't far behind. As I fished, I kept glancing over my shoulder to check where it was, and thereby missed a good many rises. Then, too, fishing illegally is not what it's cracked up to be; rather than providing a furtive, daring pleasure, it's more apt to make you feel sordid—a dirty old fisherman worthy of contempt. Even if it *were* fun, the upper Madison is no river to poach; without streamside trees, a warden can spot you a good mile away.

Which is just what happened. I was starting in on a new side channel, casting to the seam of a pool near a sheltering log, when I saw a jeep pull up behind my car back on the highway. A warden got out—there was no mistaking that hat. He shouted in my direction, but I pretended not to hear and kept on casting, working myself toward a small island and a protective screen of brush. Once past it I waded faster, hoping he would tire of chasing me and go back to his jeep. But this was a forlorn try—a last, pathetic rebellion against the irony that had me squarely in its sights.

"Excuse me, sir?" he shouted, from a short distance downstream.

My first impulse was to raise both hands in the air; my second, to play dumb.

"Oh? . . . Oh, hello there."

I reeled in and waded over to the bank. He was very nice about it—his choice of words was simple and direct.

"The governor has closed the state to fishing."

I looked into his eyes. "Why?"

"Because of the fires."

"What fires?"

"Those fires."

He turned and pointed—touché. But still, if I was going to go peaceably, I wasn't going to go without registering an objection, so I trotted out my best shot:

"Water doesn't burn."

Give the warden his due; he laughed and shook his head sympathetically, and together we waded back across the side channels like old friends ("Mister," he said, "You can't even step off the road and *pee* in Montana while the ban is on"). He had a bear trap trailered behind his jeep; the ranchers were complaining about grizzlies being chased out of the park by the flames.

"You can still fish Yellowstone," he said, when I asked him for advice. "The ban doesn't apply there."

Irony never knows when to quit. You could *fish* in Yellowstone Park, only you couldn't *drive* into Yellowstone Park, all the entrance roads being closed. But again, it was a matter of clinging to wisps now, literally and metaphorically, and so I decided to drive to West Yellowstone and wait for some shifting pattern in the fires to give me my chance.

As I drove up the highway I saw the warden wading through the river toward another fly-fisherman who cast all unsuspecting upstream—set in the glorious riverscape, the mirror image of what I had just been: a man a moment away from heartbreak, flailing away at the sky with grace, rhythm, and—dwarfed as he was by the rolling smoke clouds—a small penumbra of the absurd.

West Yellowstone must be a tawdry enough place under normal circumstances, filled as it is with vacant-eyed tourists seeking to find in the garish streets that which escaped them in the park, but in early September of 1988, with the fires making headlines everywhere, the flames just a single block away, it was against all probability one of the most interesting places in the world.

It's hard to do justice to that exaggerated, surrealistic scene. The improvised, graffiti-like signs that met me as I drove down Route 20 into town *(Welcome to Charcoal-broiled National Park);* the line of yellow fire trucks lined up ready to spring into action if the flames crossed the street separating the village from the park; the lawn sprinklers borrowed from every golf course in Montana, covering the scrubby border zone with their arcing white spray; the ghostlike emptiness of the motels; the heart-broken fishermen roaming about like me, absolutely at a loss; the legion of green-panted, yellow-shirted fire fighters, the way they crowded the restaurants and lined up at pay phones calling home they were safe; the army jeeps swerving around corners on two wheels as if under fire; the way the T-shirt factories had switched gears and were churning out designs for the current market (a fat grizzly picking his teeth with a toothpick, saying "Who needs tourists? Send more firefighters!"); the high-school football team running wind sprints under falling ash as behind them the cheering squad practiced their splits . . . It was a place under the gun, and like all such places, it had gone more than a little bit nuts.

Seeing all this, seeing the school buses taking fresh fire fighters into the park while other buses brought exhausted ones out, smelling the smoke, seeing the huge, iodine-colored cloud that kept expanding and moving closer (tending to a mush-room shape, but never quite taking it on), it was impossible not to think of combat. The enemy was out there in the hills, its whereabouts constantly shifting; there were retreats, furious counterattacks—communiqués issued hourly for the reporters and TV crews camped in the larger, luckier motels.

As with combat, it was impossible to get the story straight. Everyone you talked to had a different rumor. The town was going to be evacuated at eight that night; the town was going to be evacuated at eight-thirty; the town was going to be evacuated at nine, but only if the wind shifted to the east. The forlorn fishermen gathered in the tackle shops exchanged rumors of their own. It was going to snow on Thursday and the season would be reopened; it was going to snow on Thursday, but the season *wouldn't* be reopened; it wasn't going to snow and the season wasn't going to be reopened and the fires would never stop burning and all of us might as well pack our fly rods and go home.

The strangest rumor concerned the West Entrance Road. Was it open or wasn't it? Some insisted yes, it was; others were equally adamant in saying no way. Since the West Entrance is approximately forty-five yards from the café in which this discussion took place, I decided—now that dinner was over—to walk past the sprinklers and take a look-see.

By some miracle it *was* open—the booths were manned by rangers just as on a normal day. The woman at the booth I stopped at didn't bat an eye when I asked for a fishing permit; she gave me the standard spiel about regulations, and before I quite realized what was happening, I was driving alone into the park along the Madison in a sunset that was starting a good three hours before it was due.

As it turned out, I didn't get very far. There in the opposite lane was a convoy of campers and cars being escorted out by rangers in jeeps; the scene, in the black-and-white haziness, reminded me of newsreels I'd seen of refugees fleeing the blitz-krieg in France. I still had no idea what they were doing letting people *in* at this time (I found out later the decision to open the West Entrance Road only lasted an hour or two); it was just one of those inexplicable windows of opportunity that open even in the messiest of wars. I drove about eight miles to the point where the land on either side of the road was blackened with smolder-ing embers, and there, open road or not, decided to stop.

I didn't go back right away; in fact, I did something I'm rather ashamed to admit: I put on my waders, tiptoed around the embers, let myself down into the cool Madison water, and began to fish.

West Yellowstone craziness had gone to my head. But irony, my nemesis, played a part, too. Having allowed me by a miracle into the park, it permitted me to advance only to a point on the Mad-ison that was, I found out later, notorious for its absence of trout. I cast for an hour or more, pleased to have the river to myself, taking mental snapshots of the bizarre, otherworldly scene, only a little disappointed the fish weren't rewarding my foolhardiness with the appropriate bravos. By the time it was dark I realized something I'd been hiding from myself all along: that I wasn't enjoying myself— that with men and women being ferried in behind me to fight this awesome, unknown thing, fishing for trout seemed, as it never had before, the idle occupation of the vain.

There comes a point on any trip that is as much psychologi-cal as geographic when you've gone as far as you're going and everything else is simply return. That roadside pull-off eight miles inside a burning Yellowstone Park was that point for me. From then on in, my trip was only a kind of mopping-up exercise and I traveled without expecting much at all.

Still, I gave it one more try. When I woke up in the morning I drove south into Idaho toward the Henry's Fork, making what had been the obvious move all along. The fishing season was still open there—the rumors all agreed on that. That I had postponed going down there as long as I had was only due to my fear that every other disappointed angler in Montana would be doing exactly the same thing.

And that's pretty much how it turned out. I drove past campground after campground of troops getting ready for another day of fighting fires in the south part of the park. Crossing the state line, I stopped at Lee's Ferry for a license; the man who sold it to me said he'd issued over a hundred on the previous afternoon.

I should have turned around right there. But I didn't—I drove to the "mailbox" just upstream of the famous Railroad Ranch, parked my car, suited up, then started the long hike into the river. It was a lovely morning, or at least it would have been if it wasn't for the smoke; if anything, it was even more biting and acrid than it had been farther north (and this was the day back in New York that people noticed an even stranger pall in the air than normal—the smoke from burning forests drifting eastward across the continent).

What's there to say about the Henry's Fork that hasn't been said before? It's beautiful water, set in a glorious vale, and once the sun warms the surface, the river comes alive with flies and rising trout. I didn't catch any, of course—no one actually *catches* a Henry's Fork trout. I took a certain amount of consolation in managing a rise or two. I took a great deal more consolation in seeing none of the other forty-three fishermen I could count from where I was standing catch one either.

Forty-three fishermen—the scene resembled a New Jersey trout stream on opening day. There were fishermen everywhere, not only wading, but riding along the riverbank on their dirt bikes, rods propped up on the handlebars like the bike-riding jousters in *A Connecticut Yankee in King Arthur's Court*. Every few yards they would pull over, put their kickstands down, hop into the river, cast, then climb back out and pedal on some more.

It was all rather interesting in its way. I hated it immensely.

I walked back to the car and drove toward Montana, my spirit pretty well broken. After a few miles I came to one of those places you see so often out West—a combination restaurant/motel/gas station/bar. I parked, went over to the phone booth, and in a few quick phrases made a reservation for a flight home the next day.

There didn't seem to be too much to do after that except eat lunch. At first, I was the only customer, but then three young fire fighters came in dressed in the green pants and soft yellow shirts I was beginning to envy. They were coming off the fire line for a reason I couldn't quite pick up; that they were tired and relieved was evident from their expressions. The two bearded ones were from Wyoming, and the thinner, slighter one, the one sitting across from them with eager, ash-ringed eyes, talking rapidly, was from somewhere in Utah.

"There's no turkey today," the waitress said, handing me a menu.

"Hamburger's fine," I said, handing it back.

To my left at the other table I heard the word *Jews*. I glanced around and saw it was the thin, beardless one who had said it. He was talking even faster now, caught up in his explanation.

"From Odessa, which is in the southern part of Russia. The Black Sea? That's where the Revolution began. Did you ever see the movie *The Battleship Potemkin?* They lived there and ran a shop that sold leather stuff. My grandparents. Do you know what a pogrom is?"

The huskier of the bearded men said he didn't know what a pogrom was.

"Mobs went around killing Jews and burning their homes. It had to do with rumors they spread about ritualistic killings. Jews were supposed to go around murdering children, and it was just an excuse to take their property. The czar encouraged it."

The waitress came back with my sandwich. "Pretty bad out there, huh?" I ventured.

"We're waiting on the wind," she said, with no inflection I could catch. "It blows from the east we're going to lose some stock. Already moved them twice."

"So they left," the young man said. "You know about the Lower East Side? In New York City?"

"We lost a mule back in July," the waitress said, wiping the hair back from her forehead. "Wandered too close to the fire, I guess."

"How did they get to Utah?" one of the bearded men asked.

"Tough," I said, shaking my head.

"They were afraid of cities. After the pogroms, all those walls. My grandfather wanted to live somewhere where there were no walls. No walls and lots of leather."

"Nobody tells us anything," the waitress said softly. "All we do is have to wait."

"Is a pogrom like the holocaust?" the second of the bearded men suddenly asked.

"I came out here to fish," I told her.

"Yeah," the thin one said, chewing away at his sandwich. "Like that."

"Tough," she said. "Pie?"

And so there we were, an odd enough quintet, the boys fresh back from fighting the apocalypse, talking in casual phrases of obscure destinies and ancient wrongs; the waitress with her stoic acceptance of tragedy that was just over the ridge now; me with my silly disappointment, a fisher of the absurd glutted with his catch—the five of us slumped there at the fag end of that summer of drought and ozone depletion and global warming and a burning Yellowstone Park.

The boys were still talking when I left. I envied them, and not for their shirts this time, but for their youth—for being immersed in the center of experience while I circled the edges coughing in the smoke. But if nothing else, before leaving I could get my belly full of that. I got in the car, rolled the windows down so it would stream right in at me, then headed north on the highway toward being forty after all.

July 2

Morning swim, six-thirty a.m. The fog so thick I have to thrash through it just to find the shore of the pond. Lots of surprises emerge from that fog in the course of the summer. Snapping turtles laying their eggs, bitterns slipping through the marsh grass, raccoons tidying up the picnic area, once—miraculously—three lovely campers taking their morning baths. I make a point of coughing to warn whatever's *in* there I'm afoot, but this time the only thing that materializes is Cider, my golden, whose nose has taken her on an elliptical orbit from our car to the beach.

It's amazing how much moral credit I get for these morning swims—to hear people talk, you'd think I was flailing myself with ice. And yet there does come a time, stripping off my sweatshirt, coming skin to skin against the fog, that my every instinct is to turn around, run back to the car, and turn the heater on full blast. The fog is generated off the pond's surface so fast, with such turmoil, it creates its own damp breeze, so there's a reverse double shock in braving it—that first chilly plunge through the mist, followed by a warmer slap into the water.

So I always hesitate. If nothing else, it gives me time to check out the fishy population of the shallows. Trout, bass, contented sunfish. The pond contains them all, and there's almost always a troller out there making the rounds. Me, I prefer not to, even though it's the nearest body of water to my house. This is neutral territory in my conflict with the piscine kingdom, a buffer zone between my resolute pursuit and their resolute fleeing, a watery Switzerland where both of us can swim without worrying about who is or who isn't attached to whom.

And yet a fisherman has been at work here already—a blue heron who, seeing me now, lets out a deep, halfhearted squawk of protest, pulls its legs into its body, and flip-flops those lazy wings away into the fog. He's left his breakfast behind—a rock bass that lies spinning on its side in six inches of water, the body folded back on itself like a target that's been drilled.

A feeding heron, a dead rock bass—this is the pond's natural order at work. Still, coming upon death so suddenly on a morning so tranquil adds a deeper chill to the mist, and I hesitate there on the beach longer than usual, trying to get up the nerve to plunge through the various layers of vapory indecision and metaphysical doubt.

Deep breath, flapping of arms, stutter step, plunge, double plunge, stroke stroke stroke! There's nothing graceful about my entry, but all the splashing and yelling dissipates the fog just enough for the horizontal admittance of a man and his dog. Out I swim, rolling on my back to stretch the morning stiffness out, flopping back over and digging in freestyle, working myself gradually up to top speed. Cider, who has two speeds, mine and double mine, turns on the jets and disappears after some surface-skimming swallows, her jaws chomping open and closed like a crocodile's.

The swallows have nothing to worry about—they enjoy leading her on. In the meantime, I'm swimming in what I hope is the direction of the eastern shore, navigating between strokes by quick glances at the branches of a dead elm up on shore. The fog hides everything except that. After a while, I hardly know whether I'm swimming in water or air, the horizon is lost to me, and the fog muffles even the dipping sound of my hands as they reach, cup, and pull. With the body so disoriented, the mind retreats, too, until it hardly seems *me* swimming there at all; I'm off somewhere imagining all this, irritated at myself for dreaming up a waterscape so featureless and gray. Time to turn around before I bump into something—in this thick nebulosity, it's the only thought that coheres.

And then it happens.

I'm retracing my course, swimming through the trail of foam left by my kicks, when—my head rolling underwater—an all but imperceptible wave of pressure comes against my eyes and causes them to open. There three feet to my left and slightly deeper than the surface, moving on a parallel course to mine, is a flash of something gold. I say "flash" and "gold" as if my mind had time to register these things, shape the experience into words, but what really happened happened so fast it was over before I had time to blink. Still, re-creating it now, I remember the movement and gold coming to me in one sensory packet, like a sheaf of sunlit rays—how the gold seemed so bright and happy I wanted to fasten on to it the way a child at Christmas wants to grab an ornament off the tree . . . how my left hand reached from my normal stroke in a greedy, grabbing motion that came sweeping down toward the golden bauble, and—fluttering the shape of it—just barely missed.

These things—and how, missing, I felt both an ineffable sadness and a sudden fear. I rolled over and started treading water, gasping, all but shaking, just in time to make out, disappearing through the fog twenty yards ahead, the square stern of a fishing boat trolling the treble-hooked spinner for which I had grabbed.

A narrow miss then—my skin could all but feel those barbs sinking in. But there was as much disappointment in my reaction as there was fear, and it's only now I can make sense of it. That sudden appearance of color in the colorless element in which I swam; the tactile *definiteness* of it in my haze; the envy created by a speed that was greater than mine; the curiosity it engendered, the longing that was far more impulsive than any hunger; the nostalgic compulsion of that possessive juvenile response, *mine*. Here I'd been all season trying so hard to figure out my *why*, I'd forgotten the fish's *why*, and suddenly I had it, in a demonstration that could hardly have been clearer, more dangerous or plain.

What makes a fish take a lure?

I know now. For one fleeting moment the fog dissipates and I *know*.

Golden Age

Picture this for a golden age.

Trout that are widespread and plentiful, flourishing in waters that are perfectly suited to their rapid growth. A growing number of flyfishermen with increased leisure time to pursue their avocation. The rapid development of lightweight tackle— new fly-rod designs that are much lighter and more powerful than anything seen so far; new and innovative fly patterns tied by fishermen with a deep understanding of aquatic life. A new conservation ethic that persuades even the lowliest trout-chaser he shouldn't keep all his catch, but must return some to ensure future propagation. Growing scientific interest in the species, with much that was left to hunch and instinct now being studied and described. A literature that celebrates the trout in all its splendor with a delightfully sweet lyricism that makes books on fly fishing the proudest body of writing on any sport.

Picture all this, then try to give it a date. Eighteen ninety-eight, when Henry Van Dyke was writing essays about little rivers and it was no trick at all for a beginning flyfisherman to take fifty Catskill trout in a short afternoon? Nineteen ten, when Theodore Gordon and George M. L. La Branche were developing techniques and tactics so fundamental that they are still in use today? Certainly in our great-grandfathers' day, the glories far enough away now that they've taken on a bittersweet patina and shine through the years like the afterglow from an extinct Valhalla.

But the funny thing about golden ages is that you never realize you're in the middle of one until the gold turns to rust. Change a single word in the opening paragraph and you have, in every particular except one, a perfect description of the situation that applies today.

Change the word *trout* to *bass*.

It's a simple change, but one with wide significance. Fly fishing for bass, so long the dowdy stepsister of fly-rodding for trout, is at last coming into its own. Next to me as I write is a catalog from a leading tackle house, and on its order blank are no less than fifty different fly and bug patterns tied exclusively for bass. Beside it is a recent issue of a fly-fishing magazine, with three articles on bass, each written at a high level of technical expertise. New graphite rods make casting bugs easier than it's ever been before, and tiers are creating flies that actually resemble what the bass eat. And while organizations like Trout Unlimited are doing wonders in preserving the trout's domain, the bass's range is scarcely threatened, and there are few places in this country where good largemouth or smallmouth fishing isn't available within a convenient drive.

But it is not what links these two golden ages that's important here, but what separates them. We have the fish and the tackle and the scientists, but there is one thing we don't have and it's a pity.

Where are the writers on bass?

I don't mean the lunker and hawg boys. There's a plague of these, God knows, each with their pet little theory to sell, each with their high-powered state-of-the-art user-friendly fishing reel and high-powered state-of-the-art user-friendly prose style. I mean instead the real writers, stylists who can compare with a Haig-Brown and Howard Walden from an earlier generation, or a Nick Lyons and Robert Traver from our own. It's not hard to make a list of people writing about bass with the same kind of originality, grace, and beauty these writers bring to bear on trout. The list begins and ends with a single digit: 0. The bass, for all its familiarity, is a noble fish, well deserving of a poet laureate, and instead it's held captive by a court of illiterate jesters tearing around in sinfully overpowered boats equipped with a thousand dollars' worth of superfluous gear.

The absence of a bass literature to compare with the trout's has several reasons, some obvious, some not. The tradition from which American fly-rodding stems is a British tradition, of course, and British, too, are its literary antecedents, with Izaak Walton as patron saint. Thus, right from the start the poetic trout was deemed a proper literary subject, while the humbler bass—unknown in England—was deemed, if not beneath contempt, at least beneath dignity.

Actually, bass fishing does have a patron saint, but he's a much different sort of man than Father Walton: Dr. James A. Henshall, M.D., he of the white walrus mustache and silver pince-nez. I have the ninth edition of his classic *Book of the Black Bass* in my collection—a beautiful copy, with a golden smallmouth embossed on the cover, and above it the famous motto that, like a catchy advertising jingle, made the bass's reputation: *Inch for Inch and Pound for Pound, the Gamest Fish that Swims.*

Henshall, writing at the turn of the century, makes no pretense of his intentions. "*The Book of the Black Bass*" he writes in his introduction, "is of an entirely practical nature. . . . It has been written more with a view to instruct rather than amuse or entertain. The reader will, therefore, look in vain between its covers for those rhetorical flights, poetic descriptions, entertaining accounts and pleasing illustrations of the pleasures and vicissitudes of angling which are usually found in works of like character."

So there we have it right from the start; Dr. Henshall rules that for bass, poetry is out of bounds. It's a Philistinism he doesn't always stick to—there are lovely passages in the book where the good doctor quite forgets himself and writes most lyrically—but for the main, he puts bass writing in the technical, how-to groove it remains in to this day. Along with this, he launched that other annoying quality that still infects so much bass writing: an obnoxious jingoism; a boosterism designed as a corrective to the trout fisherman's disdain, but which in the end becomes so established and ingrained it becomes a reverse snobbery of its own.

The Kentucky bait-casting reel didn't help matters either. Its perfection (and the perfection of the spinning reel a few decades later) pushed fly-fishing for bass to the periphery of the sport, and widened the divergence between the English lyric tradition and the new American technocratese. If the best way to catch largemouth was to throw a one-ounce River Runt Spook at them, then the person doing the throwing was less apt to pick up a book of fly-casting recollections by, say, Lord Grey of Falloden, and more likely to pick up *Sports Afield* to see what Jason Lucus had to say about plug weights. Thus, the would-be bass writer had no Eugene Connets to emulate, no A. W. Millers. That bass fishing could be a beautiful experience, a balm and restorative to the soul, wasn't macho enough to be admitted; what counted in bass fishing, right through the plastic worm/tournament era, was horsing in those hawgs.

Even the bass's prolificacy worked against him. While the trout stylists cherished their fish all the more because he was so threatened, bass writers could wallow in their fish's abundance and afford all kinds of sloppiness, not only in their conservation ethic (or rather their lack of one), but in their prose. The catching of one trout became a ceremony to be celebrated, while with bass there was no use talking about it unless you came home with a full stringer. An individual trout was thought of as a miracle; an individual bass as a statistic, so there's no wonder someone with talent and sensitivity preferred writing about the former.

But if there are compelling reasons why bass writing has never produced its *A River Runs Through It* or its *Upstream and Down* in the past, there is no reason why it may not do so in the future. For there are signs of hope. Fly fishing for bass is undergoing a tremendous resurgence of interest, as witnessed by all those new fly patterns, all those new tactics. Some of our best fishermen are beginning to realize that not only is fly-rodding a good way of taking bass, at some times and at certain places it's the *best* way. Every year around the first week of July, I have the same conversation at a boat landing near my home on the Connecticut River. A jump-suited bass man will trailer out his souped-up Ranger and allow as to how he's given up for the year, since the bass have gone deep where he can't get at them, even with his fish finder. I smile at this. All summer the small-mouth will be rising freely to bugs along the shore, and the finest surface fishing of the year is only just starting as the plas-tic-tossers give up.

The resurgent popularity of bass bugging is bound to result in new writing that comes from the flyfisher's unique perspec-tive—that is, from a perspective that combines profound curi-osity with deep respect. The new breed of bass writer will not be afraid to give us those "rhetorical flights, poetic descriptions" and "entertaining accounts" that Dr. Henshall so disdained—will instead glory in them and so produce a body of bass-fishing literature that can stand proudly against our best, most lyrical writing on trout.

What kind of literature will this be? I'm playing hunches now, but they're strong ones. It will be a literature with a remarkable geographic range, taking in not only glacial lakes in Maine and farm ponds in Indiana but swamps in the Louisiana bayou country and man-made impoundments in the Nevada desert. It will be a literature set on still water more than rivers, plains more than mountains, with perspectives that are those of expanse. It will be an aural literature, splashy with sounds. It will be a literature that is tangential, full of anecdotes; things *happen* in bass fishing, crazy things that aren't necessarily con-nected to the fishing. It will be a literature that is nostalgic for a simpler era without being maudlin—a literature that treats with respect the old wooden plugs and sparrow-sized bass bugs and boats that had to be rowed. It will be an extroverted literature, the focus being on the other fishermen in the boat rather than on the fisherman telling the tale. It will be, above all, a literature that is as pugnacious and brave as the bass itself, one that comes at you with unexpected leaps and cantankerous little flourishes and a great unquenchable tug of joy.

I think of the bass writing to come, and I think of two evenings last August when I fished a small mountain lake on the height of land behind my home. It's a clear, stony lake of the kind found in northern New England, complete with its resident loons and its osprey and its deer coming down to shore at sunset for a curious stare about. There are smallmouth in it, few very big, but possessed of a brightness and energy that do ample justice to the beauty of the scene.

Near the eastern shore is an old logging dam, and from its base extends a vast shallows of boulders dark and craggy enough to gladden the heart of a Robert Frost. I was in a canoe on that first night; for reasons I'm not sure of, I'd brought along a spinning rod with a tackle box full of ancient Bass o'Renos and rusty Jitterbugs I'd used as a boy.

About seven, just as the sun touched the mountain's shoulder on the lake's far shore, smallmouth started rising on all sides, so that within seconds the surface that had been completely placid was dimpled with interconnected, outspreading rings. The effect was that of a rainstorm with no rain—I held my palm out, expecting to feel drops. As it turned out, the bass were rising to a small white mayfly I'd never seen before, and totally ignored my meatier plug. Some were leaping free of the surface and not just sipping; there was something so startling and unexpected in the explosive way they shot clear, yet so fixed and regular in the parabola described by their reentry, that I began thinking of summer fireworks and not summer rain.

I was back the following night, this time with my fly rod and some small white Irresistibles that perfectly imitated the hatch. By the time I actually saw a fish jump it was too late to cast to him, but if I kept my line in the air and waited, I'd notice a rise a few feet away, and by dropping the line a few feet from *that* I could anticipate the bass's direction and so have him.

It was fishing of the most exciting and yet gentlest sort, and by the time it became too dark to see, the pattern of the catching had become mixed with the whistly gargle of the loons and the humming crickets back in the beaver swamps and the steady lap of water against the canoe's bow, so that it seemed I was reeling these in, too, and not just fish.

Thirty bass, thirty-five. I don't remember how many I caught and it's not important. What is was that sense of levitation—the feeling that all the smallmouth in the lake were devoting themselves that night to pushing the already airy surface even higher, so that the whole experience, myself included, floated a foot above the real lake in a magic realm where anything might happen.

That was your golden age for you, right down to the sunset, which—touching the far shore now—sent a ripple across the lake that transformed itself halfway across from a ray of magenta light to a pulse of cool wind that shivered me in absolute delight.

July 24

There's luck and there's luck.

A simple illustration. We're lucky to live a short drive from the picture-perfect village of Strafford, Vermont. Set in a valley where the fields are cleared and open in the old way, its dwellings little changed in appearance since the Civil War, the village boasts what my editor friend Tom Slayton likes to call the Chartres of Vermont—the immaculate white meetinghouse set high above the west side of the common. It also boasts, a short way down the common, one of the best bike-repair shops in New England. Me being the avid bike rider and mechanical illiterate I am, I'm lucky in this proximity.

The shop's proprietor is a multitalented, sophisticated man whose world encompasses a lot more than ten-speeders. Among other things, he's a devoted bird hunter, and I always make a point of asking him how the shooting's been while he prods and pokes my gears. He tells me a hunting story or two, I lie about the fishing, and the conversation is, I like to think, conducted on a plane of mutual curiosity and respect worthy of Piscator and Venator in Izaak Walton.

We're lucky to have a man like that around. As I was leaving his shop one day, Richard—who never loses faith in one's ability to surmount one's mechanical deficiencies—yelled after me this advice: "Try fixing that yourself next time! All you need is a number-eleven wrench!"

Right. But the advice was generously offered, and I filed it away in the list of things I must do someday. I drove the dozen miles home, parked my car near the village common, cut across the grass toward the general store, felt something hard crunch below my shoe, bent down, and discovered there in the grass a wrench—a wrench that, when I lifted it and brushed off the dirt, had the number *11* engraved on its stem.

That's *luck*.

Of course, there's bad luck, too, but even this has a way of turning in unexpectedly happy directions. This afternoon I managed to clear my desk off early and drive up to the Waits after too many days away. I went in by the cemetery stretch, waved on my way by the cheerful red-bearded farmer who works the adjacent farm—seeing me, he likes to hold his hands apart, tilt his head in a question mark, and laugh. This stretch of river is set well below the road and pretty much ignored, but since it's the upper limit of brown trout range, the lower limit of brookies, it's fun discovering which ones are currently in residence.

The brookies as it turned out. On my first cast a decent ten-incher took my Royal Wulff in the pocket along a fallen, water-scoured maple. I landed him quickly, released him into the current, and was heading upstream to the next pool when my wading shoes came against a mossy rock and I slipped. Slipped, not fell; in fact, it was hardly even a "slip" more than a quick readjustment in my posture from slightly tilted to fully upright. Unluckily, what tilted the most was the hand carrying my new Orvis graphite fly rod. The butt came down on the table-sized boulder next to me, and then, with a plastic sighing, separated out into its approximately 130 constituent strands.

Strands that, luckily enough, hadn't been severed. Always before when I've broken a rod, it's been at the ferrule where the break is dramatically complete. This time the filaments, separated on the latitudinal plane, were still connected on the longitudinal one; it was as if the rod had transformed itself into an eight-and-a-half-foot assemblage of black spaghetti. That it was three hundred dollars down the tubes bothered me, of course; what hurt even more was that, weaponless, my fishing trip was prematurely over.

So, alternatives time. Cast by hand? I've seen it done, casters whipping out line as dexterously as Indiana Jones, but only as a stunt. Not fish at all, wade upstream, do some "research"? Good idea in theory, but a flyfisherman without a fly rod is like a microbe hunter without a microscope, and it's my fixed belief that it is only *through* the delicate intermediary of the fly rod that we really focus our attention on a stream's life.

There was another alternative, the one I went for. Up in my glove compartment was some electrician's tape used to patch some earlier victim of my clumsiness. I tore off a piece, wound it as tight as I could from the grip to the ferrule, waved the mended rod back and forth in a mock cast, then took it back down to the river hoping for the best.

It cast. It didn't cast pretty and it didn't cast far, but it cast. That was the lucky part. The unlucky part was that when I rose the next trout, the response time—the time it took my upward-lifting impulse to be transmitted through the tape to what was left of the fiber—was so slow the fish was long gone by the time the line tightened. The same thing happened on the next pool upstream: another good fish, another slow-motion miss.

Well, I was *almost* there. What I needed besides the tape was a splint of some kind, something that would add rigidity—a branch, say. The moment I brought my head down to look for one—the very moment!—I saw something long and cream-colored on the bank: a kid's fiberglass fishing rod, the cheap kind that costs a few bucks in the five and ten, abandoned there who knows when, absolutely perfect—when broken in half—for my splints.

It was the work of a few seconds to unwrap the tape from my rod, graft in the added section of the kid's, and wrap the bastard-ized hybrid back up. I tried a cast, and the action seemed much stiffer than before, much faster. I waded up to the next pool, worked out as much line as I dared, and—holding my breath the entire time—hooked and landed a twelve-inch trout, the nicest brookie I'd taken all summer.

That's *luck*.

But even then it wasn't finished. If you fish the Waits much you'll hear stories about an eighty-year-old woman who divides her time between tending a tag-sale table outside her simple home and fishing the river every night just long enough to catch dinner for her cat. I'd heard about her from several sources, and though I'd kept my eyes open, six years had gone by and I'd never actually seen the fish lady in person.

I don't have to tell you what happened. Driving home that night, trying to decide if it was my unlucky day because of breaking the rod or my lucky day because of mending it, I saw a movement in the twilight near the river's edge . . . pulled the car over . . . and saw emerge from the alders a little stooped-over woman carrying a spin-casting rod, a worm bucket, two long trout, and—trotting behind at a respectful distance—a smug-looking Siamese cat.

I could all but feel the scale tip—LUCKY. Getting home late, I rushed right out to the barn and rubbed the totem responsible there in its bracket above the paint: my beautiful, well-tempered number-eleven wrench.

A River of a Certain Age

In shaking a life loose from the trivia of daily routine, airing it out in the open where there's a chance for perspective, there are at least two approaches. The first is to appraise everything you do with the eye of the twelve-year-old that lurks in each one of us, delight him or her by the actual immersion in an experience that as a child was only dreamed. The other is to look at that same experience from the opposite angle, from the old person we will all too soon become, and from that perspective savor every experience for the fleeting moment it really is. At forty, you're torn between both approaches—rewarding the kid in you for all that wanting; consoling the old man in you for all those regrets.

Because I realize this—because, forty myself now, I can begin to sense the shadows cast by even the most commonplace events—I have a hunch there are certain experiences that better be stored in memory right. Moments of love, moments of labor, moments of fun. Part of the delight in these has always been to think of my twelve-year-old self romping in an adult world of endless possibility, but increasingly, with this new prescience, I find the pleasure is apt to come from that other focus, of thinking how good this will all be summoned back in leisurely remembrance.

And so in the store of these last, knowing I'll need it, I would like to enter the following: a hot and sunny mid-June afternoon in any of the years 1982–90. I've spent the morning writing and managed to finish something I've struggled over for weeks. Now, with the long afternoon ahead of me, I'm sliding my green fifteen-foot Old Town Acadia canoe (remembrance delighting in specificity!) into a lazy-flowing river a short distance from my home. Into the canoe goes an extra paddle in case I drop one; a thermos full of cranberry juice; a frozen bottle of Guinness lager; a bag of ham and cheese sandwiches; an eight-and-a-half-foot graphite Orvis fly rod; an old Almaden wine box filled with extra bugs, flies, streamers, and leaders; and—most important of all for a redhead—a six-ounce container of number-twenty-eight Johnson & Johnson sunscreen.

And yes—myself, dressed in the khaki-colored pith helmet that makes my friends kid me about safaris, orange sneakers still damp from the last time I made this trip, and green hospital scrubs I was given the morning I was coaching Celeste in labor, and—coaching aggressively—my pants split down their seams.

Everything loaded? Fine, off I go. The water—cobalt and mysterious in the center of the river, startlingly clear in the six-foot-wide fringe along the banks—is flowing downstream at a slow but perceptible pace, the gates being open at the dam fifteen miles below. I see the motion first in the way the pale green weeds off the boat landing stream in that direction, then feel it as the canoe comes fully out into the current and takes on motion itself; the effect, in water so otherwise tranquil, is like stepping out onto a moving sidewalk that frees you of any obligation but to keep to the right and glide.

Motion first, then smells. Manure up on the banks—I look up to see some Holsteins tranquilly crapping as this horizontal apparition sails past. Honeysuckle blossoms lower down—a sweet wild smell that seems broadcast and exaggerated by the heat of the sandy banks. New-cut hay, an old favorite—in a field on the far shore a red tractor finishes its sweep and turns in a wide circle around. A water smell that's not of water at all, but of earth carried down from the tributaries upstream, held in suspension, so that the whole river, in an olfactory sense, seems an enormously long furrow turned in warm and fragrant soil.

When motion and smells drop into place—a hundred yards from where I started—I touch the paddle long enough to make the canoe drift closer to shore, then, like a man reaching out to measure familiar boundaries, I work out my line in a first cast. There are trees in the water here, old spruce that crashed from the bank in the high water of spring, and from the complicated archipelago of bark formed by their branches a silver twenty-inch pike comes up to devour my Sneaky Pete popper. He fights wildly, bizarrely, fleeing out into the river *away* from safety, and for a change the leader doesn't snap in his teeth and I manage to carefully land and defeather him. Beyond, in a smaller tree, is a monstrous rock bass, a brute of a sunfish, and a cast beyond him is a fat bluegill sunbathing above a sandbar, and here it is ten minutes since I left and I already have three good fish and I haven't even started trying for the species I've come for.

They're over on the New Hampshire shore where the banks become both steeper and rockier. I have one on almost immediately, then a second and a third—smallmouth bass, absolutely frantic with energy, and they prance and splash and dive like contestants in a swim meet whose winner depends upon my scoring. Bass by the mile—there's no end to them!—and they're in tight a few inches from shore where the overhang of branches makes the taking of them require just enough preciseness to make it interesting; preciseness, and yet the casts that bring fish fastest are the bad ones that rebound off the leaves into the water like vertiginous bugs.

The rocks give way to sandier, more barren stretches, but it's no trick at all to paddle a few times on the left and let the current glide me back over to Vermont. There are all kinds of rocks here—the Boston and Maine railroad tracks run right along the river—and basses twenty, twenty-one, and twenty-two are quickly hooked, fought, boated, and released. I'd like to think there are differences between New Hampshire bass and their Vermont cousins, the latter being less reactionary, more generous and fair, but they refuse to fit my political anthropomorphism, and fight with matching splendor, free of any cant.

A pause now—a low, barely perceptible disturbance in the river makes me think a beaver is about, but then the sound loses its liquid quality and becomes established as a definite rumble in the embankment to my right. A freight train approaches from the south, chugging slowly up the tracks with the cautious side-to-side wobble a dinosaur might display returning from extinction. I have a bass on, and with a little upward nudge from my rod he obliges with a jump just as the engineer leans out of the locomotive and waves. The engineer—God bless him!—blows his horn in salute, and between the vibration of the rocks and the shadows of the boxcars and the lonely hoot of the horn, the bass, train freaks all, really go nuts, so for many yards it becomes literally impossible to retrieve the popper without having a strike.

There's a cliché about catching so many fish your arm starts to ache, but it's no cliché because my forearm throbs now like I've played six sets of tennis, and I pull over into an eddy below some spruce to recuperate over lunch. When I'm trout fishing I eat abstemiously (like Cyrano de Bergerac, a grape and a macaroon), but when I'm bass fishing I like to wallow in all the fat and alcohol I can stand—for me, a piece of strawberry cheesecake and a single twelve-ounce beer. Finishing, I take a walk along the shallows near shore. The river mud is slick and treacherous, peppered with raccoon tracks, but it's cool on my bare feet, and above me the blue spruce shadows shimmy back and forth like fans.

The afternoon is much the same. More bass, more sunshine, more of that lush, pastoral landscape with which this valley is endowed. Six hours go by and I don't see another boat or another person, not even up on shore. This beautiful river, the splendid fish, and no one has caught on yet, not a single person! After a while it doesn't seem I'm drifting in a canoe at all, but riding the crest of a blossoming something, being lifted up by the life force's outspreading petal, and not a life force that's abstract, but one comprised of those leaping bass and darting swallows and the warmth exuded from the river's center. The feeling impresses itself so deeply—the feeling of abundance, of being able to dip my hands into a well of anything I want, fish, flowers, farmland, and sky—that it stays with me long after I leave the river, so for the entire night I feel gliding, uplifted, *borne*.

All these things, and then, with a long paddle home ahead of me, the breeze switches direction and blows my canoe back upstream with the effortless, stately propulsion of an emperor's barge.

The river I'm talking about here, the ribbon of experience that ties these memories together, is the Connecticut—the longest river in New England, and, on a June day like this one, the prettiest. Starting hard by the Quebec line in a pond hardly bigger than its name, Fourth Connecticut Lake, it flows south nearly three hundred miles through four states to the whitecaps and sandbars at its mouth in Long Island Sound. For most of its course the width stays remarkably constant—the width, to compare fair to foul, of a four-lane interstate highway complete with shoulders and median. And while narrow in one sense, the river is absolutely central, drawing upon a watershed that takes in well over half of New England. You can see this best from the air. Every intersecting valley from Canada south, every parallel hill, every ridge and fold, furrow and trickle, seems to have as its purpose one goal and one goal alone: to support and nourish the low silver line looping back and forth at its center.

So essential is the river to this region that whatever allegiance local people seem to have to a "place" is to what is called the "Upper Valley"—that corridor extending from Windsor-Claremont an indefinite distance upstream. There's much logic in this—a watershed forms a better natural division than a state, and people hereabouts have much more in common with Vermonters across the river than they do with people living beyond the hills in Concord, the state capital. And while valley dwellers can be susceptible to narrowness of focus, they seem increasingly willing to acknowledge a basic truth: that we live upstream of neighbors and downstream of neighbors and in this day of environmental interdependence, we're all in one valley together.

Just as the Connecticut is central to this region, it's central to our town, even though few who live here seem aware of the fact. The village itself is set a mile east of the river where its plain meets the first big hills; the town owns no land on the riverbank, there is no place to launch a boat, and it's my guess that the majority of townspeople have never ventured out onto its water even once in their lives. This includes our local fishermen. They will spend hour after hour trolling circles around our swimming pond for hatchery trout, while only a short distance away is one of the best wild-bass fisheries in New England, which is almost totally ignored.

This seems exactly opposite to how things should be. Meeting a neighbor casually on the common I'm tempted to begin every conversation with the query "How's the river today?"— make a ritual acknowledgment of its presence. Even apart from the fishing it forms the best wildlife habitat in town, though people hereabouts, for all the lip service they pay to "country" life, are too suburbanized in outlook to care much about that. When the town does notice the river it's usually to destroy it; there was a grassy knoll at the mouth of a tributary where fathers would take their kids fishing, but our local developer has seen fit to build himself a boathouse there, a monstrosity straight out of Disney World, and so the families can't go there anymore and another bit of riverine beauty is chipped maliciously away.

The town did not always ignore the Connecticut this way. In the years when the fields were all cleared many of the farmers would have been along the banks for the better part of a working day, and a good proportion of men and boys worked during the winter rolling logs onto the frozen river from cuttings up in the hills. There are pictures of crowds lining the bank in the spring to watch the log drives, which must have been the great event of the year. One picture shows them on the North Thetford Bridge (swept out in the ruinous 1936 flood, so only the classic stonework of its supports now remains), peering down in happy curiosity at some bedraggled river men standing wearily amid a logjam with their cant dogs and pikes.

The bridges were private in those days, crossed by paying a toll, and there's a story they tell from Civil War days about the town contingent of 16th New Hampshire volunteers marching away with a splendid send-off toward the railroad station across the river in Vermont. When they got to the toll bridge, the collector—a true Yankee—wouldn't let them cross until they paid their toll, thereby putting things like patriotism and martial glory in their proper place.

The last log drive was in 1927, and it's been years since the river was worked here. Upstream by the paper mill in Groveton you can still see traces of what it was like heavily used—tawdry and nondescript—and it's these mills starting at Saint Johnsbury that explain in part why our town has so relentlessly turned its back on its essential geographic fact. Pollution—the filth that once made cynics call the Connecticut "the most beautifully landscaped sewer in the world."

There's an irony here—thanks to the heroic labors of river advocates, the Connecticut is being cleaned up. But the cleaner it gets, the more people find their way to its water, and what was once spoiled by sewage now becomes spoiled by fleets of power-erboats and homes built too close to the banks. It's the familiar

American paradox—neglect or crush, neglect or crush, with no possibility of a sensible in-between.

I've strayed a long way from that perfect June afternoon. But it's one of the characteristics of big rivers that anything puny tends to get swamped, and I suppose measured against the weight of those 250 miles, all the dreams and defeats of the human landscape through which this water runs, my own moment of quiet enjoyment forms barely a molecule. Rivers flow two ways, at least the big ones, and even here in rural New Hampshire the Connecticut carries the sense of Springfield's concrete and Hartford's sprawl and all the various forms of ugliness and indifference to be found from here to the river's mouth.

Big river. I can all but hear the snort of contempt from those who know really big rivers—in Mississippi terms, the Connecticut is an irrigation ditch for watering the cows. But there are other ways for a river to be big besides size—big in history, big in spirit—and in these measures, the Connecticut, New England's locus, has always been world-class.

And even if it wasn't, in my mind, on my own personal scale of river size, the Connecticut would still rank as big, and for a reason I'm reluctant to admit: I'm afraid of it. In the narcotic lull of that perfect June afternoon, fishing late on moonlit summer nights, casting for bass in September's bayou-like fog. Nine tenths of me is aware of nothing but sheer joy in being out there, but that last tenth, the wary, too-imaginative tenth, is vaguely waiting for the river to pounce.

There, I've said it: big rivers are the ones that make us scared.

Part of me is afraid of the Connecticut, though I'm not even sure what it is that makes me feel this way. There are objective dangers of a kind here. The dam down at Wilder backs up the river a distance of forty miles into a long and very narrow lake; unlike most lakes, there is no gradual drop-off from shore—six feet out, you're in water over your head. Deep, the river stays colder longer into spring, so even in June, a capsize can spell trouble. Not too long ago a canoe was found floating empty here, it's owner, a champion white-water racer, discovered drowned a good distance downstream. Similar things are always happening—the Connecticut seems to have the evil knack of taking the young, gifted, and strong.

What's more, the Connecticut *looks* dangerous, at least up close. There are logs in the water, the heavy business ends two-thirds submerged in the sardonic manner of alligators and icebergs; chunks of collapsed bank with those bad-looking sweepers; weed beds whose strands are so long and oddly tropical they could be the abode of man-eating clams; enough pollution, on rainy days, to turn the river a shade too brown. Added to these is a haunted quality that gives the sensation you get on a man-made lake created over an abandoned village—the sense you're floating over a vanished epoch and can all but hear the ancient fiddles tuning up for a ghostly dance. Rural self-sufficiency, pastoral isolation. What was here is no longer and never will be again—the Connecticut knows this, and there's something resonant in the riverscape that can send a frisson of regret down the neck of even the dullest.

But I think in the end what my fear stems from is the reading of another message the river is constantly doing its best to transmit: that harnessed and tamed as it is, reduced from its wild glory, a Samson in chains, it still aches to burst loose from its channel, regain its freedom, destroy the dams, and until the day that happens, it will erode a bit, haunt a little, wreak its vengeance on one unfortunate canoeist at a time.

The Connecticut, then, is a channel of secret beauty running through the plain of everyday—a suggestive layer of remembrance superimposed over our amnesic age. The exploration of its riches should be enough to fill up the leisure hours of even a non-introspective man, and yet in my case—God forgive me!—it is not. Like a boy reaching into a cereal box for the toy at the bottom, I ask more from the Connecticut than just the spiritual nourishment that comes with silence, scenery, and space: I want, want even desperately, a prize.

Smallmouth bass. It's their inhabitance that fascinates me, their pursuit that lures me out. The river is full of them here, fish that take on the same green-gold darkness as the water, so you can say of them what Thoreau said of Walden's pickerel, that they seem the "animal *nuclei*" of the river—Connecticut "all over and all through." Not large in the average, they more than make up for it with the spirit in which they fight. We're talking strong fish here, wild fish, and they react to the curtailment of their liberty with more instinctive rebellion than almost any creature that exists. Their huge indiscriminate mouths (smallmouth is only a relative term), the flexible armor of their gills, their squat fullback bodies, and the muscular spring of their hurdler's tails—these are fish that are superbly equipped to eat, run, and jump, and to be fastened to one for even a few seconds is to feel plugged into the life force at its maximum voltage.

When I moved here I was slow to find out just how good the bass fishing was. There were trout streams to fish, ponds to explore, and it wasn't until my third summer that I began trying to understand what the Connecticut was all about. Even then, I did most of my early fishing with spinning tackle and plugs, and I soon got bored with the assembly-line monotony of that kind of fishing. It was only when a friend gave me a fly rod heavy enough for serious bugging and a tackle box crammed full of poppers that I began to find the proper methodology—began to see how the disciplined ethic of fly-fishing I'd managed to teach myself over twenty years of chasing trout could be expanded to take in this new kind of river, this different kind of fish. Spin casting is casting *at* a fish, but fly casting is casting *to* them, and the difference, small as it sounds, is enough to elevate a recreation into a craft.

The fly rod is an epistemological tool the wielding of which gains us entry into a river's life—this is just as true on a slow-moving bass river as it is on a freestone stream. On the latter, with long experience and if things go right, fly-fishing can give you the feeling that every secret in the river is potentially graspable, all it takes is a little more care, a little more sharpness. On big rivers like the Connecticut, the knowing is much more tentative; with our casts covering so small a proportion of the total water, it's like chipping away at a secret with a chisel. And while bass fishing is invariably compared to trout fishing without either being particularly illuminated, I find the two fishings, these two ways of knowing, complement each other perfectly. There is a quality to trout fishing that doesn't bother me while I'm at it, but which I become aware of when I'm fishing for something else—something cramped in it all, the necessarily small scale (at least here in New England) of fish and river size, and the corresponding mind-set of fitting ourselves into something thus circumscribed. On the Connecticut, with no trees to entangle backcasts, with the views extending far in every direction, with the potential, especially in the backwaters, for seriously large fish, I'm aware of being released somehow—of exercising that part of me that finds joy in expansion, power, and force. Anyone who alternates between freshwater and saltwater fishing will know what I'm talking about here—how refreshing it can be after delicate casting to put all your strength into a powerful rod and really start to *haul*.

Sloppiness comes as a relief at times, in fishing just as in life. River bass are earthy fish, generously forgiving, and if you have the time and place down right, they will overlook a certain exuberance in your method. Here in the Connecticut their abundance is such that you're almost certain to find one who's in the mood for whichever fly you're using, be it a swallow-sized Dhalberg Diver, a moth-sized Bass King, or a streamer with eight inches of marabou trailing backward over the shank. There are just enough contaminants in the water (as if I'm praising them!) that people are reluctant to eat their fish, and so release them; with this, the coolness of the water, and the extensive cover, catches of twenty-five or thirty bass are common, at least in early summer. By August they're lazier, but bigger, and there always seems to be a spurt in September when the largest fish of the year become susceptible to yellow Woolly Worms jigged close to shore. But this is only a general trend. There are days even in August when some trick of rain or temperature will produce daytime fishing every bit as fast and exciting as June's.

The Connecticut, generous as it is, has certain peculiarities as a bass fishery, and anyone fishing my stretch of river will have to come to terms with these before getting into the heavy catches. Backed up by the dam as it is, with the dropoff so sudden, the fish hang in tighter to shore than any fish in any water I know. The cover is there—the bankside rocks and protective blowdowns—and between these, the availability of crayfish on the sandy bottom, the insects falling off the overhanging trees, the relative warmth of the sunny "shallows," the nearness of deep-water safety, you get a fishery that, in essence, isn't much wider than a small mountain brook. Many times, in fishing this strip, I've had the uncanny feeling I wasn't fishing water at all, but dry land. One of the most effective casts is to drop your popper on the rocky shingle, then pull it abruptly into the water. Six inches from shore may mean water two feet deep, and the bass, with excellent visibility, will often take the fly before it travels even a millimeter farther. How *far* they will come is something that varies tremendously from week to week; early in the season they seem to shy away from leaving the bank at all, but later in the summer they will often trail a lure ten yards and more, and the biggest have the trick of taking just as you're starting your next cast.

There are other peculiarities. Unlike the bass lakes only a few miles away, Connecticut fishing seems to improve in direct proportion to the thermometer, so the hotter it gets the faster the bass feed. This has it limits, of course. We had a heat wave last year that was either one of those unpredictable bumps in the weather pattern or a foretaste of what global warming will do to our summers. In either case, it pretty much put an end to the fishing by early July. But in most years the hot weather brings the fish up, particularly at the beginning of a season or the finish. Conversely, a cold front is enough to spoil the fishing for a day or two; on those crisp, invigorating days of northwest wind, I leave my canoe on the lawn and head for a trout stream instead, finding—after all that wide-open athleticism—the delicate preciseness to be just what I need.

There's the weather to take into account, and there's the tide—the daily rise and fall of the water level as the gates are opened at Wilder Dam fifteen miles to the south. The usual pattern is for the river to be at its highest in the morning, then to start dropping as the power demand peaks with the heat of the afternoon, rising again in the evening. Depending on the weather, the range can be extreme; I've seen mornings when the river seemed an inch from flooding over its banks, afternoons when there were mud flats along shore littered with sunburnt crayfish. And while I've spent many hours trying to find the link between these fluctuations and the fishing, I've never come to any conclusions I have much faith in. Is the fishing best when the water level is highest, offering more cover? Not particularly. Is it better at dead low, when the fish have fewer places to hide? No, I don't think so. If anything, it seems best at slack tide—the water neither too high nor too low, with perhaps just a suggestion of a downstream current.

Lures? I'm tempted to say any standard bass popper will do, but there's one so superior it deserves special mention: the chartreuse Sneaky Pete. Small and bullet-shaped, with long spidery legs and a pert, feathery tail, it takes more and bigger bass than any other lure I've tried ("Did you catch them on Sneaky Pete, Daddy?" my three-year-old daughter will ask the moment I come home). What's more, it casts well, not like those heavy bass bugs that make you feel, hauling it out there, that you and your lure are traveling in different time zones. You could fish exclusively with Sneaky up on top, pack along a few Woolly Buggers or Zonkers for times when they're deep, and be set for anything.

But careful here. Whenever I start to offer advice this way I feel the same flush of arrogant guilt I experience whenever I talk about technique in fiction—as if anyone can take something so magical and reduce it to formulas! There are general parameters for bass fishing, hunches and intuitions, but no rules. And whereas in trout fishing the tactics are so complicated and structured that for many fishermen method serves as its own reward, in bass fishing a much more pragmatic ethic is at work: the goal is to get out there and get some fish.

And what fish! Much more delicate than their lake-dwelling cousins, they have the knack of sipping in a popper so quietly you'd swear it was being attacked by a bubble—delicately, but once the line tightens all hell breaks loose, as if by some thermal bassy reaction their fastidiousness has been transformed into sheer bravado. Up they go exploding from the water, then submarining down into the depths, then skyrocketing upward again, this time out on the other side of the canoe, *kapowie!* . . . Well, as you can see, it's practically impossible to write about smallmouth without falling into a pinball-machine, italicized kind of prose (just as it's impossible to talk about them without wiggling your hand back and forth like a Spitfire pilot at a debriefing). They deserve better from a writer, much more lyricism and grace, and my literary resolution holds fast until I have one on the end of my line again, and then . . . *Zap! Zap! Powie!* Up they go! It's a great fish to catch on a fly rod, but a lot harder one to capture in prose.

It's odd to think how many of the happiest moments of my life, literally the happiest, have been spent chasing these feisty little bombshells with the squat, take-it-or-leave-it kind of name. The time I took my father out on the river one morning shortly after the birth of his granddaughter; how instead of our usual skunking we caught fish after fish, and my father's face lit up in surprise, wonder, and delight. Celeste and I out in *Bismarck*, our toy inflatable boat; how we caught not bass but one of those fringe benefits you often come across in pursuing bass, a walleye, a big four-pounder that towed us a good hundred yards along shore. Celeste again, this time reeling in a perch only to have a monstrous pike appear from the weeds to sever it in two. Owls, a whole parliament of them, barn, screech, and short-eared, twisting their necks around to watch us at twilight until you'd swear they were about to come unscrewed. All the flotsam and jetsam the river carries, finding among the half-submerged cornstalks Frisbees of all sizes and lollipop colors; Frisbees from new pizza shops opening in villages upstream, Frisbees left behind after river picnics, Frisbees lost in the water by teary-eyed kids—a whole river of Frisbees! The covered bridge at Clay Brook; how one July evening fishing alone in the endless dusk, I thought of writing a short story about a fourteen-year-old boy who must choose between the girl of his longing and the bass of his dreams. All these things, and where did they come from? The intense delight I find in spending a few seconds attached to a smallmouth bass.

We started out on the river this trip, stayed there for the most part, and we'll soon finish where we began—there in the sunlight catching fish. In a fraternal way I hope I've explained, the Connecticut has been my silent partner in these episodes, so when I come home at night it's not with the feeling that an "I" has caught these experiences, but this much more essential, satisfying "we."

Me and the Connecticut, brothers unto death. It's the kind of feeling a big river leaves in you, the endless downstream flow of it being such an obvious metaphor for time's own inevitable rhythm. Here in New England this note is played even more explicitly than it is elsewhere. Thinking back on its history, remembering the Puritans who settled here with their burden of piety and guilt, it's hard not to picture New England being born old, and living through the centuries, not toward senescence but toward a much delayed and much welcome youth.

And maybe this explains the fellow feeling—that here at the end of the twentieth century, the Connecticut River has at last reached a mature middle age, and so it's no wonder I identify with its complicated intermingling of freshness and hope, pollution and neglect—those alterations between wild surges of energy and lazier, more introspective driftings. *Old Man*, Faulkner called the Mississippi, but it's different on the Connecticut, and if either of us, river or man, is headed toward old age, I'm the one, and the Connecticut—cherished, protected, valued as the irreplaceable treasure it is—is on its way toward a well-deserved youth when it will flourish as the centerpiece of the first region in America that puts aside greed as the only ethic and ugliness as the only aesthetic and recovers this beautiful wonder world that on first try we spoiled.

Or so I hope. Me, I'm headed the opposite way, but that's all right—as long as the river flows in that direction for me, and for a few hours now and then I can float along with its current and gain vicariously my own small measure of renewal and hope.

October now, and the bass have long since gone to their deep-water haunts, but then a day of warm and radiant sunshine makes me take the canoe down from the loft of our barn, where I've already stored it for the winter. A quick gathering of rods and tackle, a note for my wife, a drive down the mountain, and out onto the Connecticut I go.

The river is full of leaves, leaves of every size, shape, and color, from vivid gold to impeccable green, the preponderance being double-pronged pine needles of burnt yellow pointing like delicate arrowheads downstream. It's no trick at all to align the canoe so it drifts parallel to this autumnal procession. My fly sinks between leaves and shore, hangs there in the thick sunlight like a jewel set in honey. Seconds go by, I'm just about to twitch it, when a bass separates itself from its own exaggerated shadow there by the rocks, lured by the same sun that's lured me. The moment I see him I realize his attention is focused on something in the water, and the moment I realize that something is the streamer the streamer is disappearing, and the moment I realize disappearance and bass have some essential interconnection there's a jolt as the fish takes hold, and then he's soaring through the air, higher and higher, up over the rocks, up over the banks, up over the spruce trees into the realm of sky-colored remembrance where, if I'm lucky, if I ease off on the pressure and don't pull too hard, he will never, not in a dozen years, not in a hundred, come down.

August 13

Summer ritual is a sacred thing, but nowhere more than on Cape Cod. We've come down this weekend for a badly needed fix of sand, sea, and sky—for these, and to touch bases with the much-loved traditions of summers past.

Arriving at our friends' house shortly after breakfast, we're immediately taken on the rounds. The garden to see the state of the corn, the deck to see how far David's extension has proceeded, the aquarium to see John-David's periwinkles, the kitchen to see the crabs Katherine has shredded for a lunchtime salad. Finally, after we've seen everything else—after the summer's adventures and misadventures have been quickly chronicled, to be elaborated upon and embroidered that night over dinner—we're taken down the oak-covered bank to see the biggest surprise of all. There, nestled comfortably against the weathered dock, a spanking new eighteen-foot Boston Whaler, heavy spinning rods mounted in the gimbals, silver gaff propped behind the steering wheel, green landing net—sized for whales—fluttering limply over the flagpole in the stern.

John-David, at twelve, has the fishing bug and has it badly. It's good to watch him caught up in it—to see myself in the obsessive way he ties and reties knots, his agonized indecision when it comes to lures, the importance attached to wearing just the right kind of battered straw hat . . . better still to watch his dad bring to this the same kind of patience, bewilderment, and grace my father brought to my own equally dogmatic boyhood fussings.

Sandwiches packed? Plenty of juice? How's the gas? The nonfishers come down to see us off, and for a time there's enough excitement and merriment on the side of the dock to see off the QEII. Our boasts become mixed with their best wishes, then the water is separating us, until finally all that can be heard is the hoarse bark of the family Chesapeake, in despair at being left behind, and we're on our way down the pond, ducking our heads as we go under the low causeway that crosses the inlet, then standing straight again, grabbing onto the side rails as the boat comes bow-first into the choppy waters of Vineyard Sound.

David sets a course alongshore in the smoothest water, but even so, we're in for a good bumping. Out to port is the Vineyard; "like a low smoky cloud," I once described it in a story, but today the haze is blown away and the cloud has become a felt-tipped line of green and tan.

It's nice to play guest for a change, have someone else be in charge of figuring out where the fish might be. Father and son confer over the sound of the motor, decide we're best off in the lee of Nobska Lighthouse toward Wood's Hole. Fine with me—some of the best moments of my life have been spent in and around that busy harbor, and bouncing off it in a small boat is the one perspective I haven't tried.

Any doubt we have is overcome by the sight of gulls and terns sniping at the water off a buoy-marked reef straight out from the Steamship Authority pier. Baitfish are everywhere— they shoot across the surface like silver darts. David brings the boat up to where they're thickest while John-David and I ready our rods. Three or four other boats have raced out from Eel Pond, attracted by these same birds. We form a ring around them—these fish are surrounded!—and in between casts glance around to see who wins this instant, undeclared derby and catches the first blue.

Woods Hole is an interesting enough place to fish, what with ferries coming in from the islands, a fleet of yachts running past, the tide that springs furiously between Buzzards Bay and the Sound. These are all fairly routine, of course, but then the *Oceanus* comes out, the Oceanographic Institute's famous research vessel bound who knows where, and cradled in the stern, its name clearly legible, is the *Alvin*, the homely submersible that found the *Titanic*. To a rube used to fishing the quiet places of the country, it's all quite a show, and it takes the hard, vicious strike of a blue-fish to recall me to the water.

It's a modest blue, two pounds at the most, and nowhere near as big as the twelve-pounder John-David landed earlier in the

summer. But still, it's the only fish taken, and upholds the unde-
served reputation I have after writing a fishing book or two.
We bounce around some more, try spots closer in toward shore,
then, with not much cooking, turn around and race back along
the beaches toward home.

Later that evening, reading the paper, we learn we're not the
only ones to have gone blue fishing on this perfect August day.
Down in Maine, the president has been taking out his power-
boat in the hopes of getting some fish. The papers have been
keeping score; to date, it's seven vacation days for the president
with not a single blue landed or hooked.

The president, questioned about this, has an excuse. Is it a
knowledgeable explanation of bluefish migratory patterns, a
normal fisherman-type rationale, a shrug at the wrong kind of
weather or the fickleness of fate? No, not at all. The president,
having used "environment" as a buzzword during his election
campaign, having tried his hardest to open the Gulf of Maine
to offshore drilling, having done everything he can to sabotage
international efforts to come to grips with global warming and
the devastation of acid rain, having placed people in charge of
this country's wilderness who are dedicated exploiters of that wilderness, having, in short, done everything he possibly can do to
destroy the natural world in which the bluefish swims, now voices
his displeasure at not catching one by blaming the press boats,
which, in his words, "Come too close and scare the fish away."

I feel bad for the president. But not to despair; two days later,
on the last afternoon before he's due to return to Washington,
he manages to catch a solitary bluefish, which is then held up for
the despised press to record on film.

It's an angry-looking fish, like all blues, but seems angrier
than most I've seen, even in death; it's sharp bullet mouth is

drawn back in a contemptuous sneer toward the aging man that lifts it. Perhaps it's my imagination at work here, but I see that bluefish as heroic—as the agent of the natural world the president and his cronies have declared war on in their greedy crusade . . . a fish sent on a suicide mission to penetrate the circle of Secret Service boats and press launches and the barges of the president's flunkies—to penetrate and deliver to the president as it's removed from the hook a sharp nip on the hand. Not a fatal nip—nature is too generous for that and there are laws forbidding anything greater—but just enough to make him pay attention.

Did it succeed? Well, in the newspaper pictures the president looks just as inattentive as ever. But it's a sign of rebellious stirrings, a straw in the wind, and makes me feel better about the future of this country than I have in a long time.

Glory and honor onto you, O noble blue!

Two Places Well:
Notes from the West Highlands

That Scotland has a secret becomes apparent to any traveler driving north from the Great Glen. The way the landscape is held back under the serene mist, the hills with their convoluted folds and cloud-draped summits, the open heather that both exaggerates distance and diminishes it, the one-track roads that seem to swallow up cars, literally erase them, the abandoned crofts with their missing roofs, the odd sensation, all but unique on this overcrowded planet, of being in a place that for two centuries has been losing population. It's a secret kept by offering so many possibilities it's impossible to determine which holds the key. Not for nothing is Loch Ness situated in the Highlands—this is a place where surfaces, alluring as they are, only make you want to plunge deeper to grasp what's beneath.

It's a familiar note to any New Englander, at least one who can remember the old days before the interstates when the abandoned hill farms and overgrown meadows suggested both a great loneliness and a great calm. Montana would be the closest you could come to it in the States today—that high, sky-drenched plateau fit for ruminants and ruminators, philosophers and sheep.

Introspection, of course, can be a troublesome thing. There are those who hate the Highlands, hate the way the hills seem to offer something they immediately—the weather being what it is—take back. There are still others who are sensitive to these moods, but vaguely afraid of them; the endless gift shops with their tartan plaids and heather sprigs and shortbread tins seemed designed just for them. "My God, Willa, will you look at that sunset!"

"Yes, Donald, but shall we bring Alice home the porridge or this box of Edinburgh Rock?"

But not to laugh at these tourists—the emigrant Scots among them are homesick, the Sassenachs merely confused. Even someone sensitive to landscape has a tough enough time of it here. The weather and terrain change so fast it's possible to read into Highland scenery any conclusion you want. Life is this, life is that, and so many in-betweens it makes you dizzy.

So much weight for a land so small! But it's exactly the West Highlands' charm, this association of opposites, the intimate grandeur, this cozy expanse. Take the road south along the coast from Ullapool and you'll see what I mean. There to the right is the ocean, wild and cold-looking; there to the left, mountains even wilder and colder; in between along the roadside, a jungle of lush rhododendron that seems lifted from Henri Rousseau. Better yet, screw up your courage and drive the Pass of the Cattle inland from Applecross farther down the coast, glancing up at the scenery in those brief intervals when the road straightens from its switch-backing descent. Hills on one side, sea on the other, lochs in between, the three elements repeated in endless superimpositions of color, line, and plane.

And if the land is dense in scenery, it is even denser in history, so that the past in Scotland is as exposed and palpable as the heather and rocks. These human associations are always poignant, often tragic—too many seem to memorialize farewells. The plaques in village kirks commemorating soldiers dead in foreign wars; those shortbread tins showing Bonnie Prince Charlie bidding a respectful adieu to Flora Macdonald; the marker indicating the spot Mary Stuart left Scotland on her way to being axed; the emigrant ports with their sad reminders of the Clearances, when crofters were forced off the land by their lairds to make way for sheep. . . . Travel through these glens and you're never far from a goodbye that was forced.

Clearance, war, emigration, neglect—such has been the Highland lot since the Jacobite insurrection and the bitter Culloden defeat. Bad enough in the past, there is a new round of clearances under way today, the so-called "Second Clearance" as the current lairds (who when it comes to insensitive greed could teach American developers a thing or two) clear the sheep off the hills in order to plant more profitable spruce.

The one who would know about this cycle best—the man around whose bronze shoulders the secret of Scotland seems to drape—stands with an old model Lee-Enfield rifle on the outskirts of Glenelg, his kilted legs planted firmly on the pebbly marge of the shingle, his mustached face, tarnished by salt water, looking out toward the mountains of Skye across the narrow, whitecapped Sound of Sleat. He stands there for a reason—to commemorate the final chapter in the Scots diaspora, the half-forced, half-voluntary emigration to the trenches of Flanders and France in what is still known in the Highlands as the Great War.

Never was a statue better placed. Remote, solitary, its loneliness set against scenery that is almost unbearable in its perfection, it evokes as no words can the tragic loss of those years 1914–18, when the Highlander, the man who had withstood all history could throw at him, was all but destroyed as a separate proud being by the wicked expediency of Maxim machine guns and coiled concertina wire.

Glenelg is neither an easy place to find nor to drive to—it's as if to approach the statue you must first traverse enough Highland landscape that it settles deep into your understanding. The stoic and bitter—these are plain enough in the erect way the soldier stands there, the simple inscription on the plate. But there's beauty in it, too, the other half of the secret, and if you stand there long enough, waiting for that slow summer sun to get below the Cullins, you'll see the secret toward which everything in the Highlands seems trending—the dark bittersweet shadow of a place history has blessed by leaving behind.

I visited Glenelg last year, spent my hour at the base of the statue, then wandered down to the water to see if I couldn't skim a rock all the way to Skye. Celeste was with me—I had spent the first years of our marriage attempting to describe to her the beauty of the Highlands, deciding in the end the only way to do it was to let her see for herself. And though we spent a lot of time at it, we weren't there simply to define what it was we found so alluring in the landscape, but to actually immerse ourselves *in* some. For the first half of our trip this meant climbing, or as they more correctly call it in this part of the world, "hill walking." We'd gone up Lochnagar from the Spittal of Glen Muick on a brutally hot afternoon, and had been rewarded at the top by a view of the famous Black Spout gully and the silvery lochan nestled below its sheer walls. We hill walked around Glencoe, too, getting lost just long enough in a snow squall to be able to laugh about it later as we nursed some Courage in a Fort William pub.

Now here we were in the West Highlands turning our attention from hills to trout lochs—the lochs that had, on my earlier visit, both enchanted me and, having neither the time nor means to fish them, tormented me as well. We made our base at the fishing lodge in Shieldaig near Gair loch; situated right on the ocean, they have the rights to the fishing on a dozen hill lochs scattered back a good ten miles inland.

It's beyond expectation that a place that suits me so well in every other respect should have trout in it as well. The Highlands are full of fish, browns brightly colored and wild. Such is their abundance that bags over a hundred are not uncommon, at least up in Sutherland, and nobody thinks the worst of you for keeping all you want. Add to this the salmon rivers, sea trout streams, and hill burns, not only on the mainland but in the Hebrides, the Shetlands, and Orkney, and you have a place where the fly-fishing opportunities are endless. Read the Brit fishing magazines (which are wonderfully chatty and specific compared to ours), and you can get a quick overview of all this and the names of generous fishermen who are more than willing to help you with advice.

This was my first experience of British fishing, and I was more than a little intimidated by what I'd read of its tradition. Wasn't this where you were guilty of terribly bad manners if you used anything besides the fly the trout were actually taking? Where people called river "keepers" lurked behind the box-berry, the better to catch you out? Where—for all I knew—you were expected to bow to other fishermen you passed, or maybe not bow at all, but put your nose up in the air and snort, "Good nymphing, what?," failing which you were taken off the water and expelled to the rude place whence you came?

Maybe this is so in England, but up north in the hills there's a more relaxed ethic at work. In the Shieldaig lodge's lobby is a list of all the lochs, and you pick out one that's free, write your name down beside it, help yourself to the keys to its rowboat, and you're in business. Arriving late in the afternoon as we did, we were too late to bid, but this was no problem either; Colin, the lodge's owner, explained we were free to fish any loch we wanted, as long as we cast from shore and didn't use a boat.

Fine. I put our rods together, Celeste grabbed her pack, and into it we stuffed gammon sandwiches put up by the hotel's chef, some scones, and—the pack having just enough room—a bottle of white Hungarian wine.

We decided to try the closest loch first. It's an uphill two-mile walk, and we took our time with it since the sun was as bright and hot as it had been our entire trip (at dinner that night the other fishermen complained bitterly about the weather being *too good*). Spring lambing was over, and the lambs were every-where—they were just old enough to leave their mothers' sides, but would stumble back in confusion the moment they saw us. Somewhere along the way

I glanced down at my watch; it was four on the button, and to prove it the watch cuckooed.

It wasn't the watch, of course, but a real cuckoo, whose call, though we'd heard it often on our walks, we still couldn't convince ourselves was real.

"It's over there," I said, pointing.

Celeste listened with her head tilted. "No, further away. Over . . . there."

"It could make you cuckoo playing this game."

"Cu-kooo. Cu-kooo." This from the bird.

The loch, once we got there, was larger than I'd pictured, the size of water that would have been crowded with cottages back home. Here, there was no sign of any human presence, nothing except a rowboat on the far shore with a solitary flyfisherman whose rod, enlarged by the sun, lay tilted like a stirrer in a punch bowl of gold.

I was worried about the fishing-from-shore business, but there were no trees here, nothing but heather, and when it came to backcasting room the sky was literally the limit. On my second cast, a brown came up from the peat-colored depths, curled its body around the fly, then—just when I thought he had missed it—came tight against the line. He wasn't big, perhaps half a pound at the most, but even from the distance I could see the butter-crimson blend of his color, and he fought in an exuberant, bulldogging manner reminiscent of smallmouth bass.

I caught three more after that; initiated, I rock-hopped along shore to where Celeste was trying her best to keep her line free of the heather. It was hot, the fish were feeding just out of her range, my advice wasn't particularly tactful, and between one thing and the other it was suggested I walk a little way off so she could fish alone. Meaning to save her the effort, I swung the rucksack up on my back; a little farther along, I bent over to tie my boots and out the opened flap of the pack directly into the water dropped Celeste's favorite Nikon camera.

I fished it out again, but the lens and viewfinder were soaked. Celeste, hearing the splash, came over to see what I had caught.

"We can let it dry," I said lamely.

"It's ruined. Absolutely ruined."

"I guess you should have tied the flap up."

Counterattacking is always a big mistake. Celeste dropped her rod into the heather, grabbed the camera, and stalked off in the direction of the lodge. Under any other circumstances I would have hurried after her, but behind me the trout were beginning to rise, and not just occasionally but *everywhere*. I was mad at her for leaving, madder yet at my clumsiness, but grateful, too—at least she had left the rod! Thus equipped, I could switch from a sinking line to a floating one without changing spools.

Despite the rises, the trout preferred taking the fly just as it became waterlogged and sank. Once I figured this out, I caught fish regularly. The sun setting so late in Scotland, it was tempting to stay long enough to bring the total up to two dozen or three, but I was worried about Celeste, and after my thirteenth I put the rods up and walked back to the lodge.

Things smoothed out over a dinner of trout and the bottle of wine. We talked to Colin and decided to reserve the farthest loch for the next day. It was a two-hour hike, but supposedly the fishing was worth it.

We got an early start in the morning, or at least tried to— when we went to fetch the key to the boat on our loch, it couldn't be found. We asked Colin, who asked the night clerk, who asked the chambermaid, but without success—the key had gone missing. I suspect we upstart Yanks were being none too subtly bumped off a loch, but there didn't seem to be much we could do about it. The only loch still available was the one we had already fished, but maybe, we told ourselves, the sacrifice of the camera would have propitiated the gods there in our favor.

And apparently it had—our day there was perfect, from the moment I pushed Celeste out from the beach in the skiff and jumped in after her, to the moment eight hours later when we slid the boat back into the sandy impression left by the keel. We caught trout, a large number, and they seemed the vibrant, living underline to the generous blue sky and the easy June breeze and a waterscape set like liquid heather against the hills.

The skiff was a heavy one of traditional design, with thick green planking, iron oarlocks, and a healthy amount of daylight showing between her ribs. She was heavy to push out, a lot heavier to row—a good heavy, I decided. It slowed down the drifting and got me thinking.

"You know," I said, digging in the oars. "This American fascination . . . *puff* . . . for lightweight equipment . . . *puff* . . . has gotten out of hand. There's a lot to be said for old-fashioned solid construction . . . *puff* . . . as exemplified . . . *puff* . . . by this skiff."

"Hmmmmn?" Celeste responded, looking up from her fly. "Could you please row a little faster, dear? I think Scots trout prefer more speed."

"Certainly. But what I meant to say . . . *puff puff puff* . . . is that less is not necessarily . . . Just let me rest here for a moment . . . *phew* . . . more."

With a boat like that, anchoring was almost redundant. I gave a final desperate yank on the oars and we glided to a stop in a cove where the shoreline dropped sheer in a mica-flecked cliff. Celeste immediately caught a nice one-pound brown that ran toward the rock as if to climb it. My arms ached so much from rowing it was all I could do to cast at all, but then I caught one, too, and immediately decided—now that the ice was broken—to tie on something I'd been wanting to try for a long time.

It was a cast—a leader—of three wet flies. Once upon a time it was a common way to fish in the States, and there were passionate arguments concerning which order the flies should be arranged in and why. There's probably not a Yank under the age of eighty-five who remembers this method, but in Scotland it's still a common way to fish, and at a tackle store in Edinburgh I'd bought several of the dropper-festooned leaders and a handful of appropriate flies.

I rummaged through them now, picked out three I thought offered the fish the most variety, thereby emphasizing their smorgasbord attraction. They weren't easy to cast (not just for the wind do the Scots use those heavy rods), but I finally managed to get the slow, deliberate roll of it and work out line.

The trout, as if to encourage me in my first clumsy attempt to speak Scots, immediately responded. A fat speedy fish came a fantastic distance to take the red fly at the end, and before I could bring him in, another had taken a swipe at the brown fly in the middle. Whether it was the processional quality of the flies, their resemblance to a school of baitfish, or simply the greater odds of the multiple offerings, the trout kept slashing at my rig with happy abandon. It was fascinating to see which fly caught the most; as it turned out, it was the red one at the end.

The fish, having seen the first two sail by, couldn't resist a shot at the shimmery third.

At lunchtime, we rowed across the loch to where a burn spilled across a broken weir, and ate our sandwiches looking toward the grayish blue hills in the east. They were twenty miles away, but such was the transparency of the air, the treeless intervention, they seemed much closer. They had an airy, detached look, as if they were hovering above the moors; the sight, combined with the spray of the burn, took the place of the vanished breeze to cool us off.

A sea gull drifted in from the ocean to look us over. Watching it, we saw a raven circling even slower, in a higher orbit, and watching the raven, trying to focus against the sun, we saw a still-higher shape, an eagle, all but motionless it was so high, as if loch, hills, and birds all circled around the brown fixed center of its wings.

The afternoon was largely an expansion of the morning, with more trout, more sun, and the funny footnote of lambs coming down to the edge of the loch to look us over. On our way back to the lodge, on a whim, we detoured off on a trail to what are called the Fairy Lochs—three interconnected lochs set high on a miniature plateau.

"Hear it?" Celeste said, as we paused to catch our breaths.

I glanced at my watch. "Four o'clock. Right on schedule."

There were no jokes about cuckoos this time—we kept on climbing. The lochs, once we got there, reminded me of the remote ponds we have back in New England, minus the trees. Celeste stretched out on the heather to nap while I made my way around the perimeter of each one, trying a few casts, exploring, not really caring if I caught fish or not.

As I completed my circuit and made my way back I noticed something scattered in the heather and by it partially obscured:

bright shiny pieces of metal. Some of them were small and curled like shavings, but some were ruler-sized, and one piece was as long as my arm and violently bent.

What I was looking at was the scattered wreckage of an army transport that had crashed on its way back to the States in June of 1945. We got the story later from Colin. The plane had been full of returning GIs, and it had hit against the plateau's summit during a storm, killing all thirty aboard. A band of local farmers and ghillies had climbed through the snow and gotten to the bodies first; a shred of brown fabric had been their first clue, and then there was more of it, until it was as if they were following a deliberately laid trail of torn uniforms.

It's a sad and eerie sight, that unstainable silver metal. It's American, but the touch is unmistakably Highland—the bitter under the sweet, the farewell that is tragic, the ghosts amid lochans meant for fairies, fishermen, and trout.

I can catch wild one-pound trout for a long time without getting bored, but after another day on the lochs we decided to take a break from the fishing in order to make a literary pilgrimage to a place I had wanted to see since I was a boy: Camusfearna, the remote coastal home made famous by Gavin Maxwell in his 1960 best-seller about otters, *Ring of Bright Water.*

Maxwell is all but forgotten in America, I suppose, but he's still in print in Britain, and thirty years ago his books were as popular as Joy Adamson's *Born Free* series about Elsa and her cubs. It was a time of dawning environmental consciousness, an awakening to the fact we were exterminating so many species, and at some level people probably wanted to be told the animals forgave us for this—that lions would lie beside our cots at night in perfect contentment; that otters, for all our sins, bore us no grudge.

Maxwell was a lyrical writer, and reading his books as a child I was even more enchanted with his descriptions of the lonely Highland setting of Camusfearna than I was by the otters. An old sea-weathered house set on a beach where no one could bother you, with nothing to do all day but the chores of running the place, a spot of beachcombing, then long, slow evenings filled with books? It was the kind of place Holden Caulfield was looking for; it was the kind of place *I* was looking for, even at twelve, and the magic of his evocation settled so deeply it became at least partially responsible for who I turned out to be.

Camusfearna wasn't its real name, but a protective alias. "This is from no desire to create mystery," Maxwell wrote, "but because identification in print would seem in some sense a sacrifice, a betrayal of its remoteness and isolation, as if by doing so I were to bring nearer its enemies of industry and urban life. Camusfearna, I have called it, the Bay of the Alders."

Maxwell could have had no way of knowing, writing those lines, how immensely popular his book was to become—and how many thousands of readers would take it into their heads not only to discover where Camusfearna was located, but to visit it in person. He was dogged by sightseers for the next eight years; there is no law of trespass in Scotland, and anyone who happened along had to be put up with. By the time he came to write the third book in the Camusfearna trilogy, *Raven Seek Thy Brother*, the disguise hardly seemed worth the effort. "It will be obvious to any interested reader that Camusfearna is Sandaig, by Sandaig Lighthouse, on the mainland of Scotland some five miles south of Glenelg village."

And five miles south of Glenelg village is where we were driving, visors down to keep the sun from our eyes, Maxwell's book open on the dashboard like a compass pointing the way. There over the cliff on our right was a sand-fringed promontory jutting out into the Sound of Sleat—Sandaig Lighthouse, we decided—and a little farther up the road stood a simple green cottage that was boarded up and empty.

"This must be the Macleods' house," I said, slowing down to park.

"The who?" Celeste asked.

"The family who lived here when Maxwell did. He was always writing about them. They were his support system. No, more than that. They were his link to the human race."

The next part should have been easy, but wasn't. We knew where Sandaig Lighthouse was—we had the cottage at our backs—but that still left a large space in between with nothing to point the way. Since Maxwell's day the bare, bracken-covered cliff has grown over with Sitka and larch, and the forest is high and thick enough to obscure the views in every direction.

There were some overgrown woods roads, nothing more. We took the one that pointed most directly toward the ocean, and almost immediately came upon our next clue: a burn, a narrow, primrose-lined burn that dropped out of sight in the direction of the coast.

Anyone who's read Maxwell remembers All Na Fearna, the Alder burn—how important it was to the life of Camusfearna, both as a source of drinking water and as a playground for the otters Edal and Mij in *Ring of Bright Water* he describes balancing his way down it when he first came here to live.

"Presently the burn became narrower, and afforded no foot-holds on its steep banks, then it tilted sharply seaward between rock walls, and below me I could hear the roar of a high water-fall. I climbed out from the ravine, and found myself on a bluff of heather and red bracken looking down upon the sea and upon Camusfearna."

This was the fastest way down then, but the waterfall part made me hesitate—despite the drought, the burn was high with snowmelt from nearby Ben Sgriol—and so we decided to try and find an alternate route. I won't list all our false starts and disappointed backtrackings, other than to say that finally, just when we were about to give up, we found something all but miraculous scratched there in the dirt beneath our feet: an arrow pointing toward a vague break in the Sitka near the cliff's edge.

"Shall we try it?" Celeste asked.

"Someone must have drawn it for their friends to follow," I said. Then, shrugging: "Sure, why not?"

The gap in the Sitka grew larger, we came upon some poles carrying a single strand of wire, the path widened and dipped, and then suddenly there we were on the edge of the cliff staring down at the scene that had greeted Maxwell the morning of his first glorious descent.

The landscape and seascape that lay spread below me was of such beauty that I had no room for it all at once; my eyes flickered from the house to the islands, from the white sands to the flat green pasture round the croft, from the wheeling gulls to the pale satin sea and on to the snow-tipped Cuillins of Skye in the distance. . . . Immediately below me the steep hillside of heather and ochre mounting grasses fell to a broad green field, almost an island, for the burn flanked it at the right and then curved round seaward in a glittering horseshoe. The sea took up where the burn left off, and its foreshore formed the whole frontage of the field, running up nearest to me in a bay of rocks and sand. At the edge of this bay, a stone's throw from the sea on one side and the burn on the other, the house of Camusfearna stood unfenced in green grass.

Staring down at this my mind raced with the frantic regauging that comes when you finally see a place in person you've fallen in love with through books. There below us was a grassy meadow waving in the breeze, a corner of sea that was almost tropic in its turquoise, the bright, pebbly curve of burn that suggested Maxwell's title—all these, and not just flat as they come off the page, but round and splashy and colored, with the rolling bass note of incoming breakers and the sandier hiss of their retreat. Beyond the burn were the ridges of the miniature islands, and beyond these, repeating their anticlines with more emphasis, the first blue mountains of Skye.

It was just as Maxwell described—with the exception of the house. On January 20, 1968, it burned to the ground, and the ruins were later bulldozed over, so that except for a small memorial marking the spot where Maxwell's ashes were spread when he died the next year, there is nothing left of it whatsoever, not even its foundation.

We climbed the rest of the way down to the grass, instinctively lowering our voices, not so much out of respect, but at the pure shattering beauty of the spot. Meadow, beach, ocean, burn. Here in front of us were perfect specimens of each, as if nature had decided to show exactly what she could do with each form in the briefest possible compass, and then display them beneath a sun and sky that were perfect, too.

Knowing nothing of Maxwell, coming here quite by chance, you would still sense something bittersweet in this scene, breathtaking as it is. Simply put, it's hard to look at all this and not want in some way to *want* it. No, not want it. Want never to *leave*—to have the ability to open one's eyes each morning on exactly this landscape, and not just for an afternoon, not just for a summer or even a lifetime, but *forever*.

It's too much to want of a place—if nothing else, Maxwell's life here was evidence of this. His books, for all their delight, read like an endless shopping list of misfortune. Lawsuits, accidents, sinkings, divorce, illness, the killing of Mijibal, his first otter, more accidents, more illness, more sinkings—not without reason, Maxwell ended up believing he was cursed.

These calamities have an unintended effect, as depressing as they are—they reinforce his picture of Camusfearna as sanctuary, a preserve surrounded by danger on every side. Even at twelve I responded to this, and it's clear, the modern world being what it is, this note gave the book much of its appeal. "Whatever you're going to do in the future," a reader wrote him, "please never say that the Camusfearna of *Ring of Bright Water* never was. Say that it's gone, if you like, but not that you lied. I couldn't take that, because it was the only evidence I had that Paradise existed somewhere."

Well, Maxwell did in effect say all this—that in the end life was too much for him, and even the love of otters couldn't pull him through. There can't be too many examples of a writer creating a dream in so many hearts and then taking such pains to shatter it, but perhaps Maxwell can only be blamed for not shattering it correctly—for not taking pains to explain that Camusfearna, seen on an afternoon like this one, was so perfect it made you all but sob at the limitations of mortality.

We didn't sob. We stared at all this, felt these things, then went down to the beach to take a closer look. It's to the left of where the house was located, curving inward for a longer distance than I had pictured. The breeze was just strong enough to add manes to the waves lazing in through the turquoise—again, the effect was tropical. Celeste took off her shoes and waded across the burn's mouth to the first miniature island; an old boat was cast up and neglected there on the rocks, undoubtedly one of Maxwell's shipwrecked fleet, though her name had long since been weathered off the stern.

We spent an hour or more beyond the burn, bending down to examine the wild roses, picking up pieces of shell and brightly colored pebbles, turning over the wooden fish boxes that had drifted ashore (in Maxwell's time, they had been the chief source of Camusfearna's furniture). When the tide turned, we retraced our footsteps back across the burn. There was an English couple sitting in the grass beside Maxwell's stone; the man was reading a paperback edition of *Ring of Bright Water*. We talked for a while. No, he had never heard of the book before, not until coming up to Scotland. Yes, it was good to look up from the page and see illustrations, as it were, of what he was reading.

To the rear of the meadow, tucked in a fold of the cliff, is the waterfall and the basin that served as Camusfearna's swimming hole, not just for its human inhabitants, but the otters as well. It's high and serene and rocky, so that resting on the ferns by its edge, smelling the wild garlic, it's hard to remember you're not deep in mountains but only a Frisbee toss from the sea.

We plunked our toes into the frigid water, then pulled them quickly back out. Sitting there we could summon up a happier Camusfearna, the haven where Maxwell brought his otters to let them roam free.

"She rejoiced in the waves," he says, writing of Edal, his second otter.

She would hurl herself straight as an arrow right into the great roaring gray wall of an oncoming breaker and go clean through it as if it had neither weight nor momentum; she would swim far out to sea through wave after wave until the black dot of her head was lost among the distant white manes, and more than once I thought that some wild urge to seek new land had dizzied her and that she would go on swimming west in the Sea of the Hebrides and that I should not see her again.

Eventually, with all the disasters that befell Camusfearna and its owner, Edal had to be kept locked up in the house. In *Raven Seek Thy Brother*, Maxwell describes the gradual reestablishment of their trust, and how they were at last able to resume much of their old life together . . . a life that was destroyed when, after so many new beginnings, the house burned and Edal with it. She is buried beside the burn underneath a rowan tree; on the flat top of the rocky monument is cut the epitaph *Edal, the otter of Ring of Bright Water, 1958–68. Whatever joy she gave to you, give back to nature.*

On the weathered metal beside these words we found earlier visitors had left their small tributes—a shell, a twist of flower, a small blue feather shed by a bird. Celeste walked over to the beach, found a stone that was white and perfectly oval, then— tapping the other gifts gently aside to make room—added its brightness to Edal's collection.

Maxwell wasn't the only one we were reading on the hills. There was John Inglis Hall's *Fishing a Highland Stream*, about the Truim,

Robin Ade's *Fisher in the Hills*, about the burns and lochans of Galloway, and, with special enjoyment, the novels of a writer who was famous in Scotland yet all but unknown in the states, Neil Gunn. Read his *Blood Hunt* and you'll see what a talented novelist could do with this landscape—a landscape where people have enough space between them that they stand out as men and women should stand out, craggy and individual and proud.

Between reading these, driving past salmon rivers and sea trout streams we wouldn't have time for, hearing stories in the pubs about the fabulous lochs in Sutherland and the Orkneys, we were storing up resolutions about where we would fish on our next trip. As for *this* one, there were only two days left now before our plane left Prestwick—just enough time to take care of what for me was some very important unfinished business.

It didn't concern trout this time, but mountains—one mountain in particular. On my first trip to Scotland, nine years before, traveling mainly by bus and foot, I had splurged one morning, rented a car in Inverness, and driven northwestward toward the coast. I ended up in Ullapool around three—it was November and the shops and hotels were shuttered closed. I found a chips shop down by the harbor, and nursed a cup of coffee while I watched a rusty trawler unload its catch. Finishing, I decided to drive a bit farther on, look the scenery over, then turn back toward Inverness.

I hadn't gone far when I saw a man beside the road with his thumb stuck out. Ordinarily, I'm wary of picking up hitchhikers, but in this kind of emptiness it seemed a moral imperative to stop.

"How far you going?" I asked, rolling down the window.

The man was already opening the passenger door, sliding himself in. "Not far," he said, or something like it. "Oh, just up the road a way."

He was an angular, ruddy-faced man in his twenties, dressed in a brown duffle coat patched with tape. His "just up the road" turned out to be twenty miles along a one-track road through the grandest hill scenery I had ever seen in my life—grandest, and with the sun going down, the road getting twistier, loneliest. It turned out he was a mason working in a village called Achiltibuie on the coast facing the Summer Islands, a small chain of the Inner Hebrides. In the usual Highland pattern, the government was moving everyone off these islands into the equivalent of council houses on the mainland—houses he was involved with building.

"What does Achiltibuie mean?" I asked him.

"The place where the fair-haired boy lives," he answered.

I nodded. "Does he live there still?"

It was a throwaway line, but its effect was as if I had just stuck my finger in his ribs and started twisting. He laughed so hard he toppled sideways against the car door. For minutes he laughed; he would recover himself, take a deep breath, remember what I'd said, then start off laughing again, his whole body wracked with spasms. For all I know they speak of my reply in Achiltibuie to this day as the wittiest thing ever said there; "Aye, he was a grand comedian, that Yank," someone will say, shaking his head in nostalgic admiration.

Despite the communication gap of his Gallic swallowings and my New Yorkese, we were old buddies by the time we made it to the village. I stayed long enough for a mug of whiskey, then started back along the road far faster than I'd driven up it, trying to reach pavement before the light disappeared.

"And what happened then?" Celeste asked. We were driving the opposite way along this same road now, on a bright sunny day nine years later.

"My left front tire went flat."

"Right here?"

"Up ahead somewhere, I think. It was almost dark. Luckily, there was a spare in the boot. I changed it, then just before I got back in the car saw something that had been there right behind me all along."

"A sheep?"

I shook my head. "A mountain."

And not just any mountain, but one so unusual and compelling I fell in love with it at first sight. There rising above me in the darkness from a slope of scree, its sides barely outlined as a richer shade of black against the dark northern sky, was a crenellated ridge of abrupt towers and weird spires that in variety and steepness would have made a fit playground for trolls. It was like looking up at the walls of a fantasy castle in Spain, a bit of Yosemite transported to the Highlands, a . . . Well, all my comparisons were feeble. It wasn't the highest mountain I'd ever seen, not even the most spectacular, but between its isolation there by the sea and the abruptness of those towers, it was impossible to look at it and not want to stand on top.

It wasn't until the following morning back in Inverness that I discovered this beautiful and suggestive peak had a beautiful and suggestive name: Stac Polly. The book I found it in was called *The Scottish Peaks* by one W. A. Poucher, who describes it lovingly thus:

> This peak with its bristling summit ridge of sandstone pinnacles is the favorite of all mountaineers visiting Coigach. Bold and steep buttresses rise at each end of the mountain; the weird formations of sandstone are a great attraction and those crowning the terminal points

of some of the very narrow spurs can only be reached by a sensational scramble. The whole of Stac Polly is the delight of the photographer, and is the most rewarding and sensational subject in all Scotland.

I brought the book back to the States with me, glanced at Stac Polly's picture surprisingly often in the intervening years, day-dreamed about going back one day and climbing it. Gradually, it became one of those lesser ambitions even a happy life becomes littered with, and yet fate took a lucky turn with this one, and here I was nine years later parking my car in the turnoff at its base and tying on my hiking boots and starting toward its ridge with my wife.

Again, we were blessed with the sunshine that had drenched us every minute of the trip. Between the darkness of the night I'd first seen it and the natural exaggeration of memory, I was prepared to be disappointed by Stac Polly's size, but if anything the sun only emphasized it, throwing the towers and spires into even bolder relief. I understood now the appropriateness of the name. Weathered indents made the towers look stacked rather than carved, and homely as the mountain was, there was a wild, merry impudence in the way it rose there from the scree—a perfect Polly through and through.

Our legs were in that happy condition that comes after a week's strenuous climbing, when up hardly seems up at all, and we made good time along the dry bed of a burn. There were lots of sheep about with their lambs; in a short while we were above them, or at least all but one.

"Hear that bleating?" Celeste asked. "It's a lamb. He's stranded up there on the cliff."

"He'll be all right," I said.

"That must be his mother down below. I think you should climb up and chase him back to her."

I wasn't worried about the lamb; he was perched on a ledge fifty yards above us, as rigid and proud as the hood ornament on a '53 Buick. We were out to climb Stac Polly—why deny that privilege to him? But unluckily for the lamb, I was in a frisky mood, and the idea of chasing him from his smugness was irresistible.

Off I went. Within seconds I was in among the lesser towers and buttresses that make up Stac Polly's flank. It was hard to keep sight of the lamb from in close. Celeste, below me on the bulge of scree, kept up a running play-by-play.

"He's still there. . . . No, he's moving through the heather. He's coming your way. He sees you. . . . He's heading uphill. He's trotting. . . . He's trotting faster."

Each time I drew even with him, he took off again, climbing those rocks as daintily as a mountain goat. I doubled back under him, came at him from the steep slope to his left, hid behind a boulder to let him settle, then traversed to the right to take him unawares.

"Gotcha!" I yelled, all but springing.

There was nothing behind the rock. Above me, a long way above me, the lamb stuck out its tongue.

We played this game for an hour in all. When I finally gave up, I was panting from effort, my knickers were torn from briars, Celeste was doubled over with laughter, and the lamb was back in the exact spot he had started, bleating in happiness as his mother trotted past us to fetch him.

"You did good, honey," Celeste said, patting the spot on the shoulders where my ego resides. "Real good."

Chasing lambs doesn't leave much strength for climbing mountains, but we'd come too far to quit now. The trail leveled off, then swung to the right to get around onto the north face. As we turned the corner a whole new view opened up—the country unrolling into Sutherland—but the footing was becoming dicier as the slope steepened, and we couldn't take our eyes off the ground other than to peek.

Toward the top the trail left off switchbacking and went directly up the rocks. The last ten yards would have been rock climbing in the States, but is called "scrambling" in Scotland—scrambling and kicking and scratching and clawing. Celeste got up first, let out a delighted yell, then reached down to help me up the last bit of rock. In a second I was beside her, and together we were looking out at the world falling away beneath our feet.

There to our left were the lower round pillars of Stac Polly, grooved brown by the weather, aligned so they pointed like a gunsight toward the sea. At our backs was the twisting line of the road up which we had driven—in one coil was a loch with a fisherman's rowboat moving at the apex of a green, outspreading V. Directly in front of us, seemingly endless, stretched the wild country north of the mountain—a furrowed, treeless expanse of loch and lochan, moor and hill, with the sea on one side, mountains on the other, and in between nothing that hinted at the presence of man. In the stillness of that windless day only one sound could be heard, and it seemed the very call of that landscape, impossible to locate, distant, unutterably sweet.

"Hear it?" I said.

Celeste smiled. "Cuckoo, our old friend."

In the afternoon slant of sun, the misty softening provided by the sea, it was at the same time the wildest landscape I'd ever seen and the gentlest. I thought of Thoreau's happy phrase: "A breadth of view equivalent to motion"—just looking at it made you soar.

"What's that one called over there?" Celeste said, pointing to the nearest mountain, the one with snow in its gullies.

I turned through the guidebook. "Cul Mor," I said. Then, flipping to the glossary: "Great Nook."

There were no foothills to these mountains—they rose directly from the moorland, so they seemed many times their actual height. The most impressive was wedge-shaped Suilven directly opposite us over Loch Sionscaig; as often as we spun around to point at something new, we kept coming back to it, and when we finally sat down to eat our sandwiches, it was facing Suilven's direction.

We stayed on top with the light. My legs were tired with satisfaction at having completed the climb, and it was matched by the kind of contentment that comes when you find—from the height of years—that one of your ambitions was worth the dreaming after all. For a long time the view alone was enough to occupy me, but then mountains being the meta-phoric prompters they are, I tried focusing on some thoughts that seemed as large and compelling as distant Suilven. Story ideas, a rush of remembrance from that earlier, lonelier visit, resolutions for the future, not just about travels, but ambitions and difficult, all but unobtainable goals. I tried capturing them, but they floated off into the soft air, where, measured against that scenery, they popped apart into the fine, scattered mist of insignificance.

But that was all right. One did stay intact, the one I brought down with me, my one and only Highland souvenir. The things we had seen, our small adventures, the sense we'd had in all our circling of coming closer to the secret of these hills. We weren't

there yet, not by a long shot, but the challenge was clear now—
to take home from the landscape a new breadth of perspective;
to keep it in memory; to someday come back again; to learn this
key to wisdom . . . to know two places well.

September 30

My hunch is that we flyfishers, away from the water, measure rather less gullible than average. Fly fishing, after all, attracts many of its practitioners from the professions that deal with precise measurement of fact on one hand and intuitive gropings toward truth on the other—actuaries and historians, engineers and poets, draftsmen and bakers, scientists and philosophers. Then, too, it's not in front of the television set swallowing lies that we choose to spend our leisure time. No, on the whole, we're rather less gullible than the norm.

We overcompensate for this skepticism once you get us out on the water. There, when it comes to gullibility, we're the biggest suckers there are. You can test this yourself easily enough. Next time you see another flyfisherman walking along your favorite stream, stop him thus:

"Good morning." (You say.)

"Hi. How's the fishing?" (He says.)

"Not so hot. But I'll tell you what. There's this blonde sunbathing up there in that meadow, I believe she said her name is Miss June or Miss July, something like that, but anyway she needs someone to help her with her suntan lotion. . . ."

Or, as a variation:

"Not so hot. But I'll tell you what. There's this wildcat oil well up there in the meadow all ready to start pumping, all it needs is someone to invest a little more capital. . . ."

Now an ersatz flyfisherman will perhaps rise to these baits, but a skeptical flyfisherman, a *genuine* flyfisherman, won't bat an eye. This is where the real test comes, variation number three:

"Not so hot. But tell you what. There's a three-pound brown sitting in tight by an alder up there in that first pool. I gave him my best shot, but nothing doing. He's all yours."

And off our skeptical flyfisherman will run, hurrying past you so fast you can all but feel the slipstream of his credulity.

Fiction writers have a term for this: *the willing suspension of disbelief.* What makes it possible, I suppose, is the mystery of the watery element we probe. Measured in cosmological terms, it wasn't that long ago we were water dwellers ourselves, and our hunch that a huge fish might be lurking just beyond that outcrop of coral was the defensive safety mechanism by which our species thrived. Now, emerged, our other instincts dulled, we still remember this one ancestral lesson: in the water, as in the dark, *anything goes.*

Not all waters are created equal in this respect. I find, fishing a dark muddy pond, that it's hard to believe there are fish in the murkiness; conversely, fishing the Caribbean, where it's no trick at all to see bottom fifty feet down, I find it just as difficult to believe there are fish in such clarity. Hope requires neither transparency nor opaqueness, but flourishes best in exactly the right blend—the transparency of a trout stream, say, where we can see just far enough into the bright swirls of color to make of them huge fishy forms.

I was given a good refresher lesson in all this yesterday afternoon. I was down on the White River, famous water in New England, but for me—with all the best intentions in the world—a stream with which I've never quite hit it off. The water's always too high when I get there, or too low; there are lots of fishermen about, lots of canoes, and the presence of the interstate, in an already sloppy valley, pretty well spoils most of its charm. Still, there are serious fish in the White, big rainbows I've seen racing away from my boots, and the salmon restoration effort has, if nothing else, drawn to its banks a loyal band of river advocates I admire very much. Between this and the undeniable beauty of the remoter stretches, the White and I have reached a grudging truce over the years: it gives me a trout or two each time I visit; I don't push it and don't bad-mouth it to my friends.

Yesterday I drove up past Stockbridge, where the river narrows to a width you can pretty well cover in one cast. Even so, I had to watch my footing; as relaxed as the river is there, there are surprisingly deep holes. For the first hour I spent most of my time freeing my hook from the salmon parr that throw themselves on even the biggest dry fly with maniacal persistence, as if demonstrating they have the moxie it takes to swim round-trip to Greenland. There was a trout where the flow was smoothest, not a big one, but rising so perfectly to dusty white midges, with such fastidious grace, I felt honored just to share a seat at the same table.

I was wading a little deeper out into the current to try and see if I couldn't cover him with less drag, when I heard something upstream and to my right—heard it the way you hear a skyrocket going off, first in the gut, then in the ears. Recovering, jolted, I realized what I'd heard was a tremendous splash—a splash that resolved itself into outspreading ripples almost seismic in their velocity.

My first reaction was the skeptical one—some kid had thrown a rock. But there was no kid, only some innocent-looking Holsteins a hundred yards back from the bank. I was wondering if something that loud could possibly be what I hoped it might be when the sound came again, perhaps not as explosive as the first time, but—in that narrow glen—sufficient to shatter apart what remained of my doubt.

A trout! And not just any trout, but the Queen of the White River, Miss Stockbridge herself. This was the chance I'd been waiting for all season. I immediately forgot about the feeding trout in front of me, waded clumsily past him toward the far bank, then—just before sinking—got control of myself and started plotting things out.

The fish, wily monster that she was, had stationed herself in a deep channel hard against the shady bank. I couldn't wade directly over but had to backtrack fifty yards, then ease my way up through the shallows until I came within range. I did this carefully, keeping my eye on the spot the sound had come from, but—damn! A dicey spot made me glance away for a moment just as the fish splashed again.

I looked up, and this time managed to spot the epicenter of the rings, the place the fish had surfaced. It was within casting range—a long cast, but makeable. I was fishing a Light Cahill, and it made sense to stick with that. I tied a few more half hitches into my blood knot, then—my hands shaking—worked out line.

First cast—nothing.

Second cast—nothing.

Third cast—my God! I brought my arm up in a reflex motion, literally gasped from the force of striking, and clenched my teeth waiting for the monster's weight to come tight against the line.

Nothing happened.

Five minutes went by.

"Trout?" I felt like saying. "O trout? Are you there, trout?"

I was so surprised to have missed, so speechless, the disappointment in my stomach was so sudden and cold, that I didn't even try casting again, but bulled my way through the current to the place she had rose, trying to at least get a glimpse of what I had missed.

I was there looking down into the water when she rose again, this time so close it made me jump. I spun around, and was just in time to see, splashing into the water at my back, a beautifully ripe, beautifully crimsoned McIntosh apple, dropping from the highest branch of the outspreading apple tree that shaded the lie. Again, I glanced down into the water. There they were, bobbing just beneath the surface—splashes one, two, and three. I scooped one out and took a vicious bite of its middle, determined to have my vengeance on something's flesh. I understood immediately the ludicrousness of what had happened; it's hard enough to be had by a trout, but to be had by a McIntosh apple?

That was yesterday. Now, looking back from the perspective of my typewriter, 1 have only one regret—that the apple didn't hit me on the head. It worked, after all, for Newton, and God knows he was *not* a gullible man.

The Bigger They Come

My friends know me as a man who likes to exaggerate, but for the next five thousand words I'll stick to a sober recitation of the facts, the better to deal with events that are themselves sufficiently exaggerated. What I'm referring to are the two most extraordinary fish of my angling career, the first extraordinary for the circumstances of its capture, the second, for the circumstances of its capture and the extraordinariness of its size.

There are two schools of thought on catching big fish. One school holds that you fish for them deliberately, use outsize lures and streamers, fish only those lies capable of sheltering fish of weight. The second maintains the best way to catch big fish is to work your way through as many lesser fish as possible, harness the laws of probability to your cause. This last may be called the lottery school of fly-fishing, and it's the one to which I belong, since it pretty well matches what I've learned of life. The big things come unexpectedly amid the ordinariness of daily routine, and to deliberately go hunting Joy or Love with a metaphoric net would be to doom yourself to failure by the very nature of the quest. No, I'm a small-fish fisher, a small-fate man, who hopes, like we all do, for miraculous things.

But this by way of preface. From here on in I'll adhere to the Joe Friday school of angling literature: the facts, ma'am, just the facts.

It wasn't meant to be a fishing trip at all. Nova Scotia for two weeks—a trip we could manage with our baby. That I packed a small fly rod was of no significance; it goes into my duffle bag the automatic way my razor does; it wouldn't matter if my destination were Bahrain. That Nova Scotia has some fine fishing is something I was aware of, of course, but that only added a vaguely illicit interest I wasn't going to allow myself to pursue.

Nova Scotia is not your undiscovered, off-the-beaten-track gem, but it's still lovely for all that; the descriptions that speak of it as "Vermont surrounded by ocean," or "New England thirty years ago," are both true. With its mix of Acadian, Loyalist, and

Scots traditions, its coastline that out-craggys Maine's, and its laid-back Canadian citizenry, it's the perfect spot for the kind of relaxed family vacation we were after. Starting in Halifax, we were going to travel around toward Cape Breton, staying at bed and breakfasts, driving in the morning, hiking and picnicking in the afternoon.

Our first night was spent near the Saint Marys, a famous salmon river, but only because it's where we happened to be when evening caught up to us. And though I may have briefly entertained the notion of trying a cast or two, the south-coast rivers were already closed for the season, the victims of a summer-long drought that was the worst on record. Still, after we settled in, there was no reason not to stroll over to the river and have a look-see; our landlady told us about a bald eagle who made his home in a spruce above the iron bridge, and we wanted to try and spot him.

The facts—and yet already a digression. My attitude toward salmon, to this point in my life, could pretty well be summed up by the term *reverse snobbery*. Yes, I knew about the mystique—about how Atlantic salmon were the king of game fish, strong, brave, beautiful, and scarce; of Lord Grey of Falloden and Edward Ringwood Hewitt and Lee Wulff and Ted Williams, and all the famous flyfishers who dedicated their lives to its pursuit. And yes, I knew about the efforts of conservationists not only to preserve the salmon in their present range, but to bring them back to the New England rivers they once inhabited. I even, God forgive me!, knew what it was to carve into a side of smoked salmon, curl off a piece, and drop it on rye bread with a whisper of onion, wash it down with good Danish beer. I knew all these things, which isn't bad for a man who hadn't, until this moment, seen an Atlantic salmon that was actually alive.

The reverse snobbery? Well, weren't all salmon fishers rich bastards who mouthed pieties about protecting the fish (protecting them, that is, from fishermen whose bank accounts weren't as large as theirs), while back at work they were presidents of corporations that were despoiling the environment as fast as possible? And even the local effort to return salmon to New England rivers—wasn't that a misuse of scarce conservation dollars, trying to bring something so fragile back to a region where fish and game laws still reflected the ethos of the eighteenth century? Just before our trip a man had been arrested for catching and killing one of the first Atlantic salmon to make it all the way up to the White River in Vermont; the man had been previously charged with beating his wife, and was to shoot himself before he could be brought to trial for killing the salmon. In a bizarre kind of way it all fit in—the violence done the salmon, the violence done to man. No mystique for me, thank you—when it came to my attitude toward salmon, I was very skeptical and confused.

At least until that walk along the Saint Marys. We found the eagle fast enough—he was soaring in a spiral from bank to bank, with the majestic, disdainful quality all eagles possess. We stood on the bridge trying to get our daughter to share in the excitement—"See, Erin? See nice pretty eagley?"—when fifty yards upstream there was a splashing sound with an odd uplift to it, as if someone were throwing rocks *out* of the water. I forgot about the eagle, and shifted my focus to a lower plain. There it was again, and this time there was no mistaking the fluid, bright shape that appeared a second before the splashing sound and disappeared a second before its echo.

Salmon! In the drought-ravaged river, they were in the one pool big enough to shelter them, and seemed—when we balanced our way along the bank to it—not overly concerned by their plight. The water was deep and dark enough that it was hard to make them out, at least until they jumped. They went straight up in the air then, and it was so sudden and joyous our hearts lifted with them, so we laughed out loud at their sheer exuberance. There were no falls there, no dams—if anything, they seemed to be jumping out of the depths of their content-ment, as if remembering in intervals they *were* salmon and were expected to do so for our delight.

By the time it was too dark to watch any longer, I was, if not converted to the mystique, at least firmly in the salmon's corner as a devoted fan. Unlike other big fish I'd seen, I was not immediately possessed by the desire to be attached to one; it was subtler, more a wanting to be *around* them, the way people swim with dolphins.

Next morning we stopped briefly to see if the salmon were still there; if they were, they weren't jumping, and we contented ourselves with another good look at the eagle. Later in the morning was the restored village of Sherbrooke, then beautiful, lonely Wine Cove, and then our trip was fully in gear, and we made our way in a back-and-forth looping toward Cape Breton and the dramatic headlands of that coast.

The weather, with the drought, was gloriously sunny and hot. Here on the watersheds flowing into the Gulf of Saint Law-rence the salmon season was still open, though the rivers looked just as low and hopeless as they had in the south. I thought about fishing, went so far as purchasing a license, but between my flimsy trout rod, a few battered trout flies, and a wife and child, it seemed better to concentrate on the hiking and beachcombing we could all do together.

And then I got my chance—at some brook trout fishing. We were passing the Cheticamp River, a beautifully clear stream flowing seaward from some bread-loaf-shaped hills a short way above the Acadian town of the same name. It was a hot Sunday afternoon, half of Cape Breton seemed to be out enjoying the sunshine, and we had already stopped in a roadside store for the makings of a picnic. Leaving our car at the campground, we slipped Erin into the backpack, then started through the dappled sunlight of the old woods road that parallels the river's bank.

The first salmon pool is a forty-minute walk in from the road, and this is where we decided to stop—*not* because of the salmon (the river was too low to think about that) but because the granite ledge that shelved down into the pool was a perfect spot for a picnic. While things were readied, I waded down below the pool to the only fast water in sight. I was wading wet—in that heat, it was the only comfort available—and I had nothing stronger than my featherweight pack rod—perfect for seeking out the small brook trout I hoped to find.

Small fish, small fly. I was tying on a number-fourteen Royal Wulff when behind me in the pool was a tremendous splash, as if someone had just dove headfirst off the ledge. I spun around, startled, and was just in time to see my wife pointing down toward the pool with what can only be described as an expression of total dumbstruck awe. Any doubt about what had caused the sound disappeared instantly—again, there was a tremendous splash, only this time at the center of it, breaking the pool's surface, becoming detached from it, hanging there like the froth of a silver geyser, hanging there for what seemed like minutes, hanging . . . hanging . . . tilting . . . falling . . . knifing back in, was a . . .

"Salmon!" we yelled, simultaneously.

The salmon was jumping, not rolling—I was told later a jumping salmon will never take a fly. But I was too inexperienced to know this; my hands shaking, I finished tying on the fly, added two more half hitches, then waded the six or seven steps to the lip of the pool. The salmon had come up seventy feet away—a heroic cast for a little rod—but I was afraid coming any closer would frighten him off. I worked out line as quickly as I could, then—David with a slingshot—let the fly shoot forward in what was undoubtedly the longest, luckiest cast of my life.

The fly landed perfectly, its tail pert on the water, its hackles puffed and upright. There was barely any current in the pool, so it floated back toward me slowly, my emotions traveling with it in the classic emotional pattern of a drift—anticipation and alertness flowing imperceptibly toward disappointment as the fly came back untouched. Not on this cast, I decided, but just as the thought formed there was a saucer-sized dip in the water below the fly, then something yearning up toward it, and faster than my thoughts could operate, my rod arm was high above me and with an amazing, exhilarating tightening—a tightening with a *bottom* to it—the salmon was on.

I reacted very coolly to this: I shouted "Holy fuck!" and immediately fell down.

But even reduced to a state of blithering idiocy, there was a surer instinct at work, and the tight arc in the rod never softened, even as I thrashed my way to my feet. The fight that ensued lasted nearly a half hour, and while there wasn't a moment during that time I wasn't terrified the salmon would break off, I also knew, in the strange contradiction only fishermen will understand, that I *had* him, and unless I blundered badly the fish was mine.

For even with that toy rod, the odds were all in my favor. With the water so low, there was no way the salmon was going to leave the pool, which was fine with me, since I had no backing on my reel, and had already proved my inability to chase after him. Our fight consisted of short, strong runs wherein the salmon proved he could take line out anytime he wanted, and continued stubborn pressure on my part, proving I was not without power myself. With the rod being so light, the tippet so frail, the exact ratio between the salmon's force and my force was delicately balanced, and if there was any skill involved it was the adjustment and readjustment needed to keep the equation constant.

After each surge, I managed to get the salmon closer, to the point where I could see him now, angled down in the crystal green water of the pool, the fly right in his jaw where it should be, his flanks a buttered silver color, his tail powerful and square. He was a good fish, not a huge one, but not a grilse either, and I estimated his length at over two feet. Up on shore my wife and baby were cheering me on, only they had been joined now by another forty people at least. Picnickers, bikers, fishermen, hikers—the woods had been empty when I hooked the salmon, but now people were materializing from the trees as if summoned by bush telegraph, and they alternated between calling out advice to me and discussing among themselves the chances of the fish getting away. Here I wanted to be alone with the experience— my first salmon!—and I had a cheering section, and it made it all ludicrous somehow, the mob up on shore adding a harder tug I wasn't sure I could handle.

Between the lip of the pool and the granite shelf was a towel-sized patch of sand, and—netless—this is where I decided to try and beach the fish. Each time he came in, I brought him a bit closer, letting him get used to seeing the sand, not bothering him when he turned back toward the pool's center. I had learned the first time I fought a fish his size (see below) that a long battle becomes psychological as much as physical—exhausted, you become indifferent to the outcome, and you're apt to try and snap out of it by forcing the fish. I was fighting this temptation more than the fish now, and after about ten near approaches I decided enough was enough and pulled the salmon toward the sand as hard as I dared.

And, to my surprise, it worked—the salmon with hardly a protest slid himself up on the beach and lay still. There is no use trying to describe my emotions—anyone who has landed a big fish will know the mingled triumph and relief, and anyone who hasn't will find it impossible to imagine what a bizarre sick feeling it leaves in your gut. I was happy of course—I turned toward my audience and threw my arms up like a hockey player celebrating a goal—but almost immediately I was faced with a new problem, this one the thorniest yet.

What to do with the fish. During our fight I'd acted under the assumption I was going to release him unharmed— unharmed, that is, if he survived the acid buildup that causes so many released salmon to later die. If anything, this resolution became firmer as the fight wore on, since it seemed ridiculous to think of a fish that had come so far, past gill nets and trawlers and oil spills and so many other perils, dying at the hands of a picnicking vacationer.

The crowd, though, thought otherwise; all through the fight they were operating under the assumption I was going to not only keep the fish but eat him as well. It's hard to say how this feeling manifested itself, but it did, and though I've withstood my share of peer pressure in my day, this was about the most concentrated dose I was ever subjected to at once. These were local people, good Acadians, and the only logical destination for a migrating salmon was their pot. That didn't square with my own philosophy, but I was on their home ground, a visitor, only it was my fish, to do with what I pleased—wasn't it? Back and forth I went, and there were several times during the fight when I was tempted to deliberately snap the leader, disburden myself of this ethical dilemma.

The fish landed now, I was quickly running out of time. Keep him and maintain hero status with the crowd? Release him and keep the sense of my immaculate self? It would have taken Immanuel Kant to reason through this, but then I was saved by a man calling out from the hemlocks where the crowd was thickest.

"You have your salmon permit, don't you, mister?"

I had no such thing. There was an audible sign of disappointment with that—obviously, the fish would have to be put back before a warden arrived. Relieved, I took the fly out of the salmon's jaw and began working him back and forth through the water. Ten minutes later, when I released him, only my wife and daughter remained to watch.

But still, the news traveled fast. A few minutes later, when we were walking back down the path toward the campground, happy, hot, and tired, a man met us carrying an old steel fly rod with a huge automatic reel. He was small and wiry, and looked to be in his seventies; he had a pipe in his mouth and wore an old stocking cap, and there was something stooped in his posture that made you think he was portaging an invisible canoe.

"Are you the man who caught the salmon?" he asked.

I allowed as it was indeed me.

"Your first salmon?"

I nodded.

"On your first cast?"

I nodded again.

"On your first salmon river?"

"Well, yes," I said, and there's no describing the look of amazement and envy that came over the man's face.

"Mister," he said, his head sinking toward his chest as if the canoe had just gotten heavier. "I've been fishing this river for twenty-five years and never caught even one."

In the late 1970s, learning to write, single, broke, I spent the year making a slow counterclockwise progression between temporary homes. Cape Cod in the summers, stretching fall there until the pipes in my unheated cabin began to freeze, then—throwing manuscripts, typewriters, and fishing tackle into my Volkswagen—the winter renting various houses in the quiet hills of northwestern Connecticut. In between were periods of rest and recuperation at my parents' home in New York. One of these intervals was in November, and looking around for something to fill up my time, I decided upon a little trout fishing out in Suffolk County on Long Island's eastern end.

That Long Island—the ancestral home of concrete—even has trout fishing will come as a surprise to many. Back in the nineteenth century it was an unspoiled pastoral landscape of surpassing beauty, and among its delights was trout fishing of a very high order indeed. The early American fishing writer Frank Forester, in an appendix to a revised edition of *The Compleat Angler*, raved on and on about the delights of Island trout fishing.

Long Island has been for many years the utopia of New York sportsmen ... trout fishing still flourishes there and is likely to flourish as long as grass grows and water runs ...

it abounds in small rivulets, which, rising in the elevations midway along the Island's length, make their way without receiving any tributary waters into their respective seas . . . the brook trout are found in abundance and in a degree of perfection which I have seen equaled in no other waters either American or British.

Poor Forester! He must be thrashing about in his grave to see what man has wrought there, and yet in what can only be described as a miracle, a fragment of this idyllic fishery remains: the Connetquot River on the Island's south shore. Located within a defunct private club, managed now by the state, the beautifully clear Connetquot is a river I fished often once upon a time, and I've never visited a place that in its unspoiled perfection, its lost-world kind of atmosphere, gave me such a sense of time suspended, the past regained. If Proust were a flyfisher, this would be his stream—it's the madeleine of trout rivers, and I loved it very much.

The Connetquot is run, very sensibly, on the British beat system. You call, make a reservation, then check in at the gatehouse and select your stretch of water. In November, the pressure falls off, and this particular day was so cold and ominous I was the only fisherman who showed up; there was a note tacked to the gatehouse door instructing anyone who stumbled along to leave their five dollars in the box and help themselves to the river. Swaddled in thermal underwear and sweaters, toting a thermos of tea and bourbon, I did just that.

Past the gatehouse is the clubhouse, a weathered old building that even abandoned suggests a kind of leisured elegance, so you half expect Jay Gatsby to pull up in a shiny Stutz roadster. It faces the lake where the Connetquot opens behind a small dam; the road crosses the dam, and on the abrupt downstream side is one of the best beats on the river: a broad pool flanked by a picturesque old mill. Unlike the water above the dam, the pool can be reached by sea-run browns, and I'd heard rumors about fish so big they were scarcely credible. Rumors—only back in the spring, crossing above the pool on my way upriver, a fisherman fighting a small trout asked me to hold the net for him, and as I dipped it in, a monstrous shape appeared from the pool's depths, took a swipe at the hooked trout, missed, and vanished back whence it had come.

There was no one fishing the pool, but I decided to save it for later. I hiked around the lake through the pitch pine forest, fished the stream above, and caught several decent rainbows. The weather, bad to begin with, now turned vile, with snow mixed in with sleet, and aside from what the frigid air and water were doing to my torso, there was the added inconvenience of having the guides of my rod freeze up, so that casting was like whipping slush.

I was a tougher fisherman in those days, but even so there were limits. Toward noon, I'd had enough, and started back toward the gatehouse. Walking helped warm me up—between this and the "one last cast" theory, I decided to fish the pool below the dam.

I went in on the left bank. It's an abrupt drop-off there, but being right-handed, fishing downstream, it would allow me to get the longest drift. The water comes into the pool in a heavy gray surge from the spillway, churns through the middle, then widens into the broad, placid tail. I tied on a brown Matuka, the New Zealand pattern that was all the rage, then, with the steep bank rising behind me, I roll cast out into the current and let the streamer swing down.

I hadn't been casting long when a brown caught hold of the Matuka and skittered across the pool toward me. He was small, and I was hardly paying any attention to bringing him in, when between one moment and the next the middle of the pool fell away, as if a petcock had suddenly been opened in the river bottom. But no—that simile isn't violent enough. As if a depth charge had gone off in the pool's center, so what I was aware of was the odd, backward sensation of seeing the water implode.

If the rise of that salmon on the Cheticamp was so measured and graceful it gave me time to see it all in slow motion, this was exactly the opposite experience—it happened so fast it's recorded in my memory as a bewildering blur. At about the same instant I realized something had slashed toward the trout I was playing—a rogue alligator? a misplaced shark?—my rod bent double and nearly snapped, and I remembered, with an emotion that nearly snapped *me* double, the monstrous trout that had frightened me back in the spring.

If it wasn't he, it was surely his brother—his *big* brother. I'd always heard browns turned cannibal when they reached the right size, and this was evidence of the strongest, most vicious sort. Engorged with the smaller trout, the brown turned toward the middle of the pool, giving me a good view of his huge, incredibly powerful tail—in turning, he left a shadow in the water that was part silver, part cream. That it was the largest trout I'd ever seen or even thought about was obvious at once; that I was attached to it seemed a hallucination.

Fight back, I told myself. Fight back! I was charged up now, ready to follow him down through the marshes to the Atlantic, but he hardly seemed concerned with what little pressure I dared apply. He lived in the center of that pool and in the center of that pool he was going to stay, and we both knew my leader was too miserably light to do anything about it. I thought about changing my stance, applying pressure from another direction, but with the bank so steep, the drop-off so sudden, I was stuck. The best thing to do, at least for the time being, was to stay where I was, keep the line tight, and await developments.

These were not long in coming.

(Remembering my disclaimer at the beginning of this essay, I write the following two paragraphs in the full knowledge not a single one of my readers will believe them, yet every word is true. The only thing I ask you to remember is how the laws of probability necessarily imply the improbable—that a tossed penny, tossed frequently enough, will eventually land on its edge.)

The trout was toward the middle, placid part of the pool, deep, but not so deep I couldn't see him. There was no sign of the smaller trout he had swallowed or the fly the smaller trout had swallowed to start the chain off, yet my leader ran straight down the big fish's mouth (I remember wondering if, when it came time to brag of him, it would be more accurate to say I caught him on bait or the fly). My pressure, light as it was, irritated him enough that he swung his head around and started calmly back in my direction, thereby changing the angle enough that the hook came loose.

I stripped in line furiously, unable to come to terms with the fact the big trout was gone. Instinctively, doing it faster than I write these words, I swung line, leader, and trout-impaled fly back into the center of the pool. Again, the bottom of the water seemed to drop away, again the rod bent double, and not more than ten seconds after I lost him, the big trout—the big cannibalistic gluttonous suicidal trout—was on again.

There the two of us were, bound tight to each other in a swirl of frigid gray water, fish and man. The snow had dropped back again, stinging my eyes; my legs were numb from iciness, my arms all but palsied from the effort of holding the rod. A few yards away was the trout, bothered himself now, the hook embedded at an angle that must have plugged directly into his nervous system and hurt something essential, coming back to me with grudging reluctance, his thoughts filled with—what? Anger? Homesick memories of the ocean where he had spent his adolescence? Guilty reminiscences of all the smaller trout he must have eaten to obtain his weight? Or was his entire awareness centered in that sore, relentless ache in the jaw that meant his time was up? We swam in our misery together, danced our stubborn dance, and for upwards of an hour stayed attached in that partly sweet, oddly bitter symbiosis that is playing a fish of size.

The rest of the story doesn't take long to tell. Gradually, over the space of that hour, we were both weakening, and it was merely a question of who would reach exhaustion first. As in any epic of endurance, there were minor battles won and lost, various swings in the pendulum of fate, but twenty years later these have all been lost in the predominant, simplified memory of my tug versus the trout's.

Toward the end another fisherman appeared. With over forty beats on the river to choose from, he had reserved the pool by the dam, and he didn't act pleased to find me there.

He was a cool customer altogether; looking down from the spillway, he could see the trout quite clearly, but he hardly seemed impressed. I asked to borrow his net and he scaled it over to me, then, with a sullen expression, starting casting as if neither I nor the fish were there.

The trout was coming closer now, to the point I could start worrying about how to land him. The net was far too small to do the job, which left beaching him as the only alternative— beaching him, only there wasn't any beach. Behind me was the steep mud of the bank; to my right, the deep water near the dam; to my left, bushes and saplings that overhung the bank far enough to push me out over my head.

It was the bank then—that or my arms. I had the fish close to me now—he was so large I was shy of looking at him directly—and by increasing the pressure just a little I was able to swim him around so he rested between my waist and the bank. Coaxing my legs into motion, I waded in toward him, gradually narrowing the space he had left to swim, until there was less than a yard between him and shore. Again, there was no shelf here—it was like backing him against a wall. Finally, with a dipping, scooping motion, I got my arms under his belly, lifted him clear of the water . . . held him for a moment . . . then, just as I tensed my muscles prior to hurling him up the bank, watched helplessly as he gave that last proverbial flopping motion, broke the leader, and rolled back free into the pool from whence he came.

How did I feel? How would *you* feel?—that multiplied by ten. While obviously I never had the chance to put the fish on the scales, I'd had him in my arms for a few seconds, and kept a clear view of him for over an hour before that. I put his weight at eight pounds (no, I put it at *twelve* pounds, but I'm going to reduce it to cling to what credibility I have left, though reducing it is the only lie in this essay). An eight-pound brown trout—a fish that would be large for Argentina, let alone Long Island. I knew, with a feeling beyond words, that it was the biggest trout I would ever have a chance for, and that the rest of my angling career would be nothing but a futile search among lesser fish for his peer.

Melodramatic, perhaps, but I was slow to snap out of the bitter aftertaste losing him had left. In one sense I had landed the trout, if landing meant getting him out of the water into my arms, and in any case I'd decided during the midst of our fight to release him. There was some comfort in this, but when I shuffled my way out from the pool onto dry land, I was shaking with cold and stiffness and disappointment, and something even more intense I didn't believe existed until then: buck fever.

To be that close to something immense, to fight it for what from the trout's point of view was life or death, to have it and lose it in the very same instant—these were the ingredients tangled together at the emotion's core. But there was more that's harder to explain. It was as if during those minutes I was attached to him, all the civilized, dulling layers that separate me from my ancestral, elemental self—the hunter and gatherer that, reach back far enough, dwells in us all—had been tugged away, giving instinct its chance to romp through my nervous system in the old half-remembered patterns, so what I felt was the sick nauseous *human* emotion of a hunter at the end of the chase.

It didn't last very long, at least in one respect. In five minutes I was back at my car, dumping ice out of my waders, pouring the warm tea and bourbon directly over my toes. And yet a trace of that emotion lingers on to this day, as if the trout had been attached so long and fought so determinedly he welded a circuit between myself and that ancient, vaguely suspected self—the self that once fought giants and defeated a few and knew what disappointment was right down to the thrilling marrow of the bones.

October 15

T o the river.

The leaves were blown down in a Columbus Day gale, and what foliage is left drifts just beneath the surface of the current like a separate soggy river of red and gold. Now, in the brilliant sunshine of the storm's passing, with no shade, the color is blinding, stronger off the water than at any time during the summer. But no—*off is* not quite the word. The brightness is *in* the water, as if the usual laws of reflection have been suspended, the sun taken in rather than mirrored, the subtlety washed out into something that is already closer to December's steel than to August's velvet. The sun is tossed up in the rapids and aerated, stirred out in the pools and cooled, turning even the most familiar lies into mysteries of impenetrable radiance, so—wading into all this, trying to get my bearings, flipping down my Polaroids—I immediately feel at a loss. Brightness to the left of me, brightness to the right—it's as if the water has turned molten, and I have no idea where to cast. When the radiance gets into the water the fishing is over—it's Wetherell's Third Law of Fishing, and I try to take comfort from it, since it's apparent in the way my line and fly disappear in the hard beauty that this will be an afternoon without trout.

For all the times I've fished the river, there are stretches I still haven't tried. This is one of them—a quarter mile of riffles and pools backing the overgrown acreage of a newly abandoned farm. It's the classic New England scene, of course. Stone walls choked with briars, a rusty thresher obscured in milkweed, the ungrazed fields going back to ivy and birch. Up on a knoll is the abandoned farmhouse and barn, the boards already sagging into a closer, snugger fit to the land, though it's only a month since the last struggling farmer failed there and moved on. New England's landscape, at its purest, has a genius for nature's soft reclamation—ashes turn to ashes nowhere prettier than here.

There are stories in all this—it's the classic New England literary landscape as well. Ruined dreams, vanished villages, the bittersweet suggestion of an apple tree growing beside an old cellar hole—these have been the staples of the region's fiction through Frost and Jewett and Wharton and Howells all the way back to Hawthorne, whose genius not only captured the lonely shadows over these hills but cast his own that lingers in our imaginations to this day. Many talented writers have worked this terrain; many talented writers work it still, mopping up the tragic leftovers—the last farmers struggling to stay afloat; the irony of a flinty land dying through prosperity—though it's clear that here as the twentieth century lurches and stumbles its way toward a finish, New England has become a literary backwater, and its writers of fiction will have to turn their attention outward from our old familiar parish if they are to avoid total irrelevancy. Me, when I see the birches I think of Russia and copses and Tolstoy—my imagination glances off.

Fishing? No, but the kind of thing I'm apt to consider when I'm not catching fish. For all the perfection of the water behind the farm, despite the generosity of an afternoon that gives me, in quick succession, sights of hawks, grouse, mink, vultures, and deer (plus a rarity, a turtle sunbathing in the stream!), it's obvious my first instinct was right—that I could change from using a Gold-Ribbed Hare's Ear to TNT and still catch nothing.

The realization that you will be skunked is one of the hardest things in the fishing life; when in the day that moment comes is one of the diciest timings. Sometimes the signs are so ominous you know with the first cast you're going to strike out all day; other times, conditions are so ripe you can work for hours, and, fishless, still feel certain your next cast will bring a rise. I've had my share of both experiences, particularly the former. In September, just before leaving for an overnight trip to the upper Connecticut, I was met with the following weather report: "The eye of Hurricane Hugo will pass over Pittsburg, New Hampshire (our destination!), sometime during the morning Saturday, bringing torrential rain, followed by an Arctic cold front that will leave up to six inches of snow by Sunday morning." Maybe it's the pessimist in me, but I had a strong presentiment—subsequently confirmed—that it was not going to be a trip rich in trout.

There was one obscure period in my life when I used to venture into singles bars; I remember the disappointment that came, usually with the third vodka and tonic, when I swallowed the fact I would be leaving alone. A similar disappointment is what I'm talking about here; we put so much behind us when we go fishing, work, trivialities, worries, that, with disappointment, we risk having it all flood back. That the fish isn't everything, that it's enough merely being outside surrounded by beauty, up to our waists in living water, is certainly true, of course, but it's amazing how much truer it seems if we've caught at least one trout. Fish-less, the temptation is to fish longer than conditions warrant, thereby setting up a vicious cycle—the longer you fish without a fish, the more you need one; the more you need one, the more your disappointment grows; the longer you fish, et cetera, et cetera.

Flyfishers differ in nothing so much as they do this, the willingness to admit defeat. It's one of the trickiest things in a fishing friendship, the fatalist ready to throw in the towel too quickly, the optimist fishing far beyond hope's outer bound. The best partnerships work out a code to face facts gently . . . "Anything doing down your way? . . . What do you make of this cold front? . . . Does that store down the road sell Molson's?" . . . and with mutual commiseration agree the moment has come to transfer hope to the next day out, take down the rods, and quit.

Alone, it's a harder decision for me, since it means not only ending the day, but the season. Between the empty brightness of the water (my thermometer measures it as forty-nine degrees), my fishless conviction, the sense of regret and finale suggested by the abandoned farm, my thoughts change focus, so somewhere between the log-sheltered pool at the start of the run and the undercut bank at the finish, I've turned from hoping what the next cast will bring to remembering what the long season has brought.

A good year, I decide—no monsters, but even so. There was the spring when I finally got the hang of fishing a nymph; a June morning when I caught two dozen smallmouth, the slightest of which was two pounds; the discovery of a secret brook trout stream no wider than a sidewalk; the start of some new fishing friendships (to this habitual loner, a miraculous thing); the rediscovery of my river after a year of drought and too long a time away.

The season was over; as they say in Hollywood, "That's a wrap," and then as I turned to climb up onto the bank a brown trout tugged on my trailing Muddler, re-creating for the time he was on the hope I had already given up. But what was odd, as careful as I handled things, it hardly seemed like I was playing him in the present tense at all, but off in the future somewhere—that beautiful as he was, he was pulling at me from April of the coming year, so at last, when I landed him on the rocks, knelt down, and released him, I was faced the right way for winter, with the right spirit, with just enough hope to pamper toward spring.

Why Fish?

I have an uncle for whom I have a great deal of affection, despite the fact we have very little in common. Over the years, by default, most of our conversations have been about his bowling, the only subject I've ever found that will take us past the uncomfortable silence after preliminary remarks about weather and health have quickly been exhausted. People need a tag, a quick label, to make it easy for insensitive dullards like myself to work up some chit-chat. Mine—now that the tables have been turned and I'm an uncle myself, with nieces and nephews faced with the daunting prospect of making me talk—is fishing. "So, how's the fishing been, Walter?"—this in lieu of asking me about my latest novel, or the condition of my back, or all those murky, complicated things that might, with unpredictable consequence, get me started.

So I tell them—so I tell you—that by and large the fishing has been very good, thank you. A balm and supportive to the soul, an antidote to bitterness, a relief and a restorative and a reward. What I don't tell them, though I'm tempted to, is that I'm going to quit it any day now and take up bowling myself.

It's amazing, now that I think of it, how much time I spend dreaming, not about fishing, but about *quitting* fishing—of selling off my tackle at a tag sale, ripping up my waders to use as chaffing *around* our fruit trees, donating my fishing books to a responsible charity, turning my canoe into a planter. For all the gentleness of the sport, it has the maddening trick of suddenly turning on you, becoming a burr and an irritant, a breeder of bitterness, a plague and a problem and a pox.

These manic attitude swings have been a feature of my fishing right from the start. I remember once as a fourteen-year-old being deposited by my parents near a river that was said to have monstrous bass, and being picked up again in tears four hours later, driven to despair by the dozen lures I had lost on the brush-choked bottom, the wet clay I had foundered in, the sweat that poured over my face, the branches that knocked off my glasses, the terrible disappointment of catching, for all my agony, absolutely naught. Even closer than that, even yesterday. After three days of rain, three days of being locked in the house, I was desperate to go fishing, to the point where I talked myself into believing the rivers wouldn't be flooded, though I knew in the suppressed half of me they would be exactly that. Forty miles later, arrived at the river I had inexplicably chosen, I saw the situation was exactly as I foresaw: the river was over its banks and unfishable. Nothing daunted, I drove on to another river, fooling myself into thinking it hadn't rained as much over there; that river, of course, turned out to be flooded, too, and there I was at eight in the evening a hundred miles from home, exhausted, disappointed, and so mad at myself I feared for my sanity.

As unnerving as this type of thing can be, it's the natural downside of anything that is pursued passionately over any length of time. If worse comes to worst and I give in to my peevish irritation, make good my threat to quit, no one will be the loser except for me. But it's one thing to give up something cherished through your own free will, quite another to have something cherished taken away from you by force.

Let me backtrack here to an incident that happened this summer. I was teaching at a writer's conference, feeling, as you do at these things, that I was a minnow of some small knowledge pursued by voracious muskellunge hungry for same. To escape, I went fishing. A few miles from the campus is a surprisingly good trout stream, replete with pools and riffles that stay cold even in July. I fished it regularly for a week, got into some nice browns each morning (including a monster that broke off during a thunderstorm I had no right being out in—but that's another story), enjoyed some Vermont scenery at its most pastoral, and in general had a delicious time. On the seventh day, though the water was just as perfect and clear, I caught nothing. Walking back to my car, puzzled, I saw a highway crew leaning over a bridge downstream of the stretch I'd fished; they had long-handled nets with them, and were leaning over the water to scoop up dead, colorless trout, tossing them into their truck as if they were cans of Budweiser thrown there by slobs.

The explanation wasn't long in coming. A valve had been turned the wrong way at the municipal swimming pool six miles upstream, releasing chlorine and other chemicals into the river, killing upwards of fifteen thousand fish—demonstrating, among other things, how even the clearest trout stream is nothing more than another pipe in our municipal waste system; one twist of the dial and trout, mystique, and purity are all flushed away.

Now it seems to me this episode is both a perfect literal description and a perfect metaphor for the present condition of American trout fishing. There I was fishing that gloriously pristine river, oblivious to the fact the water that shined so brilliantly was in reality poisoned—that the browns I had caught earlier in the week and released so carefully were now being hauled off to the dump. We cherish our traditions, do the best we can to leave no imprint on the stream, and despite our best efforts the water is dying anyway, to the point where we realize how pathetic the enterprise has become, and fish less often, and eventually find excuses not to face this irony at all.

People whose backs are against the wall, pressed hard enough, will eventually lash out with their fists, and if there's any good news to be had in the depressing roll call of environmental catastrophe, it is this: that lovers of nature, flyfishers among them, are beginning to fight back. I have a friend who spends many hours each week working on behalf of Trout Unlimited, traveling around the country spreading their message of wise and measured use of our fishery resources. I have another friend who puts his talents as a lawyer to use in suing those who would dam and harness every molecule of moving water they can find. Still another friend, while having neither the time nor temperament to work so aggressively, goes out of his way to contribute money to conservation organizations, and isn't shy about lambasting senators, representatives, and wardens for the primitive fishing regulations still in effect. I have another friend—a real favorite—who does none of these things, but fights underground, pouring syrup into the tanks of bulldozers he comes upon deep in the forest, ripping out survey stakes, and in general making good use of those monkey-wrenching tactics made famous by the late, great Edward Abbey.

There are those who would shake their heads at my last friend, counsel moderation, but I am not one of them. It is clear, after a century of lip service to "conservation" matched by environmental disasters of unparalleled scope that the time has come for those who care for natural beauty to think in terms of revolution, consider using the guerrilla hit-and-run tactics that are a prelude to any full-scale revolt. While it's certain the bulk of measurable results are being garnered by friends one and two, supported by the dollars of friend three, it's equally clear it's time to start adopting the tactics of friend four, to see whether civil disobedience might not be more effective. The environmental movement needs its radical left, and not only that, but a radical right, an organization that would fight with the same fanatic devotion for the fish lobby (with over seventy-five million fishermen on this continent, how formidable it would be!) with the same fanatic devotion as the NRA fights for the gun lobby.

Me, I've torn down my share of survey ribbons in my day, finding the little shredding tug as they come apart to be among nature's most delightful sensations. But still, at my age, in my circumstances, I haven't yet grown into the radical I aspire to become when my courage matures. Those who write of nature in this country are given a different task: to carefully explain what it is in beauty that is worth saving, and thereby give those who fight in the trenches a clearer sight of what they defend.

Add that to the list of devastation wrought by developers and highway builders and politicians and our own wasteful sloth:

that even someone who writes about something as innocent as fishing must adopt the vocabulary of apocalypse and confrontation, deviate as far from the pastoral style of a Charles Cotton—patron saint of fly fishing—as our threatened streams differ from his untroubled Dove. To be written honestly in this day and age, a fishing book has to acknowledge the threats squarely, or hide behind a nostalgic obscuration—has to take on an edge, as it were, and sacrifice a portion of its lyricism to the hard blade of truth.

A portion—but not all. If nothing else in this book, I hope I've conveyed the delights flyfishers can find in the practice of their incredibly simple, incredibly sophisticated art. Here at the end it seems appropriate to be quite explicit about what prompts me to spend a good portion of half the year trying to convince trout and bass and pike the bauble I am floating across their narrow cone of vision is in reality a morsel of food—to make, as an affirmation of faith, a list of the reasons I fish. For convenience, I will separate out the constituent motives, and not only that, try to rank them in order of personal importance, but only with the disclaimer that in fishing, like life, everything comes in one overwhelming jumble, lists and categories be damned.

Why, then, fish?

1. *Geographic Discovery*

A real surprise for starters, a very personal reason, and one I didn't appreciate the force of until I sat down to make this list. Simply stated, the prime motivation for my fishing is to explore rivers, lakes, oceans, and ponds—explore them, in my small way, like La Salle or Champlain or one of those early explorers whose eyes had first crack at this continent; explore with a global kind of curiosity the small hidden corners of the world.

In practice, this works on two modest levels: my continually wanting to try new rivers, not so much to discover whether they have any fish, but simply to see where they *go;* my returning again and again to familiar water, to explore it a little further, try that pool that's always been a little too remote. The first has resulted in many happy discoveries of places I would never have seen without fishing as my ostensible purpose (for instance, the wild scrub forest of Cape Cod, which I stumbled into in my pursuit of its elusive salter trout); the second, in my continual amazement at how the familiar can yield so much that is brand-new (yesterday on the Waits, again stumbling, I came upon a small tributary that doesn't appear on any map).

I have a deep curiosity about land and waterscape, which, trace it back far enough, probably has something to do with the infant Wetherell's delight in exploring the steadily expanding boundaries of cradle, bassinet, nursery, and yard. It's almost impossible to exaggerate the adult dimensions of this delight; I want to swallow terrain whole, sink my teeth into it, so when I travel, even to a stream half a mile away, I'm possessed by a restlessness and curiosity that both propels me and leaves me drained. It has another, sadder effect: it makes me a much worse fisherman than I would be if I could linger with more patience. Sure the trout are rising right there in the pool ahead of me, but what is that compared to the allure of the canyon or waterfall that might be around the next bend?

Closely allied to geographic discovery is the exploration of time; indeed, it would be more accurate to speak of the space-time continuum in all the above. Time of day is one of the things a fisherman learns best, in all its subtle shading, from that first riverine curl of gray in the east that comes before true dawn, to the slow clockwise spin of the Great Bear over a bass lake in total dark. Even here I can tune the list finer: of all the times of day, it is dusk—summer dusk—that interests me most, and I often go fishing simply to immerse myself in some, let its settling curtain bring the gentle shadows and increasing stillness I love so well.

2. A Role in the Natural World

Going fishing to be "outside," going fishing to see "nature." These are familiar explanations for something more subtle, the compelling reason I put second on my list, but which could equally be first. In this industrialized age of ours, man—only a few generations removed from coaxing his living from the farm, the forest, or the water—is sick to death because of the artificial divisions he has established between himself and the natural world. Anything that gets us past these divisions is worthy of passionate pursuit, whether it be the flowers of the suburban gardener or the birds of the amateur ornithologist.

What is special about fishing in general and fly fishing in particular is that the pursuit of fish alone, with no other object in view, brings with it all kinds of attendant marvels, from sights of hawks and ospreys and foxes, to the more intimate miracles of tiny wildflowers and insects that to anyone but a flyfisher and a trout would be invisible (I think of Thoreau's phrase, "All this is apparent to the observant eye, but would pass unnoticed by most"). Just being outside in nature is not as good a means of discovering nature as it is to *ask* something of it; we have to pose specific questions to nature for it to answer; we have to sharpen our senses to search for trout, and, sharpened, those senses are available to take in the mysteries our duller selves would miss.

But to put the motivation more clearly, I can do no better than to quote the naturalist Henry Beston. Asked what understanding he gained from his year alone in the "outermost house" on the dunes of Cape Cod, he replied: "I would answer that one's first appreciation is a sense that the creation is still going on, that the creative forces are as great and active to-day as they have ever been, and that to-morrow's mornings will be as heroic as any in the world." This at some level is what every fisherman learns when he spends time on the water, and the spirit of this in our pessimistic age is intoxicating and one of the prime reasons that makes us fish.

3. Tactileness

There's almost nothing that feels as good against the skin as water, which is what all those beaches and water slides and hot tubs and pools and showers and bathtubs are all about. Even the most sedentary bait fisher will dangle his bare toes over the rowboat to establish contact with its coolness, and one of the consistent delights of fly fishing is to be immersed in this element at varying depths. It's a hard pleasure at times, to be sure; to stand chest deep in an April river slightly over freezing is something only a masochist would find pleasure in, but even here, the numbness in the body creates a sharpness in the mind, and lets you know, as few other tingles can, that you are alive.

But usually it's much better than that. A May river on the back of one's legs, cooling pleasantly through the wader fabric, supporting by its force, lightening by its buoyancy—if there's anything as sensuously rich it's only the same river in July, when the waders are gone and the current comes directly against bare legs. Add to this a breeze against the neck, a fishing breeze from the south carrying with it the earthy damp of fiddlehead ferns, the slippery firmness of a trout against the palm, the dust of mayflies blowing against your cheek during a good hatch, the pleasant, loosening tug on the shoulders caused by casting . . . there can be few pastimes that in their normal execution feel as good as this.

4. Fish

Anyone who's come this far with me will know I admire fish greatly, spend a great deal of time longing to be connected to one, study their habits and habitat with a good deal of attention, and the only thing to do here is explain why I haven't listed them first on my list. For me, the fish is not the be-all and end-all of the fishing process, though I feel like the Mad Hatter in writing this down. I have an intense curiosity about fish, but it has its limits, while the first three listings come without bounds.

That fish are hard animals to love (love, say, like I love swallows) will come as no surprise to anyone who thinks about it; their cold-blooded status creates a barrier our mammalian solipsism finds difficult to bridge. Then, too, they are quarry; to even the most sophisticated of anglers, the strictest conservationist, the most devoted catch-and- releaser, they are quarry, something hunted, and while respect, insight, and empathy can flourish in the hunting process, it's a perversion of the term to speak of love. No matter what fishing represents to us, to fish it's a grim life-and-death struggle, and though I've caught my share of fish that winked at me, I've never seen one that smiled.

I have a passion for fishing, a lesser passion for the fish themselves. But passion is passion, and if fish aren't first in my motives, they are still high up there on the chart. If catching fish involved none of the first three entries, but meant instead you had to wade foul urban alleys beset by rats, I would still pursue them intently. Land a good trout or bass, hold it for a second on the wet skin of your hand, and you have, in one compact bundle, as beautiful and bewildering a combination of opposites as it's possible to imagine; strength and litheness, fragility and toughness, intelligence and obtuseness, fastidiousness and voraciousness, boldness and stealth. And even if you're not as fond of contradictions as I am, what other creature comes close to a fish in color and fluid grace? Offered a shot at reincarnation, I would opt for being a trout without any hesitation at all—a wild twelve-inch brook trout, say, at home in a small brook that made me slightly bigger than my peers, living out my days with detachment and a certain world-weary wisdom that would perfectly complement my size.

Perhaps I would be a better fisherman if I didn't admire fish so greatly; I've never been able to turn them completely into objects, never been willing to apply any science to them, preferring, like the stars, that they swarm about me with their mysteriousness intact.

5. *Texture of Memory*

Number five now, but climbing higher with each year. More and more I fish to reestablish contact with places, times, and events I have in memory; so present fishes for past, as it were, and when a memory takes hold hard its current flows up the line and lives in all its intensity again. Fifteen years ago, this wasn't the case—I simply hadn't fished long enough, my experiences were too scattered to take on any texture. It takes five or more years' fishing the same water under a variety of conditions to create a dense enough association that your fishing becomes enriched; fishing the Waits, I think of the young man I was ten years ago wading into the same river without knowing where any of its trout were, hardly knowing where to look; fishing Franklin Pond above my home, I think of springs a decade in the past when I caught trout that even now stand out vividly enough in my recollection that

I can picture every spot. The time my wife bailed a leaky row-boat three inches from swamping, while I, sitting oblivious in the stern, fought and landed a five-pound largemouth; the patient way my mother used to take me fishing at our Connecticut summer home when my father was working; a slow, lazy trip down a bass river with two good friends, eating carrot cake on a sandbar under a warm summer rain. I remember these hardly ever when I'm not fishing—it takes being on a reminiscent body of water, fishing in a similar evening light, to bring the memory back, and this explains the allure of familiar water, the reason we never tire of it though we fish it again and again.

6. Literature and Tradition

Saint Peter, Dame Julian Berners, Leonard Macall, Gervase Markham, Izaak Walton, Charles Cotton, Sir Edward Grey, George M. L. La Branche, G. E. M. Skues, Edward Ringwood Hewitt, Theodore Gordon, Dolly Varden, William Scrope, J. W. Hill, Huck Finn, Plunket Greene, Patrick Chalmers, H. T. Sheringham, John Burroughs, Queequeg, Eugene Connet, John Taintor Foote, Eric Taverner, Preston Jennings, Ernest Hemingway, Zane Gray, Caroline Gordon, the Darbees, A. W. Miller, Odell Shephard, Robert Traver, Nick Lyons, Norman Maclean, Arnold Gingrich, Ed Zern, Roderick L. Haig-Brown, Pogo, Red Smith, Angus Cameron, Ted Hughes, Elizabeth Bishop, Lee Wulff, Charles Ritz, Paul Young, Charles Fox, William Humphrey, Vincent Mariano, et al.

7. Art and Craft

Art is not a word to toss around lightly, and it's important to remember fly fishing is not an art in the same way painting the Sistine Chapel is, or writing *The Charterhouse of Parma*. The kind of patience a fisherman needs is similar to that of the artist—a passionate, active patience, the kind that knows when to search and when to wait—and of course imagination and talent also play their part. The *art* of fly fishing, though, leans more toward the *craft* side of the term; we speak of the art of holding a runner on first base, the art of putting, the art of fishing a size-twenty-eight midge, when the word *craft* would work better. Fly fishing differs from most sports in the almost infinite variety of art-crafts that come into play even routinely. There's the art of fine rod making, the art of fly-tying (here if anywhere the word art means ART), the art of casting, the art of reading a river, the art of hooking a trout in fast water, the art of playing a heavy fish.

Fly fishing is enough like art that aesthetic satisfaction is an important ingredient when you total up its delights.

What's more, there's a mechanical satisfaction that comes from the execution of perfect technique, the intellectual satisfaction that is similar to solving a hard chess problem, the athletic satisfaction that—with the hand-eye coordination involved in casting—is similar to shooting baskets. When things go right, that is. What a day on the river usually becomes is an amalgam of mechanical triumph and mechanical fiasco, aesthetic disaster and aesthetic bliss, and it's this dizzying roller coaster that resembles art most of all, so defeat is there in all our minor victories, victory there in all our major defeats.

8. *Toys*

It's hard not to get carried away here. Is there any adult pastime that brings with it such a delightful treasure chest of toys as fly fishing? Reels that go clickety-clackety-clack, rods that whip the air about and magically extend our reach, waders we go clomping around in, hooks adorned with feathers (feathers of guinea hen, fur of polar bear, tinsel from a Christmas tree!), little springy things, pastes and scissors and sharp instruments our mothers would have in no circumstances let us touch . . . the playroom was never as good as this.

Fishing tackle brings us back to the days when our only work was play, our toys the means by which we explored our limited and infinite world. Toys, and yet there's more to it than that; reels not only go clickety-clack, but purr exquisitely, and there are satisfactions in owning a fine bamboo fly rod that mimic the satisfactions in owning a Stradivarius; indeed, there are people who don't fish at all, but spend many hours and dollars assembling collections of rare rods and reels.

My own passion is for lures; I don't think there has been a time in my life when I wasn't enamored of one variety or another. When I was younger it alternated between River Run Spooks, those scoop-nosed, hook-festooned plugs that resemble aquiline minnows, and Jitterbugs, the platter-faced marvels I spent too much of my allowance on when I was twelve. Since turning flyfisher, I've run through a whole parade of favorite flies: Muddlers, Honey Blondes, Brown Bivisibiles, Gray Fox Variants, Royal Wulffs. It's no exaggeration to say I can stare at a perfectly tied Royal Wulff for minutes at a time, delighting in the deer-hair puff of it, the crisp red and white color. Just the word lure is alone enough to fascinate me; how many lures of any kind does man have in his arsenal? And how many of those are as bright and purposeful as a number-sixteen dry fly?

There are fishermen who overdose on tackle; almost all do during some stage of their fishing career, and what is means can too easily become ends. Winter is the time to indulge this passion—late winter when the tackle companies are canny enough to send out their catalogs. Once the season comes it's best to simplify things as much as possible. Anyone who's been a kid knows the very best thing to do with toys is make a cache of them, a chest or drawer no one else can touch, and I advise the same for the novice fly-fisher; buy all you want, but when you go out to the river, leave all but the essential tackle at home and concentrate your passion on the fish.

9. Solitude

In this day and age solitude runs to two extremes. To people who are locked in by it, unable to make contact with any human no matter how ardently they try, it must seem an evil spell they would do anything to shatter; to those caught up in the vortex, physically and psychologically hemmed in and supported by a network of friends, relatives, lovers, and colleagues, with all the mental battering that happily and unhappily results, solitude must seem an impossible dream, something longed for with just as much intensity as the lonely bring to its detestation.

So it's a condition to speak about carefully, lest its gate abruptly swing down and block our retreat. Suffice it to say that here in the industrialized West, solitude, spatial solitude and silence, is next to impossible to find; we retreat to our homes, but the television lies waiting; we try to find it in sleep, but outside the horns keep blaring, the sirens rush past. Fly fishing for trout, done properly, requires much time alone on the stream; one of the few rules that seems to hold true in all circumstances is that the farther from the road you go, the better the fishing becomes. Countless times I've followed trout from pool to pool, catching one here, one there, until I've been led deep into the forest like Hansel and Gretel toward the witch's house, only it's a good witch this time, and, when I remember to break for lunch, I'm amazed at what silence I've managed to reach—how between one pool and the next the sounds of the mechanized world have dropped away and I'm as isolated and solitary as if I stood on a peak in the Hindu Kush.

But perhaps even this experience is too solitary and enchanted to speak of in print. Just say that being alone is a rare pleasure to those lucky enough not to be alone, and fly fishing, notwithstanding entry number ten, is still best pursued in as much solitude as you can stand.

10. *Lingua Franca*

While I don't have any statistics, fishing must be responsible for more cross-generational, cross-occupational, cross-societal, cross-geographical, and cross-just-about-any-boundary-you-can-mention *friendships* than any activity you can compare against it. Golfers tend to golf with people from the same office; bowlers bowl with people from the same plant, but fishing friendships seem to flourish amid what would seem the unlikeliest of dissimilarities, and there's no better tribute to the richness of our sport. What I've been struck with time and time again is how two very different people, united by this one passion, can begin talking in a common language from the first sentence of their conversation, exchanging secrets, trading battle stories, instantly getting to a stage of intimacy that would take many hours if not for this key. I don't speak French, yet I still feel certain that if I were plopped down next to one of those patient Seine fishermen I could have a pretty good conversation going inside of minutes, even if it was exchanged solely with our hands.

Add fishing partnerships to this entry, those happy combinations when to the instant communication of the above is added long shared experiences on rivers and ponds. For many fishermen it will come first in the fishing motives, and should I ever come back to revise this list, I would hope—if present trends continue, if people continue to ignore my foibles and invite me out—that it would be first on mine.

11. Retribution

There can't be many activities where sins of commission and omission are punished as instantly and inevitably as in fishing. A hasty knot in a leader will surely find a trout to snap it; an unsharpened hook will find a bass's jaw too hard to penetrate; a clumsy step in a deep pool and over our heads we go. I am just enough of a Puritan to find this comforting; again, it goes against the grain of our century, where the wages of sin are higher than the rewards of virtue. Keenness of attention, discipline of method, fussiness over details—these are dull attributes to list, but every good fisherman has them, so there you are.

The only thing better than being a Puritan, of course, is being a lapsed Puritan—to not give a damn about knots or imitation or prudence, and just chuck the fly out there. Make that number eleven and a half on the list—a halfway step to:

12. Chance

The throw of the dice, the spin of the wheel, the play of a card— fly fishing is as chancy as one of these, and gambling is unquestionably one of its delights, and goes far to explain the compulsive ardor many fishermen bring to its pursuit. To anyone who's made the high-wire gamble of a writing life, any lesser chance, by a cautious backlash, seems unbearably risky, and I've never been one for football pools or raffle tickets or bingo. Still, when I go out on a river I like the fact so many chances are taken—taken in big ways when the wading gets dicey or a thunderstorm brews up; taken in lesser ways almost continually: the chance there may be a trout lying in that riffle where none has ever lay before; the chance he might be in the mood for a Blue Winged Olive; the chance we can land him if we pare down to a 7X leader with a breaking strength of less than a pound. The best fisherman I know giggles a lot when he fishes—giggles, I suspect, at so many of his risks coming off. We all do this at some level—laugh at our good luck, curse at our bad, so that a day on the water is a kind of catharsis, and I often come back home at night with a throat scratchy and sore from sheer exclamation.

13. *Hope*

Mountain climbing has been described as "the alternation of hope and despair," and while flyfishers in the ordinary course of their game do not risk rockfall or avalanche, this definition still goes a long way to explain the intensity of the fishing passion. Despair—well, there's plenty of that, even on a good day. Small tangles become monstrous backlashes; leaders snap from the clumsiness of our knots; trout are rising to a hatch that is unmatchable, until we're locked out by our ineptitude from the moment when nature exhibits itself at its very richest.

But even that maddening, unmatchable hatch fulfills one of the hopes we bring to the river in the first place: to see it at the peak of vibrant life. Hope is the one prerequisite in angling, the best part of the sport, and, I'd like to think, the coda that has underlined this book all along. In a century where hope has pretty well had its face smashed in, even to wear the small hope of a fisherman is in its way a victory—to hope for anything at all. And further—where in this age can even small hopes be satisfied as readily and innocently as in fishing? Estranged from nature, what other portion of it responds even occasionally to our coaxing?

Coming to the end of *Walden* Thoreau summed up his experiment in living thus: "That if one advances confidently in the direction of his dreams . . . he will meet with a success unexpected in common hours." This was written from an optimism that seems amazing to us now, and yet there are people who every day learn the truth of this, and among them are fishermen, who, in their precious hours on the water, possess an optimism and strength of purpose worthy of Thoreau. Try it the next time you go out on your favorite river. See how the four-count rhythm of fly casting synchronizes itself to the surge of hope welling up in your chest.

I . . . fly off the water . . . real Ay . . . line uncoiling back of us . . . HOPE . . . line shooting forward.

I . . . real-ly . . . HOPE.

That the twelve-inch rainbow there ahead of me sees the Spent Wing Adams floating down past his sheltering log.

I . . . real-ly . . . HOPE.

That the rain lets up. That the wind doesn't collapse this cast around my head. That the Hendrickson hatch starts at two o'clock on schedule.

I . . . real-ly . . . HOPE.

That my daughter and son will learn to love fly-fishing. That I introduce them to it with the right measure of gentle patience. That they find in it what I have found and more. That they remember to take their old man out with them when the passion takes hold.

I . . . real-ly . . . HOPE.

That they decide not to build a freeway across the river. That the state institutes a catch-and-release stretch before the trout disappear. That the coal plants cap off their emissions and reduce acid rain. That the farmers stay in business. That flood plains are not built on or developed.

I . . . real-ly . . . HOPE.

That trout streams run pure and wild forever. That trout and bass and every fish that swims flourishes mightily in the coming century. That man calls a truce with nature, starts the long patient healing and rejoining the lack of which dooms us all. That in the future even to talk about a separation this way will seem an ungrammatical impossibility. That the lion of man lies down with the lamb of nature, not in an allegory, but in a new realistic symbiosis.

I . . . real-ly . . . HOPE.

Add your own here—add the minor and major hopes that go into the fishing passion and so unite us once and for all. "Our tradition," wrote Roderick Haig-Brown, "is that of the first man who sneaked away to the creek when the tribe did not really need a fish, a tradition developed for us through thousands of years and millions of river lovers. We fish for pleasure, and fishing becomes pleasure from within ourselves in proportion to the skill and knowledge, to the imagination and flexibility of soul, that we bring to it." This is correctly and splendidly said, and the only thing left to do in finishing is to wish you all the best fishing in the world—wish, as intently as it's possible to wish something off the page, that once in your life the fates conspire in your favor, the planets pause in their circling, the waters part, and there beneath your uncoiling line will rise something miraculous, something worth all your longing, something extraordinarily fine.

One River More

Part One:
Early Days

The Waiting Game

Every flyfisher knows there are two fishing seasons: the official one set by the fish and game department, and the richer, more fluid one set by your heart. In most northern states the first comes in mid-April, which is a joke for everyone except the worm fishermen, and with the streams so high and cloudy, not a particularly funny one even for them. The second starts—Well, take your pick. When the first tackle catalogs come in January, just when you're at your weakest, so spending money on equipment seems a plausible substitute for actually fishing? Sometime after Christmas when, using that new vise Santa brought, you tie up your first pattern for the coming year? When brochures are sent for from

Montana, Alaska, Argentina, or, better yet, when a deposit is actually mailed? Everyone picks their date, and for me, though I've tried every psychological trick there is, every coaxing, I've never been able to get the season of expectation to open any sooner than the first week of March.

January and February, the long weeks leading up to the equinox. These are strictly working months here, the time I earn my fishing time, literally put it in the bank—and not only a real bank, but that more complex lending institution that revolves around family goodwill. When I do go outdoors its usually to ski through the mixed softwoods that start behind our house, and the only thing this has to do with fishing is that occasionally I'll catch that low, throaty surge of water as I cross a frozen stream—a sound no river lover can hear without sensing a matching pulse coursing through their blood. I'll even try poking at the snow with my ski pole just to see if I can't liberate some watery brightness; once, doing this on a day of extreme cold, I pulled back out a perfect popsicle, my pole frozen from the tip over the basket into a clear blue ball of ice.

Other than these little foretastes, there's not much going on. The sun gets brighter, the days get longer, and if you wake up early enough you can see Vega and the summer constellations rising over the low mountains to our east like coming attractions scrolled over a dark orange screen. But when you live in northern New England as long as I have, you develop a little damper on your hope, try not to get excited. Another month until fishing is even a remote possibility; two months until I'll actually venture out; three months until hatches start and conditions become halfway decent; four months until the glory days of June and early July. It's simply too much hard time left in the sentence, so, like a prisoner facing freedom, I find its better not to think about it at all.

If I do give in to temptation, it's still retrospectively; it's last year's fishing from remembering, getting out the pictures, glancing at my fishing calendar, taking solace from modest triumphs that have only been enhanced by the intervening months. I notice the same backward inclination in talking with my fishing partners. Meeting in January, we're still talking about *last* summer on the Yellowstone, not *next* summer on the Androscoggin.

As I said, all this changes around March first when I start giving myself permission to think about the coming season. The winter seems endless at this stage, the storms we always get around town meeting day being among our most ferocious, and what robins or blackbirds manage to find their way up here are often blown right back to Massachusetts by the frigid northwest wind. But still, there's something in the air now—a vague earthy scent, little trills and whispers from meltwater, a growing confidence in the sun—that at least enables you to pronounce the word *spring,* not like a remote, half-imagined abstraction, but as a reality, the appearance of which won't be spooked by mentioning its name out loud.

In short, late winter is very much a waiting game, one every flyfisher has to play as best they can. There are time-honored means for doing so, of course, some of which I take part in, others I prefer to sit out. One of these is ice-fishing. Our local pond will have its little village of companionable shacks most winters, at least when the ice has a chance to thicken before being covered by an insulating blanket of snow. The fact I've never actually gotten up the energy to dig a hole, let a line down, hoist a flag shouldn't obscure the fact I can understand perfectly the motives of those doing so. The hard crystalline beauty of a frozen pond in winter; the polar bear companionship of people who are as thickly booted, mitted, and hatted as you are yourself; the restorative dashes back to the shed for whatever is in the thermos or flask. Dig me a trench, get a hatch started, oil a fly line with antifreeze, and I'd be out there in a second.

Fly tying is another form of winter fishing, one I have all the respect for in the world, but don't have the knack for and probably never shall. It's an art and a demanding one; Carrie Stevens, Helen Shaw, Roy Steenrod, the Darbees: these are great and honored names, and rightly so, for the skill these tyers bring to their work, the combination of preciseness and flair, experience and imagination, can only be compared with the work of the great nature artists or the most skilled jewelers.

For me, those long hours hunched over a tying bench are a little too similar to the long hours hunched over a writing desk, a little too much for my back, eyes, and nerves to handle. But as something to tide you over between seasons, I don't see how it can be beat.

Neither ice fisherman nor fly tyer, I'm left with a lot of winter hours to fill, or at least would be if it wasn't for the fact there are plenty of other fishing surrogates, stopgaps, and pacifiers waiting on line. The following is a short list, both of the kinds of things I personally find helpful in waiting out March and suggestions for anyone faced with the same predicament.

1. FORM RESOLUTIONS

I have this terrible habit I'm half-ashamed to admit: I'm the kind who keeps their New Year's resolutions. Of course this is absurdly anal of me, priggish, straight-arrowish to a fault, and wins me more suspicion and disgust than it does approbation. So I'm always careful with my resolves, since, as with wishes, they very well may come true.

I think I'm on safe ground this year, at least with fishing. For I've formed two resolutions, one on the practical side, one on the practical-spiritual.

The first is never to lose a fish this season through a badly tied knot. Adding an extra half-hitch when you tie on your fly; sitting down out of the wind and concentrating as you fashion a blood knot; checking the breaking strength of your tippets. In theory, these are the easiest preventatives in the world—and yet how tedious and slow that extra care can seem when actually fishing. The trout are rising, your hands are shaking from excitement or cold, you realize it's been a while since you last checked connections, but. . . . No, it's simply one task too much, like getting back out of a warm, cozy bed to floss your teeth. Trout, of course, ask for nothing better, and will undo a bad knot with what always seems a particularly gleeful, tah-dah kind of flourish—trout as disappearing act, trout unbound.

The second resolution may be a little harder to keep, for all my self-discipline. Last year my friend Tom Ciardelli and I finished salmon season up in Maine, fishing the Rapid River for landlocks. What with logging roads going everywhere now, four-wheel drive and ATVs, the lower Rangeleys aren't as remote as they once were, and we had more company than either of us would have liked. So, with no alternative open, we pretty much stayed on one pool, the one neglected pool, the entire day.

This was something of a precedent for a fisherman who, like a salmon himself, always forges relentlessly upstream. A revelation, too, since I discovered how rewarding it can be to concentrate on one small stretch of river and yet concentrate on this intensely, getting to know it in all its moods—the different ways the sunlight comes off the water at dawn, midday, and dusk; the movement offish within a pool, their feeding cycle so exuberantly on and so stubbornly off; insect emergence and how much life comes off the water if you have the patience to sit and watch. And narrowing the focus paid off in fish—we learned that too, sight-fishing for salmon who came up to small gray midges with interest, respect, and, finally, acceptance.

Hence my resolution. To slow it down this year, my fishing, my pace upstream. Not go chasing after the river, but, waiting patiently, to let the river come to me.

2. FIGHT THE GOOD FIGHT

Conservation groups like to hold their annual banquets in March, the month when their members are unlikely to be off fishing and are most eager to hear a speaker wax informative on the subject. And while I'm not a banquet type of guy, I do try to send in money for raffle tickets, donate a book or two, help out where I can. If nothing else, the invitations that come in the mail are good reminders of something I think should become *the* off-season activity for all devoted flyfishers: working to make sure there is a trout stream to go back to when the snow disappears.

This winter several such campaigns have concerned me enough to warrant my involvement. Across the river in Vermont, trout fishers are fighting the ski industry again, this time over the industry's plans to loot water from headwater streams to use in snowmaking, and to make snow from treated wastewater (conservationists, prompted by this last folly, have bumper stickers reading *Effluent for the Affluent!*).

I've departed from my usual shyness about such things to go to a meeting on the subject, give a talk. At the same time, I'm talking to people here in town about saving a remote pond at the base of our local mountain. Grunt work mostly, stuffing envelopes, writing appeals, asking for donations. There's a land trust that owns it now, having obtained it in a complicated three-way trade, but they're holding it only temporarily, and it's up to the town to raise the funds to preserve it forever.

That's locally. Nationally, I'm distressed to read about the gold mine planned on the Blackfoot in Montana and on other mountain streams, the poisonous leachings and what they would do. With less of a direct role open for me, I've ponied up the fifty dollars for membership in a coalition fighting the threats, trying via this modest but necessary means to lend my support. Again, it feels right to do so; when I wade into my own river this spring, I want to be able to look it in the eye.

3. PERUSE CATALOGS

Not quite the off-season activity it used to be for me, since with great effort I've gotten past the acquisitive, tackle-mania stage everyone goes through at least once in their fishing career. Between a back-to-basics mind-set, a longing to continually simplify, a bank account that is always challenged, skimming through fishing catalogs has become mostly a spectator sport for me. Still, I spend some time at it, since the mail carries them in on a springtime freshet of gloss, hype, and exaggeration, and I'm still not immune to being swept along.

If nothing else, they're a good way to keep up with the state of the sport, what's in and what's out. Thus, going through this year's batch, I see that the once humble fly reel has now been elevated to equal status with the fly rod, with prices to match (insane in my view); that saltwater fly fishing is exploding in popularity (good! spread everyone out!); that videos have shoved aside books (reading being an endangered activity); that fly-fishing luggage has become a serious status item (no one fishes at home anymore; the trout are always two thousand miles away); that the commercialization and deification of Norman Maclean proceeds apace a decade after his death (enough already!); that it's getting harder to find flies with barbless hooks (bring them back, please); that women are being looked upon as the new frontier by the merchandisers (designer waders, special rods, vests with tampon pockets: male condescension at work here, or sensible adaptations?); and that whoever is writing catalog copy should in the name of truth and decency be hung.

A healthy corrective to all this and a far more interesting pastime is going back to look at fishing catalogs from an earlier era. Beside me as I write is something I've saved for thirty years: a catalog from Norm Thompson Inc. in Oregon back in the days when the company still sold fishing tackle.

A couple of things are at work here. First is the price of bamboo rods (pre-graphite days these), which sets my mouth watering with retrospective greed. A Winston eight-footer with two tips comes in at an even $100; an Orvis seven-footer at $67.50 (postpaid!). New fly lines are $11; a Hardy silk line is $19; a Hardy LRH reel, $27 (extra spools for $10). It only gets better as the pages go on. An assortment of dries tied by the famous Art Flick is $4.50 for ten; Muddlers tied by Don Gapen, their inventor are $6.50 each. The catalog is printed with a kind of modest, understated dignity; it includes, among other interesting pieces of advice, an excellent article on casting by the late great Jon Tarantino.

A golden age, surely, but in truth the prices were just as out of reach for me as a teenager as today's are out of reach for me as an adult. I did manage to save $39 for a Hardy fiberglass rod, which has served me well ever since, but I don't remember ever having enough for anything else.

Nowadays what I mostly order from catalogs are flies, since, as mentioned, I'm no tyer. This year I notice, scanning back over my list, that I've pretty well abandoned standard mayfly imitations altogether, except in their parachute versions, the rest of my dries trending toward caddis patterns, midges, and attractors. For nymphs, I favor Pheasant Tails, weighted mostly, a few with bead heads, most without. In streamers, Woolly Buggers have pretty much replaced traditional patterns for me, except for the Golden Demon (death on brookies up here) and the Muddler. The chief oddity on my list are wet flies; I'm one of the last to fish them with any frequency, and I have to scrounge around some before finding catalogs that stock them.

When I added up this year's total it came to $253—a little too much, what with my daughter needing braces, my son wanting to go to soccer camp, various bills becoming due. I went back to the drawing board, crossed out ruthlessly. This time, I told myself, I would scrape it down to a bare-bones essential list, no vagaries, no experiments, no gambles, just the working everyday flies I absolutely needed. . . . Did so, added them back up, came to a grand total of $346.68.

4. DO LUNCH

Talking about trout fishing has always been a substitute for the actual act; some people are more adept at the former, some are good at both. I enjoy it under two circumstances: trading battle stories with old friends who share many memories; and talking with complete strangers, seeing how quickly we can find common ground in rivers, landscapes, and fish.

It's a large and complex subject, conversational fishing, but here 111 say only this: how endearingly eager so many of my friends are to launch right into their latest fish stories, to the point where even the usual conversational staples—how's the family? how goes work?—are skipped entirely. One of my friends, having returned from fishing in Argentina, called me up the other night with a full report, in the course of which it became clear that he had been home only seconds—that his very first act when the taxi dropped him off wasn't playing with the kids or checking in with his wife, but calling a buddy with all the glorious details.

So, come March, I'm more than ready to go out to lunch with anyone who calls, knowing full well what the agenda will be, willing to do my share of listening, expecting some patience in return. There's a lot of planning and scheming that goes on during these lunches. I've noticed the deeper in winter the date is, the wilder and crazier are our schemes (We'll fish in Bosnia, take advantage of those brown trout streams no one's fished in years), and that the closer to spring we get, the slightly more realistic they become (Hey, rainbows feed on walleye eggs, right? We tie off some egg imitations, head right down to Kenny Dam, and—bingo!).

But lunches can booby-trap you, too. Last week a friend who never steers me wrong called with an interesting proposition. He was sponsoring a Russian fishing guide who was in this country for a month-long internship at a tackle shop, the better to learn about the business end of fly fishing and acquire lessons he could apply to his budding capitalistic enterprise back on the salmon rivers of the Kola peninsula.

Would I have lunch with him? my friend wanted to know. He wouldn't be able to stay more than a minute himself, but he was certain the two of us would hit it off.

All my fishing lunches are at the same venue: a large, friendly Chinese restaurant one town south of here. Two minutes after sitting down, my friend arrived with Andrey. He was a stocky man with a drooping mustache, dressed in a leisure suit of black denim. With a smile that was more of a grimace, he shook my hand—with his *left* hand, his right being stuck, like Napoleon's, at a right angle into his jacket.

My friend grabbed a wonton and left, leaving Andrey and me alone.

"Have you enjoyed your stay here, Andrey?"

He scowled. "Of course," he mumbled, with great sarcasm. Whoops.

"Uh, it's a shame you're not here during the trout season. I could have taken you out."

He shrugged. "On my river, we have salmon of fifteen pounds. The small ones."

Whoops again. Time to order, try to get communication back on track . . . but we never did. For some reason, he and I started out on different wavelengths and never managed to find a common one. For him, this was one blind date that was obviously a bore, the only redeeming factor being the Chinese food or, better yet, the Chinese service, which amazed him with its attentiveness; he kept glancing at his water glass, amazed to find it was forever filled.

I did my best to carry the conversation along—English wasn't the problem, since he spoke it perfectly—then we pretty much gave up and ate in silence. The situation was saved by the lucky intervention of my pal Tom C., who happened to come in and did somewhat better with Andrey than I had. We finally managed to learn something of Russian fly fishing; we were interested to hear that, according to Andrey, the same scoundrels who ruled things under the Communists now ruled things under democracy, and that the chances of his getting a fishing lodge established on his river without paying massive bribes was slim. Which explained his gloominess, I suppose.

After what seemed like hours, the waiter brought our check and the fortune cookies. We had to explain to Andrey what they were.

"My future, yes?" he said with the first real animation he had displayed. Breaking the cookie apart he read his, read it twice, then, with a snort of disgust, crumpled it up and threw it at the lo mein.

5. Buy a License

We usually get a big snowstorm the first week of March, and often we'll get a second hard upon this, but by the last third of the month winter seems to have broken its back. The robins return for good, ditto the bluebirds; the sap is running, not only in trees, but in human beings, so it's hard not to feel the anticipatory exhilaration of spring.

You'd have to be made of granite not to give in to this. The new lightness in the air seems to require an appropriate tribute, and one of mine is to stop off at our local country store, plunk my twenty dollars down for a fishing license.

"Early this year, aren't you?" Tammy says, rustling behind the counter for the proper form.

I shrug. "Figure I'd nudge spring along."

Tammy, speaking of spring, is very obviously pregnant, happy with it, excited, but a bit on edge as well. Since I'm the first one to buy a license this year, she has some trouble with the new form, and what's worse, there's suddenly a long line of customers, the phone is ringing, and there's no one else to help.

"You want the cold-water species license?" she asks distractedly, searching the form for the right box to check off.

"Yep."

"Hunting, too?"

"Just fishing."

"Shellfishing?"

We both laugh.

Finishing, she pushes it across the counter for my signature, then hands it back with the little booklet listing the rules and regulations—and there, Wetherell is official once again.

"When's the big day?" I ask, tucking it in my wallet.

She smiles at her stomach—a bit ruefully. "Tomorrow!"

Buying a license up here, while I fully support it, is something of a formality, since with the fish and game budget being so strapped, warders at a premium, I'm never checked. Thus, a month later, wading into the cold shallows of a favorite brook trout pond, I was more than a little amazed to see a green-jacketed warden emerge from the puckerbrush behind me. "Gotcha!" his expression seemed to say—or maybe it was just the quick flash of guilt that comes over you in these situations, innocent or not.

"How's the fishing?" he asked. Then, a second later, "Can I see your license?"

I thought he looked at it with more than usual concentration, glancing up now and then to compare description and reality. Hmmmn. Red hair? Yep. One hundred and ninety pounds? Yep. Six foot three? Yep. That left only one thing.

"There aren't any clams in this pond," he said. "Lobster neither."

Say what?

"Here," he said, pointing to the upper corner of my license. "You've got yourself a shellfish license, mister." He hesitated. "And I *bet* you have a story to go with it."

6. ANSWER LETTERS

One of the best fringe benefits of writing about fishing is that you get lots of mail from people telling you how much your book meant, far more letters than you receive when you publish a novel. Flyfishers tend to be literate folk, so enthusiastic about their passion their letters all but bubble over, and of course there's that ancient and venerable swapping instinct at work as well; since I've told a story or two of my own, it's only fitting that I share theirs.

Fair enough, especially since receiving such letters is one of the real highs March brings (and for whatever reason, late winter is when most of the mail comes in). I always answer each one. I'm pleasantly surprised by how many turn out to be from people who don't fish at all, readers whose letters begin "Dear Mr. Wetherell, I've never fished in my life, but something made me pick up your book and I just want to tell you how much it meant."

This is not to pat myself on the back, but to try and understand exactly who my readers are. That books are one of the oldest, most successful collaborations in the world—a collaboration between writer *and* reader—is perhaps so obvious it doesn't need mentioning, but it's a blind collaboration, between people who in most cases never set eyes on each other, their only meeting ground being those words.

The people who respond best to the ones I'm responsible for seem to be those who, in loving the natural world, rivers, lakes, and ponds, respond passionately to a note of celebration played even as wobbly and discordantly as mine. Dogmatic, know-it-all flyfisherman, pompous technocrats, the macho boys or jet-setters: I never get letters from these, and I suspect if they read me it's with a mix of bewilderment, incomprehension, and anger . . . but now I am bragging, wearing their disapproval like a badge.

Give me readers of simple hearts and subtle minds! Readers who know what a river feels like full on the chest! Readers who see in trout the richness of the living world, and find in books something of the same wonder!

But here, let me quote from a handwritten letter I received just this week; see for yourself what I'm talking about.

Dear Mr. Wetherell,

My name is John Grienan. I'm 61 yrs. of age. And recently retired from my Sales job w/a Tool Co. after 32 years.

I have owned a camp on Sheckle Pond in Vermont for close to 27 yrs. My Wife of 38 yrs. & I purchased this Piece of Heaven when my 2 Sons were Young & Still at Home. Outside of my Wife, 2 Sons & 5 grandchildren it's my most precious possession.

Your book is the first & only book I ever read. I'm not proud of that but it is a fact none the Less. I read Magazines, Short Stories & the paper cover to cover; but till your book I never finished a Book.

Mr. Wetherell I'm writing to you to tell you how you put on paper all that I thought & felt while walking my river. I've sat like you on the Bank or dreamed of someday putting into words all the feelings I have about my River; but you have said it all I guess I needn't put mine on paper. I'll just Read & Talk about yours.

If you ever want to Try my River; please contact me. I would be proud to Guide you through & maybe even catch a few Browns, Rainbows or Brookies to Boot & Introduce you to some of the wonderful People I have met on my river.

Thank you.

p.s. Please forward to Mr. Wetherell.

That's a collaborator for you, my partner already, the two of us putting our backs to the words and together wrenching out some meaning, then some more, than still more, until finally we've built something where the words disappear—a riverine world in which we dwell simultaneously, if only for the space of a page. Thank you, Mr. Wetherell? No, it's thank you, Mr. Grienan, for a high so unexpected and delightful it has brightened what is otherwise a cold dreary day here, lumined my spirits with it, so I feel like a man should feel heading into spring—alive and giddy, silly with sap, madcap, coltish, corny, ready to foxtrot, jitterbug, levitate, soar.

Hey, I'm a fishing writer! Drop me a line!

7. WRITE A BOOK

What's important to remember about fishing stopgaps is that none of them work, not entirely, not for very long. Substitute fishing is substitute fishing; its pleasures, though real enough, are like solitary notes waiting for a melody to sweep them along. What they're up against is not just the frustration of waiting for that oh-so-distant opening day, but the lingering regret from the season having ended the year before—for me, a real downer that colors my mood well into winter. Here for a six-month cycle fishing and all the joys that come with it has been woven into my everyday life, and then suddenly—just because the northern half of the planet happens to be tilting on its axis away from the sun—*it* isn't, and the bittersweet emotion attendant upon this is not easily assuaged by anything but another year immersed in the same cycle.

And the weather doesn't help. That first spell of warmth never lasts in these hills, nor does the second, and the storms seem to get fiercer and more perverse the further it gets into spring. Worse, each fair interval is more beautiful than the last, until anyone who is at all sensitive to fluctuations of the vernal mood feels like they're being embraced by a skillful and experienced lover (there is no other analogy) who knows how to tease and stroke until you're all but crying from desire . . . and yet the climax never seems to come, so the stroking, pleasant as it is, loses its point.

Spring, when it does arrive, with its chorus of bird calls, its high-pitched choir of peepers, the warmth that not only pours down from above but wells up from below, seems so new and overwhelming it demands an extravagant response. For my children, it's going outside with a kite, or kicking through last year's leaves in search of balls and Frisbees abandoned there in the fall; for our retriever, it's kicking up her heels like a puppy, chasing her tail; for my wife, it's digging in the top inches of soil, the miraculous inches, so warm, so particulate, so suggestive of bursting life. Kissing a pretty girl, driving with the top down, knocking out fungoes, painting the birdhouse, caulking a boat. Spring is response time, always the response.

Writers, too, even those most thickly ensconced behind impervious study walls, are asked for a springtime response. Often, this can take the form of starting a book. For this writer (for whom study walls tend to be more like drafty, permeable membranes), it can sometimes take the form of writing a book on fishing, a journey which—having made it twice before, seen what I wanted to see, shown my slides, written my postcards, paid my entry fees, left my tips, gotten home healthier, less wealthy, more wise—I never thought I would embark on again.

My determination to *not* write about fishing became, in the seven years I stuck with it, something like the ice that covers the Connecticut River near my home. Glacier-like, solid, seemingly immune to change, caring not a whit for the variations in warmth and light that create such longing in humans, it appears in March like something that will literally be there forever, having forgotten how to be anything but what it is: *ice*. And yet, even in the deepest recess of winter, there are other forces, less spectacular, less obvious, and by themselves less powerful, that work invisibly to erode and chip at it from all directions, until, between one day and the next, the ice is gone, and anyone staring at the blue, sparkling water where it had been could only with the greatest difficulty be able to imagine there ever having been ice there in the first place.

As in ice, so in writers, and the only thing left to do here is explain as best I can those little nudgings and chippings that have once again caused things to flow.

The first of these is that my fishing days have gotten into the habit of coalescing themselves around stories, and it's a tendency I enjoy and approve of, to the point where I'm not sure I could call a halt to it even if I wanted to. Yes, I enjoy fly fishing, but I also enjoy thinking about myself fly fishing, and it's just this added bit of refinement that gets my stories started. Or put it another way. I've a habit of noting things on rivers I wouldn't notice if I wasn't interested in getting them down on paper, sharing them, and I find that if I throttle this urge, I see less, notice less, enjoy less, even *catch* less . . . and so the selfish and unselfish motives are pretty well mixed.

And as a close corollary to the above, I feel I'm not quite done with sharing my adventures with my collaborators, feel their own interest quite strongly, and—again like that ice—find I'm not proof to it, not by a long shot. It's not just those letters, the pleasure they bring, but the fact that I sense my readers so clearly, me who hardly ever meets any of them face to face. In writing novels, I've always found the dreaded creative isolation to be a real and painful fact, one that has to be struggled with constantly, and yet I feel none of that strain in writing about rivers and the natural world, and I'm just human enough to find this comforting.

And more experience is waiting on line, demanding to be described so as to come fully to life. This is another motive and a strong one. Trips to western rivers; new friends made fishing; watching my children learn to fish; a new river I've fallen head over heels in love with or, rather, a new portion of a river I've known for years. Runoff, current, sunshine . . . the ice starts to crack.

And there's another nudge, a strictly personal one this time. Having written two books on fly fishing, I want to write a third partly because of the magic that resides in the number three. Troika, trio, triad, trilogy, trinity, *trico*. The first book on the left, exuberant and rambling, an unabashed love letter to my favorite stream; the second in the middle, more realistic and sober, an examination of the fishing motive and why it takes hold; the third here on the right, impelled by a reformer's zeal this time, the feeling that the tremendous surge in popularity that fly fishing has undergone in the last ten years has seen much lost in terms of quietude and contentment, modesty and simplicity, solidarity and fellowship, and since these are the qualities at the very heart of my own love for fly fishing, I want to do what I can to preserve them, sing their virtues. A desire, that is, to steer fly fishing back to its roots, when Izaak Walton, in all tranquillity and fullness of heart, could describe fishing as "a rest to the mind, a cheerer of spirits, a diverter of sadness, a calmer of unquiet thoughts, a moderator of passions, a procurer of contentedness that begats habits of peace and patience in those that profess'd and practis'd it."

Thus, my intentions. What kind of book will it actually turn out to be? I honestly don't know, not at this stage, not when the long season of commitment a book represents hasn't properly started yet, other than these preliminary jottings, this slushy March of good intentions. *Humble* is the operative word here. Someone starting out to fish the Battenkill or the Madison would hardly say, "I'm going to catch three rainbows sixteen inches long, then top things off with a brace of twenty-inch browns"—not a fisherman I would care to know, at any rate. No, what he or she would say is, I'll be fishing the river tonight, and my hopes are high, but it's a funny game, fishing, so you never know, though at a minimum I bet I'll catch a delightful helping of earth, water, and sky."

It's the attitude that motivates this book—to find words fit to match the beauty of the locales it inhabits. I want it to be a random, artless kind of book, not one that is shaped too deliberately; I want to give the writing a chance to wind (as fishing writers of an earlier age might phrase it) hither and yon, pooling up eddies when it needs to, forming broad slow oxbows that double back on themselves, sluicing off the rocks into wild, chaotic chutes, carving its way through a willing landscape of collaborative hearts.

This may involve being a cheerleader at times, celebrating the joys of rivers, lakes, bays, and ponds just for the sake of celebration; there will be other times when this is not possible, and the cheerleader in me will give way to the Cassandra, the

Jeremiah. This is the writer's double role now, since here at
the millennium it's impossible to write honestly about nature
without confronting many hard things. Yes, a trout is the most
beautiful example of sentient life I know, so perfect in its adap-
tation, so colorful, so strong, that merely to see one finning in
the shallows, taking a mayfly with that delicate rise, tip, and
fall is enough to anchor an entire book on; this same trout, scientists warn us, can contain enough poison in its tissue that a
person concerned about their health should eat no more than
two or three a year. No, celebration alone is impossible, but only
the worst pessimist would be blind to the beauty of the natural
world that still surrounds us, though we try so hard to spoil it,
tame it, beat it back.

In angling terms, this book will stick to the middle ground.
I'm neither expert nor duffer, but someone who is lucky enough
to have made fishing a part of their everyday life. Hence, there
will be many detours into other subjects, other ground; my best
fishing days are often those where fishing barely fits, and I see
no reason to change this pattern when it comes to writing about
fishing.

So be it! Here is the source—my hands on this keyboard,
this head full of memories, this surge of happy intention—and
there out this window are the granite hills and limestone meadows down which all this will run. Where the current will cut
deepest, whither it will lead, no man, least of all this one, can
know.

And one more thing before starting, the answer to the question I didn't quite solve at the chapters start. When exactly is
that border when the fishing season in imagination becomes
the fishing season in fact? In the quirky, stubborn state I live
in you're allowed to fish beginning January first, but this, in a

personal-responsibility kind of way, only throws the decision back onto the individual, makes the answer an impressionistic one, having little to do with the calendar and everything to do with mood and feel.

I can't give a precise opening day, but I can give a precise opening moment. Taking a break from writing around ten when the sun warms my study window, I wander out into our meadow where one last snow drift rises like a humpbacked island from the sea of flattened grass. Down the side of this island runs a rivulet of water, cutting a small bluish channel through the wood-flecked snow, fanning out when it touches earth, thinning to transparency, then collecting itself again, running down the all but imperceptible declination formed by our hill. I've watched this before, but now, straddling it, staring down, blinking in the sunny brightness, with a sudden intuitive knowing that must match an animal's or bird's, I realize there is no refreezing in store for this drift, no more storms waiting to add to its bulk, nothing in this landscape but a myriad of such trickles running down the hills in perpendicular interminglings, restoring to full and vibrant motion the brooks they fall into, the streams, the rivers, the life in the rivers, the life in whoever loves that life— and that it's the wide and exhilarating sense of these contained in the trickle at my feet that, for this flyfisher at any rate, starts the season once again.

Times Seven

It was a good day, not a great one. Only three trout, but one each of the species we catch here, and so victory enough to commemorate in some appropriately small way. On the inside of our kitchen door, hung high for convenient jotting, is a calendar—the family kind, with pictures of grazing holsteins and date squares so fat and open they seem to generate appointments on their own. On impulse, I took out a green marker from the drawer near the stove and printed my own message in what little space remained on May 20 between Dentist appointment 9:00 *and* Return IRS call late p.m.

Three trout. Sugar River. Brook, Brown, Rainbow.

On impulse—and yet more than that, too. It was my way of saying "Take that!" to the messages already scribbled like a maze across the month, giving them the metaphorical finger—the appointments to have the brakes checked, the boring lunch dates, the nagging reminders to do this and that. The following day, managing to sneak out for an hour before breakfast, I crammed in another entry beneath those already written across May 21.

Two smallmouth Clarkson Pond.

This was surprising in a way, because I've never been one to keep a fishing journal. Every few years I receive one for Christmas, beautifully bound, often gorgeously illustrated, with lines for recording stream, species, fly, water temperature, and hatches—even space at the bottom for what is referred to in the more expensive editions as *Musings*. Each year I resolve to start making entries in these, but always wimp out at the last moment; there's something too business-like and precise about it, a note that is only exacerbated when friends who do keep fishing diaries tell me how valuable they are in forming a "data base."

No thanks. But the quick, harmless jottings on the family calendar—these soon become my regular habit, the brief formality of taking out a pen, finding the proper date, squeezing my little triumph in what space remained, becoming—like a beer from the fridge—part of the ceremonial withdrawal from fishing to nonfishing.

Any habit needs limits and bounds. Mine is that only game-fish can be listed, which here in northern New England means the three trouts, largemouth and smallmouth bass, landlocked salmon, and pike. When circumstances warrant I may add the size and appropriate punctuation to the entry, as on July 15: One brown 22 inches Connecticut River! Once, teased and toyed with by a big northern for a good twenty minutes, only to lose him at the net, I felt justified in listing *A pike!* There's only one more rule—any size counts, so a two-inch trout goes on the calendar beside the large one, all fish, within species, being equal.

I can sense purists objecting already—numbers and fishing do *not* go along. There's a danger of turning our pastime, like so much else in this culture, into a matter of keeping score. Those big squares on my calendar. What do they resemble if not the inning squares of an old-fashioned baseball scoreboard, the kind that once in fond memory rose above the bleachers at Ebbets Field? But, to my credit, I've resisted the temptation to think of it in those terms, count every fish as another run. No, the pleasure for me is in marking and acknowledging the seasonal rhythm of a fishing year—the two or three trout wrested from a grudging April, the sudden surge in numbers during late May, the June so crowded with entries I begin to write sideways along the calendar's edge. And reassurance is there, too. No brookies yet from Franklin Pond? Well here, rummage through my bookcase until I find last year's calendar, flip quickly to May and discover I didn't catch my first one until the 15th, the year before on the 17th, so nothing to worry about, right on schedule.

Beside me on the desk is the calendar from the season just completed. It was an excellent year. I managed to get out often, the weather was cooperative, and by playing some lucky hunches I was able to find fish all the way through the first week of November. At the end of each month I added things up. June was the leader with ninety-seven fish; August, with family trips, the slow spot with only thirteen. Totaling up each month in turn, I find I caught and released a grand total of 356 fish.

Now, this is a modest enough figure—roughly a fish for every day of the year, which, considering how many of those days are actually fishless, seems a most appropriate figure to shoot for. It's the total of someone who goes out two or three times a week two or three hours at a time. Certainly, on the right water, fishing hard, you could match this figure in three or four days of good fishing, and there are anglers who do just that. But it occurs to me that my total, so definite and final on the calendar where I inked it in, is of and by itself a completely misleading number, one that doesn't begin to convey the complexity and richness of a fishing year. For starters, it represents only gamefish: bass, trout, and pike. If I were to count *every* fish landed—the pugnacious bluegills that swerve about like flying saucers, the rock bass that punch so hard before collapsing, the gregarious perch and misanthropic pickerel, the chubs that rise so annoyingly to a fly—I would have to double the total, which in one swift calculation brings me from 356 fish caught per year to a more realistic 712.

But stay with me a bit further here. Even this figure isn't the end of it, and if were talking not of fish beached or netted, but fish I was somehow *involved* with, the number grows even higher. What about all those fish that rose and I missed? The deep strikes that never resulted in a hookup? These were part of the experience, too, often the most exciting part. In midsummer, fishing in desultory fashion on a slow-moving river near my home, I made a just-for-the-hell-of-it cast toward the center in featureless water over fifty feet deep. Instantly, as if the fish had been waiting there for just that very thing, the water burst apart, the uplift so violent the popper came spitting back at my face, causing *me* to duck so violently the canoe nearly overturned.

Nothing. The pull with no bottom to it; the grasp that comes up empty.

A big fish certainly, but what? An adventurous bass roaming far from shore? A stray salmon on his lonely, homesick way back to the Ammonoosuc? One of those mysterious trout that are rumored to live in the river, slow and weedy as it is? The fish we miss are the ones whose shades we remember longest, and there are hundreds of them each year, surely at least three for each fish actually landed, which—going back to my original 356—adds another 1,068 to our total, bringing it up now to 1,780 fish I was busy with last year, in one way or the other.

And what about those fish we manage to hook, but lose on the fight? There was a big, heartbreaking one on the Upper Connecticut last autumn—a monstrous rainbow that took a Royal Wulff five yards from where I was casting, stayed attached for the first jump, but snapped the tippet on the second as I stumbled frantically to get downstream. Even a modest computation would include at least one fish escaped for every one landed, another 356, swelling the year's total to 2,136 fish.

The iceberg is emerging past the tip now, with more yet to come. What about all those fish seen in the shallows that despite all our efforts refuse to strike? I'm not particularly adept at spotting fish in a river, even with Polaroids, finding my myopia no match for the complex shadows on the bottom, all of which I'm more than willing to believe are trout, but even so, there are dozens I *do* see in the course of a year, managing inevitably to scatter them apart on my first reckless cast. Bass, too—there are days after a high-pressure system moves through when they roam the shallows with their jaws set in a puckered and painful way, as if they had locks through their jaws, locks no key of mine can possibly turn. How many of these fish are there each season, seen but not caught? Let's keep it on the conservative side, a quarter of my 356, which still swells the larger figure to 2,225.

I fish with my family a lot. Anyone who has young children knows how strenuous an operation this can be. Child Number One's rig readied, bobber adjusted, worm attached, the whole to be tossed gently sidearm to a likely looking spot. Repeat operation with Child Number Two's outfit, only the process is interrupted by Child Number One's bobber disappearing . . . frantic instructions to reel in, landing the perch for her, rebaiting the hook, casting it gently out again . . . back to Child Number Two, who meanwhile is near tears from impatience; get his outfit rigged now, but before it can be cast Child Number One has managed to get her hook caught on some weeds, go over to free her, then back to Child Number Two, who really is crying this time . . . soothe him, cast his rig out, keep watch on both bobbers simultaneously . . . rebait, recast, detach perch, apply sunscreen, rebait, recast, feed, and water . . . In comparison, wading upstream on the Madison near Slide Inn seems easy, an effortless stroll.

I have to be tactful here, and a loose accounting is in effect, but let's say Dad has a hand in catching just about every fish. That's easily another hundred fish a year, and a new subtotal of 2,325.

Had enough? What about partners I go fishing with, all the fish I net, or even the battles where I merely sit and cheer them on? I have a friend who took two rainbows over twenty-five inches from the Bechler River in Yellowstone last year, fishing hoppers in a wind hard enough to knock us down, and watching him play those fish on a 6X tippet from the bank, intent as a heron, balanced right on the border between panic and calm but balanced there perfectly, was one of the high points of the season.

Fish with the right person, someone who shares the excitement with you, and the fish soon become joint property; stories told subsequently are apt to begin, "Remember that first rainbow we caught on the Bechler?," that expansion in pronoun, *I* to *we,* being the identifying mark of a real fishing partnership. Certainly there are 150 of these *mutual* fish a year, enough to bring us up to 2,475.

And maybe this is where we should let the figure rest, though there is another category that would at least double the figure, perhaps even triple it. We see the fish landed, of course, even many of the ones that get away, but what about that surely larger class, the unseen fish that spot our lures, follow them for a second, but then turn away in boredom or contempt? There must be hundreds of these a year. Occasionally you'll see some sign . . . a brief swirl well back of the fly; a shadow deep beneath your streamer as it's withdrawn from the water for the next cast . . . but for the most part they remain invisible, the great fishy majority of the unconvinced.

But let them go. Two thousand four hundred and seventy-five fish landed, lost, spotted, felt, or shared is still a huge number to be in any way involved with, and yet a much more accurate representation of the fishing year than my original and too modest 356. A season turns out to be not grudging and niggardly, but full of fish, fish won and lost, opportunities squandered, near misses, vicarious success—fish everywhere, fish by the thousands, fish galore! Any diarist, any calendar jotter like myself, should keep these in mind, even if choosing to commemorate the few in honor of the many. I picture them there right now, the trout and bass recorded in those calendars from 1990 and 1991 and 1992, squeezed in what space remains beside the exhortations to Pay mortgage! *or* Change shocks!, reducing these forgotten and burdensome chores to their proper insignificance, feeding on the quotidian like it was a new and tasty form of crustacea, until the decades go by, the calendars yellow, and all that remains in the record of those years is water and fish and those generous moments stolen from the trivial when against all odds we manage to connect.

May 29

It wasn't my kind of fishing, which is why I said yes. My kind of fishing had been consistently lousy; with the rivers so high, the ponds so cold, I hadn't caught anything longer than a salamander all month. So yes, by the time my friend Ray Chapin called with his unexpected invite, fishing for shad immediately below a nuclear power plant in the middle of a mob under a broiling May sun seemed the very thing.

Words can attract you even more powerfully than fish, and this was the determining factor. *Shad.* That's a word worth saying out loud, with its sibilant start so suggestive of speed and stealth; it's hard, rakish and sound, rhyming with had and cad; its quick, compact finish, suggesting a fish that packs a considerable punch. Free-associate with all the fine old American connotations . . . shadbush, shad roe, shad bake, shadfly; shadberry; shadrach . . . and you have something that exerts a pretty strong fascination, even though, at the moment Ray called, I had never seen one in the flesh.

Neither one of us had the slightest idea how to catch one either, but what the hell. We hitched Ray's boat trailer to the back of his car, stopped at Wings for some meatball subs, drove an hour south to the big dam that crosses the Connecticut just below the nuke, kicked the winch loose, shoved the boat in, hopped aboard. The shad run, exterminated by the early dams, has pretty well been re-established, and now substantial numbers of fish are finding their way ever further north.

Were we in time to hit the run at its height? For once in my life I was hoping for a crowd, not only as evidence that the shad were there, but to steal some hints as how to catch them. The dam forms a huge pool here, the cement of the spillway merging into bankside cliffs that are even higher. In the middle of the current a flashy runabout was anchored, monofilament lines stretched taut out the back like thinner versions of the power lines that crisscrossed overhead; around and behind it, zipping in and out from the dams base, was a smaller aluminum skiff with a big antenna mounted in the middle, a man sitting in the stern with earphones, squinting in concentration; closer, on the rocks, were (not to put too fine a point on it) a shirtless redneck bully and his entourage of Budweiser-swilling friends. With the pylons, the cooling towers of the nuke, the nearby traffic, all this seemed perversely appropriate. Put a couple of effete fly-fishing sissies in the middle and *voilà*—the scene was complete.

"What do we do now?" I asked. Caught in a whirlpool, our boat was spinning around out of control—but it takes more than this to break Ray's concentration.

"We put on one of these," he said, tossing me something that, compared with trout flies, seems lurid in its redness. "Shad dart. I tied some up last night."

You're supposed to fish these slow and deep, something we didn't know at the time, so we fished them fast and shallow, since, as mentioned, the very notion of *shad* seems to demand speed and haste. Over on the Vermont side of the river was the fishway, and we could see a family peering over the fence, staring down and pointing, so it seemed pretty clear that there were indeed shad passing within reach of our darts, probably shad in great numbers, and yet two hours went by and we had nothing to show for it but sunburn.

There was a saltwater kind of feel to this fishing, what with our long casts, the expanse of the river, the anchored boats—even the sunbathers on what passed for a sandy beach. The longer we went without catching a shad, the greater my respect for them became. Shad are so powerfully anadromous that even the presence of them in the general vicinity carries the flavor of salt air, far horizons, wheeling gulls. Standing in the bow of the runabout, trying to keep my balance, hauling away, furiously stripping, I felt stretched, mentally and physically both, and it felt good to be so.

When it came time for lunch we put-putted downstream until we found a sandy island shaded by some huge silver maples. Up by the dam all was commotion and hurry, the river industrial, but a few hundred yards away a much more quiet, pastoral mood was in effect, and both of us were pleasantly surprised by how lush and rich the landscape was on both sides of the river. Three states come together here, but they all seem invisible; there you are down on the water hardly aware of anything but the steep and sandy banks, the swallows darting out from them, the trees silhouetted obliquely against the sky, a glimpse now and then of wide, darkly furrowed fields, the rush of current against the boat's bottom.

Exploring, we thought we might stumble into some fish, and we did—but not shad. Tying on a chartreuse Sneaky Pete, I tossed it out to where a sandbar cut abruptly down into the current, and immediately found a nice three-pound smallmouth. They were stacked up there in line, strong, gutsy river fish, just waiting for our poppers; as I've noticed before, they always seem to hit these, not from hunger, but from an outraged, betrayed kind of anger, as if the poppers didn't represent food at all, but little totems or miniature gods the bass had once worshipped, but then had been disappointed by in some essential way (allowing the invention of bass boats?), to the point where the fish struck back at them every chance they got.

Which, of course, is a lot to read into a bass hitting a popper, but how else to explain that ferocious explosion? I've been searching for the perfect analogy to describe it for many years now, and—since I love smallmouth so passionately—perhaps always shall.

Once the sun got lower we went back up to the dam to take another crack at the shad, though by now the day had the feel of going fishless (at least with shad), and that's a pretty hard notion to shake.

Then a funny incident happened (and yes, it also had the feel of being a funny-incident type of day). A pontoon boat festooned with fishing rods steamed into view from downriver, heading right for the center of our little flotilla. There was a suntanned man steering—in age and demeanor he looked like someone who had retired too early and was having trouble filling up his days. In the bow stood his attractive, suntanned wife, ready with the heavy anchor. Reaching us, he had her heave it . . . but apparently it wasn't the right spot for him, because not two minutes later he shouted for her to pull the anchor back up. A second spot they tried, closer to the dam in the heavy current, but this wasn't quite to his liking either, because no sooner had the boat come taut on the anchor line than he had her pull it up again, hand over straining hand.

This went on at least six times—which was obviously one time too many. Suddenly the wife turned her head, said something we couldn't hear, something especially pungent and to the point, and the next thing we knew the pontoon boat was disappearing downriver the way it had come. We looked at the fishermen in the boat next to us; they looked at us—we all burst out laughing.

Yeah, that kind of easy, relaxed day. Holding each other's gunwales, we talked for a while with the man in the antenna boat, discovered he was doing research on the salmon smolt released upstream, seeing how many made it through the dam intact, then, on our way in, drifted over closer to the Budweiser boys, and found them to be pussycats, all excited about the shad they had caught the day before. Pulling the boat out, breaking down our fly rods, we took our own beer out of the cooler and strolled over to the concrete fish ladder to see what we could see.

There were shad all right, hundreds of them, three or four pounds each, as compact and purposeful as their name suggests. That each one of these had sailed right past our shad darts without interest seemed beside the point now; it was wonderful just to watch them, admire the way they turned, turned a second time, then shot over the next step on their way up and across the dam. Their color, a silvery brown that veered toward yellow, seemed peculiarly foreign and exotic, emphasizing their migratory quality, as if they were indeed emissaries from a watery kingdom far more colorful than the one we knew.

"Incredible," Ray said, pointing at the biggest. "Beautiful, huh? Wonder what they feel like on the end of a line?"

I shrugged—but at the same time felt those little sensor muscles in the middle of my forearm, that higher, vital fishing pulse, go taut in sympathetic vibration as I imagined their power . . . the power to run three hundred miles up a once polluted river and gladden us on a perfect May afternoon.

Part Two:
The New River

The New River (I)

It wasn't love at first sight or second or even third. Seen early in June, its water still busy with springtime cleansing, the river has the gray-silver color of a playground slide—a dangerous, slippery one, with treacherous steps and no handrails, something a prudent mother wouldn't let her child on alone. And while a river that has the potential to kill you is in many respects more interesting than a river that doesn't, on this perfect late spring morning, as I pulled on my waders, looked around at the radiant bowl of mountains, meadow, and field, smelled the mica sharpness of rushing water, sensed that vernal crescendo of bursting and triumphant life, I was even more strongly than usual in no mood to drown.

So *gently* was the operative word. To the river, this silver-colored, unknown thing racing past the alders twenty feet below, I would bring gentleness, stealth, efficiency, calm—this though my skin had already tightened in anticipation of its temperature, my heart was thumping in anticipation of its force. Anyone with a sense of prudence, anyone approaching the down slope of life, will always be respectfully frightened of a strange and powerful river; its perhaps a tribute to the fact I wasn't quite over the hill yet that this fear, though real enough, only contributed to the fun.

Booted, wadered, armed with the lance of my fly rod, the visor-like brim of my fishing hat pulled low against the mid-day sun, I clanked toward the banks ready for battle—and then, remembering the prudent part, found a boulder and sat down to look things over. I had picked the most obvious spot to start: a dirt pull-off where the river first came into sight from the road. Of course this was the spot most likely to be fished most often, but this sometimes can mean it's the spot most deserving of fishing often—and in any case, this is exactly the kind of self-serving logic you start playing around with on a river where otherwise you don't have the slightest clue.

What I was looking at as I sat there shaping up my nerve was a river twenty yards in breadth, with a current fast enough to form haystacks against the granite boulders that forced it into a curve. On the far side, the New Hampshire side, was a cornfield that had just been planted; in the middle distance I could see the red tractor, the sunburned farmer, moving at the head of a vertical halo of chocolate brown dust. Higher, looking up, were the northern peaks of the White Mountains—pyramids, a child's perfect drawing, and yet jumbled, lying in a plane that seemed remote from the one the river ran through, pictures hung on a separate wall. The Vermont bank, the one I sat on, was steeper, with enough alder and raspberry vines to make getting into the river a challenge. A bit to my right—the water that had drawn my immediate interest when I parked—the current pushed hard into the bank to form a long sluice flecked with bubbles, running between a corridor of smaller, sun-bleached boulders, their tips white with bird droppings and the dried skeletons of bugs. There were no insects showing, but the air had the humid softness that generates mayflies. And, while this is a hard concept for the nonfisherman to grasp, over everything—sky, fields, boulders, even mountains—hung the distinct and unmistakable aura of trout.

And it was all new to me—that's the important part. I was badly in need of a new river. The one I've fished religiously for ten good years had declined to the point where I could no longer pretend the poor fishing was due to seasonal fluctuations—fool myself, that is, that it would someday bring me the rewards and pleasures it had in its prime. Too many houses had gone up too close to its banks; too many lawns had received too much fertilizer; too many trees had been felled; too much shade had been hacked away by the highway crews; too many gravel pits were now gouged into the hillsides, too many trout decorated too many stringers—too much of the kind of abuse and neglect whose effects are malicious, downright criminal. Its native trout had disappeared completely, and even the stocked ones were gone by July, so what had been a living, thriving miracle was now nondescript and empty, any stream USA.

But that wasn't all. Even when the fishing was still good I found myself getting bored with its challenges; they came to resemble pieces of a dearly loved puzzle, assembled and assembled again, but always in the same pattern, so it's solving became too static, simple and flat. The rainbows in the Aquarium pool were suckers for a Royal Wulff twitched across the current, but that was just the problem—they were suckers for it, time and time again. The longer we fish for trout, the more we want them to come to us from behind strong defenses—and the more we realize that those rivers where the defensive is strongest form, in trout fishing terms, the major leagues. This new river at my feet was most definitely the major leagues, perhaps the only river in New England that could be mentioned in the same breath as the rivers out West. To take the analogy a bit further, it's what I was feeling as I sat there tying on a fly—like a rookie stepping up for his first at bat in the Fenway Park of his dreams.

And even that, when it came to motives, wasn't all that was at work. For many years I had ridden the boyish bubble of sheer animal exuberance that can last well into a man's thirties—and long past this as well, but only if we actively work at it, seek out new challenges, ones that are taken seriously, but not grimly so, our motives trending toward, at least in this one area, the care and nurturing of pure delight. Many fishermen change wives at this point in their lives; me, I was ready to fall head over heels for a gorgeous new river, a trophy river, one I could grow old with in perfect content.

Strictly speaking, this wasn't a new river at all. If I waded across here, set out downstream along the eastern bank, in less than a hundred miles I would come to my home, set on a gentle slope above the river and facing past a farm. The water there was deeper and slow, thick with smallmouth, pike, and walleye, but no trout, other than the occasionally stray monster that stumbled down from one of the tributaries. A hundred miles is a sizeable gap in a river; that the bright rushing water here had some connection to the lazy river downstream would have been hard to accept, other than for the strong circumstantial evidence of their having the same name. And yet there were other threads, now that I looked. Here the banks were steep and sandy, the resort of swallows, just like at home; silver maples leaned out over the shallows, just like at home; like at home, honeysuckle blossomed wild right down to the water. The farmland, what I could see of it, seemed every bit as rich and fertile as it did further downstream, the river s gift to an otherwise flinty land.

And yet it was a trout stream here, not much more than a good cast wide, something I could wade across if I picked my spot, get to know with my feet, thighs, and chest—a river that came in flashes and swirls rather than a broad, seamless pushing; not a silent film, but a river with a sound track. The transparency was different, too. At home the river was opaque, mysterious; here it was clear and mysterious—mysterious in the way of a mirror, hiding as much as it reflects. I edged my way into the current behind the shelter of the first large boulder, felt for the first time the water on my legs; felt a cold chilling power that even the neoprene of my waders did little to stop; felt that prodding downstream nudge on the back of my knees; found I could withstand it; found, half to my amazement, that this river, like other rivers, would accept my intrusion after all.

Again, gentle was the key word. One of the things that occurred to me as I waded my way out was that slip in the wrong place, hit my head on a rock, and the river would give me a fast ride home. Working out my line with fussy little shakings, coming at last to a comfortable stance on firm gravel, pivoting, stretching, I tossed a Muddler toward the gray-white seam where the bubbles swept past the rocks . . .

And immediately caught a fat fourteen-inch brown trout.

Well no—but that's the way the paragraph is supposed to end. It is impossible for anyone possessed of the genetic minimum of hope necessary to be a fisherman to step into a new river without expecting a fish on their first cast. Since this so rarely happens, it's best to get the little bump of disappointment over with early; I stripped in fast, loaded up my fly rod, sent the Muddler back to resume searching, fantasy stage over, ready now to deal with the bright, flashing reality spreading out past my legs.

Fun reality—I'd forgotten how much fun. Right from those first exploratory casts I was caught up in what for an experienced flyfisher is probably the purest delight of fishing a new stream: applying those generalities experience has taught us elsewhere to an entirely new set of specific conditions. In general, current surging against a bank, channeling itself into a deep run, is a prime spot for trout, offering shelter, shade, and a reliable conveyor belt of drifting food. The experienced fisherman sees this at once, makes for it, hardly gives it any thought. So too with pools—our eye seeks them out, finds them even in what, to the casual observer, appears hardly more than a vague slackening in a current that seems uniform. Of course, each river has exceptions, spots that don't conform to these patterns at all, or do so in quirky variations that aren't at first apparent; one of the interesting things about fishing a new river is learning not only how the general rules hold, but how they don't. But, in lieu of specific tips, the a priori rules and patterns come first, giving a comprehensible frame within which to find the intensely specific. It is why, if luck stays neutral, the experienced flyfisher can catch trout faster than someone who doesn't have those miles of wading, probing, questing under his or her belt.

Reading the water is one of the few talents in my very small arsenal. Partly because I've been doing this for nearly forty years, partly from intuition, I seem to be able to sense where fish are holding, though, of course, catching these is an entirely different matter. In theory, the spot I'd picked out to start was a good one; in reality, the current was far too fast, sweeping my streamer along before it had a chance to sink to the trout's level of interest. And I was fishing downstream with a steep bank on my right—for a right-handed caster, a tough, uncomfortable position. Across the river was an inside curve where the river was slower, but to get there I'd have to tiptoe from sunken boulder to sunken boulder, in water well over my head; in other words, though with a lower water level it would definitely be worth trying, I was fishing something of a dead end. So okay, I was learning. Chalk it up to experience, file for future reference, and, cutting my losses, climb back out onto the bank, pull my waders down, finish off the blueberry muffin left over from breakfast, drive further upstream.

This random in-and-out probing is one of the ways you get to know a new river; you have to pay your dues with lots of wrong hunches, air balls, sheer and maddening dead ends. As I drove along I kept one eye on the river, trying to determine where to try next. From the highway the water had that intimidating silver color that had so impressed me earlier, so I still felt wary of trying just anywhere. But in trout-holding terms, it looked more seducing the further away the road curved, and this made it even harder to pick out a spot than if it had all looked barren.

But this is no way to scout out a river, no way to drive. After about a mile I spotted what I'd been looking for all morning, put on my directional signal, turned onto another sandy pulloff, this one leading right down to the river through a cut in the bank, as if there had once been a crossing here for wagons or carts.

It was a fly fisherman who had caught my attention—the first one I'd seen. He was barging through the alders toward his pickup, his waders dripping in wetness like the fur of a sleek young moose. Not so many years ago the profile of your typical flyfisher was bulky and endearingly plump, what with those crammed-in fly vests, those baggy waders that never quite fit. This has changed in the last decade, thanks to neoprene, designer vests, Gore-Tex, and pile; this fisherman was taut in the contemporary, fascist style in sportswear, everything a uniform, everything a statement. You can picture this type of flyfisher not only getting dressed before a mirror, but saluting when he's done.

So I should have known. Right from the start I should have known. But being the fool I am, I rolled down my window, came out with that time-honored opening line. "Any luck?"

The flyfisher—he looked to be in his thirties—grimaced and mumbled something I couldn't hear.

"I saw some caddis down below," I said. "Anything showing?"

A real scowl this time. He continued past my window to the pickup, threw his rod in, backed up with a squeal of brakes, drove off.

Screw you, buddy—I didn't have to be clairvoyant to read his thoughts. It's the prevailing attitude of too many flyfishers you meet on the stream these days, their competitive fires fully stoked, every fisherman looked upon as an intruder, so you find yourself facing not a companion in a gentle, carefree sport, not a fellow pilgrim, but a competitor, naked and brutal and in-your-face.

I'm not that old, and yet I can remember a time when this was different. Any luck? Well yeah, not too bad, a nice fifteen-incher and lost something bigger besides. Midges, small gray fellows. Here, you might put this on if you get a chance. Tied it myself last night. How about you?

Nice river; huh? You know it well? Let me suggest a place you might want to try a little further upstream.

Fantasy? No, since it's happened to me often, and once upon a time led to some of my best moments on the water. Sure, fishermen have always been secretive, but they once were secretive with panache, and an encounter like this would have been ornamented by some imaginative fibbing, all of which would have been part of the game, perfectly understood on my part, returned in good measure, a decoration of the essential good advice we both swapped.

Not anymore. Rule that out as a means of getting to know a new river: asking another flyfisher for advice. Luckily, I had another card up my sleeve, and I decided to play it now, my one real bona fide tip, given me by a friend from the old school when he heard I was heading north.

"There's that old grass landing strip up past Lemington. Army used it for emergencies during the war, and the town still keeps it cleared, God knows why. Anywhere along there is good. Nymph water mostly. Fish down from the windsock and watch out for that bull."

You can't miss it, he added, and naturally I should have understood that to mean the place was hidden in vines, invisible from the road, impossible to locate short of chartering a plane. After many wrong turns into pull-offs that petered out in mud or rocks, a bumpy driveway leading to a landlocked farm, I finally stumbled onto the obscure landing strip and its ancient windsock. This last was fastened to a corroded hoop mounted on a rusty iron pole; the windsock itself, condom shaped, was full of holes, so in the light breeze it could only manage to flop forlornly, not stream out erect. Between this the *temps perdu* atmosphere the landing strip cast off (I thought of Spitfires, vintage planes), I had a good feeling about the place even before I climbed down the bank.

As it turned out, my friend had steered me to as prime looking a fishing spot as any I'd seen in a very long time. Here a river that was forty yards wide narrowed to a uniform twenty-five, deepening with that concentration, going from just barely wadable ten yards out to well over my head in midstream. This deepening ate up the current—the surface moved in the kind of even, controlled pace that is perfect for a drifting fly.

The approach was made easy by a long sheltering island on the Vermont side; it was no trick at all to cross the narrow channel that led out to this, then, using the island as my combination base camp, observation spot, and lunchroom, fish upstream or down. Over on the New Hampshire side, perched there like a watchtower deliberately erected to spy into the pools center, was a small summer cabin, a man outside cutting wood. Upstream was Vermont's tall Mount Monadnock, tilting the horizon into a greenish slant. Downstream, backed by the twin Percy Peaks, was more of that wonderful riverine farmland, shaggy with unbaled hay that, judging by the smell that wafted upstream, had just been cut. Though I looked carefully in all directions, there was no sign of any bull.

What struck me right from the first moment was the combination of power and intimacy contained in this stretch; here was a river that had thirty miles behind it and four hundred left to run, compressed into a channel I could almost cast across, and yet it was quiet, easy, in no hurry whatsoever, easily wadable over a perfect gravel bottom—a place possessing that trouty atmosphere even more intensely than the first spot I tried, so I knew that I would *have* to catch a fish here, and probably a good one.

I waded out to where the current was strongest, pumped my rod up and down like a drum major leading off a parade, then dropped a weighted stonefly at the bottom of the scrappy cliff on which sat the little cabin. The current bellied the line downstream, slowly straightened it, and then, just when I decided *nothing,* pulled much harder and faster than the current could have managed on its own. A trout, a fine trout, but what occurred to me right from that first instant was how sharp and compelling that first strike was, out of all proportion to the trout's eventual weight—that what was really taking hold in that instant was the new river itself, its promise, its beauty, the joys it would soon bring; that if it's not correct to speak of W. D. Wetherell falling in love with the Upper Connecticut River at first sight, its eminently fitting to speak of his falling in love at first tug.

Indulge me for a moment while I write into that tug everything I can. For while half of me, the part that resides in hands, arms, muscles, and eyes, was busy keeping just the right amount of pressure on what was turning out to be a thick-bodied, headstrong rainbow, the other half was listening to the kind of voice we never hear except in retrospect, and then hear so clearly we can't believe we didn't actually hear it at the time. *Enjoy this, fella* was what the voice was saying, in a baritone so musical and strong it could have been the river's. You're going to catch lots more fish here over the years, this is only the first, so concentrate, enjoy it, savor it right from the start. You're going to make friends with the man who owns that cabin, though you'll never exchange words—a pantomime kind of friendship, where he'll spread his arms apart and shrug a question mark when you first wade into the pool, point down emphatically when he spots a good fish, clasp his hands over his head like a prizefighter if you catch it, shrug his shoulders and frown if you scare it back under the bank. You'll fish here often with your fishing partners, rotate through the pool with them, have fish on simultaneously, call out to each other those little telegraph messages of advice, disappointment, victory, interrogation. Here in a few weeks you'll be up to your neck in hatching caddis, the pool alive with trout, so their rises spread into one another and you can arrange your drift to cover three fish at once. You'll camp here this fall, know what it's like to tumble out of the tent into the cold damp fog of morning, see it with a whistling sound be pierced by a squadron of mergansers racing upstream, the fog in tatters on their backs. You're going to find this pool, this river, an excellent antidote to the staleness that creeps into a forty-something life even in the best of life's circumstances—an aphrodisiac of fishing that makes you discover new delights in a sport you were almost beginning to lose interest in. You're going to sit on that sandy dip in the middle of the island, find it a perfect backrest, pour yourself countless mugs from your thermos of tea as you sit there watching your friends fish, or the trout rise, or the play of sunlight off the water when it's too hot to do anything else. You're going to forget to be careful going down the muddy bank and slide in like an otter, not once but a dozen times, get your waders soaked, shiver in autumn snowstorms, catch fish almost every time you come here, and take it in stride when you don t. Enjoy fella, throw your strength against that fish, push your belly into the current, overwrite all you want. Enjoy fella, because life can be ironic and bitter and cruel, and it's only moments and places like these that redeem it, so watching carefully; putting your heart into it, for God's sake get it right.

Which, of course, is a lot of portent for one trout to carry. He was up to it and then some; after that first long run, he came slanting back toward me, still stubborn, still likely any second to run—and there, that's exactly what he did, leaping clear of the water just when I decided he wouldn't jump at all. Holding my rod high, stepping carefully over a bottom with contours my boots weren't used to, I found a comfortable stance at the head of the island and brought him in. A good fish, the kind with shoulders, the color oddly pale on its flanks (the pink washed out into a watery silver), but more than made up for it by a dark shield of reddish-maroon over his gills—a color that made me think, when I first saw him flashing, that it was a brook trout, not a rainbow at all.

A wild fish, too—there was no mistaking that kind of robust good health. I put my thumb on his jaw, widened my fingers along his flanks, then, pivoting on my pinky, extended my thumb again. A span and a half, or nearly fifteen inches.

Soon I would learn that this was the kind of fish you were looking for on the Connecticut. There were bigger trout (state-record size, ten and eleven pounds), but for the most part this was the quarry that made the trip worthwhile—strong, wild fish with just enough heft that you couldn't take them for granted, boss them around. I've noticed this before, how critical the inch is that separates the almost good fish from the really good. A thirteen-inch trout is a decent fish in this day and age, but give him just one more inch, add on the correspond-ing depth and maturity that starts to kick in at that length, and you're talking about a serious fish, one that seems, though com-posed of familiar elements, an entirely different compound, with four times the explosive punch.

Releasing him, I waded back out into the pool and worked my way downstream, throwing that black stonefly out toward New Hampshire, then letting it swing in the current back toward Vermont. There were three more good fish within the overlap of a dozen casts. Toward the tail of the pool, where the water thinned and quickened, the fish were smaller, brook trout, small wild browns. On my last cast, just before heading back to the island for some R & R, something hit the nymph even harder than that first rainbow, so hard that when, missing him, I stripped the line back in, I found the hook had broken at its bend.

In its way, this first fish lost was as symbolic as the first one landed, suggesting that my future with the river would include many disappointments to go along with its many pleasures. Making the long drive north only to find the river the color of a chocolate milkshake from a thunderstorm during the night. Seasons of drought when the trout, the best ones, turned belly up and died. Days when fish were everywhere, and yet I fished badly, making them flee in aesthetic horror. Good fish gone on the strike, leaving me with that desperate feeling of loss that makes up in intensity what it lacks in duration—the feeling that if you hadn't been so quick or so slow or so stupid, not only the fish but happiness itself would have been landed, redeeming everything that happened to be wrong with your life at the time in question. Yes, it was good to have this reminder early, find it to be a real river, not one flowing in dreams.

It was late enough now that the Vermont side was deep in blue shadows from the bankside pines. I continued downstream through the edge of the rapids, then down through another series of riffles and pools, knowing it was a long walk back to the car, but keeping on anyway, even though I was no longer fishing. I'd found what was obviously an excellent stretch of river, caught enough trout that my first day was a success, and now I wanted to top things off with a last bit of reconnaissance, start linking the scattered stretches of river I had seen so far into a comprehensible chain.

One aspect about this portion of the Connecticut immediately enchanted me. Over the years the current has cut deep
through the surrounding clay and loam, so, wading, you can be
a good twenty feet below the level of the surrounding countryside, making it feel like you're fishing in secret within a self-contained groove of water, rock, and sky. There on the banks are
vines and creepers, great clumps of hay the tractors can't reach,
trees in the muddy spots, the raspberries and sumac that help
hold things together. By June these are already high enough
to add to the tunnel effect, their leading tendrils curving out
toward the river so the banks are doubled. Still higher, above
the vegetation, above the willows, the sky seems channeled in
the same narrow blueness, so the entire world, not just the river,
is rolled into that flowing north-south line. Occasionally, one
bank will crumble away of its own weight, giving you a glimpse
over farmland toward mountains, but for the most part the outer
world remains invisible, except for the smell of hay, the rumble
of tractors, a distant chainsaw, the harmless rush of invisible cars.
More than anything, this serene, self-contained effect is what
causes the bittersweet feeling I have when climbing back out
at the end of the day; it's a narrow strip of paradise you've been
wading through, but paradise all the same.

Time to go? Not quite. Up in the sky the light was still
yellow enough to pass as afternoon, but down on the river the
shadows had already joined from both banks, so what I waded
through was the last V of sunlight left on the water, my waders separating this into a smaller, darker arrowhead that stayed
in close to my waist. With dusk, in that perfect June stillness,
mayflies were hatching and caddis, too, enough that I had to
blink as they brushed against my eyes. I'd been wading along
gravel all the way down from the landing strip, but here near

an enormous silver maple, in what I would learn was one of the river's characteristic tricks, the bottom suddenly turned to mud, the water deepened, and I had a difficult time scrambling back to the bank.

But no matter. I had spent the whole day trying to read the river by various clues, portents, indications, trendings, and now between one moment and the next, in the fullness of that hatch, the river was revealing itself to me for free. Trout were rising everywhere in the water I had immediately judged fish-less—good, deep-bodied sips, the kind that make it seem like it's not invisibly small flies the trout are sucking down, but the river itself, saucer-sized sections they take away as trophies, cast in bronze, stash who knows where. *Voilà*—they could have been shouting this out loud. One over by the sloppy beaver lodge; another dead center ahead of me; still another under that leaning, fungus-scarred birch.

It's one of the most splendid things about trout, this rising to feed visibly out in the open; the effect is what you would experience in Vegas if the blackjack cards, as you watched them in despair, ready to give up, started giving quick little flips so you could see their faces. Here we are, come and catch us; as graceful as these rises are, you can't help but imagine them being made without a certain nah nah nah-nah-nah tone that can drive you mad.

This tone was uncalled for, at least tonight. I wasn't going to fish for them at all, but sit there watching on the bank, absorbing the day's late lessons. The fish were unreachable anyway, not without a float tube or canoe. So, put that down on the list of resolutions that had been growing longer all afternoon. Come back with canoe, evening, Sulphur Duns, Olive Caddis, long leaders, 6X, stealth.

I needed my flashlight to get back to the car. As I stumbled through the brush, one of the briars managed to strip the flashlight away, but even in the dark the grassy runway was unmistakable; a half hour later I was back at the car, taking apart my rod, gulping down the dregs of tea still left in the thermos, and with it some aspirin for my overworked back. I could hear the river now—realized that as intensely as I'd been staring at it, I hadn't taken the time to adequately listen. It was a soft noise, surprising in a month when everything in nature has its voice turned up full blast, muted even further by all that meadow grass, so the effect was like silk being poured over velvet, poured in a tall pitcher, shaken on the rocks.

Back next week on Tuesday if I could finish work on time? Maybe spend the night, wake up early? It was good to think in those terms, good to feel the old kind of excitement kick in. I had done what I had to—given the river the chance to work on me—and it had made of it a thorough job, so if it wasn't love on that first intimidating sight, not love on that first chilling immersion, it was certainly love now—or how else to explain that intense and happy sorrow I took away with me home?

The New River (2)

Since that first afternoon on the Upper Connecticut, in the ten years since, I've been back well over a hundred times—a statistic that probably carries no significance for anyone but me, yet one I'm childishly pleased with as a mark of my devotion; it's as though I've entered upon a marriage so perfect I renew my vows every chance I get. And—why not admit this?—I'm head over heels in love with the river still, think about it often while I'm away, pine for it, dream about it, rave about its virtues to family and friends, soberly come to terms with its imperfections (which in any case are of a kind to make me love it all the more), take solace from the

memory of past assignations even as I find excitement in plotting
my next. When it comes to infatuation, the Connecticut and me,
it's the heart's whole nine yards.

And it's remarkable, looking back on that first introductory
season, how fast the routines started to form that have served me
well in the years since, with little variation. The early-morning
start, often in darkness, the stars bright out the window as I go
around the kitchen on tiptoes trying to bag together a lunch.
Tom driving up in his pickup right on schedule, or maybe Ray
in his little Volkswagen—the quick stowing of rods, vest, and
waders, the brief remarks about the weather, always putting a
good face on it, at least at this stage, when even snowflakes on
the windshield can be given a propitious slant. The drive up the
interstate, high on its ridge overlooking the valley, the two of us
talking over prospects, all but rubbing our hands together and
chortling in anticipation of the swath well cut among these trout.
The sunrise over the White Mountains to the east, the summits capped by lenticular clouds that multiply their dimensions
in purple-gray swellings . . . The radio, the news, fading out
in static, the last noisome whispers of the world we're leaving
behind . . . Breakfast at our favorite truck stop, the eggs and
home fries and homemade toast appearing so fast on our table it's
as though the short-order chef has gotten word of our coming
through CB radio, anticipated our order well in advance. . . .
Leaving the interstate for slow, stately old Route 2, route of the
logging truck, the school bus, the moose. The first view of the
Connecticut near Lancaster, giving us a clue as to what kind of
water level we'll be fishing in—the banks sandy here, the water
slow, but a reliable guide all the same. On through Guildhall, the
neat, compact little village where the road cuts north. The vexing question of whether to continue up the west, forgotten side

of the river or cross over to busier New Hampshire for the added speed . . . Northumberland, Groveton, North Stratford. . . . Trout water at last, the river not slow, sleepy, and deep anymore, but fast, broken, and rushing, so even through the window glass, in the eight a.m. sunshine, it gives the effect of well-shaken champagne poured down a silver-bronze chute. Fishable? Yes! A bit high, but not too high, and transparently clear from bank to bank, the boulders on the bottom doubled by their own blue shadows. . . . The talk about where to start in, not abstract and hypothetical like it was two hours ago in the darkness, but urgent now, needing a fast decision. Trophy Hole? Perfect. Slug our way up to it while we have all our energy, fish it while the sun has the stoneflies rock and rolling up a storm, then the current on our backs for the long wade back. . . . Parking, unpacking, getting dressed—stopping now and then to blow on our hands, our breath in front of us in crystal balloons that pop apart on anything but the softest syllables. Socks on, waders on, vest on, rod strung up—the ritual that is so important a part of the fly fisher's start. . . . And then the river itself, stepping into it—hardly feeling anything at first, not even coolness, not until we're well out into the current and sense that old familiar pressure on the back of our waders, like a reassuring pat on the rump as the river welcomes us for the 101st time.

There are other rituals in the course of a fishing day, but it's the river that's setting the agenda now, with much more variation, so things never again become quite so formalized as they are when starting out. I've gotten to the point where I need every one of those steps along the way, feel, rightly or wrongly, that if one or two are left out then I won't be able to catch as many fish, or at least not quite as much enjoyment—that substituting apple jelly for marmalade at breakfast will result in botched casts, missed strikes, and overall futility. In life, ritual seems to work best in small things and big things, coffee breaks or weddings, and for me, fishing the river is a mix of both—and yet the small comes first, to the point where I think a fishing day could be described not in terms of fish landed, but solely by all those small, dearly loved familiarities woven into the fabric of a fishing life. The downward, not unpleasant tug a fishing vest gives on the shoulders when you first put it on; the sharp taste of split shot as you bite it closed; the gossamer shine of tippet material blowing in the wind; the fine, almost invisible spray of wetness that comes off a fly line as it shoots forward and drops. "All this is perfectly distinct to the observant eye," Thoreau wrote of delights just as small, "but could easily pass unnoticed by most."

With all this by way of introduction, starting now on the second stage of my exploration, it's time to come forward with what is simultaneously the most extreme and yet sincere bias in my entire arsenal of fishing beliefs: that the most important factor in fly fishing for trout is not casting ability or streamcraft or entomology, but coming to appreciate and understand something of the landscape, terrain, history, and culture of the region through which your river flows.

This is heresy of course—suggesting that anyone setting out to fish the Henry's Fork might do better to bone up on local history than consult guidebooks to the various pools; that sitting in bars and diners listening to the locals talk weather, politics, or crop prices ultimately might be more useful than hiring a guide; that time spent loafing beside a river looking out at the distant views is in many respects even more valuable than time spent studying the water. All this not only flies counter to prevailing wisdom, but hardly makes up a corner of it at all—and yet I'm absolutely convinced it's true.

Why? Remember, we're talking bias here, personal hunch and intuition, and it would be hard to isolate the direct causative factors between understanding the region and understanding the fish. Certainly, to try to come to an appreciation of the larger scape a river runs through demands of a person a certain investment of time and attention—and its exactly the ones who are willing to do this who are most likely to bring the same qualities to their fishing. Then, too, it slows a flyfisher down, looking outward like this, and in fishing, slowing down is half the battle. Too often we come to the river caught up in the fast, frantic pace of the artificial world were seeking to escape, and this man-made schedule is the first and most onerous burden we must shed. A river can't be rushed—this is the first rule of fishing, the second, and the third—and so any time spent along its banks *not* fishing is a worthy investment, slowing, quite literally, the speeding hands of our inner, overwound clocks.

Listening to the locals, trying to learn who they are, what their lives are like, pays off, too, since these are the people you will encounter along the stream, and there is simply no talking to them unless you're willing to make some effort to share their world. Fly fishing is more art than science (though fully neither), and one of the criteria for being good at it is the ability to take into simultaneous consideration many varied threads. Local knowledge is one of the most important of these elements—and how else to tap it except by meeting it halfway?

I could back up my theoretical arguments with a more pragmatic one, point out that the best flyfishers I know happen to be the ones who have an instinct toward the elusive "feel" of the region they fish in. I could also point out examples of flyfishers for whom none of this counts—those who are too wrapped up in their own passion to focus on anything but the fish there in front of them. Not understanding the country's rhythms, they're locked into the rhythm they bring from home, so there's a clash right from the start; not catching very much understanding, they will not catch very many trout. Not catching many trout, they will hire a guide next time, or buy yet another book on fishing how-to, and, because they are mistaken in their basic assumptions, the river will always run away from them and never be grasped.

This kind of larger understanding and empathy is even more important when the region through which the river flows is an unusual, even quirky one, not at all what it first appears. The Connecticut River, starting as a small beaver pond only a few yards from the Canadian line, flows through a series of four mountain lakes of increasing diameter before spilling through Murphy Dam and becoming a full-fledged trout river in the town of Pittsburg, New Hampshire. Little bigger than a good cast across, fast, weed-slick, and rapid, it's not until it reaches Stewartstown and works the west out from its southwest trending that it becomes prime fishing water; from here on in, for the next 235 miles, it forms the border between Vermont and New Hampshire, though in a compromise that goes back to the former state's admission to the union in 1791, New Hampshire law still governs the river itself. Between Pittsburg and the vicinity of Lancaster the valley remains in the same overall pattern and can be spoken of as one; this is the region, the hard, gritty, difficult region, that in the course of my fishing trips I gradually began to know.

There's no shorthand name for this land, or rather, there are two names, both of which testify to the fact that it's a world apart. The Vermont side of the river, not without some irony, is called "the Northeast Kingdom"—a broad upland of granite hills and boreal forest, with a sparse, hard-working population settled in a few, well-scattered villages. Across the river in New Hampshire it's called "the North Country"—a similar landscape, only with higher, steeper mountains and, if anything, even poorer, more nondescript towns. The river valley proper, the broad floodplain, manages to seem as pastoral and gentle as anything further south (the white farmhouses, the old ones, are the most prosperous looking, best-kept buildings in sight and have been for two hundred years); a mile from the river on either side it's a different story. Here the upland begins, and it gives a rougher, grittier kind of feel, both in the landscape and in the habitation. Trailers covered in plastic; log cabins that are never quite finished and look horribly out of place; suburban-style ranch houses built from kits; sagging tourist cabins long since gone bust. This is as far from the familiar Currier & Ives stereotype of New England as it's possible to be, and much closer in feel to Appalachia, or timber country out West. Many of the towns, even in summer, manage to give off the worn, tired feel of perpetual November; Colebrook, the market town in the regions center, has the wide main street and slapdash, unfinished feel of a small town in Wyoming, though its origins date back two centuries. Like the river, the money has always flowed south here and probably always will.

An intimidating land, in the end—a region everyone agrees is "different," though without any of them quite agreeing where exactly the difference lies. Some would point to the terrain, those mountains that aren't as high as the Whites or as approachable as the Greens, but humpbacked and shaggy, less visited, more remote. Others might point out that, geographically speaking, this is very much a dead end—all the roads seem to end at border crossings which, for lack of traffic, always seem to be closed. There's the prominent French influence, or rather the Quebecois; the convenience stores have names like DeBannville's, the tackle shops Ducrets, and the churches are more apt to be cement, workaday Catholic ones than the stately Congregational churches associated with townscapes further south. Others, the wiseacres, might have fun with the moose, point out that moose-watching is the favorite (some would say the only) after-dinner activity. Sensitive observers, those who like to gauge a region in the faces of its inhabitants, might point to the people you see in diners or waiting by their trucks as they fill up with gas—their beaten mien and shabby clothes, the hill-country strength that stays hidden from strangers, yet you know must be there.

The difference is as much good as it is bad—people who linger here, make the attempt to know the region intimately, agree on this, too. There's the Connecticut, of course, its winding beauty, the locus for all that is soft and easy in the landscape, at least in summer. The beaver ponds lost in the ridges near the Quebec line, the brook trout lost and lonely in their centers, splashing to a fly like drowning swimmers to a life ring. Those moose that are everywhere—the wildness that clings to them like a second, more exotic pelt. The sense the surrounding forest gives of true northing—of boreal spareness and boreal flint, hills scraped as clean of ornament as the people who by stubbornness or inertia make it their home. The fact that it's a yuppie-free zone and always will be—that even its lakes haven't been gentrified or tamed.

You can take the difference even deeper. Living in most parts of America is like living on an inclined plane or gigantic slide, one that's tipped in only one direction, toward the great American middle ground—middle in jobs, middle in culture, middle in aspirations—so all you can hope for, growing up in it, is to drop pinball-like into one of several inevitable and ready-made slots. Here in this forgotten corner, up high on the height of land where the watersheds begin slanting over toward the St. Lawrence, the sense is of sliding away from America altogether, lives running in a totally opposite direction. Those radio talk shows in French. The poverty so pervasive the Depression is remembered as a prosperous time. The legends of bootleggers, draft exiles, and smugglers. The roll call of hermits and loners and misfits who have fit in here and nowhere else. The old communes and forgotten marijuana fields rotting away deep in the woods. The cranky politics. Yes, in a nothing direction entirely.

Cranky politics? For anyone driving through the region this is most apparent in the local custom of planting your property every four years with an orchard of campaign signs, ones that, once staked, are only reluctantly removed, so, feeling in something of a time warp already, seeing those signs, you're apt to think Ford/Dole is still running against Carter/Mondale. The shabbier the house, the more likely it is these signs will be for Republicans, though many are hand-lettered and crude, warning the US out of the UN, or vowing fidelity to guns. This is your basic old-fashioned cranky New Hampshire reactionary right, the kind you might have thought had crept up here to Coos County to die, were it not for the fact it seems to be spreading. There's an anarchistic flavor to it all; you get the feeling, talking to them even casually, that what these people really hate is any government interference whatsoever, though in the same breath they're berating it, they complain about how the state government down in Concord (or Montpelier) hardly seems aware of their existence.

It's a strange, potent brew. Who should stumble into its middle a few years back but Newt Gingrich himself, at the height of his power and influence, up north to do a little moose spotting, his euphemism for testing the waters in the primary state for a possible presidential run. Followed by an entourage of doting reporters, he stopped beside the Androscoggin near Errol for a photo op, started chatting up a flyfisherman waist-deep in the river (I picture the stampede scaring away a nice trout the fisherman was just on the verge of catching), who looked up at him, the cameras, the tape recorders, and scowled.

"You're the meanest thing that ever happened in Washington," the flyfisherman said, making the most of his opportunity. "Jesus, if it was up to you and your cronies there wouldn't even be a river here. Go home now—get."

Newt seemed considerably taken back at this—and as history records, shortly thereafter decided *not* to run for president that year.

This independent streak goes back to the region's start. Upper Coos County was once an independent country of sorts, the Indian Stream Republic of the early 1830s, when a free-spirited assortment of settlers, crooks on the lam, and wildcat speculators took advantage of a border dispute with Canada to create an "independent" country with its own laws and courts—an independence that lasted until 1842, with the signing of the Webster-Ashburton Treaty between the United States and Britain, and the arrival of the first militia units from New Hampshire to enforce the new boundary.

The only thing left of all this, beside the independent streak mentioned, is a historic marker on Route 3 and a good, characteristic story—a story about how a reporter was sent north by a Boston newspaper to interview a local Vermont farmer, who, when the reporter informed him the boundary had been redrawn and he now lived in New Hampshire, scratched his chin whiskers for a moment, pondered on the implications, then trotted out in his best laconic drawl, "Well, young fella. Mighty glad to hear it. Couldn't have stood another one of those Vermont wintahs!"

There's tourism here, of an old-fashioned blue-collar sort—northern New Hampshire is one of the last refuges of your basic twenty-eight-dollars-a-night tourist cabin—but nowhere near the kind that overwhelms the White Mountains every summer. Over on the Vermont side of the river there's even less in the way of visitors, and it's possible to drive the roads in October at the height of foliage season and never see another out-of-state car. What the region does experience in the way of mass invasion comes in appropriately bizarre fashion; the biggest event of the year in Colebrook, for instance, is the "Blessing of the Bikes" in May, when thousands of motorcyclists from all over New England drive their machines past a Catholic shrine set in a little grotto off Route 3. The shape of the two states accounts for a difference in the tourist flow; when you drive north in Vermont, you're driving toward the broad base of its inverted triangle, spreading everyone out; when you drive north in New Hampshire, you're driving into the apex, so everyone becomes concentrated.

Logging is the main industry here and always has been. It's an important part of the economy in the lower parts of both states, but up here it's the only industry and so it's more visible, with logging trucks as common as cars, tote roads going everywhere, scars on the mountainsides from recent cuts, and, in mill towns like Groveton, mountains of sawdust and the sweet, heavy smell of boiling pulp.

Skidders, forwarders, and whole-log "harvesters" have made logging into a humdrum, brutally efficient business, though one that still carries with it more than its share of danger. It has its romance, too, or at least its history of romance. A hundred years ago the Upper Connecticut was the starting point for the great logging drives on the river (still the longest in world history), wherein the timber cut from the surrounding hills was sledded over the snow every winter, piled on the river's ice, then—with the help of a great deal of manpower—floated on the springtime head of water down to the mills in Massachusetts, three hundred miles to the south.

Log driving was one of those hard, miserably paid jobs that, like cow punching and whaling, seems more glamorous in retrospect than it probably did at the time. Look closely at those old photos of rivermen posing by their bateaux or waist-deep in a river full of logs: along with the pride and cockiness, you see a great deal of plain old bone-weary exhaustion. For logging was a brutal way to make a buck, one requiring agility and great strength, accomplished by a mix of Yankee woodsmen, immigrant Finns, and itinerant Québécois. Rising before dawn to spend fourteen hours up to their waists in forty-degree water, ordered about by dictatorial woods bosses, preyed upon by hustlers of every stripe—it's no wonder rivermen were famous for their brawls (caulked boots festooned with case-hardened spikes three-quarters of an inch long were their weapon of choice, the flying leap toward the face their favorite tactic); the not uncommon murder (Canaan, Vermont, once had a lawless, rock 'em-sock 'em reputation to rival Abilene's or Dodge's); the dev-il-may-care attitude that made them spend their money as fast as they took it in (brothels, even up here at the drive's start); their chilblains, lumbago, and TB.

There have been attempts over the years to put a sheen over all this, make of these men heroic Paul Bunyans, but it's never really caught on, not with the Connecticut River log drive, since if anything the real interest and awe comes from remembering it realistically, as a remarkable example of the partnership between man's cleverness and the sheer driving force of nature. This was before the internal combustion engine, before paved roads. The Connecticut was the highway south, and every April the river was crammed bank to bank with rough, potato-colored logs, poked at by quiet, deadly earnest men—the logs jamming fre-quently (including the infamous North Stratford jam of April 1914, when thirty-five million feet of wood piled up in one extended jam thirty feet high), getting blown up when these jams proved recalcitrant, the drive sweeping downriver and tak-ing with it every spring its sacrificial quota of a dozen or more lives. The bodies, those who no one claimed, were buried in pork barrels by the side of the river—in some cases, the victims' spiked shoes were hung on a branch by way of tribute.

The men in charge of these drives were not chosen for their compassion or sensitivity. The most infamous was George Van Dyke, a notorious bastard who saw nothing wrong with paying the men starvation wages, then finding every opportunity to cheat them out of those. But fate had its ironic way with him in the end. As he was watching the finish of the drive down in Massachusetts from his chauffeured touring car, the brake slipped and down he went over the steep bank into the river, never to rise again—the river's final sacrifice, for after this, with the interruption of the Kaiser's war and the introduction of the first trucks, the Connecticut River drives were never again the same, though pulp wood continued to be driven in the upper reaches until 1948.

There remain few visible traces of those days. At Lyman Falls you can see what's left of an old wooden dam and sluice; detouring into the woods to get to better fishing positions, you'll sometimes stumble upon the rusty old cables that held boomed logs in place . . . but thats about it. At least once during my fishing day I find myself wondering what the river looked like full of logs (and what it did to the trout—did they just hunker down until all the confusion swept past?), but it's a tough feat for imagination to pull off. Partly this is due to the fact that my fishing is in the clement months, so the river seems too relaxed and gentle to have ever been involved with anything so chaotic; partly because, on this side of the mythic enlargement time brings, the river now seems far too small.

But there are other moments when I can picture the log drives perfectly—autumn days, for instance, when the water is high and the leaves are gone from the trees, when the water seems darker, more furious, capable of something mighty, waiting only its chance. You can also sense something of the atmosphere of log-drive days just by cruising the roads, looking at the hardscrabble towns, sensing the feeling that something essential about the region, its very heart, has long ago been swept downstream.

The kind of man who found the log drives his escape—you can picture him, too. Earlier this season, after fishing just above the covered bridge at Columbia, climbing back up to my car, I discovered my keys were missing. I gave myself the usual frantic shakedown, then, thinking I had left them locked in the car, started prying at the window trying to get my hand far enough in to pull up the lock.

I had just found them (in the most obvious spot, naturally—the toes of my waders) when a pickup pulled over and a young man in a T-shirt and jeans jumped out, ready and eager to help. He was no more than nineteen, short and wiry, with a large French nose, bright blue eyes, and a restless, blinking kind of expression that couldn't stay fixed in one mood for long.

"Stupid of me," I said, holding up the keys. "Thought we were going to have to smash that window."

The young man grinned. "Why I stopped! Wouldn't have been the first time I smashed one."

I pointed to the chainsaw and gasoline cans in the back of his truck. "Looks like you're pretty busy in the woods."

"Nope. Not anymore. Got laid off"—he glanced down at his watch—"two hours ago."

"Christ. Sorry."

He grinned even wider. "No problem. They'll hire me back if I want. Old man Toller, he lays off everyone after nineteen weeks so we don't get enough consecutive in for unemployment. Then he hires us back, starts it over." He looked toward the river, spat without any particular malice, added by way of afterthought, "He's a bastard. Anyway, it don't matter. This time Sunday I'm out of here."

I played a hunch. "Army?"

"Marines."

Well, there it was, the North Country's other industry, the export trade that works full-time in so many of the forgotten places of the world, the beautiful places—sending its children to places less beautiful, less forgotten, less hard. With time, if he serves enough years for a pension, perhaps he will come back again to hunt and fish out his retirement, be able to enjoy the land without having to wrest a living from it, fight that particular battle at such long odds.

But he was excited with the future the way any young person gets excited when it comes time to tell the place you grew up in to go to hell. He pointed to the river, bent his head over so he could peer under the first tree limbs upstream.

"Always wanted to try a fly rod, see if I can keep myself from strangling in all that line. But up there's where you want to be fishing. Base of that little island, current scrapes out a big hole. Go there at night sometime. That's my secret spot, and here I am handing it over free of charge." He shook his head, ruefully this time. "What good is it to me? Hell, you can have them all. Up there by the town hall—good spot, too. You go down to where you see those cows, there's a little sandbar that'll take you right out in the middle of the river like a causeway. Rest is mud, so that's the only way. Good spot for browns. You know the old gravel pit down by the airport?"

On and on he went—my brain raced to take all this down; I kept wishing I had a tape recorder—going over his favorite spots, all the stories that went with them, so it was as if this were another part of the burden he had to shed before he could be free of the place and leave. Light, wiry, tough already at nineteen—it was easy to picture him growing up by the river in the days of the great drives, begging each year to go, being reined in by his mother as long as possible, until finally comes the day—and off he goes with his stagged kersey pants cut short in river-man fashion, the black felt hat, the peavey or cant dog, the spiked boots . . . and with a last farewell glance or, more likely still, without any backward glance whatsoever, away he floats down that river, never to return.

If getting to know a region helps you to get to know the fishing, the converse is true as well—there are few better ways to get to know a region than spending your time fishing it. Out in all weathers through six months of the year; poking your nose into all kinds of unexpected venues as you seek out new water; spending long hours in what is often someone's backyard; relaxing on the bank near a road, watching the traffic stream past; helping yourself to wild raspberries; learning where the old apple trees are that still bear fruit, if only by snagging your backcast on their branches; having the local flotsam and jetsam drift past your waist (red Frisbees, a blue Styrofoam "noodle"—whatever water toy is currently the rage); sliding down the midden heaps that river banks often become, so the archaeological perspective comes into play; talking to the local fishermen, the occasional duck hunter, the kids who come down to the river to throw stones in the current or hunt crayfish; being involved in a common pursuit people enjoy asking you about; making friends in the diners where you break for coffee or the bars where you go to celebrate your success. After a while, all this adds up. This is even more true if you go about your fishing quietly and modestly, so you all but become a part of the riverscape yourself—a tree, a willow, albeit one with eyes and ears and understanding.

I've often thought a good book could come out of this—a collection of tales on the order of Ivan Turgenev's *Sportsman's Sketches,* changing the hunter into a flyfisher who in the course of his or her exploring learns much about the local people and their customs, their heartbreaks, and sadness, their losses and their loves (Coos County, New Hampshire, badly needs its own poet or novelist; Frost never got this far north, and all the fiction writers seem to be concentrated on the Vermont side of the river). Just last week, fishing the river in the course of a long June day, I came away with enough locales to fill the book s first half. I started fishing behind the county old folks' home, a Gothic pile straight out of Dickens, where people in wheelchairs sunning themselves on the terrace waved as I waded past; a hundred yards downstream (the state liking to put all its institutional eggs in one convenient basket), I passed the county "farm" that serves as the reformatory—young men this time, too busy piling up hay to wave, hardly noticing as, right below them, I landed a good brown. A little later, driving upstream, I fished behind some abandoned factories, had my thoughts filled with a *temps perdu* kind of moodiness that made me think again of the region's boom-and-bust history. In late afternoon I was caught in a sudden hailstorm, took shelter in DeBannville's, where French memeres in curlers shook their heads and clucked in sympathy as the ice melted down from my hair. At dusk, waiting for the sulphurs to get going, I ran into a ninety-two-year-old bait fisherman, pumped him shamelessly, not only for information about the fishing, but for his memories of the old days (these took a morbid turn; most of his stories were of young men and women who had drowned in the Connecticut and people he knew who had helped pull them out).

And, just for the record, it's the bait fishermen you want to talk to if you're interested in learning equally about the fish and the region. Too many flyfishers these days are too narrowly focused on their pursuit, too businesslike and competitive to spare much time for my random kind of sightseeing; then, too, flyfishers you see on the river are apt to be from elsewhere, without much in the way of local knowledge. Spin fishermen, many of them, are pretty much just out for the afternoon, and when it comes to learning about the river, few have paid the requisite dues. No, what you want is the classic worm-chucking old-timer (by old-timer I mean anyone between the ages of fourteen and a hundred who fishes alone and obsessively and ponders the implications of what they discover), though once upon a recent time, to flyfishers with illusions of purity, these were apt to be viewed as our enemy. Secretive when they're fishing, they're talkative when you catch them at ease, and, like the teenager leaving me his secrets or the old man with his tragic stories, they're invaluable sources of information on the river you're trying your damnedest to figure out.

The hatch I was waiting for has started now right on schedule—little sulphur duns whose color is halfway between the white of a Cahill and the yellow of a daffodil just past its prime. The pool I'm fishing is a slow, even one, where the current, running broken along the Vermont bank, slides to the east, widens and slows, creating a living-room-sized terrace (with boulders for armchairs) that is almost always dappled with feeding trout. Catchable trout—for a change I feel pretty certain of this, and thus take my time getting ready, giving me the opportunity to go back again to one of the points I made earlier.

It concerns the river being the one locus of beauty in an otherwise hard-pressed land. Fishing the tributary streams, hiking the woods, driving the back roads, spending much time in town, you get the feeling that there is indeed much in the way of beauty here in this northern wedge of land, and yet it seems to come at you through a gauze, a scrim, that all but makes you rub your eyes in bewilderment, trying to clear them so you can see things plain. It's partially a scrim of poverty: the sense you have, even today, of what brutalities can be inflicted upon a land where the growing season is six weeks too short; a recognition that beauty is not a word that can be tossed around lightly in this kind of world, not with the shortcuts, stopgaps, and scraping that is visible on every hand. And yet, go down to the river, spend your days in its pastoral corridor, and the scrim literally dissolves; words like lush or lovely, prissy absurdities when applied anywhere else in the north country, suddenly become fully applicable, so it makes you see not just the Connecticut, but the entire region with a gentler, more forgiving kind of appreciation.

Wading out toward those fish, tugging line down from my reel preparatory to casting, picking out my spot, I'm aware not only of the merging cobalt rings spread across the current by the trouts' inhalations, not only the yellow-blue surge of water where the lowering sun hits the river and thickens it, but the tall, seed-heavy meadow grass that begins on the bank, the bristly hedgerow of sumac, black cherry, and ash, the first sloping esker with its birch and white pine, the staircase of spruce-covered mountains that leads toward the coral-dark sky—Vega at the top of it, the high steady beacon of a midsummer's eve.

"What a land!" I say to myself, not for the first time. "What a river!" I want to shout.

Ten minutes left of dusk in which to appreciate it all—just time enough to end on a personal note, expose to light what my mind kept chewing over when it should have been concentrating on those trout. It was about the boy I met earlier in the season, the logger who was bailing out for the Marines. I thought of him, and in a strange way that surprised me; I realized I envied him, and not just a little.

What's going on here? A dead-end job, telling the boss to shove it, going off to the tender mercies of boot camp—no, it wasn't envy of any of these. Envy instead of what he probably hated most in himself: of having this hard, bitter land as the place he grew up in, the region he will—for better or worse—compare every other with for the rest of his days. I suppose it's a mixed blessing—mixed for those who leave, just as it is for those who hunker down and stay. Live your whole life in such a landscape and between tears and exhaustion and familiarity, the beauty disappears; it's someone like me, neither local nor stranger, who, when it comes to appreciation, has the priceless vantage point of standing halfway in between.

In this respect—and here again I'm speaking most person-ally—almost anything would be better than being from the sub-urbs. When that boy searches his memory one day it will be of dark forests and impetuous rivers and snowstorms in October; when I search mine, it's of patios and split-levels and manicured front lawns, spiced with nothing more romantic than the occa-sional vacant lot. I think of Chekhov, born into a family of peas-ants, vowing to squeeze the serf from his soul drop by hateful drop—and remember as a young man vowing in much the same way that I would force everything suburban from my soul or die trying. Hence, I suppose, those long hours on the river in all kinds of weather, fishing long past the point of exhaustion, dreaming about the river when I'm away, coming back every chance I get. Much has changed in my life—and yet the cleansing still goes on.

And maybe all this helps explain the feeling that comes over me sometimes that this hard northern land, with the river as its mouthpiece, is speaking to me quite plainly and directly—that if I haven't succeeded in articulating its message here, it's my own fault, not the regions. Certainly, having this feeling . . . of embrace, of acceptance, of an odd and powerful kind of pity . . . is a good, reassuring sign that I'm that much closer to understanding the river, making it, in the vain way we speak of such things, mine. If stage one was that first specific reconnaissance, then stage two is this working toward a more general, wider appreciation . . . and this is what I flattered myself that I had now, as, a tall shadow in a forest of round ones, I climbed out of the current, reached the crest of the bank, then turned my head quickly back toward the river like a man trying to catch it unawares.

June 9

J ust when you think you've seen it all is the time to start admitting you've seen nothing. This is as true with sporting atrocities as it is with cultural ones, though I'm not sure which to file the following under. Twenty-four hours after the event, I'm still fuming, and write this partly in the hopes it will prove therapeutic.

Perfect weather. June and gloriously so, temperature topping out at seventy, the water at a perfect fifty-five. Lilacs at their peak—bouquets line the road. Mayflies on our windshield so dense and yet so airy it's as if a special welcoming committee is draping my Toyota in a fine muslin sheet. Visions of plentitude, visions of grandeur. Thirty-fish day? Thirty epiphanies? Both feel in reach.

Then, the fall to earth. Our favorite spot, our secret spot, a gray Mercedes parked there in its insufferably squat, arrogant way. Empty rod cases in back. Silver nails in our golden hopes.

Ray and I make a good team. He's good at speechless indignation; I like to curse. "Fuck!"

(A quick calming reminder to myself from Father Walton: "I would you were a brother of the Angle, for a companion that is cheerful, and free from swearing and scurrilous discourse, is worth gold.")

Nothing for it but to saddle up and wade right in; the situation is a bit similar to finding someone else in bed with your lover—a fatal compulsion draws you on to see the worst. Two flyfishermen, right in the current where, without any surface indication, it deepens into a long narrow run full of some of the largest, feistiest trout in the entire river. "How you doing, Doctor?" one of the fishermen shouts, as he starts a new cast. "Fine, Doctor, how you doing over there?" his friend shouts back. "Just fine, Doctor! You nail 'em, hear?" "Okay, Doctor! Hit 'em hard yourself!"

Ray and I are sitting on the bank taking all this in. "What does this mean?" I ask quietly. Ray shrugs. "Maybe they're doctors?"

Noisy ones. They shout back and forth in that macho small talk you hear a lot of on the river these days—it's as if everyone not only is being fed their lines from the Saturday-morning fishing shows, but have adopted the Southern accent to match.

Ray is crestfallen and angry; this is his spot more than it is mine, the one he discovered by many hours of exploration and the divining rod of his own splendid intuition. In all the times we've fished here we've never had company, so I'm pissed, too. What both of us suffer from, ultimately, is the fact that we're lucky or unlucky enough to have fallen in love with fly fishing many years before it became a fad, setting up that familiar and not very pleasant syndrome (seven parts protective jealousy, two parts sincere amazement, one part snobbery in reverse) of having the rest of the world discover something you've been in love with all along.

But that's not the atrocity. The atrocity is this.

Both men catch fish. That these are chub—that the fishermen loudly identify these with exuberant whoops of victory as trout—adds a little ironic frisson to our indignation, but does little to erase the scar. As they fish, they become further separated, so the younger of the two, the one with the waxed cotton hat, is now directly below us, backlit by the sun, which is still not quite clear of the trees on the New Hampshire bank.

"He's got something wrong with his neck," Ray says. "Watch." I watch—and realize it's not a crick in his neck at all, but that he has his head tucked in tight toward his shoulder, holding by this pressure, as he continues to cast, a cellular phone.

"He's on the phone."

"On the what!"

Ray squints, sees for himself, blinks, blinks again, sighs— collapses backward in a faint that seems real.

Who's this man calling? His patients, telling them he'll be late? His friends, telling them where he is, feeding them the exact coordinates of his fishing position? He catches another chub now, reels it in while he continues talking, then, releasing the chub, bringing the phone down, presses in a number, sticks it back there against his neck, resumes talking. His casual absorption reminds me, more than anything, of a secretary talking on the phone as she polishes her nails.

A beautiful river, a perfect day, a tonic to the senses. All this means nothing to him—for him, it's just another in the endless series of places where he can be reached.

(Flash again to Father Izaak: "And for you that have heard many grave serious men pity Anglers; let me tell you, Sir; there are many men that are by others taken to be serious and grave men, which we condemn and pity.")

By the time anyone reads this, the phenomenon of flyfishers talking on the phone in the middle of the river will probably be old hat, with catalogs offering special waterproof models just for this purpose, your choice of camouflage or dark Orvis green. I realize that many people probably see absolutely nothing wrong with conducting business or making social calls while they stalk trout, or, to put it another way, feel vulnerable and disconnected if their phone isn't constantly in reach. I also realize that many people like to fly fish via the Internet, transform their favorite fishing spots into digits that are broadcast around the world. I realize there are guidebooks and videos available for every major river in North America, taking you by the hand and leading you pool by pool in great detail. I realize, too, that one of this country's most successful businesses is the manufacture and sale of electronic fish finders—that there are millions of people who, spending their working day in front of marching electrons, enjoy spending their leisure hours sitting in boats watching electrons fish for them.

I could have some ironic fun with this, or change gears and wax bitter; better, perhaps, to bite my tongue in silence and slink back toward the 1940s, where I belong. But there does seem to be one point in all this worth extracting once again:

that secrecy, long considered to be among a fisherman's most characteristic and endearing traits, seems to be taking it on the chin these days, and I think it's time it was restored as one of the highest of fishing virtues.

Late yesterday afternoon, as we were eating dinner at the Wilderness Restaurant in Colebrook before going back out, still mad over the phone stuff, who should amble over to our table but a couple of fly fishermen I know casually from home.

"How's the fishing?" they asked.

"Great," I said (for we'd done well once the doctors had left). "Six trout each, decent size, all on top."

Their eyes lit up—it hadn't been a good day for them. "Where?" they demanded.

"Well, you go—" I felt a telepathic something in the air, hesitated, looked up to see Ray staring at me *very* intently; if eyes were feet, his pupils were kicking me on the shin.

"You go down—that way," and I pointed.

"That way?" they asked.

"Yeah, you know. Down that way by where the river is."

"Oh, that way," they said, and nodded.

All four of us sat there over our coffees not saying much, not having to. These were experienced flyfishers after all. They had probed, we had defended, so what else was there to say?

That someone who not only talks about the rivers he loves, but writes about them, is a bit vulnerable in the secrecy department is something, believe me, I'm fully aware of. In my defense, I'm known for including my share of protective obscuration; one of the most frequent responses I get to my books, when meeting someone who knows them, is having them shake their head, say something to the effect of, "That pool you call The Pet Store. I couldn't quite figure out exactly where you meant."

Damn straight you couldn't figure out where I meant, I feel like saying, I'm dumb, but not that dumb.

(Regarding Ray's secret run, it's worth mentioning that I've made it up entirely. It's not on the Connecticut at all, not even in New England, not even in the Western Hemisphere; nope, not even on this planet, so there's no use you're searching for it this side of heaven. That okay, Ray?)

So, my fellow flyfishers, the time has come to bring secrecy back into our gentle pastime—the tight lips, the polite shrug, the knowing wink. Be generous with your help to beginners, praise a river all you want, help strangers out with tactics and flies, try to show them by word and deed what fly-fishing ethics are all about, but when it comes to your favorite spots, cherish them in secret, keep your mouth shut—and leave the godamn electronics at home.

The New River (3)

Some lessons I've learned ...

That there is a special way flyfishers talk about a river, see a river; regard it, that it is all but incomprehensible to someone who doesn't share our obsession. The argot of line weight, tippet diameter, a rod's pliability; tackle craft and the complicated minutiae that goes with it; the specialized references to insects, with their erudite flavoring of Latin; the shop talk of flies, referred to now by the name of their inventors, now by their descriptive nicknames, generating words that are as colorful and vivid as any in our language; the fascination with current and depth, bottom and cover, the geological lingo, the fluvial one; the calendar that has nothing to do with the Gregorian, but marks off the season in hatches, stream temperatures, water levels, and spawnings; the map, the vivid and raised map, of fishing success and fishing failure, superimposed over a graph of good days and bad, endlessly perused for its lessons; the body language of leaping hands, painful grimaces, melodramatic shudders—the puzzled frown, the slow rueful shake of the head, the shrug that says it all. All these contribute, so it's quite possible for two fishermen, comparing notes on a river, to talk in a language that to the uninitiated sounds as arcane as Greek, and yet to flyfishers is remarkably universal, an Esperanto of the fishing passion.

This language has only one goal: to speak of the river in a way that leads to the catching of more and bigger trout. The verbs, the nouns, the adjectives—all these are used like an abstract kind of fly, one we toss around fairly wildly at times, yet which must be chosen with intelligence and deliberation, carefully fastened to our purpose, thoughtfully delivered, attentively followed as it works its way across the water toward the fish it's meant to snare.

That the most important and vexing factor in fishing the Connecticut is water level. The upper part of the river drains a large and turbulent watershed, with tributaries that come down from high soggy plateaus on the Vermont side and snowy uplands on the New Hampshire, so in most seasons the river doesn't become fishable until the second week of June. Even then, things are dicey. It's a tailwater fishery, and the release from Murphy Dam is usually reliable enough that there is little fluctuation in the course of a normal day. No, the tricky things are the summer thunderstorms that can be remarkably isolated, and yet so violent they dirty up the river fast enough to eliminate all fishing.

We've learned over the years to expect these, keep our tactics flexible. Even if the weather has been good down here I make a point of calling Ducret's and asking about local conditions; all it takes is for whoever answers the phone to go over to the window and look out at Mohawk Stream, the tributary that runs right by the shop. It dirties up fast—but if it's clear, the chances are the main river is clear as well.

Even if we receive the green light, were still faced with a two-hour drive to get there—time for a lot to change. If the water is high but clear, it's worth fishing, though there will be many places we can't reach; if it's dirty and brown, it's still worth prospecting to see if we can't get above the offending tributary, or, changing tactics, head downstream far and fast enough to beat the silt, get an hour or two of clarity before we have to quit.

If worse comes to worst, there are the tributaries to fish. Sometimes we'll drive up to the headwaters between the lakes, try there. If it looks like the entire river is up, we can bail out completely, head over to the Androscoggin, which is only thirty miles east—though this, of course, means raising the stakes for a long disappointing drive home if it turns out to be muddy there as well.

Low water can also be a problem, particularly in drought years like 1988 and 1995, or when the power company forgets its corporate responsibility toward the health and well-being of the fish. The river looks ugly and exposed at these times, and if hot weather kicks in you'll see dead rainbows. But this is exceptional—most years, July is perfect.

Between high water and low, there are at least five or six weeks each season when the river is completely unfishable, making for what is in effect a closed season within the open one—and yet when it's over, when the level goes back up or falls back down, the fishing can be the best of the entire year.

That partly because of the difficult, sometimes dangerous water conditions, partly due to the fact that it's inhabited by wild and moody trout, the Connecticut is not a river for beginners or the casual once-in-a-whiler. It's a river that is constantly asking you to *reach*—reach with your cast, reach with your patience, reach with your wit—and someone who is inexperienced may find they're being asked riddles they're not quite ready to solve. The two most common fishing situations here are casting to rising trout in slow water where a single clumsy cast is enough to drive them sulking back to the depths, and fishing fast, turbulent pocket water where it can be hard not only to hook fish, but to even detect their strikes. Then, too, wading is difficult at the best of times; there's that high water which will hold the timid in close to the banks, or the low water where the rocks become covered with weedy slime.

Does this mean it's a river for experts? No, because in all my years of fly fishing I've never encountered an expert, have come to believe they don't exist. The good flyfishers I know are the ones who, competent with the basics, put most of their energy into many hours of local investigation; the *best* flyfishers I know add to this large resources of intuition, the kind of imagination that likes to tinker and probe, excellent vision, a gentle way with water, the gift of attention—or, in short, qualities that have nothing whatsoever to do with expertise, but everything to do with grace.

That a five-weight rod with backbone is what you want to be fishing with here. The Connecticut offers a lot of variety; a hundred yards of fishing might call for drifting midges in slow water at the top of the run, dredging stoneflies across the bottom when you reach the middle, flicking attractors in the choppy shallows where the current picks up. Because of the size of the river, the depth, you frequently get into situations where you've waded out to your limit, cast to your limit, and yet still need a few feet more—and the only way to do this is by having in hand some extra graphite oomph. I fish with an Orvis Henry's Fork, their jack of all tasks, but find myself vowing each year to switch to a ten-foot rod, not only for the extra power, but to hold more line clear of the current and cut down on drag.

I've gone up and down in this respect, but always come back again to the five-weight. A two-weight is a delight to fish, but the trout are seldom close enough here to make it practical, and in slow water where the light line would work best you want to bring in trout fast so as not to spook the next one waiting on line. I've gone up to a seven-weight in high water, one of those stiff, expensive, high-tech jobs, but find it simply too much rod; it crosses that crucial border between stroking the rivers back and flailing it.

And I always carry a spare—a cheap pack rod I stick in my rucksack with my lunch. Perhaps it's only me, but I find graphite rods surprisingly brittle—I've broken two or three in as many years. But then again, I'm an aggressive, absentminded caster, am always asking of my rods too much, and they tend to answer, with a little sighing sound, by breaking at the ferrule.

That when it comes to flies you would be well advised to carry a large assortment of the usual old reliables, but then spend all your time trying to discover which particular pattern the trout prefer as their flavor of the month. For there is a flavor of the month, or rather, a flavor of the season—we've discovered this again and again. What makes it interesting is that this flavor will vary from year to year so when you start on the river in June, last year's flavor means little and the search has to start all over again. ("You don't want vanilla? How about cherry vanilla? Maple walnut? My, you're fussy today, little fella. Mint chocolate chip?" . . . I bite my tongue, dig out another scoop, wait for that appreciative and greedy swallow.)

The first year I fished the Connecticut it would have been foolish to use anything on the surface besides small Light Cahills. For that endearingly reliable *stenacron canadense* was everywhere that year, and if they started to slow down in midsummer, then something very similar took their place; it was as if the river were sending up an airy ginger-yellow froth to gladden man and trout. I came back the following season armed with dozens, but went the entire summer without seeing anything on the water but caddis—small brown-gray ones that came off the water in unbelievable numbers. Other years it's been the darker mayflies or caddis again, only this time in white or olive. I don't have enough entomology to explain this phenomenon, but whatever surface pattern you discover early seems to be the one you'll be fishing five months in a row.

There are some more specialized considerations. Emergers are worth trying; quite often, especially in slow pools with little current, you'll see trout rising to what seems thin air.

For a long time I thought they were sipping midges, but even something as small as a 24 wouldn't interest them—they want a meaty emerger that never quite manages to break the surface film, and they want it fished with a tantalizing little twitch just as it comes into view. There are times when they *are* feeding on midges, and when this happens you might as well bite the bullet and go right down to a 22 or 24—18s and 20s are hardly worth bothering with. You would think it would be a good terrestrial stream, rushing past meadows overhung with trees, but in ten years of fishing I've never caught anything on a grasshopper or beetle, though I keep trying them, especially when not much else is happening. Every August there is a hatch of flying ants that lasts the length of one afternoon; I've always managed to be elsewhere that day, with timing that is impeccable.

I've had a lot of success fishing attractors over the years, though my friends laugh when I tie one on. To a generation weaned on match the hatch, these gaudy generic patterns are *infra dig,* the feathery equivalents of Big Macs . . . but I like them for that reason, spend so much time fussing, it's fun now and then to fish in sheer bad taste. The Royal Wulff is my favorite; it seems to provoke a response from trout that doesn't depend on color and silhouette as much as it does something chemical— if they want it, they want it, and I'll never tire of seeing that splashy all-or-nothing kind of rise it provokes. If Wulffs aren't working, I'll put on a Schroeder's Hare's Ear Parachute, which has the nice trick of vaguely resembling a caddis and vaguely resembling a mayfly, combined with that Hare's Ear kind of nondescriptness fish love. If neither of these are working, then I'll switch to a Yellow Humpy, more out of my perverse sense of humor than anything; I'm convinced fish strike it out of their own sense of humor (or to bulk up on roughage?), thinking it harmless, showing off.

More? I like Zonkers, but they don't work up here. Muddlers take hatchery trout, Woolly Buggers take natives. Hornbergs are a waste of time. Stonefly imitations are useful. Wet flies are definitely worth trying, too, particularly Hare's Ears or Cahills. As mentioned, the trout up here have a sense of humor, and appreciate a little movement in a floating fly; you should be fishing caddis sloppy, for instance, with all the crosscurrent drag you can muster. I've never seen a river where trolling works so well, by which I mean dangling your line absentmindedly behind you as you wade upstream. This always seems to get a bite, even from water you've fished carefully for an hour with no success. Why? No explanation, other than the trout's ironic take on life—and a trout's sensibility is nothing if not ironic, especially a brown's.

That it's a beautiful river to float with a canoe, taking you away from the road, away from the competition, in and under and through a tunnel of maple, ashy sumac, and birch, a bower of vines laced with moving water that is to the rockier, faster stretches of the river as the Amazon is to the Madison. Even if it wasn't for the beauty, a canoe can take you to water that can't be reached wading, especially those characteristically deep, slow, featureless pools that even to an experienced eye look fishless. In spring, there's enough inertia in the current so that you'll be fishing downstream all the way on a moving ramp that allows for no second thoughts, but later in the summer the current slows, and with a little paddling you can backtrack to spots you missed coming down or those pockets deserving of being fished twice. Still, even in these conditions you'll often be casting downstream to rising fish; this is extraordinarily difficult, especially when there's not enough current to give the fly any movement, so you have to drop it on their noses without spooking them. But what I like about a canoe (or even a drift boat) is that it makes you into an angling version of mounted infantry—transports you pool to pool in luxury, then lets you climb out and do the harder fighting on foot.

Spotting a canoe, shuttling around cars, can be an awful waste of time. Our trick is to lock a rusty old mountain bike to a tree where we're going to take out, and then the youngest, most energetic of the duo (defined as the one highest from catching the most trout) pedals back five miles to our starting point to fetch the car.

That on this kind of river with its wild, strong fish, it's insanity to fish with a 6X leader; hubris to fish with a 5X, prudence to fish a 4X, caution to fish a 3X, sloth to fish a 2X . . . and optimism to fish a IX.

That it's a good river on which to hit for the cycle, take a rainbow, brookie, and brown, even do it on three successive casts. The rainbows will be the most common of the trio—if you catch ten fish, seven will be rainbows, two will be browns, one a brookie. The best of these will be wild fish, which becomes apparent the moment you tighten on them—no stocked fish will fight like that. The river *is* stocked and stocked fairly heavily, but only in those spots where the truck can back up to the river without sliding in. This allows you to avoid the industrial fish entirely, not suffer the embarrassment of catching those three-pound brood fish New

Hampshire likes to dump into the river to inflate its reputation—salting a gold mine that is already full of fish.

What fish these wild ones are! The rainbows thick and full-bodied, their pink taken up by muscle so it's more of an added enhancement than it is a definite marking, their gills having the healthy red shading you see on their cousins out West. The browns, butter-colored just like they're supposed to be, with that iridescent spotting I can never see without wanting to stroke. The brook trout, small but willing, the river s original inhabitants and so always welcome, particularly in autumn when the males, to my eye, take on the most fluid, delightful color nature can create—those coral fins, those copper bodies!

In all the years I've fished here I've never been able to come to a definite conclusion as to which locale each variety prefers. Browns, of course, are said to favor slow water, but I've also found them in the heaviest current, albeit with a rock or log nearby to absorb the worst of the brunt; rainbows, going somewhat against their usual grain, are the fish you find rising in those slow, lazy pools, even in summer; brook trout can be found almost anywhere, but seem to favor best those scooped-out hollows downstream of islands, where they'll congregate in happy schools, caper about like kids on recess.

That some of these fish will be big—that the Connecticut is a big-fish river, with all that implies regarding mystery and excitement and keeping you on your toes.

This is important. Many rivers have the gift of charm; only a few have the gift of depth. The Connecticut is one of these, and much of it comes from the sense you have, even without immediate evidence, that there are big fish lurking about. Those deep back eddies that, judging by their appearance (their swirling vortices that swallow branches whole, let alone flies) must be bottomless; the logs sticking out of the water like the sharp outerworks of an unconquerable fort; those stretches so fast and deep and unfishable they function like a combination wildlife refuge, nursery, and old-age home where trout may flourish unbothered by man. All these create a certain aura—and if they aren't enough, then there are those grainy black-and-white photographs that show up in the newspapers just often enough to keep things interesting: ten- and eleven-pound browns, held up by someone who's caught them on Rapalas or worms.

One morning last summer, fishing further downstream than we normally venture, my pal Ray Chapin caught four fish, two rainbows and two browns, the smallest of which was nineteen inches long. Had anyone else, I wondered, anyone else in the continental United States, fishing the same day, taken such a glorious quartet? I don't think so, and if you qualify that to east of the Mississippi, almost certainly not.

Hearing of these fish, seeing them on the end of someone else's line, drooling over those pictures, I began to feel more than a little bit left out. Here for four or five solid seasons I'd been working hard to get to know the river, grasp its secrets, and now I couldn't help feeling it was time for the river to repay my devotion and grab hold of me. A big fish would do nicely in this respect, acting as the emissary, the embodiment, of the depth and gravity I'd sensed in the river right from the start.

Knowing the next fish that takes your fly might be five or six pounds enhances the fishing experience in all kinds of ways. It makes you think much more about tackle, measure your rod and tippet in terms of what they can do against a really strong fish; it keeps you from taking anything for granted—makes you fasten on fish more gently, knowing what kind of power you might suddenly be attached to. It makes you scan the water differently, searching out places a big trout could break you off, readying yourself for chaos. Most of all, it makes you regard the river with a double focus, appraising it not just for where the trout might be hiding, but where the *big* trout might lie—the effect is that of reading one of those novels or poems that work well on two levels, the everyday and the mythic, so the river is acting continuously on your imagination, expanding it in airy fantasies even while it solidifies that expectant base.

And then the river did fasten on me, fastened twice, the second time hard enough even a slippery fellow like myself was hooked. It came about like this . . .

Ray and I were fishing some pocket water we hadn't fished before, working on the theory that on a hot summer day the trout would be hungrier and more active in current that was broken and oxygenated than they would be where it wasn't. For once, it turned out to be the correct assumption, and with the sun at just the right angle it was easy to pick up the quick, desperate splashings as the trout came up to chase, tip, and grab.

It was a good day to be out. The water ran in those broken surges of gold that brings out the kid in you, makes you happy to be alive. Ray found a chute where the water, hitting the roadblock of a ledge, flowed in a channel perpendicular to the current's main thrust, and he was busy taking one small rainbow after another along the rim. I stayed out in the middle, doing just as well, the trout leading me upward pocket by pocket and ever so slowly across toward the Vermont side.

I was fishing a 5X tippet, a small, heavily greased Royal Wulff. I was also half-asleep out of sheer contentedness—with a twelve-inch trout sitting behind every boulder, I felt I could go on enjoying them all day. As I came closer to the bank I had to veer back out again to get past a heavy stretch of rapids; past this, I resumed my westward inclination, to the point where I was within casting distance of the bank. Sleepy, but with my instinct still working, I became aware that the pocket ahead of me and slightly to my left was much deeper than anything I'd seen so far—deeper and longer, so there was a ten-foot wide band of smooth water extending from an upstream boulder to the head of the heavy rapids. Again, acting purely from instinct, not quite realizing the implications, I tossed my fly over, expecting nothing more exciting than another twelve-incher.

The rainbow that came up to the fly was much bigger than that. The rainbow that came up from below the fly, reached for it, took it, and kept going through the surface film to the altitude of my forehead was a trout of four or five pounds. But here I'm already racing ahead of the moment itself. What I was aware of first was hardly its size at all, but a shocking and over-powering sense of reality—finding out reality, truth, was a hell of a lot different than I had heretofore thought it to be; realizing I had been nowhere near understanding the rivers capabilities to generate living, healthy, vibrant flesh, and that what I was now faced with was the sudden and overwhelming need to get back in touch with this new reality, at odds that, thanks to my casualness, were impossibly long.

Ray, who had been following me upstream, saw the fish jump and we both yelled together. It came back into the water flank first, making us both think (we discovered later when we compared notes) of the most ludicrous, yet inevitable analogy, given its splash—of a bowling ball dumped into the river from great height. *I must get below him before he reaches that rapid*—as in all violent situations, I was given an instant of remarkable clarity before things started to fall apart. On the first leap I managed to stay attached, but at the second—at the precise moment I remembered my tippet was far too thin—the tippet parted and that was that.

"Jeezus!" Again, we both yelled this in unison and—after standing there staring at the black hole carved in the river by the trout's escape—waded together over to the Vermont side, immediately starting in on the yearlong analysis called what I should have done different.

It was winter before the regret softened enough that I could see I'd done something right—found what was probably the best ten yards of fishing on the entire river, a spot we were calling the Trophy Hole even before we waded back out. Again, I couldn't get over how the smaller trout had led me over there fish by fish; it was as if I'd whispered, "Take me to your leader," and they had responded instantly. As for losing the monster—well, there was this consolation: it's almost impossible to practice catching fish that size, and if I'd made a crucial error it was in not recognizing the water's potential just by looking, and changing instantly to a heavier leader.

Armed with those most precious of weapons, hindsight and expectancy, I would catch him next year—or so I thought. All through the following spring the water was too high to let me get across to the hole, or even to tell where it was located in the bank-to-bank dance of rushing white peaks. It was the middle of July before I had my chance—a soft rainy day when the sky and weather blended into the same pewter grayness and anything seemed possible.

Tom Ciardelli was with me—he was the only one we had let in on our discovery. Still, he seemed skeptical . . . it was all that talk about bowling balls . . . and stayed downstream to fish the pockets while I plowed on upstream.

I found my way to the hole all right. I stood there gauging it, trying to figure out a game plan to use if and when the trout took again. The rapid below me was the crucial factor; no way could I hold anything immersed in its force. If I stayed on the outside of the rapid, though, I would have difficulty following anything in the treacherous footing of those rocks. After thinking about it for a while, experimenting with various stances, I decided my best bet was to plunge through the waist-deep current and get on the Vermont side of the fast water; if worse came to worst and I had something too strong to hold, I could step up onto the bank and follow him on dry ground.

I'd checked and rechecked my leader before starting and felt pretty confident in that respect. I had a Wulff on, since I wanted to repeat as nearly as possible every step that had worked last time. Nervous, knowing it was unlikely anything would come up the first cast, but knowing I had to be ready just in case, I worked out some line, then dropped the fly just below the boulder that marked the holes upstream start.

The strike was instantaneous, solid and hard; I'd seen the snout appear below the fly and was already lifting up my rod when it took hold. It's difficult remembering which came first, my amazement that fate had come through again in such classic fashion, or my surprise that this wasn't my rainbow at all, but—as if by a miraculous feat of transfiguration—a large, a very large, *brawn*.

I'll spare you the details of the fight, other than to say this: how delightfully rare it is in New England to fight a fish that is a *long* way off, making you feel like you're flying a remote-control airplane, something that's attached to you but remains almost entirely independent, so you marvel at being able to exercise even a modicum of influence. It was a powerful fish, but nowhere near as fast and dangerous as the rainbow; I had the sense, even as I fought him, that it was an old fish, a year or two past its prime. It got in the fast water just as I feared, but the second part of my plan worked to perfection; by hopping up onto the bank and hurdling various boulders I managed to stay below him and slowly led him over to a gravel shingle that sloped into the water as gradually as a boat ramp.

Tom, hearing me yell, seeing the commotion, had hurried up to meet me, and with his help we had it measured, photographed, and released in the space of a few seconds. Twenty-four inches from snout to tail, with a big angry hooked jaw, a yellow that was brighter than any I'd seen on a fish, and just a trace of slackness on what was still a fine, thick flank. That I was pleased to have found him goes without saying, but what pleased me even more was the feeling that the river had come through for me big-time. I had explored and experimented for a good five years, tested and probed in all kinds of weather, watched and observed, tried my best to divine its secrets, and here in the middle of a rainy July day I had at last been deemed worthy of initiation, been accepted by the river into its bright and wondrous fold.

A fitting end to my journey of discovery—and yet I can't quite end this here, feel reluctant to sever myself even temporarily from the river of delight that runs so strongly it's as if I can feel its energy pulsing through these keys. But in sharing the wonders of my new river I haven't yet mentioned my favorite spot of all, something that sits on the western bank a short distance downstream of the town of Canaan, Vermont, beside one of the river's best pools. It's a sewage-treatment plant, squat and unlovely, resembling with its cement severity and flat storage tanks a service station for UFOs, and yet from it, and from its cousins downstream, flows everything beautiful I've described.

The best landscaped sewer in the world. This was the Connecticut's reputation just a few years ago, when so bad was the pollution and neglect no one would go near it, let alone write rhapsodies in its honor. That this has changed is directly attributable to the enormous collective effort to win back the river undertaken in the late-middle years of this century, including the federal legislation known as the Clean Waters Act. A long story, full of villains and heroes, successes and setbacks, but one I'll draw a simple moral from, including with it as deep and heartfelt a thank-you as I know how to write. Ray, Tom, and I. The fishermen we've met on the stream. The canoeists, the picnickers, the hunters, and the birders. Our children and our friends. We're the first generation to reap the benefits from the efforts of the generation just before, and it's because the fight was made to restore the river to health that everything follows. The trout, the mayflies, the otters, mergansers, and moose. All the enjoyment, the mystery, and joy. Conservation works . . . that's the motto I'll end on . . . and the task it works best at is the creation of delight in the human heart.

Part Three: Full Season

Cohorts

Like I came late to friendship. Like many people who reinvent
themselves after their teenage years, I was ruthless in cutting off
the friends I grew up with, and it was a long time before I found
anyone to take their places. Suffering badly from the form of ego-
ism called shyness, with a stern and idealistic view of the novelist's
task (Proust called friendship an abdication of the writer's duty
and I fully agreed), I felt friendship was simply not on my list of
life's requisites. When I eventually softened in this regard, began

to feel the need for friends after all, life wasn't willing to accommodate me just like that. I was living in the country, cut off from
anyone I knew, and though northern New England's reputation
for iciness is in many ways unjustified, it is and always has been a
place where friendship doesn't come easy.

The upshot of this is that for over twenty years whenever I
went fly fishing I went fly fishing alone. I mentioned this in an
earlier book and it won me a certain amount of pity—perhaps
the reason I mentioned it in the first place. But I can say now
that nothing in my fishing has changed as much as my habits
in this regard, to the point where I now pal around with the
best of them, have become, at least compared with my earlier
standard, as gregarious as a Rotarian. Like a reformed drinker
or exsmoker, I feel compelled to mount a platform, testify to
the evils of my former ways, and thank with all my heart the
two men who are largely responsible for converting me from
fly-fishing loner into fly-fishing friend.

First, a few words about fishing friendships in general. It's
not as easy a relationship as the nonfisher might think, since
anyone with a passion likes to approach that passion in a certain
way. I don't know how many times I've had people try to set me
up with the fishing equivalent of blind dates—"Oh, you have
to go out with Ranald, he just loves fishing!"—only to discover
that Ranald and I come at fishing with a very different set of
assumptions and expectations, so our day on the river is a disaster right from the start.

A fishing friendship is a hard and demanding thing—a
good, lasting one something that is rare and priceless. So much
goes into it. A tacit agreement on how much seriousness to put
into the enterprise, how much fun; an admiration and respect
for the friend's abilities; a competitiveness that is playful, not

corrosive—the ability to tease and the ability to commiserate; a genuine delight in the other's successes; a telepathy that works even when you're far apart on a stream, so understandings about lunch breaks, quitting times, and meeting places always seem to take care of themselves; a shared willingness to put up with disappointment, not let it get you too far down; facing a certain amount of discomfort together, even danger, giving the friendship some of the enduring loyalty known by soldiers in combat; the ability, most of all, to be young together, if only for the space of an afternoon, to work like men or women at being boys or girls.

I met Tom Ciardelli after our wives had already become friends. In the same aerobics class together, they had discovered that both their husbands were passionate about fly fishing, thereby setting the stage for us all having dinner together, and—for this is the way the women pictured it as they burned up those carbs—the men to become friends as well.

I resisted—my first impulse toward any social invitation is to turn it down. I'm sure Tom resisted, too; I'd published a book on fly fishing by then, and it was easy for him to picture some egotistical know-it-all arrogant yuppie scum snob. But Celeste worked on me (there was talk about a private one-acre pond), Andrea worked on Tom (couldn't he steal from me some secrets?), and the matter was settled—we would be going over to their place Saturday night at five.

We surprised ourselves by hitting it off, at least after the first awkward moments. Tom was not a man who put much energy into the social graces, and I can be stubborn in this regard, too. What saved us was that all these greetings and introductions took place outside—that ten yards away, shining in the soft way of semigloss paint that hasn't quite dried, was a gray-green expanse of water, Tom's famous pond.

We walked over together, stood in the shade of a tall white pine watching as out in the middle of the pond trout rose toward wispy brown mayflies. I commented on how healthy and strong the fish looked; "There's bigger than that," Tom said, with a little laugh. He reached down in the grass for some fish pellets that had spilled, tossed a handful out, and for the next few minutes we watched a feeding frenzy that would have done justice to sharks. Talking about his pond led us to talk about other ponds in the area, then streams, then rivers, our separate experiences on each overlapping like the rings sent up by those trout, until without really thinking about it, standing there with our Molsons, we began a dialogue about fishing that is still going strong thirteen years later. And right from the start I was struck with one thing; that Tom is one of those surprisingly rare fishermen who admire and value trout on their own and not just as quarry, finding trout the one species that really speaks to them about nature and wonder and the large scheme of things, so it's quite accurate to say, without irony, that trout represent to them something spiritual in life, not just sporting.

Tom looks not only like the kind of man who would be good at fishing, but the kind of man who would be good at almost anything, as long as it involves hard, largely solitary effort. He's not easy to know—there's very little to read on his surface—but this is more than made up for by the kind of granite toughness you see a lot of in these hills, if not always in scientists of his caliber. Biochemistry is his field, pure research; like many talented people who live up here, he disdains the glitz and perks of a showy kind of career in return for being able to remain in the place he loves. He's of medium height, broad chested, walks in the even measured way of a good athlete (power volleyball was his game), and it's only his beard that gives any indication of his anarchistic leanings—he's not a man who has much use for the usual orthodoxies, not in politics, not in science, not in fishing. He and I are the same age, born within a couple of weeks of each other, and this has proven not the least of the strands that make up our friendship—the synchronization of outlook and expectation that comes between people who started out on this planet at exactly the same moment.

Before dinner was over we had made plans to go out fishing. There's a pond over in New Hampshire he wanted to show me; it was one of the few bodies of water he'd found that had a significant hatch of *hexagenia,* those humongous mayflies that drive trout wild. Since I had never actually seen one of these, I was more than happy to go along.

It was an interesting enough night, though I don't remember catching anything. Tom proved to be a good man with a canoe, and a generous guide; when we did see a rise, he maneuvered so I could get the best shot. I think both of us were a bit nervous those first few moments; okay, we both talked a good game, but how would we do when the money was on the line? Sitting in the bow, I found it hard to judge his casting style, though I did notice how gently his line landed on the water, and I was impressed by his ability to identify what minutiae the fish were taking. We broke for sandwiches and beer, then paddled around the shallows waiting for the *Hex* to show. And finally they did— eight or nine of them anyway, big and yellow, looking like swallows in comparison to the flies we'd seen until then, drying their wings with the kind of deliberately slow macho flappings you see in weight lifters, then taking to the air—to be immediately snared by *real* swallows, so not even one *Hex* managed to escape as far as the trees.

In the years since I've fished with Tom many dozens of times; we've covered quite a bit together in the way of river, stream, and pond, been skunked on occasions when we should have clobbered them and clobbered them in situations where by rights we should have gone fishless. I think we've grown as fishermen in the course of all this, not so much in our tactical understanding as in the delight we find in our sport. Like a lot of people who work very hard to get time out on the water, Tom was once apt to let a fishless day bring him down, knowing it might be a long while before he could get out again. Now he seems more relaxed in this respect, having learned to accept, even relish, the bittersweet kinds of defeat trout can toss at you—though they don't defeat him very often. Ten years ago, I wouldn't have dared tease him about losing a fish; now he kids himself, clears the air with the kind of loud clear "Damn!" that does the heart good.

He's one of the three best fishermen I know. So strong is my faith in his talent that I often shamelessly take advantage, feel perfectly comfortable, come late afternoon, with lazing on the bank while Tom checks out whether the fish are still interested.

"Anything showing, Tom?" I'll call, lying there in the shade.

"A decent rainbow over there by the bank. Want to try him?"

"With what?"

"Bluewing Olive."

"You sure?"

"Try it."

Yawning, moving slowly, I let myself be coaxed . . .

Tom has an even more important role: he acts as my reality checker. If he can't catch them, then I know they can't be caught, thereby absolving me from any requirement to try.

I've tried to analyze over the years what makes him so good—why he takes the most trout when we go out and usually the biggest. I think the chief of his gifts is a superb patience. And by this I don't mean the lazy kind of patience most nonfishers think you need, sitting motionless on the bank watching a bobber and worm, but an active patience that combines an energetic seeking and probing with an understanding that the rewards for these might not come all at once; a willingness, in other words, to wait fate out. This is the one trait that reveals the scientist in him; he does not like to leave a problem behind, but meets it squarely, determined to find a solution before moving on.

What this means, put him on the river, is that he concentrates on just one or two spots, working them thoroughly, blotting out from his consciousness the fact there's more fishable water just upstream or down. He refuses to give in to the easiest and most dangerous of fishing temptations—believing that the fish are biting just one pool away—but digs in and fights it out on turf of his own choosing. Me, if I haven't connected within an hour, I'm out of there; Tom, after an hour, is just getting warmed up, and—having noted patterns in the water, flashes, hints, threads—will be a more dangerous, sharper fisherman at the very moment when other fishermen begin getting sloppy, lazy, and bored.

Patience carried on a few casts too long becomes stubbornness, but Tom is smart enough to avoid this; stuck, at a complete dead end, he accepts it and switches over to a more improvisational, hunch-based kind of fishing. Last summer, floating the Connecticut, I was doing fair with Hendricksons, but Tom wasn't quite satisfied, and switched to a Blue Quill—not an unknown fly, but one few fishermen carry in their box, even an expert tyer like Tom. But it proved to be just the ticket—the slight variation in color between his fly and mine was enough to overcome all the trouts' inhibitions. I've seen him do similar many times: catch fish with the grain, then catch just as many cutting across it.

I admire Tom for all these talents, but what I admire most is the sheer beauty and grace of his casting. Tired of fishing, or even just glancing up between casts, I'll become totally absorbed in watching him work out line over a far and fussy fish—decide, not for the first time, that his casting seems a kind of elegant handwriting against the sky. Those forward downstrokes so precise and measured, like bold Gothic Is; the great coil of script as the line comes back; that extended question mark it briefly becomes . . . and then the downstroke again, another signature letter added to the blue tablet on which his line falls.

It's casting of the old school, when a flyfisher's ability was measured not in how far he drove a fly, but in how effortlessly.

Tom's casting is wonderfully effortless, so, watching from the distance, you wouldn't think he was putting muscle into the process at all, so much as merely wishing the line forward, and wishing it forward in the most fluid and perfect loop nylon is capable of assuming. Not once have I seen him strain to complete a cast—not once. Yes, I've seen him make sloppy casts (though damn few), but these are only the natural little imperfections that, rather than spoiling great art, are its surest indications. He looks genuinely surprised at these moments—surprised, I think, that there turns out to have been effort involved in the process after all.

When you watch Tom cast you end up watching his hands, particularly his left one. Many fly casters will tug and yank with their left hand, but never quite manage to seesaw it into synchronization with what their right hand is doing with the rod (someone who looks like they're constantly tossing sticky stuff from off their fingertips is doing it too vigorously). Tom's left hand seems linked to his right one by some telepathic and infallible sensing, so with the most economical, even negligent of downward motions it's adding power, force, and speed while the right one handles direction. There's a weaving kind of motion to it; once in Switzerland, watching local women demonstrate the particularly difficult kind of hand looming they were famous for, I saw in the rhythmic sweep, sweep, and pause of their hands much that reminded me of Tom.

I don't think I ever fully understood how intensely he loves fishing, not until last fall when we finished the season together—a slow, regretful kind of day, both in the heavy, Brueghel kind of grayness that had possession of the landscape and in our knowing it was goodbye to the river for another eight long months. Tom's not a man to let his feelings show, and yet just once, as we got into his truck and started the long drive home, I heard him whisper, to himself and with more poignance than the words alone can convey, "Now I have nothing left to look forward to . . ."

He's a good man to fish with, Tom Ciardelli. I think if I were ever to look back on our friendship and try to pinpoint the moments that were best, I wouldn't remember any day in particular, but something that happens in almost all our days together. Tom will be working hard on his favorite pool, and I will have roamed upstream, checking things out . . . and then an hour or two later I'll be back again, or he will have moved upstream to meet me, and we have one of those fishing reunions that come in midstream, with the simple, even banal vocabulary that is familiar to anyone who ever divvied up a river with a friend. "Any luck?" "Nope. Anything up here?" "A couple of brookies. Nothing spectacular." "I saw something. Down there by that log." "Coming up to caddis?" "Brown ones. You give him a shot." . . . Which, I suppose, are the kinds of things flyfishers say when they can't say, "Hey, I missed you, pal! It's good to be together again, eh?"

There's lots men say without saying it directly. Three years ago Tom and I were fishing a tailwater river up north. We had called ahead and gotten the tape-recorded message on when the dam would and wouldn't be releasing water, and so felt reasonably safe in what was otherwise a dangerous enough position. We waded across a shallow channel to a sandbar where we could cast the rest of the way across the river; we had been fishing there not more than fifteen minutes when we both noticed something seemed different.

"Hey, Tom," I said, pointing to the rocks. "Am I imagining things, or is the water going back up again?"

Tom stared toward the stick we'd planted in the sand to measure any such fluctuation. "It's going up. Let's go!"

Instantly, without discussing it further, we started back across the shallow channel—the channel that was already full of rushing water as high as our waists. Tom, holding his vest high like a fussy old woman but moving powerfully for all that, made it across to shallower water, then looked back toward where I was struggling. My hat fell off—I grabbed for it too late—and then I realized I had a lot more to worry about than hats. The water was gaining vertically on my horizontal shoving—a second later and the current pushed my boots off the gravel and I began to be swept downstream. It was then I felt Tom's hand reach out and fasten on my shoulder—so strong, so secure, it's as if I can feel that same arm reach out and steady me now as I type these words, a tower of strength leaning out from that bank to bring me back to safety, to standing on the bank feeling relief and gratitude and admiration, and—because we're men—trying to express these things without using any of those words.

"Thanks," I finally managed, gasping for breath, the river pouring off of me. Then, scowling: "Why the hell didn't you save my hat!"

I've always had the feeling, watching Tom on the river, that I can understand quite clearly the talents that make him such a good fisherman. It's a different story with my other fishing partner, Ray Chapin. He's a marvelous fisherman, every bit as good as Tom, yet study and analyze his talent all you want and there will always be an aspect that can't be explained, at least not without sounding like a mystic.

We met at a party at a mutual friend's; I was sipping bourbon off to one side when a young man whose beard couldn't quite disguise a boyish, handsome face came over and introduced himself. He had read one of my books, was himself just at the point where he was abandoning spinning for the fly rod, and was full of questions. Ray is the kind of person you feel you know instantly; struck by the soft earnestness of his manner, much against my usual habit, I asked if he would be interested in trying out his new fly rod on one of my favorite local streams.

Ray is ten years younger than I am, so there was something of the master and apprentice in our relationship—at least that first time out. He was still clumsy with his casting, but after ten minutes of fishing I could see he had all the tools to be extraordinarily good. Athletic, sure-sighted, passionately interested, and a native Vermonter with a real affinity for the terrain, he immediately put me in mind of James's definition of a writer: "He on whom nothing is lost."

He was working two jobs at the time, as a draftsman designing houses and, on weekends, as an orderly in our local hospital so his family would be covered by health insurance. I admired him for this, his hard and continuing effort to reinvent himself—an effort that a few years later had him going to college with kids half his age, taking the opportunity he never had as a youngster to grab the learning he craved and deserved.

It's been one of the most rewarding things in my fishing life, watching Ray develop as a flyfisher, come into his own as a man who loves the sport and does it honor. I remember that first year fishing together up north, Ray rushing downstream to where I stood casting, a bow wave cresting out ahead of his waders, so excited he could hardly talk.

"There's something happening up there. You've got to come see!"

"Happening? Like fish happening?"

"I think it's a ha-ha-ha . . . a *hatch*)."

And that's what it was, the first Ray had ever seen, and he did just fine with it, though not without some coaching; when he turned his back on the river and started to wade toward shore, I yelled "There's one!", whereupon Ray hooked the trout backwards over his shoulder, spun like a matador, and brought him in.

He's a superb caster, with a good ten feet of distance on me, more if he wants to reach (he's a basketball player, and basketball players, spending long hours coordinating hands and eyes to work at distance, often make the best fly casters). He's tireless, often wins on the river from sheer endurance. Unlike a lot of fishermen, he's comfortable talking aesthetics, or sitting back and just drinking in the views (I remember once lying on the grass along the bank, the two of us watching spellbound as the crests of the birch trees high across the river became aglow with swarming caddis, so it was as if each tree were lit by a lambent flame of spontaneous generation). He's an efficient, businesslike fly tyer, especially with the patterns he's devoted to: the olive Hare's Ear, a little black nymph with a wisp of sparkle, a ratty brown caddis. I've seldom seen him fish streamers, though now and then, not without grumbling, he can be persuaded to chuck and duck with a Woolly Bugger. He can wade a river with a risky kind of prudence—there's no machismo in him, but he enjoys pushing the envelope of what can be crossed. And he's a fast learner; I've seen him make mistakes over the years, but never the same mistake twice.

As I suggested earlier, all these only partly explain Ray's success. He brings to fishing another quality, one I'd be tempted to call pure luck, were it not for the fact that the quality is much more reliable than luck alone. After thinking about it for a long time now, having seen Ray in action on all kinds of water from Maine to Montana, I've become absolutely convinced that in some subtle and yet compelling way fish *like* Ray, enjoy being caught by him, will seek him out in a river full of anglers, as if they can sense that this is the one whose heart they should gladden first.

For Ray not only always takes the first fish, but always takes the last—fish like saying goodbye to him just like they like saying hello—and almost always finds the biggest one as well. We've fished Slough Creek together several times, have covered the same pool with the same flies, alternating casts, and—the polls are definite on this—the cutthroat prefer Chapin three to one. The same is true on the Yellowstone or the Connecticut or wherever we fish. Ray would blush if he heard me say this, and people will probably think I'm nuts, but again it's the absolute truth: fish like Ray and are forever coming over just to revel in his presence.

And perhaps because I've seen him do it so many times, my enduring memory of Ray Chapin will be of him hooking still another good trout. That quick upward glance that always manages to seem surprised; the instant switch to total, her-on-like concentration; the rod going up as far as he can reach; the smooth and furious cranking to get the fish on the reel; that instinctive first step backward into shallower water . . . and then, without ever taking his eyes off the fish, the slow dance over to the spot where he'll bring him in; the smooth reach back over his shoulder for the net; the prayerful stoop to land him; the grateful little shove of release; the long, half-wistful glance as the fish swims off . . . and then the happy, embarrassed smile as he looks up and finds me staring in absolute wonder once again.

The only regretful part of my friendship with Ray and Tom is that so seldom do I get to fish with both of them at the same time. Last September we managed to pull this off, all three of us on Maine's Rapid River going after landlocks on dry flies. We had spent most of the day on different parts of the river, but now, after lunch, we converged on that lovely slow pool where the river slackens into Pond-in-the-River. For a change I figured out the salmon first, called over to the other two what they were taking, but then the fish switched over to something smaller, and this time Tom was the one who picked up on it, and then a half hour later when they went back to something medium-sized and a different color it was Ray calling out the pattern, so between the three of us, communicating instantly, positioned in an arc, it was like we were holding a net between us and those salmon never had a chance.

Who's the better fisherman, Ray or Tom? Sometimes I play around with this, try imagining which one I would choose to wade out into the river to try for an extraordinarily large and difficult fish, knowing only one person would have a crack at him before he took off. Choose Ray with his instinct or Tom with his patience? I think about this, compare their approaches, and for the life of me I can never pick out which one would get the nod—and so, as in the case of all such ties, there's only one option left.

"Hey, Tom," I would say, glancing over to where he's stringing up his rod, all but drooling in anticipation of that trout. "Remember all those times I've paddled you around in a canoe, muscled us upstream just to get you in a good casting position? Remember those picnics I've thrown together, the nachos, the roast beef, the salami? Remember how I've always field-tested the concoctions that come off your tying bench, including those Clouser Minnows that are borderline legal? Remember all the books I've loaned you over the years, the times I've given you what turned out to be good advice?"

"Yeah, sure I remember," he would say, his forehead creasing up in suspicion.

"Hey Ray," I would say, turning the other way toward where Ray is tying on a caddis. "Remember who was responsible for introducing you to this sport? Remember all the times I've shared my thermos of hot tea with you, those cold rainy afternoons? Remember all the good fish I've stepped aside from to let you have your chance?"

"Uh, yes," he would say, frowning, beginning to catch my drift.

I'd have my own rod strung up now, my fly ready, my leader stretched tight. "Tom, Ray. You guys are the greatest friends a man ever had. I want you to sit here on the bank, relax in comfort, and enjoy watching a *real* fisherman strut his stuff."

And as my partners gape in admiration, I would wade out into the river and make friends with that trout.

July 4

I crossed the divide, but not a great one. The road climbed just enough for me to downshift into third, then there was a level stretch, then it started down. Flashing out the window like little silver mirrors signaling me to stop was a stream hardly wider than a yardstick, but it was dropping westward now, not eastward like the stream I had been following up to the height of land. The sources of both were beaver ponds so close to each other that a child could lob a beach ball from one to the other without strain, and yet the difference was dramatic for all that, at least when it came to flowage, trendings, and ultimate destinations.

Behind me the water ran abruptly down to the Waits River, then straight ahead to the Connecticut, thence three hundred miles to the placid, overused waters of Long Island Sound. Ahead of me it flowed down by many windings to the Winooski, then to Lake Champlain, thence to the Richelieu River into Canada, north to the St. Lawrence, and down that river to the wild and tempestuous ocean off Newfoundland. Or, in other words, what was a difference of a few yards on a nondescript patch of green Vermont hillside became, given gravity time to operate: a global spread of some twelve degrees of latitude and nearly a thousand nautical miles.

It's the kind of thing I enjoy thinking about as I cross this little hump. I don't make the drive often, and when I do it to fish the Dog River, my favorite medium-small stream in the state—a real charmer, whose wild fish are smart and pretty enough to make even a longer drive worthwhile. Water that stays clear and cool even in July; lush coils of vines and shrubbery that hide it under a tunnel; a rough-hewn frame of village, woodlot, and farm centered squarely against verdant hills. It's a stream best described as—Well, at the time I couldn't remember the exact word, though I was trying to. There's an old-fashioned adjective that fits the Dog perfectly, but for the life of me I couldn't come up with it, this being the only vexation in what was otherwise a perfect summer afternoon of low humidity and high nubby clouds.

I parked a hundred yards downstream from my favorite pool, then bushwhacked through the jungle of greenery that hides it from the road. I was betting July 4th would be an ideal time to fish—people off partying and the green drakes hatching right on schedule. I was right on both counts—no fishermen, plenty of mayflies—but here I'm getting ahead of myself, giving away the end before I've even gotten wet.

There's an odd quality to fishing the best Vermont trout streams; so perfect can be the surroundings that you blink and disbelieve for a moment that they're real. I pushed through the crisp mare's tails and sharp raspberry vines to a border of cinnamon ferns, then out onto the undercut gravel embankment that fronts the river proper. To my right the water ran down in a wide shallow chute that emptied into a pool deep enough for swimming; when I turned the other way I could see the rusty railroad bridge that crossed the river from bank to bank; past this, curving out of sight, was a choppy stretch of riffles that ran through high pine.

Lovely as all this was, it was only the inner core in entwined strands that were each beautiful in a different way. The surrounding farmland with its green corn that was knee-high, just like it was supposed to be on the Fourth; the two-hundred-year-old farmhouses that sat back on the first high land from the river; the railroad tracks, so serene now and forgotten; the sense all this gave you of a wise and responsible stewardship. Throw in some deer (a doe splashing across the river; its fawn shyer, staying on the bank until I passed), a red-shouldered hawk, a rare scarlet tanager (only the second I'd ever seen), some high-spirited trout, and you have a river that exudes the sense of wellbeing only the last best places on earth can.

Even the ambient sounds, usually so corrosive, only added to the overall effect. There was a tractor taking care of second haying, never mind the holiday; the distant laughter of people playing miniature golf in a simple course a farmer had put up on his spare field; the chesty booms of fireworks even more distant, even happier, a pleasant staccato in the lushness of the prevailing tune. Here for the space of a summer evening the world was staying at exactly the right distance; I hitched up my waders, shook my head to stir up the perfection some, eased my way down the bank into the light, skipping pressure of the stream.

Has anyone ever written in praise of ankle-deep rapids? They're delightful, both in sound and sensation—the smooth-moving sheen, the way your wading boots break it apart into foaming runnels that don't reform until twice your shoe size downstream. The Dog, at least when it's flavored by a setting sun, is the color of mild chamomile tea, and that amber quality was most pronounced directly at my feet. Again, and with the same vexation, I tried remembering the word that describes the rivers murmuring quality, but it still wouldn't come.

By the railroad bridge the streambed is littered with old granite blocks left over from the original construction; they've been there so long now they've become a yellowed part of the natural landscape. The rainbows like to hide in the slow water behind them, getting up the nerve with excited little spinnings, then dashing out into the current to swipe a fly. As mentioned, these are wild fish (the Dog hasn't been stocked in thirty years), and they show it the moment you hook one. Never—not in catching salmon, not in catching bass—have I seen fish jump so high proportionate to their size; an eight-inch fish will shoot out of the water so fast, so high, your head snaps back to keep it in sight. Pyrotechnics! The analogy, with those boom-hiss-booms in the background, the flaring arcs of the rainbows' parabola, is both fitting and inevitable.

After catching five or six of these, I eased on downstream, on the lookout for the drakes, trying to appraise the changes in the streambed since the last time I had fished here. These were considerable; there had been two destructive floods in the course of the spring, and a deep pool where the river hooked left was gone entirely, its bottom filled with gravel that had been deposited when the current hit the bend. I accepted this with more grace than I would have thought possible, considering it had been my favorite pool; in the give and take of floods the pool just below had been scoured out even deeper, so most of the trout had simply migrated twelve yards downstream.

The green drakes were beginning to show. As with a lot of things in fly fishing, they're not really the color they're called, but a parchment-like yellow. They're big, too. The largest Cahills in my box, size 12s, were too small to match them, though the trout—stuffed, on the lookout for lighter servings—took them readily enough. It had been a while since I had seen such a fulsome hatch on such a small stream, and after catching another rainbow, the biggest of the night, I stood hip-deep in water enjoying the way the flies appeared out of nowhere on the surface, dried their wings for a moment, then, with feathery little inhalations, took to the air like Valkyries made of papyrus and dust.

Time to move on, fish one last pool before dark. There's another old bridge site, this one much rougher and forgotten, with only a moss-covered abutment on one bank and a vague indentation in the cliff on the other to show where a cart track had once crossed. You can't wade through the pool without spooking all the fish, so the only thing to do is send a fly down from above, bouncing it off the cliff, then tossing in some slack so you get a few decent inches of drift. Browns predominate here, but they seem made of the same exuberant stuff as the rainbows, leaping to incredible heights. In the twilight, with green drakes everywhere, they weren't hard to catch, and I hoped to find a big trout before it got too dark to fish.

For a moment I thought I saw one, the largest trout in the river, swimming downstream with the wiggly, nose-first grace of a harbor seal. I wasn't far wrong, at least in my analogy. It was a beaver, one that surfaced now right below me and gave a tremendous thwack with his tail. On any night but the Fourth I might have been considerably pissed at him, putting the fish down like that, but as part of the overall celebration his cannonade fit right in. He gave me four or five of these thwacks, each a little closer; he swam closer, too, to the point where I could have jabbed a boot out and spun him around. He (or more likely she) wasn't motivated by the usual kind of territorial imperative, for on the next pass through the pool she seemed to separate into three parts, one larger, two small. Baby beavers, the first I'd ever seen, no bigger than eight-week-old retriever pups, and just as curious, tumbly, and tame.

Trout, beaver, tanagers, mayflies. The distant sounds of celebration. Not a bad way to spend a summer evening. If the setting was perfect, my little jaunt through it had turned out perfect, too, so I didn't feel separated from the landscape, but a deep, essential part. A removable part, of course. In the darkness I waded back upstream, the trout rising so freely now it was as if they were trying to nudge candy loose from my pockets. They put circles in the river's downstream surge, made the water take on even more of that quality I felt so thoroughly, yet still couldn't name.

But then an hour later, driving up over the divide toward my own familiar valley, remembering the color of the water, the even, melodious way it flowed, I came up with the right word in a flash of inspiration, so sudden and satisfying I beeped my horn twice to match its syllables: *purling*. A purling river, the Dog is. A veritable purl of watery delight.

Save the Fountain

I'm a census taker for our local streams, an unofficial, self-appointed one, someone who likes to keep track of how many wild brook trout still grace our small corner of the planet with their habitation. I go out in all weather, three seasons of the year, armed with the traditional tools of my avocation: an old fiberglass fly rod with three missing guides, a patch of fleece with half a dozen flies embedded in the marl, Polaroid sunglasses scratched and stained from long usage, a scrap of paper, a stub of pencil, and, most important of all, the long and puzzled questionnaire that passes for my brain.

As best as I can determine, there are seven wild brook trout currently residing in our town: three in Slant Brook at the base of a small waterfall where the stocked trout can't bother them; one in Whitcher Stream where it bounces down to the Connecticut; a hundred or so in Trout Pond up on the slope where our mountain begins—trout so tiny, so miniaturized, you could put them all end to end and still only count them as three.

Not many fish, of course, but perhaps the miracle is that there are any left at all. Twenty years ago, when I moved to New Hampshire and began my survey, there were hundreds of brookies in all these locales—enough that the counting of them kept several dedicated census takers working full-time. I'd come upon them in the woods, secretive men apt to shy away at your approach, stubby rods pressed under their arms, their faces greasy with fly dope, favoring dark green work clothes, the only splash of color being the bandannas around their necks. Interesting men to talk to if you found 'em in the right mood; theirs was an intimate association with the landscape and its creatures, and they were less apt to talk about entire rivers or streams than they were individual pockets, boulders, and holes. Most of them valued wild trout greatly, yet possessed one self-destructive habit: they thought of their subjects as food—and not just for thought.

These men are largely gone now. If the trout are down to seven, then the census takers are down to one—me, probably the last one in the neighborhood who realizes wild trout are still among our inhabitants. I've taken to wearing green work clothes myself now, that same red bandanna, honoring by imitation a dying kind of breed. And even I don't go out surveying as much as I used to—I'm tired of walking, knocking, and finding no one is home.

But here I am veering off into bitterness when a census taker should stick to the facts. The trout I know best are the three in Slant Brook. This is as typical a New England trout stream as you're likely to find. Starting high on the side of our town's one steep mountain, it plunges down through the forest in an exuberant rush of brightness, sluicing westward through the uplands, carving a channel for itself through granite bedrock, dropping over two sizable waterfalls and the ruins of old mills, crossing under the highway in a giant culvert, then taking on new life as a meadow stream in the last mile left to it before joining the Connecticut in a marshy bay.

The lower three miles have trout in them, lots of trout, for two weeks a year. These are brook trout that have been raised in cement tanks in another part of the state, transported here by heavy truck, poured into the brook where it meets the road, caught immediately by people who fish no other time of year, the trout that survive being swept downstream by the first heavy rain, to end up as pike and pickerel feed in that marshy bay mentioned above. Stocking fish has been going on so long now in this part of the country it's become part of the natural order of things, so you have to step back a bit to realize how odd, how truly bizarre the whole business is. I mean, phony trout? Cement trout? Trout from the city turned loose to entertain the rubes?

I encounter these trout sometimes in the course of my rounds, and am appalled, not by their meekness, but at their savagery. They strike a fly with desperate fury, turn quickly if they miss and strike it again even harder, as if from an impulse that is homicidal and suicidal at the same time. Catching them, you feel like the butt of a cynical and expensive joke, the kind you see played by art forgers or the worst kind of cosmetic surgeons, those who think beauty is for manufacture and sale. That there is just enough color and energy in these trout to convince the gullible that they *are* real makes the joke more bitter; it's only in comparison to the genuine article that the forgery becomes apparent.

Here's where the miracle comes in. Despite hatchery trout, the nearness of the road, wanton destruction of shade trees, the way the brook's most important tributary is looted for snow-making by our local ski area, the sloppy leach fields of too many houses, the penchant previous census takers had of eating their subjects—despite, that is, every wanton and cruel trick man can play on it, Slant Brook still manages to harbor at least three genuine wild brook trout, huddled together in a thirty-foot stretch of habitat like genuine flowers in the middle of a plastic garden.

How wild trout manage to survive here is partly a matter of luck, partly a testament to what, despite their fragility as a species, is an individual toughness that is as much a part of them as their beauty. A few yards downstream of the looted tributary, replenished by what water trickles in, is a pool no larger than a dining-room table, formed by water falling over a burnished log. A plunge pool you call this—the coolest spot on the brook, thanks to that turbulence, and cooled even more by the shade of a pear-shaped boulder that sits on the bottom a foot or so from the lip of the impromptu weir. Upstream of this there is nothing but shallows for a good hundred yards; downstream are more shallows, so the pool, in brook trout terms, sits like an oasis in the middle of a desert. It's far enough from the road that the stock truck goes elsewhere; it's shady, deep, quiet, forgotten, and in its center live the last wild trout the brook contains.

I've only interviewed these fish, face-to-face interviewed, two or three times. I pride myself on my restraint, claim it's for conservation reasons, but the truth is they're remarkably hard to catch. The stream is hemmed in by brush, making casting difficult. The trout favor the three feet of water between the fallen hemlock and the boulder, so you have a yardstick's worth of drift when they might possibly take your fly. Unlike the stocked fish, they won't rise more than once, and there's much more discrimination in the way they bite—not that greedy boardinghouse grab, but a delicate kind of aristocratic plucking.

They're beautiful, of course, drop-dead beautiful, and already in August have begun to take on that rich purple-red blush that speaks so eloquently of autumn. Only eight inches long, they have the thickness of flank you see in the healthiest wild fish, along with an iridescent luster that makes it seem they are taking the granite sparkle of the brook, the verdure of the forest, the dappled sunlight, mixing it all, internalizing it, then through a magic I never get tired of witnessing, generating these qualities back in their purest eight-inch essence, so holding a trout in your hand, for the seconds it takes to release it, is like grasping nature whole.

The biology of it—how three or four fish manage to survive and reproduce in what is otherwise a desert—mystifies me, and all I can do now is pay tribute to the fact that reproduction, growth, life, does go on here, without any help from man. The Slant Brook trout demonstrate one possibility for the native brookies future, albeit a tenuous one—living in isolated, forgotten pockets but flourishing there, like cloistered monks working on illuminated manuscripts through the worst of the Dark Ages, their most beautiful, vivid illumination coming from within.

Whitcher Stream, four miles to the south, offers another possibility. Similar in size to Slant Brook, it begins in a chain of beaver ponds in the notch between two steep hills; in times of high water the edges of these ponds lap the rocks of old cellar holes from vanished farms. A meadow stream in its upper reaches, it veers south into our neighboring town, then—as if not liking the neighborhood—immediately swerves back again, finishing its last mile to the Connecticut as a rocky, shady stream with numerous deep pools. Prime trout habitat—and yet to the best of my knowledge, only one trout remains in the entire stream.

It's a native trout; that's the only good news in what is otherwise a depressing enough story. The state stocks only one stream per town, and so any trout in Whitcher Stream is perforce a native. Ten years ago there were hundreds of fish here, two or three in each pool, but each autumn when I went back, there were fewer and fewer, to the point where there's only one left now, in the deepest, most brush-tangled of the pools—a pool that seems, such are the implications, the haunted graveyard where the last of a species goes to die.

I caught it last year and I'm sorry I did. It's an emaciated fish, with the kind of pale, muted coloration you see in creatures who live without hope. This, of course, is anthropomorphism of the worst sort, but there you are—it's impossible to understand what the last trout in a river must feel without taking into consideration what must surely be a cosmic kind of loneliness. For a moment I was tempted to put it out of its misery, break its neck with a little pressure of my hand, but I found I couldn't do this. If the trout in the brook hovered on the point of extinction, I wasn't going to be the one to give them the final shove, or at least pretend I wasn't, me who drives a car, consumes too much energy, accepts too meekly the prevailing order of things.

Nowhere else in town do I feel such a direct connection between the fate of trout and the fate of man. The Whitcher family after whom the stream is named, among the first settlers here once the French and Indian Wars ended, is down to one surviving male member—a young man of nineteen who was just arrested for what in some respects was a meaningless crime: shooting at a minivan with his deer rifle. He's been sent off to prison for this; am I the only one in town who senses a linkage between his fate and that of the Whitcher Stream trout? Dispossession is dispossession is dispossession, no matter which link on the chain snaps first.

There's lots more here for our local census taker (taking a break at our village lunch counter, staring down at the one wretched check mark scribbled down on his pad) to mull over. Alongside Whitcher Stream, on a grassy level patch above the ruins of an old box mill, sits an unusual kind of development. Our local millionaire, as sort of a hobby, bought up decaying old houses all over New England, had them trucked here, then reassembled them in a cluster of upscale offices, shops, and an expensive private school. The backdrop of all this is the stream— valued for its scenery, its atmosphere, but otherwise ignored.

The irony of this hardly bears underlining—that so much effort and money could be poured into rehabilitating a portion of New England's past while the *living* symbol of that past, the wild brook trout, is left to die out without anyone noticing or caring. And there are other ironies in this line. Over on the Connecticut millions have been poured into a salmon-restoration effort that, sadly, has shown very little signs of having worked. All this money to bring back something that's been extinct here for nearly two centuries, and not one penny spent on preserving the salmonoid that's been here all along, leaving to future generations the hard task of restoring it, an effort that will undoubtedly be as futile as trying to call the salmon back with our impotent whistles of regret.

And this, I suppose, is the Whitcher Stream possibility for the brook trout's future: the river as background noise, local color, pretty dead stuff, inhabited only by chub, water spiders, and millionaires.

To write about a third possibility for our local trout I may have to swerve over into magic realism. The eastern part of town is a wild, high province of softwood forest, beaver meadows, and bright open ponds. One of the largest of these is Trout Pond, reached by a half-hour hike along a shaded woods road the years have pressed deep into the earth. Forty years ago the pond was poisoned by the state to "reclaim" it from the trash fish, then stocked by helicopter with brook trout fingerlings. This was a very fifties kind of operation—the helicopter, the faith in technology, the belief in the quick fix. And yet it worked—for a time. When I first moved here and discovered the pond (it's hard to find and the locals kept their mouths shut when it came to directions) the trout had established themselves as a self-sustaining population, and—if you could lug in some sort of boat—you could count on several fat fish over twelve inches, coming up with discrimination to the tiniest of flies.

This was *not* a fly-fishing-only pond; fishermen would dump their bait buckets in the pond when they were done fishing, and a new generation of "trash" fish grew to maturity with those brookies. For a few years both populations maintained a rough sort of balance—and then suddenly, in some ecological battle too obscure to follow, the chub got the upper hand, so they were everywhere, huge ones, attacking a fly the moment it landed so you could hardly keep them off.

As the chub flourished, the brookies declined. I caught fewer each time I went, and found their size was declining, too, so an eight-incher became a real trophy. The good news is that the town obtained control of the pond and saved it from development; the bad news is that no one has the slightest idea how to reestablish the fishery as it once was. Poisoning is out in this day and age, and my own suggestion—backpacking in some chain pickerel to act as hit men on those chub—hasn't won much support either, for the obvious reason: those enforcers are just as likely to eat up the good guys as they are the bad, finish those brookies off once and for all.

What's going on up there is very odd. If you were to have asked me two years ago I would have sworn there were no trout left in the pond at all. I went back anyway last October, lured by the beauty of the pond itself (no mirror reflects foliage better than those three level acres of gray-green glass), and decided, such is the force of habit, to bring along my rod. Someone had dragged in an old aluminum skiff and tipped it against a pine where the inlet comes in. It reminded me of the *Merrimack*—there were bullet holes everywhere, some perilously close to the waterline—but I decided to take a chance. Using some broken hemlock limbs for paddles, I managed to coax it over to the cove on the pond's eastern shore.

I didn't catch fish, not at first, other than those hateful chub. The problem was that my imagination was totally out of sync with the ponds reality; it was still picturing twelve-inch trout, or eight-inch trout, and fishing accordingly. A couple of hours went by . . . I was at the point you can get to too fast in this day and age, when the beauty of the surroundings begins to deflate without some vibrant life at its core . . . when I noticed a vague upswelling in the water by a sunken log—not a rise so much as the ghost of a rise. I searched through my fly box for the smallest pheasant-tail nymph I could find, tied it on with some 6X tippet, then sent it out to see if it could summon that ghost.

It could. Something nudged the wind knot in my leader, then came a tug on the fly itself. I lifted my rod in a reflex gesture—and then ducked as a fish came shooting back toward my face.

This was a lot in the way of gymnastics for a trout that turned out to be two inches long. A brookie, beautifully formed but all in miniature, so for the few seconds he lay in my palm I had the uncanny sensation I was looking down at him through the wrong end of binoculars. Clearly, this wasn't a baby trout but a mature adult—a male, judging by the spawning colors, the vague jut in the underside of its microscopic jaw. I cast the nymph out a little farther and immediately caught another one, a female this time, Mrs. Tom Thumb, just as perfect, just as small. Realizing that two-inch fish were what I was fishing for, I scaled back on my notions, began looking at the pond differently, saw that what I had assumed were the disturbances left by water spiders and caddis were actually bona fide rises—that there were dozens of trout left in the pond after all, at least in this one deep cove.

Good news and bad. Good in that I was pleased for purely linguistic reasons there were still trout residing in a place called Trout Pond; bad in that the race had become miniaturized, so it was hardly correct to speak of them as gamefish at all, but rather as the miniature markers used in a game, toy trout, nostalgic centimeters. And yet I admit I enjoyed catching them, felt these germs of trout create a germ of delight in my eyes, hand, and wrist.

I've been thinking about these trout a lot over the winter. Obviously, the chub are crowding them out, making it impossible for them to find enough food, stunting their growth. But it's hard not to think that the trout are up to a deeper game. It's as if they've deliberately decided, from motives of self-preservation, to become small and smaller, thereby escaping man's attention altogether, to flourish on as a race of midgets no one bothers catching. Trout as leprechauns only the fortunate ever see? Yes, something like this. Philosophers of an earlier age insisted everything evolves toward pure spirit, and this may be the local trout's only salvation, to ruthlessly shut down whatever gene controls growth, evolve into something that is little more than a brightly colored minnow, the bonsai of salmonoids, ignored, unsought for, but at long last *safe*.

Thus my survey the three possibilities for the familiar neighborhood brook trout of rural New England. Hermitage, extinction, miniaturization—and a fourth possibility I've not explicitly mentioned, but that underlies all my hopes: that mankind (or at least the concerned part of it known as flyfishers) realizes what treasures are on the verge of being lost and spearheads an effort to bring our brookies back, quite literally, into the mainstream of local life.

Census taking, while meant to be a precise science, has built-in limitations, and my methods are not infallible by any means; surveying with a worm, for instance, would undoubtedly result in a more accurate tally, even as it killed my subjects off. Then, too, any census taker, even one who's been at this game many years, has their instinctive biases, and these must be taken into account in digesting their reports. My own bias is this: I believe the native brook trout, the wild brook trout, *Salvelinus fontinalis* (which in my pidgin English becomes *save the fountain*) is the quintessential New England creature, the one whose health or lack of health best reflects the health of the natural world here, the being upon whose slender back—not to put too fine a point on it—the whole health of our rural culture depends. Without brook trout, a stream is dead no matter how pretty it looks from the highway; beauty, dead, turns ugly very fast; ugliness, piled high enough, corrodes the soul. There must be a thousand streams in New England capable of supporting wild brookies. Stripped of them, these form a thousand cemeteries, complete with headstones and the keening wail of empty water. Graced with trout, they become springs of delight, reservoirs of solace, fountains of well-being—and not just for trout.

But then census takers aren't supposed to get so involved with their subjects, draw any conclusions from statistics alone.

I count, the number is seven, and unless things change dramatically, in a few years the last lonely searcher through these hills will be able to do all his counting on the trembling fingers of one gnarled and arthritic hand.

Fishing the Millennium

I know the man who helped invent fly-fishing schools. This, in his defense, seemed like a good idea at the time. He was working for Orvis back in the '60s, a decade when fly fishing was at something of a low ebb, at least in mercantile terms. It was a sport your father did, or your grandfather—the baby boomers were too busy exploring other options. What better way to stimulate sales and interest than by holding weekend seminars in which the fundamentals of the sport were taught? Get students casting with instructors, have some lectures on entomology and flies, take them to the river and talk about streamcraft, then give them some time to roam loose about the tackle shop. Great idea, right?

Thirty years later the answer is yes and no. Randy himself doesn't fish much anymore, at least on his beloved Battenkill; the crowds, many of them graduates of the Orvis school or one of its imitators, line up three deep on the banks every June to wait for their chance at eight-inch fish. Randy shakes his head over this, rues the irony of his having been at least partly responsible. If in the '60s he was one of the smart, energetic young men on the cusp of fly fishing's boom, he's now one of those burned-out cases you see a lot of today, those who *used* to fly fish, but have been driven away by the mobs, with nothing left but stories of the good old days, their poignant and sterile regrets.

Sometimes I'll see these schools in action—an instructor wading down the middle of the stream followed by eight or nine acolytes dressed in neoprene and pile. They remind me of a mother duck and her chicks, charming and harmless, though at other times—times when, frowning, they stay in close to the bushes and superseriously *stalk*—they make me think of a patrol in the Mekong Delta, up to no good at all.

But then I'm a self-taught fly fisherman, have the scorn of the autodidact toward everything academic. There's something vaguely unseemly about seeing grown men and women still in grade school—everything seems out of scale. But when I get control of my prejudices I realize I'm of two minds about the whole enterprise. Surely these people have every right to enjoy fly fishing as much as I do; certainly it's a difficult sport to learn by yourself, and what harm is there in getting some coaching?

When it comes to the larger picture, the huge explosion in fly fishing's popularity of which the schools are partly cause, partly effect, I'm much more uncomfortable, to the point where

I have to fight through all kinds of emotions before I can even begin to comprehend the avalanche that has caught us old-timers unawares. Avalanche? Yep, a biggy, when the mass of snow that lay undisturbed for generations began to creak and groan and shift along about 1978 or so, gathered momentum in the '80s, then swept on down the mountainside in full irresistible force. Here at the century's turn *everyone* is fly fishing or talking about fly fishing, fishing vicariously on television or the Internet, signing up for expensive trips, going to fishing school, crowding up our rivers, wearing fish on their T-shirts, their baseball caps, their jewelry, the trout turned into a totem, the flyfisher, at least when compared with his older, rather comic, and endearing persona, being in like Flynn.

How does this kind of mass longing come about? How does a sport for loners and traditionalists and the few suddenly become yet another fad in the massive, exaggerated way of American fads? To go back to the avalanche simile, it would take an expert on snow pack to give the correct reasons, but some factors are clearly visible, even to an amateur like me.

Spinning peaked in the '70s; after that its chief allure, its mechanical simplicity, became its chief drawback in an era when a lot of folks were looking for the challenging way to do things. Then, too, fly-fishing tackle was being improved by the introduction of new fibers, so the challenge wasn't *too* extreme. Hunting was taking it on the chin as a morally incorrect activity, so the catch-and-release aspect of fly fishing (a blood sport without blood) exerted a strong attraction to those who would otherwise worry about the philosophic implications. Norman Maclean's brilliant novella A *River Runs Through It* and the movie made of it did a lot to glamorize the sport, giving it not only a trendy literary respectability but a glitzy Hollywood sheen. Women were demanding their place on the water—a genuine, grass-roots kind of movement. Saltwater fly fishing kicked in with the return of the stripers to the Northeast. Ted and Jane were seen fly fishing—with Jimmy or Dan or Tom, or whoever was the celebrity of the moment. Once the avalanche started rolling, of course, the hucksters were there to throw in their own snowballs, swelling the mass, smoothing its way with their facile lubricity.

Anyone who's been around for a while has seen many fads come and go, from guitar playing to windsurfing. Many sports seem to go through a boom when everyone does it, then a point where only the diehards are left—cross-country skiing for example. Many of those attracted to fly fishing by its faddish allure *(you too can have this epiphany)* will surely drop out when they discover—despite the fishing schools, the assurances from the tackle companies—that it is indeed a very difficult sport to master, providing gratification that is far from instant and often no gratification at all. This is what my fishing partners long for, a crest to the wave, a gradual diminuation, so we can have the sport once again to ourselves ("I think it's crested," they'll say, when we find three fishermen on our pool, not seven). This may certainly happen; you have to wonder if there is enough water or fish out there to sustain this kind of mass attack. On the other hand, many cultural and sporting booms seem to die out a bit, then start up again in a second, even larger wave, so the worst may still be yet to come.

The saddest part of this has been the commercialization of a sport that should offer a refreshing antidote to commercialization. A modest dose of material interest has always been one of fly fishing's subsidiary delights . . . the old cluttered tackle shop; the catalog crammed full of gadgets . . . but, as with so many other things, it becomes a matter of scale. Soon, thousand-dollar rods will become de rigueur for all of us; already, reels come in at three hundred dollars, and that's not counting an extra spool. Magazines, the worst of them, create fly-fishing "personalities" who are then used to sell things no one needs, and even publications having nothing whatsoever to do with the sport feature fly fishing in their ads, using it to move everything from Jeeps to whiskey. (In the old days, if you saw a flyfisher in an ad, guaranteed he was holding the reel wrong side up; nowadays the ad men are slicker and everything looks authentic, albeit far too prissy and neat.) Fly fishing, like so much else in our culture, becomes a mystique that's for sale.

American consumerism at full throttle is not a pretty sight. A good many are confused by all the glitz, yet attracted to the sport just the same; they sense something spiritual may be had in being out on a river, something they can't find anymore in their boardroom, their bedroom, or their church. These are the pilgrims, and it's hard not to sympathize with them, even while, on their way to Canterbury, they let themselves be fleeced.

Between them, the nabobs and the pilgrims, they've created a new style of flyfisher, one who wants gratification *now*; and is willing and able to spend plenty in order to accomplish this. Three hundred dollars a day for a guide, plus tip? No problem. Argentina, a lavish lodge, an imported American guide, a picnic hamper with three varieties of wine? Sign me right up. These men and women are very serious about their sport, grimly so, and, managing a joyless competence, building their resume of rivers, they're always in a rush toward the next experience waiting on line, and have time to neither smell the flowers nor practice the ethical niceties of fishing etiquette.

Just a few days ago, as I was working the river under a hot midday sun, a couple of the new breed blundered into my pool.

One came in directly opposite me and maybe fifteen yards away; the other, the one with the teal-colored vest, came in just below me on the same side, giving me the ominous sense that like professional hit men they were deliberately boxing me in. In the old days etiquette would have required they ask my permission before venturing into either spot, or that they sit on the bank waiting until I had fished through the pool (the same etiquette demanding that I do so with considerate regard for their patience). Of course, they didn't know about this, or perhaps they did, because neither one said anything to me at all, or even acknowledged my presence.

"Hello." I said it quietly at first, then much louder. "Hello!"

This got the one opposite me to turn; he glared, remembered he wasn't supposed to know I was there, put some surprise in his expression, managed a weak little wave. Sharing a pool with two boisterously eager interlopers is one thing, sharing it with two sullen time-servers is something else again, so I reeled in my line, went back to the bank, and started through the meadow downstream.

An unsavory incident now became something worse. Having fished the pool for all of five minutes, the two darted back into the woods, got into their Jeep, drove downstream in order to beat me to the pool I was walking toward; they were already out there flailing away by the time I arrived, having positioned themselves so there was no room left for me to fish, even if by this stage I had still wanted to.

Thinking back on this a few days later, I'm of two minds. Okay, idiots exist, in whatever sport, whatever pastime you care to name. Perhaps they were merely ignorant. Perhaps they fish so seldom, have so many pressures on them back at home, that they'll do anything to catch a fish. Perhaps their fly-fishing school was a little weak in the ethics department. Perhaps they've read one too many of the ads or magazine articles, have bought into the competitiveness that has infected our sport (and yes, competitiveness was praised among the highest manly virtues in that little book of Mr. Maclean's). Perhaps . . .

Well, I can think of a lot of excuses for them. But there's one thing I can't excuse and that's the grimness with which they went about their fishing. Whatever else these flyfishers were, they were *not* men who were enjoying themselves, and it's this new sullenness, this new competitiveness, that's poisoning our sport, not merely its sudden popularity, not merely the numbers.

I would like to think that none of this affects my own enjoyment. I would like to think I could continue to fish the forgotten corners in the solitude I love, write my little essays of personal celebration, not have to worry about larger concerns at all. But any man or woman fully engaged in this enterprise will find they often fret and worry about the condition of their sport, eye new developments warily and with inherent distrust, so perhaps it's not inappropriate to do some speculating in this line, if only as a kind of personal therapy, wondering out loud what the hell is going on.

And what better time to draw a deep breath, take a look at the state of things, then at the change in millennium? Fishing antiquaries like to push back the dawn of fly fishing to remoter and remoter dates, instancing pyramid drawings of fishing poles with what appears to be yarn or feathers on the end, the prototype fly. But for all intents and purposes, it's a method of catching fish that was "invented" sometime in the first millennium after Christ, perfected through the long centuries (with increasing speed during the last two hundred years), and is now standing poised to enter its second thousand years with far more practitioners than it has ever known before.

At first fly fishing was valued for its *taking* qualities—the fact that when trout were feeding on the prolific insect hatches of spring it was far and away the best means of taking these fish from the river for food. Quite early in its development (at least as early as Charles Cotton, writing in 1676) it was discovered that there was a lot more to it than this taking power alone—that it was an extraordinarily interesting, graceful, and challenging sport, one that, with time, became increasingly divorced from its purely fish-taking function. By the eighteenth century it was caught up in the aristocratic sporting tradition, where doing things the hard way, simultaneously increasing the difficulties and simplifying the means, was seen to be the highest sporting virtue. The American contribution to this . . . the peculiar genius of American fly fishing . . . was to take this highfalutin sporting notion and make it available to everyman, the aristocratic grafted onto the democratic. Written up by a boisterous sporting press and several brilliant popularizers, blessed by the raw material of seemingly unlimited water and fish, American fly fishing became where the action was in the sport; in fly-fishing terms, like so many others, the twentieth century was going to be the American century, where everyone got their shot at it, at least while those supplies of water and fish lasted.

The American century is over, of course; what this means, in terms of fly fishing, is that we're witnessing a perversion of what made our sport so special, a clash of the worst qualities of both traditions rather than a symbiosis of the best—the aristocratic hauteur and snobbiness taken up by a greedy democratic mob. It's tempting to say that what American fly fishing needs is a heavy infusion of the older, purer aristocratic values, at least as regards fishing etiquette, where flyfishers who pride themselves on doing things right would disdain to enter a pool someone else was fishing, sneer in contempt at all the hucksterism, find interest in figuring things out for themselves, take their greatest pleasure from leaving the smaller environmental impact consistent with their presence on the river.

What we need—what we need constantly—is to remember why fly fishing is worth doing in the first place. The difficulties and pleasures of mastering a demanding craft; the reinforcement, the enhancement, provided by a long and proud tradition; the solace of its locales, the inspiration these offer; the healing power of water; the miraculous living beauty of the trout we seek. All these things, and with them a quality that is harder to define— an anti-establishment kind of pleasure; the different drummer aspect that makes its practitioners favor the lonely places, doing their thing away from the crowd, independently . . . the quality about fly fishing that has always appealed to the dissident part of us, that stubborn non-conforming raffish heretical freelance something that even our materialistic culture can never quite snuff out.

Perhaps this is why so many flyfishers feel uncomfortable with the current boom: fly fishing simply cannot afford to become too fashionable and still possess this alternative kind of allure. Let's remember that ours is a quiet and simple pursuit in an age that is noisy and complex; one that rewards patience and prudence in a jittery, impatient world; a sport that requires thinking and creativity in a culture that often punishes both; a pastime that seeks to conserve the places our money-grubbing, joyless economy seeks to destroy; a soothing antidote to everything in the world that so bitterly goes down.

Whosoever would be a flyfisher must be a nonconformist. A paraphrase of Emerson, but one that fits.

Confronting the problems fly fishing is faced with as it enters its second millennium is in and of itself part of the solution; its adherents are a literate and intelligent bunch, highly motivated, and merely by their keeping one honest and critical eye cocked on their sport much healthy course-correction will inevitably take place. There are ideas we should continue to think about. The ethic of catch and release; an insistence on the primacy of wild fish; stressing a low-impact style of outdoor etiquette; the effort to preserve land through trusts and conservation easements; the heavy-duty political battle of restoring the purity of our water and air. Much has been written about this; much, in spite of serious and well-financed opposition, has been accomplished.

More remains. Flyfishers have done a good job in fighting for what they love, but the brutal fact is that our future depends on our culture's attitude toward the entire natural world—the whole terms of our existence on this planet, and not just the sporting fine print. That our attitude must change and change dramatically to preserve what resources are still left goes without saying; that growth and exploitation and needlessly skimming off the earth's bounty without thought for tomorrow threatens a lot of things beside fly fishing is, again, so obvious it hardly bears mentioning. And yet even today this message has trouble being heard. That the economy is growing—that more resources, human and material, are being exploited at an ever-faster rate—is still considered by the movers and shakers who control things the very best news possible, though in reality it's often the worst. The writers and social critics who are talking about setting limits, changing our exploitative philosophy, are the ones doing the most to preserve our fishing, though they may never talk about fishing at all, may even in extreme cases look upon it caustically as a blood sport whose time is over. There's an attitude of *taking* we must hastily abandon, an attitude of *putting back* we have to speedily adopt, and it's on how soon this transformation takes place that the future of our pastime depends. We've had fifty years of warning. Only a Pollyanna, a liar, or a fool would think we have fifty years left in which to act.

And in this direction I'd like to suggest the adoption of a new fly-fishing motto, one that supplements the familiar "Catch and release." *Put, not take*—a slogan, a commandment, that should constantly inform us, and not only when fishing. Put fish back when you catch them, of course, but don't stop there. Order some willows or alders through your local nursery, plant one every time you go to your favorite stream. Put those fishing schools on an entirely new foundation, so they offer scholarships to local people or interested teenagers, help broaden fly fishing's demographic base to the point where garage mechanics are doing it, not just CEOs. Put some thought into fishing etiquette and whether your presence on the river, your manner there, is causing it harm. Put more effort into forming coalitions with other groups that are similarly motivated to save the natural world, and forget about all the various differences that otherwise weaken us—let the birders lie down with the duck hunters, the flyfishers make pals with the bass boys, so united we holler up a storm. Put those new masses to work, so we don't rue fly fishing's popularity but harness it, thinking of all these newcomers as valuable, badly needed reinforcements. Put aside the whole mind-set of *taking* that has infected our sport since its earliest days; start thinking about what we can give back to the river, not just what the river can give to us.

There's another practical idea that should be considered in the light of this emerging philosophy. *Put ten back*—a slogan that would urge flyfishers to place a voluntary tax on themselves, contribute ten dollars to conservation organizations for every time they go out fishing. Certainly, this would be a modest enough tithe, considering that American rivers can be fished free of charge. Followed faithfully, boosted by the fishing magazines, made easy by the establishment of statewide chapters to handle the cash, it would result in an enormous amount of money to be spent on conservation work of the most direct, pragmatic kind. In line with this I'd urge the introduction in this country of a vocation long established in Europe, that of riverkeeper—a man or woman resident on each of this country's major trout streams who functions as a combination watchdog—caretaker—public relations specialist—ombudsman—researcher—teacher. *Put ten back,* use the money to hire knowledgeable and dedicated people to live beside our rivers, and this alone would be a major step toward the moral and financial investment in our future this sport badly needs.

And a last word for those of my friends who complain that fly fishing has been ruined. Yes, some will be appalled by the mob, find they're too fastidious to deal with its pressures. Many—many of the sport's best and most faithful practitioners—will quite literally give it up. Some will retreat into nostalgia, become collectors of tackle and trinkets, hardly ever venture out onto a stream. Some will cope by fishing less, others by loudly complaining—the cynical, bitter flyfisher is someone you will meet more and more. Some, finding their local trout stream too crowded, will save up for the airfare to Montana; others, finding Montana too crowded, will dream of fishing in Russia, hope they can get there before Russia becomes too crowded, too. Some, maybe even most, will get used to the new pressure and adapt, finding new interest and energy in fighting to preserve their rivers, so there is more fishable water for everyone.

Me, I'm going to try to find in fly fishing's new millennium what I've always found in the sport—the miraculous current that connects simple pleasure to great joy—and try ten times harder to put my delight back into the river from whence it all springs.

Part Four:
Trout Country

The Grand Tour

Bozeman, Montana boasts my favorite airport in the world; a late August afternoon is my favorite time to land there. The sun will be low enough to give the mountains that surround it the kind of purple-gray color that brings them into sharpest relief, hints at majesty and mystery both, so anyone sensitive to mountain scenery, pressing their face against the window to see better, will find their adrenaline rises as the plane descends, the two emotions battling in that turbulent zone between the esophagus and the heart until they all but choke from sheer excitement.

The airport itself enhances this mood—it's one of the few I know that seems a natural portal to the experience you've come so far to find. It's low, low-keyed architecture contributes to this, with its suggestion of a comfortable bunkhouse; so do the decorative bronzes of grizzly bears, mountain men, and trout. Down by the luggage ramp a drift boat is displayed, making it seem as if you could start your fishing trip right there if you wanted; most of the people getting themselves sorted out have rod cases under their arms, and the ones who don't, judging by their clothes, the exuberant way they fling their arms around the suntanned women waiting to pick them up, look like they're headed back home to the ranch.

I'm traveling with my pal Ray Chapin this time, and for me it's something of a comeback. When I landed here in 1988 the great Yellowstone fires were raging, and even downtown Bozeman was covered by clouds of heavy, sweet-smelling smoke. An interesting enough experience, one in retrospect I wouldn't have missed, but as a fishing trip it was a disaster, and I'd spent the years since plotting my return. Ray, for his part, hasn't been in this part of the country before, and he's even more eager than I am to get our luggage together, fetch our car from the rental lot, find the quickest, most direct route to West Yellowstone, get rolling.

If Bozeman seems the welcoming portal to the classic Montana trout-fishing experience, then Highway 191 seems the yellow brick road that leads to its heart. Just south of town the mountains close in, the sky darkens, and to our left out the window is the Gallatin, looking cold and high in a late-afternoon shower. We've been talking over our plans for more than a year, and yet only now, face to face with the rushing foaming cascading reality, do we really start bringing them into focus.

"I want to fish it all," Ray says, pointing not just toward the Gallatin but toward everything that lies beyond.

"We could try," I say. "Not all of it, but a good chunk."

Pumped up by the altitude, those high peaks out the window, that Western sense of limitless possibility and expanse, we make it our plan: to fish as many rivers as we can in our week and a half, think of the trip as a grand reconnaissance wherein we'll learn as much as we can about as many rivers as possible. It won't be a race either, at least not a sprint; we'll think of it as a gentle half-marathon, and if we find ourselves rushing too fast, we'll deliberately slow things down. Eleven rivers in eleven days? There's a nice ring to it, and why the hell not?

A last meadow stretch of river, the height of land where the park cuts in, and then were driving through the semideserted streets of West Yellowstone, scoping out the tackle shops and breakfast joints, noting with interest the drift boats parked in the driveways, searching for the cheapest, quietest motel in town. We finally find one, not far from the park's entrance. Cheapest? Maybe. Quietest? Nope. Right across the street is what turns out to be the rowdiest bar in West Yellowstone—but that's okay. What I'm determined to do this trip is give my imagination free play, and that means letting the little boy in me indulge himself in all the Western playacting it can handle.

Impelled by this mood, our imaginations strumming out some lonesome, twangy kinds of chords, we mosey on downtown. The loiterers outside the bar eye us with both curiosity and disdain as we walk past, as if we're hired guns with big reputations they're more than willing to cut down to size. It puts an *amble* into your walk, this kind of thing. We pick out a shop that seems reasonably authentic, hand our money over, and come back wearing cowboy hats pulled down to what we hope is exactly the right angle over our eyes.

"Howdy, boys," one of the loiterers says, stepping aside.

Howdy, boys. We are here!

River One: Grayling Creek. It's miraculous there's any daylight left in what already seems a double-length day, but there is and we take advantage of it to go fishing. Over to the park entrance to get a fishing permit, back to Craig Mathews's fly shop to buy a state license, then the short drive to Grayling Creek, that friendly tributary stream that plays peekaboo with the parks western boundary.

I fished Grayling during the autumn of the fires, since it was one of the few streams (with a hysterical governor having slapped a ban on all outdoor activities in the state's domain) that was both legal to fish—it's partly inside the park—and safely accessible. It's a pretty stream, just the right size to get us started, and with the kind of pool-riffle-pool alternation were familiar with from home. There's lots of timber in the creek, fallen lodgepole pines, and they form an interesting network of jams, sluices, and undercut runs. In the near darkness, that adrenaline still pumping, we fish a little faster than we should—and yet the fish are there for us. That these turn out to be brook trout is both a surprise and an ironic kind of teaser—brook trout, after all, are what we have in plenty back in Vermont.

An hour of them and there's just enough light to get back to the car. We're tired, but pretty high. We woke up in our beds back in New England and now here we are finishing up a night

of Montana fishing. Talk about your magic-carpet rides! At the
edge of the creek I kneel down and splash some water on my
face just to prove to my jet lag it's really true. And it is true. I
close my eyes and shiver with it, that sense of traveling so far,
the exhilaration of having crossed a continent, felt every one
of those miles of prairie, wasteland, and foothill as a kind of
adventure . . . so far, and yet in some mysterious, essential sense,
coming via those miles to a place that is also home.

River Two: The Madison. Anyone who travels much knows the whole
experience can often present itself as a series of questions. Where
shall we eat breakfast? Try the eggs or the Texas French toast? Decaf
or regular? Fill up with gas now or take a chance on finding some
later? Cash the travelers' checks at a bank or save them for the motel?
And which motel? Do the waterfall or the scenic drive? Which way
is the rest room? Which exit do we take? Where's the turn?

To all these question marks the fisherman brings dozens of
his own. Which river to try? Which pool? Which fly? Top or
bottom or in between? Which boulder to cast to? Which side
of the boulder? Twitch it or let it drift? There are thousands of
decisions to be made, pretty much taken for granted at home,
but once on a fishing trip they present themselves in capitalized
italics, especially on a trip with no fixed itinerary when you're
traveling with a friend and these decisions have to be reached in
collaboration.

"Where do you feel like starting?" I ask Ray over breakfast.

"The Madison would be nice. Or we could head right into
the park."

"We're both anxious to get going there. But maybe we should fish outside the park first, then have Yellowstone to look forward to."

Ray knocks back the last slug of coffee, waves to the waitress for our bill. "I'll try wherever you want to try."

"Wherever you want is fine by me," I say, reaching into my wallet for the tip.

We could go on this way forever, Marty and Manny talking over how to spend their Saturday night, but after about a dozen of these exchanges it becomes obvious that what we're both thinking about is the Madison outside the park. So be it. We go across the street to a bakery to stock up on snacks, stop at a convenience store for juices, decide that we're temporarily all set for flies, then turn down Canyon Street and start north on Highway 191 out of town.

The Madison flows out of the park and under the road—a glimpse and a tantalizing one, but it's not enough to stop us.

Where Highway 287 swings west to follow Hebgen Lake the trees give way, the mountains spread open toward the divide, and for the first time we get that characteristic Western vista of drop-dead beauty and heart-stopping expanse. Hebgen Lake contributes, even though it's manmade; it's like a mirage it's so flat and still, the sight of float tubers—flyfishers with their bottoms cut off, hanging in what seems pure air—only adding to the effect. Where the mountains pinch in again comes Quake Lake with its dead, branchless trees. An eerie, haunted place, the land sliced sheer, so it's as if the earthquake that formed it happened only seconds before we arrived.

I pull some seniority here; I can remember reading about the earthquake in the newspaper when it happened, before Ray was even born. I remember how exotic the place-name seemed,

Mon-tan-a, the difficulty of trying to imagine what it was like when an entire mountain slid to one side. There are trout in the middle, judging by those rise rings, but even now it's not a place I would feel comfortable fishing—nature here is in its scornful mood, and you'd feel that dislocated mountain, the dark powers that still lurk below it, watching you on every cast.

And then the highway drops, the spillway gushes out an enormous fountain of bright water, and the mood instantly changes as the Madison, the real Madison, the river everyone dreams about, plunges down into the channels at Slide Inn, gets its act together, and roars in choppy riffleosity toward Ennis thirty-eight miles away.

We park downstream of the side channels, pull our waders on in the morning chill, then walk over to the bank, awed as we should be awed—this is Augusta, Wembly, the Eiger, the big time.

"What a river!" I say.

Ray nods, squints, then points. "What a fish!"

My first impression is that a helium balloon is drifting on the water where it edges against the bank; my second, that the river has sent a special emissary to welcome us. It's a trout, a twenty-five-inch rainbow, a dead one. Surely an omen, but of what? The impressive size of the fish were pursuing? The ominous fact that all is not well here (at this point in time neither one of us has heard of whirling disease)? Our best guess is that it's a fish that was played too long or was clumsily released—but its size, it's appearing instantly like that, gives us a second, even stronger shot of adrenaline.

The riffle aspect of the Madison can be hard for a newcomer to adjust to, and we're no exception—for that first morning we kept looking for the pools. I flush a good fish right against the bank, which should have taught me something, but we persist in fishing those vague slackenings out in the middle. At home, the fish lie behind the boulders, not in front, and we're slow picking up on this. There are some caddis about, and a few times we think we see a rise, but these are hard to pick out in the broken, windblown water.

A slow start. Back at Slide Inn to get some coffee we meet a couple of fishermen who are just getting into their car. Men in their seventies, in that kind of khaki good shape that suggests ex-military, enjoying each other's company, having a great time, judging by their smiles—the kind of old-timers Ray and I wouldn't mind being someday ourselves.

"Well, you gotta remember two things, boys," one of them says, after we sing our little song of not much luck. "First is, all these fishermen you see, all the drift boats. Most of them can't fish worth a damn, so don't feel shy about going in after they leave. The other thing is—"

His partner finishes for him. "They're there. You might not think so, but the trout are there."

Good basic advice—and it becomes our motto for the entire trip, trotted out every time we face new water without a clue about what to do with it. *They're there;* you're not fishing over empty water, and you've got to act like that with every cast. And yes, we do much better in the afternoon, moving downstream toward Lyons Bridge, waiting for the drift boats to pass, then stepping into the shallows and fishing like every twenty-four inches of water holds twenty-three inches of fish. I catch my first one (a modest brown, but I'm amused at his pretension), and hold it up for a picture; a few casts later Ray catches a rainbow and it's my turn to snap him. We're chucking and ducking with black Woolly Buggers, nothing fancy, but at least we've discovered that the fish like to hold not only in front of the boulders but also in tight along the banks.

I relax more with each fish, begin to pay attention to the surroundings, the osprey soaring brown and white over the trees, the blue, wedge-shaped mountains on the horizon to my right, the grazing horses, the exuberant rushing sensation the river gives you that you're being swept along toward happiness whether you want to go there or not. Ray has been watching the water, gauging it, working up the nerve—and there, he hitches up his vest and wades right across to the opposite bank, making a dangerous, strenuous feat look easy.

We break for lunch at the Grizzly Inn, indulge ourselves in double hamburgers and double pilsners, feel pretty rosy by the time we go back out. We finish the day on the short stretch of water where the river powers out of Hebgen Lake. There's a wide side channel where you enter from the road, then a faster, deeper stretch past a narrow island; by the time we pick out good positions the air is dusted up by tiny brown caddis. Here we stumble upon our second good source of advice. A younger fisherman this time, short, wiry, a blond cowlick leaking down from his Stetson, he's all but bubbling over with suggestions, every one of which we later follow, every one of which turns out to be right on target. Who wouldn't listen to him? He is a natural, and as the three of us sit there on the island talking things over he glances up at the water, says, "There's one," roll casts out a caddis, and hooks an eighteen-inch rainbow he leads into our laps.

River Three: The Firehole. And advice is what we're talking over at breakfast this morning; what we've managed to garner so far is forming a stepladder against the mountainous stack of our ignorance. Perhaps because there are simply more good flyfishers in Montana than elsewhere, or perhaps because they're more generous with strangers, we're finding it's worth asking almost anyone for suggestions, including our waitress. Plates balanced on her suntanned arms, in a beautifully husky voice that has a good bit of Patsy Cline, she tells us her boyfriend works as a guide and that his favorite river is the Firehole, hands down.

The Firehole has the reputation of being an expert's river—the boyfriend must know his stuff. We fish the stretch known as Biscuit Basin in intense and windless sunshine, so it's not surprising we get skunked. For once it hardly matters. We're out here to learn, and that humility turns out to be part of the lesson is eminently reasonable. Skunked—but who cares! Who, standing in a gin-clear river that winds its way in lovely sinuosity through a lush meadow that hasn't changed since the white man first saw it two hundred years ago, a meadow that features on its upstream edge an aroused elk with his head stretched out making a sound unlike any other we've ever heard, a deep, sirenlike wobble that is so rich and lonely and molten it must be coming from the center of the earth, using the elk as its bulging mouthpiece . . . a river, for that matter, that curves in and around hot geysers of white spray that suddenly spasm skyward and take on all the colors of the rainbow in cresting, shivering, draping apart . . . who, taking all this in for the first time in their life, could possibly ask that in addition a trout come over and shake their hand!

We see them anyway, holding under the fringe of meadow grass that forms a floating cover over one of the straightest runs. Beautiful fish, and maybe before our trip is over we can come back and fish a cloudy afternoon when something is hatching, at least stand a chance.

Our morning on the Firehole does manage to convey an important lesson about Western fly fishing. The difference between here and back home is one of not only scale, but degree. In the East, an experienced flyfisher will often reach the water's limit as regards trout before he or she reaches their own limit as regards ability; out West, you're much more likely to reach your own limit as regards ability before the rivers limit as regards fish. We thought, quite frankly, we were pretty good; the Firehole began teaching us how much further we still had left to go.

River Four: Nez Percé Creek. In Yellowstone you have three or four hours of morning tranquility before the elk jams ("There's an elk, Edna! Stop the car!") begin to form and driving becomes impossible. Walking, you only need a hundred yards and you're free of the tourists, the RVs, the crowds. We're hiking up Nez Percé Creek for several reasons. One, we need something simple this afternoon after the Firehole; two, I love tributary streams; three, this was the route the Nez Percé Indians followed on their famous flight through the park in 1877, and we want to get a sense of what this was like.

In its lower reaches the creek winds through open meadows similar to those along the Firehole, sans geysers, but a mile upstream the pines close in, the shadows tighten, and the stream flows through a gently graded forest. Many of these trees are blackened leftovers from the great fire, little more than vertical chunks of charcoal, and its a wonder they still stand. A wonder, too, that the fire didn't take everything; we spend a lot of time speculating about what trick of wind or rain spared some stands of trees and destroyed others. A light green carpet of vegetation underlines even the most devastated parts of the forest, so all that talk about regeneration is true.

The fish aren't hard here—nice rainbows, feisty and willing to take our nymphs. It's good to have the creek to ourselves; good to play leapfrog as we go, me in front for a trout or two, then Ray forging ahead while I slow down to work one of the deeper pools. After lunch I find a shady spot and try taking a nap. It's the first time I've ever been alone in the Yellowstone backcountry, and thus the first time I've ever really thought about grizzly bears in the way they're *meant* to be thought of— as splendid embodiments of all we cherish in wilderness on one hand, and ferocious beasties that can eat you on the other. It adds a frisson of uncertainty to even catnap like this, and yet isn't this the point? To take man down a peg or two from his top-of-the-food-chain kind of hubris and strut?

There's a noise in the woods behind me, the splitting creak of timber. Ray? Oh Ray? Is that you, Ray?

Yep, it's him, nothing like a bear at all he's grinning so much. "Thought you were a grizzly," he says, putting his hand over his heart. "Nice stream, huh? You see those little bluewings?"

Back in town that night I stop in a bookstore and buy a couple of books on the flight of the Nez Percé. Eight hundred of them, led by Chief Joseph, Looking Glass, and White Bird, crossed over to Yellowstone Lake following the north bank of Nez Percé Creek (as it later came to be called), taking with them a captured group of tourists—an English earl, two women, a music teacher, a brewer, and someone history records merely as a "blowhard"—who, needless to say, must have had the surprise of their lives. I find two aspects of this story incredible: that this was a national park that early and that you can imagine without any difficulty what this long column of warriors, ponies, women, and boys must have looked like as they passed, so little has the landscape changed in one hundred years. Isn't this one of the secrets of Yellowstone's appeal? The time-traveler aspect? Blink and it's 1877, and if the grizzlies don't get you the Nez Percé will.

River Five: The Bechler. "Hey, Ray? You know Nelson Algren, the old Chicago novelist? His rules about living, like, for instance, 'Never eat at a place called Mom's'?"

Ray glances over from the driver's seat. "'Never sleep with a woman whose problems are worse than yours'?"

"Right. And wasn't there one about 'Never take advice from a drunken bartender'?"

"Sober bartender."

"I think it was drunken."

We argue the point for the next thirty miles, since the success of our day depends on it. Last night before dinner as we sipped some beers, our friendly bartender (steady of hand, glassy of eye) had raved on and on about what a sleeper the Bechler was, down in the park's southwest corner. Hard to get to, guaranteed solitude, *big* fish. Sounded most interesting to us—but was he drunk or sober?

To get to this part of the park you have to drive through Ashton, Idaho, a town I disliked on first sight. Industrial potato fields that roll quite literally to Yellowstone's very trees—and would certainly go further if it was up to the powers that rule Ashton, right on across the entire park. This is not just an idle worry; back in the 1930s there was a plan boosted locally to build a dam across the Falls River (into which the Bechler flows), creating a huge reservoir over what is in many respects the loneliest, most beautiful corner of the entire park.

There's no entrance gate here, no highway, no tourists, no elk jams. You park at the ranger station (an old blockhouse from the days when the US Army had charge of the park), check in with the ranger if she's about, and start off on a level trail through high, well-spaced pines. It's about a two-hour hike to the Bechler. The trees abruptly end and you come out into an enormous and very flat meadow, decorated on the southeast by the unmistakable verticality of the Tetons, to the north by the closer, shaggier escarpment of the Madison plateau. Beautiful—and yet where in all this was the actual river? It flows in a deep, hidden trench, and since the hiking trail bisects the meadow's center, it's hard knowing whether to go left or go right.

Right—and after a soggy hike through flooded grass it's there: the purest, clearest water I've ever seen (or not seen), so we have to stare at the pebbles on the bottom for a long time before convincing ourselves that they are indeed covered by a flowing liquid, though to call this "water" is to give it more definition and substantiality than, on that first glance, it seems to have.

As we stand there stringing up our rods the wind picks up, strong enough, cold enough, that we plunge down the bank to escape. A little better down here, with the bluff at our backs, but still tricky to cast in, and we have to do it between gusts, loading up quickly and slinging the line out sidearm. But the nice thing about the wind is that it's blowing grasshoppers into the river; not the clouds you find here when the season is at its peak, but enough that the trout are looking *up*. Ray, using an orange-bottomed imitation, catches a rainbow of nearly twenty-five inches that leads him an enormous way down the river; on his way back, still panting from the chase, his face radiant, wind-burned, and happy, he spots another, even bigger trout finning under the overhung bank, and smoothly picks it off. Both of these are hooked, played, and landed on the same 6X tippet, which is to say on pure gossamer skill.

If the Bechler is Ray's finest hour, it turns out to be my poorest. I'm fishing badly, letting the wind bother me, pressing, and for the first time in my fishing life I learn what it's like to experience an overwhelming envy, so it's all I can do to clench my teeth, grunt out a perfunctory "Hey, nice fish."

What's going on? I'm shivering in the cold, missing strikes (and what strikes—geysers exploding out of the river when you least expect them), there are big fish about, my back is killing me, and I've come such a long way. All these combine, so the thought of being skunked, a real possibility at this stage, brings me to the point of tears.

We break for lunch on a sandbar where the bank dips away to give us a perfectly framed view of the Tetons. I let the mountains calm me down, do much better in the afternoon, even though the wind only increases. There's nothing like a fish to restore perspective, and what fish these rainbows are, possessing a mature and self-confident wildness, not the fur-tive, withered kind of wildness trout often display back East. My best fish is just short of twenty inches, thicker than the proverbial football. I miss another, even bigger, but this time I can afford to laugh, as my grasshopper imitation, at the apogee of the explosion, does a slow-motion somersault in midair, lands downstream on its back, and—another trout spotting it—is immediately sent skyward again on the crest of another geyser.

River Six: Boundary Creek. Bushed but happy, we head home about four in order to beat the dark. The cold has deepened, so that's another factor—this is a notoriously bad place for late-summer snowstorms. Boundary Creek is a smaller version of the Bechler flowing out of the forest; where the trail crosses it on a *very* flexible bridge some trout are rising, so we stop and make a few what-the-hell casts. I'm pretty exhausted by this stage, so I let Ray do most of the fishing while I lie there staring out at the enormous meadow, trying to get a deep and lasting impression to bring away with me home—and *click,* I think I have it. Meadow, sunshine, river, fish, Tetons, forest, llamas.

Llamas? Three of them in line, their arrogant, handsome heads snapping slowly back and forth as they glide effortlessly through the marshy ooze. They're led by a happy-looking llama keeper, his head swathed in a red bandanna, and behind come the hikers whose packs the beasts are carrying. There's a campsite a bit further up the creek; the llamas make for it instinctively, circle around the old campfire, crap in unison, collapse knees-first on the grass, and immediately go to sleep.

"Sober," Ray says, wading back out. "The bartender, that is." "You think so? Anyway, what difference does it make? The man's a genius. We'll go back tonight and buy him three of anything he wants."

River Seven: The Gibbon. Wiped out from the effort of fishing the Bechler, feeling a heavy sense of anticlimax, we're capable of only something modest today and the Gibbon fits the bill. It's one of those friendly riffle-and-pool streams that stays conveniently close to the road; it's longer than you would think judging by its breadth, and extends halfway across the park's middle. Above the falls it's ornamented with paint pots, plate-sized hot springs bubbling away in the shallows, so it's a beautiful combination of classic trout water and world-class exotica, the true Yellowstone mix.

The trout are small and tricky. You can get fifty strikes in fifty yards, and end up hooking only two or three, so fast do they reject a fly. But who cares! We're out to relax and get a feel for this part of the park, and the fish, at least today, are almost an afterthought.

The Madison-Norris corridor was one of the hardest hit spots in the 1988 fires, and blackened trees are everywhere. And while there's new growth prying its way up from the crusty earth (the most delicate curls of a very soft green that you can't look at without wanting to stroke), the dominant note, at least in the blackest groves, is still that of holocaust, a sudden and brutal death.

It's afternoon before the sun bakes the gloominess out of our muscles. We quit early and head back toward town, stopping only long enough to do some sightseeing along the famous park stretch of the Madison known as Seven Mile Run. ("Choice and challenging," one guidebook calls this; "the trout are more elusive and difficult here than anywhere else on the entire river.") Sightseeing, but the wide curve with its fascines of fallen timber, the weed-slicked bottom, and the protective boulders are all so trouty and promising there's no resisting, even in our exhaustion. I catch a decent brown out in the deep current as far as I can cast; it's like a free sample of goodies we'd have to pay dearly for if we really want them, and in the end we decide we've waded out far enough.

On our way back to the car we stop and take a look at the famous Grasshopper Bank on the opposite shore. I'm not impressed—it reminds me of the kind of overly manicured lawn you see in front of corporate headquarters' buildings—but that changes in a hurry when a huge trout leaps out of the river and cannonballs back in. Trout will do this to you of course. Wait until the precise moment you've taken down your rod and peeled off your waders, then *boom*—the old cannonball-in-the-water trick. It must keep them smiling for weeks on end.

River Eight: Slough Creek. Little customs and habits are quick to form, even on a fishing trip, and one of the nicest we've fallen into is strolling over after breakfast to Craig Mathews's fly shop. Craig is easily the most famous flyfisherman in these parts, something of a national celebrity for that matter, and why not, since what the man doesn't know about Yellowstone flies and fishing is not worth knowing.

We have some mutual friends. Between this and the instant rapport established between him and Ray, he's taken the time to listen to us, learn what we're after, then gotten us started with what always turns out to be infallible advice.

I say something about fishing Grebe Lake, just for the sake of its grayling—a fish I've never seen, much less captured.

"Oh, you'll catch one all right," Craig says, looking up from the counter where he's just spread some freshly dyed capes. "Small guys, no bigger than my finger. If I were fishing today"—and here a note of wistfulness creeps in; even Craig Mathews can't fish every time he wants—"I'd try Slough Creek. Here, take some of these. Mackerel Drake Emergers. You'll slaughter them."

When the Oracle suggests something, you take that suggestion. He follows us outside, goes over the directions once again. "You'll come to the first meadow and see plenty of fish, but keep on walking until you come to the second meadow. Fish there."

You'll see fish but keep on walking—it goes on the table of our trip's ten commandments, and we keep repeating it over and over again all during the long drive across the park.

A great drive. This is the first time I've ever been to the eastern side of the park, driven up the divide near Mount Washburn, seen the view of the Absarokas and the caldera of which they form the distant rim—seen this, then crested the height of land and dropped down the switchbacks to the Yellowstone near Tower Junction, where the landscape goes from thick lodgepole pine forest to those wide and rolling Rocky Mountain plains.

We park just above the Slough Creek campground, note with interest the yellow bear warnings posted on the trail register (definitely shredded—clawed?), then cram our waders into our rucksacks, start out. The hike isn't bad, not after the first steep section, and the trail is a wide one that suggests a well-worn pilgrim's way.

"Here's the meadow," Ray says, where the trees end and the ledges give way.

I stare down into the long slow curve of water that eats into our bank. There's a cutthroat holding in the current, wearing that serious, somber pout fish have when they're resting. I point toward a bigger one, and the shadow cast by my arm is enough to make both quicktail it upstream.

"You'll see some fish—"

"But keep on walking!"

We pass the ranger cabin, resist the urge to cut across the meadow toward those sinuous and sexy Slough Creek curves, stay to the right on the high, flinty trail. Have I said anything yet about the scenery? Where the next grade levels off we take a break near a park-like grove of trees, stare toward the horizon and the snowcapped mountains that rise sharp across the horizon—Granite Peak and its neighbors, the highest summits in Montana, raising the level of the scenery one notch more.

It's another hour to the second meadow. We know we're getting closer when we start encountering some second-meadow kind of guys on their way back down the trail. Young, athletic, looking more like climbers than fly fishermen, with pack rods in the loops where ice axes usually go, they're in too much of a hurry to chat, though we mange to elicit the information that all of them have caught fish.

And yes, the fishing *is* good once we arrive. What's surprising is that we get the entire river to ourselves, or at least the part we pick out. It's downstream of the trail junction—a wide slow pool where the river hooks right before dropping over a shallow ledge, with a terrace of pebbles we can relax on and look things over.

In a fit of madness we start off fishing attractors, but it's obvious the fish aren't interested. What they are interested in are those Drake Emergers we have courtesy of Mr. Mathews. Ray, as usual, catches the first fish—a beautiful copper-dark trout of nearly nineteen inches, with a pronounced yellow shading through the flanks to go along with that characteristic coral flashing on the gills. I hook one a few minutes later, but it takes two of three before I learn to control that first hard, double shake of the head. Pretty soon we've established a regular rhythm. Ray drifts an emerger at the head of the pool, hooks a trout on the rise, gets it under control, leads it through shallow water to the terrace and down the miniature falls while I step in and do exactly the same thing, beaching my fish downstream just about the time Ray has waded back around me to hook his next one.

A lot of cutthroat bashing goes on out West. Some flyfishers claim they're stupid and boring, but what they really are is patient and smart. It's hard to *spook* a cut, true, but it can also be extremely hard to *fool* one, so it's a perfect combination: a fish you get a lot of chances at, but one that's extraordinarily fussy (brook trout back East are exactly the opposite: shy to approach, easy to fool). Matching the hatch is the only option on Slough; it's clear that without Craig's flies we would have been skunked. Even later, when they switch over to size 18 *Baetis*, we're ready for them; one of us or the other is playing a fish the entire time we're there.

A long and perfect afternoon. We might be there yet if it wasn't for the thunderstorms that came up late in the day. With all those mountains and ridges, their tricky acoustics, it's hard to judge when it's time to take cover in the trees. We wait out the worst of these storms under some pines, right in the middle of what's apparently a favorite grizzly lair, judging by the whitened mounds of turds, the sun-bleached pile of half-gnarled bones. Talk about your frissons! Lightning bolts flaring down at your forehead, grizzly poop underneath your butt! What a remarkable country this is!

River Nine: The Gallatin. We've become advice junkies, and when we can't borrow or beg some, we're not above stealing our daily fix. This morning what we basically do is overhear a conversation in the next booth—a couple of guide types, judging by the gravel guards wedged around their ankles, the Polaroids tucked in at their throats. What they're talking about is the Gallatin—how crowded it is in its lower reaches, but how no one bothers fishing the meadow portion where it leaves the highway and climbs toward the mountains. There aren't any trout for the first mile of this stretch—no one knew why—but then they appeared again, and you had to keep hiking in order to locate this spot.

Was this a deliberate piece of misinformation planted to put two uppity dudes in their place? We hike a mile and then some without any sight of fish, this despite the fact that the Gallatin is perfectly clear here, and with the banks so high it would be easy to spot anything swimming about.

"Maybe we haven't gone a mile?" Ray says, mopping off his face with his hat.

I finally do spot a brown, a nice one, but he's not interested in my hopper. By this time we're halfway up the valley, hungry, hot, and tired. The only redeeming virtue is the wildlife—mule deer, a coyote, some eagles, and an elk. We also have a good conversation with a park ranger on horseback, on his way into the backcountry for a two-week patrol. Sharing a soda, he tells us some good stories about elk poachers—how smart the smart ones are, how stupid the remainder.

We've fished together a long time, Ray and I—it only takes a glance for each of us to know the other wants to turn back.

Once to the car we revive enough to spend the afternoon on the Madison. The drift boats have already floated through, so we pretty much have it to ourselves except for an osprey. We're a lot more relaxed this time, and as a result do well. A whitefish tricks me into thinking it's a brown, and after hollering Ray over to net it I feel pretty sheepish at what emerges. A few minutes later, hooking what I think is another huge whitefish, I play it casually, afraid to get my hopes up, then am surprised—and even more sheepish—to find it's a brown trout of nearly three pounds.

River Ten: The Gardner. We're here for several reasons. We haven't seen the Mammoth Hot Springs part of the park, it's on our way back to Bozeman, and we have time for one last stream before driving back to the airport. Then, too, this is by way of homage to the late Charles F. Brooks. We bought his *Fishing Yellowstone Waters* before we came out here, used it to plan our trip, and have found it a reliable and entertaining source of information all the way around the circuit. "Let's see what Charlie says" is another of our refrains. Stream-smart, literate, someone who never lost sight of the ambient beauty, he must have been a fine man to fish with.

Here's what he says about the Gardner:

> The five miles or so of stream in the Mammoth area are very pleasant miles to fish. There is just enough difficulty getting into and out of the stream and in fishing it to deter the casual. It is a prolific piece of water *for the proficient fly fisher.* The fish are larger than farther up, and there

are now and then run-up fish from the Yellowstone. You must know what you are about to do well in the lower Gardner.

It's all true. The day is a hot one, and this side of the park is more arid than anything we've seen so far, so the hike down to the river, or at least the prospect of hiking back up again, seems like a particularly grueling ordeal. But what the hell—it's our last day, and when we finish we can cool off with some beers.

Charles is right about those run-up fish. We see some on the other side of the river, dark, torpedo-like shapes perfectly aligned with one another as they face the heavy current, for all the world like cathode figures in a video game waiting for quarters to be dropped in before moving. With trees behind us and a steep bank, they're impossible to reach. Further upstream we find the fish wary, but catchable; one of these turns out to be a brook trout, a little guy who's probably run down the river from one of the beautifully named creeks that make up its headwaters, Fawn, Indian, Panther, or Obsidian. The views here are high, wide, and handsome, though you're looking *up* at them, not out or down, and this makes us feel insignificant and small. Three mountain sheep are playing on the cliffs—not a common sighting, even in Yellowstone.

Nothing major to report here, but a taste of what canyon fishing is all about, and the pleasant, relaxed kind of finale we're after. Weighted down by some extra juice cartons, my vest rips in half, dropping fly boxes into the river that Ray, wading below me, gracefully scoops up. I'm saddened; on a long trip you come to live in your vest, cramming it with sandwiches, rain gear, aspirin, candy bars, and sodas, let alone flies and tackle, so it becomes something much more essential and organic than mere fabric—it's as if a well-worn but dearly loved part of my flesh, tiring of life, has shredded away.

Time for that beer. We find a bar in Gardiner that's long, dark, and empty—the green on the pool table alone is enough to cool us off. We knock back a quick one, then take our time with the refill, talking about our trip, letting it start to settle, concerned that we do this just right. We agree that our survey, big-gulp kind of approach has worked well, giving us both the kind of wide overview that makes sense for a first trip, and a much more detailed, intimate kind of hands-on experience as well. Reading everything we could find, asking everyone questions, experimenting, exploring, we've learned quite a bit, will be much better prepared next time we come out here—a trip that's already entered its planning stage by the time that second beer goes down.

And it's a funny thing. Even sitting in that deserted bar with those beers, our muscles sore from all the hiking and wading, the rivers seem to flow into one, so the Madison in our memory becomes just a wider portion of Nez Percé Creek, the Bechler just another meadow up from the Firehole, whose headwaters drop into the Gallatin, the mouth of which forms the Gardner, with no dividing line at all, not even the narrow enough one that barely separates them in reality I think of Aldo Leopold and how he tried to find the appropriate phrase to sum up the interconnectedness of the living world, the biotic stream, and how he came up with the perfect one: *the Round River.* Yellowstone's rivers, wildlife, forest, meadows, lakes, and ponds flow into one another and are one, that's the moral; nowhere else in the world would it have been possible for us to navigate so much riverine beauty in so short a time.

There's some sadness here, the kind that comes when a good fishing trip is finished, but more than that, too. The kind that comes to an aging athlete who knows between one game and the next that the glory days are over, and while he will play on for a few more years yet, it will never be at the same intense level. Hiking to all those streams, forcing our way up rapids, taking some spills, letting the rocks knock us around, the hot press of the sun, the prying leverage of that wind. I know, sitting there in that dark cowboy bar, that I'll never be capable of such a prolonged physical effort again—know, too, that it's all right to be sad with this, since it's another part of the Round River, and I'd be a fool to wish myself free of its current.

What we need is a line to go out on, and Ray pulls one from the silence, raising his glass with the last of the beer. "You'll see fish," he says, squinting, "but keep on walking."

I nod, laugh, tilt my own glass back for its last quarter inch of foam. "You might not think they're there, but—"

We finish in unison. "They're there!"

River Eleven: The Lamar. A line to go out on—and yet there is one last river in our trip, a sunset to talk about, the kind that should by rights end any good Western. On our next-to-last night Ray stays in town to make some phone calls while I drive over to the Lamar just upstream of its canyon. While the water itself is invisible, the rivers route through the valley is marked plain enough by the declination and fold of the banks, and so it's no problem at all to walk through the sagebrush and boulders until I find a likely looking pool. There's a rainbow waiting between two rocks—he jumps when I hook him and jumps again just for fun. So close have I timed things that by the time I land him its dark enough I have to head back to the car.

From where I'm parked the land rolls toward the west like a very wide inclined plane, up which a transparent force is rolling itself toward the mountains that rise above the intersecting furrow of the Yellowstone two miles away. Even the mountains, steep as they are, seem only a higher, more rugged version of this ramp, so they, too, are helping boost this invisible something into the sky. Above the mountains, as I stare, this force manifests itself in layer upon layer of clouds, flat on the lenticular edges, billowy in their softer centers, the mass expanding upward and outward as I watch. There's hardly any variation in color from one superimposed layer to the next, and yet by the time the layers end they have gone from a base of stony gray to a ceiling that's a dramatic and vivid crimson—all this done in such gradual increments it's impossible to point to any one place on the horizon and say *there*, the color's different.

The most beautiful sunset I've ever seen? It ranks right up there. Somewhere behind the ridges the sun is just high enough to take the color and give it a name, a quality, and definition: *loneliness*. It's loneliness I'm watching, not the sad kind we feel ourselves, but the kind that has shadings of great pity and acceptance—what the land might feel for us if it bothered noticing our presence at all. It seems the whole wide untouched Yellowstone landscape is scrolling itself toward the heavens to pronounce a judgment, some final word, and then—and this was a very poignant thing to watch—the color suddenly leaves it, from bottom layer to top, and with it all the difficult meaning, so for one last moment it's the empty land itself that is mirrored there in the sky, before man could color and tame it with his own longing . . . and finally in a last flash of something that isn't quite orange, the sky rolls over into blackness, the wind comes up off the river, my shoulders start shaking, and it's time to go home.

August 25

The Yellowstone is not only the most prolific trout river in North America but also the most intimidating, especially inside the national park. Above Yellowstone Lake on the Thorofare Plateau the wading isn't bad, *if* you can get there; it's a long hike in, from whatever direction, and the country is known for its quicksand and grizzlies. Just downstream of the lake is the notorious Fishing Bridge, where the trout butchers used to do their thing, but fishing is no longer permitted there, and with the river flowing at full breadth from one of the largest lakes in the country it wouldn't be any place to wade. The water in Hayden Valley is approachable and choice, but fishing isn't permitted there either, even though it's alive with feeding trout. Further downstream are the famous falls, among the highest on the continent; below these is a thousand-foot-deep canyon with precipitous walls of smooth and friable rock. Even at Tower Junction, where the river re-emerges, the water flows past at warp speed, and this only gets worse further downstream in the hard to get to, impossible to wade section known as Black Canyon.

If you do manage to find a place to fish you can sense all this wild and lusty exuberance working on you as you step into the water—the weight of Yellowstone Lake upstream, the giddiness of the falls just below. This is the longest untamed river in the lower forty-eight states, and the water, it's very molecules, seem powered by this freedom, so they bear down on you with double the weight and energy of normal H20. This is water, cold water, that has been here a lot longer than man has and will be here rushing and tumbling and foaming downstream long after he is gone—and it's not above taking a sacrificial victim with it now and then to demonstrate this principle.

Between rapids and canyons and falls and regulations, there are very few stretches of the Yellowstone you can wade safely, let alone comfortably. One of these is called Buffalo Ford—*the* Buffalo Ford, famous for its cutthroats, pictured in all the magazines, the very epicenter of fly fishing's remarkable boom, and on a typical summer's day the most heavily fished pool in the world.

Not a place for the loner, the shy one, the fastidious. And yet on a warm and sunny late-August morning this was exactly who waded through the bright skipping water on its edge, stopped to look things over, stood rocking back and forth in his wading brogues, counting the number of fishermen he could see in the river, vowing that when he reached fifty he would turn around again and go back to his car. Something of an old hand now in this part of the world, a man who was taking a break from the family on what was otherwise a family trip all the way, he had deliberately avoided the Yellowstone on his two previous trips out West, scared off not only by the power of the water, but the power of that mob.

How many? Two fishermen just to the right of him, gearing up. Another straight ahead on the edge of an island, tight to a fish. A man and woman holding onto each other for balance, the current piling up in a golden *W* around their waists. Three scattered in the shallower water on the far and distant shore, one casting, one wading, one pointing a camera at the stolid echelon of buffalo grazing on the bank.

Seven flyfishers, not counting himself. Seven in a river that could swallow dozens and hardly show the strain. Whether because it was late August and the crowds had gone home, or because of some favorable, impossible-to-predict eddy in the current that compelled people to fish here, the fisherman had come on a day when for all intents and purposes he had the Yellowstone River to himself.

So, no excuses. He checked to see his wader belt was fastened, shuffled his boots against the pebbles on the bottom to clear them of weed, then slanted his way into the current, taking a line that would bring him above the island and into the slower water on the far side. Not hard wading, but not easy either—the Yellowstone may be fordable on four legs here, but two legs is difficult. Between the fast current, the bottom that alternates between pebbles and clay, the kind of moral vulnerability you feel when out in any big river alone, the fisherman was more than a little relieved when the bottom started shelving upward again, the pebbles came back, the water left off pushing solid on his waist and took to kicking broken on his shins.

Safe. He paused, feeling a certain triumph, then turned, startled, at a loud whuffing sound that was even deeper than the river's whoosh. Buffalo, another long file, coming into the river just behind him. They didn't seem to do this intentionally, with premeditation; they were grazing at the top of the bank, one or two stepped over, and before they understood what was happening the whole herd was caught up in a mindless inertia that carried them at a half-gallop into the river, where they stood snorting, coughing, and grunting, wondering why they were even there.

There was no exaggerating the fun of watching them. America is so full of place-names that no longer make sense—Trout Lake, with no trout in them; Cougar Canyons with no cougar— that it was good to be standing in a place that was literally being rechristened *Buffalo Ford* as he watched.

Where the bank jutted out into the river was another flyfisher, a woman this time. At this sport for well over thirty years, he'd only seen a woman fishing by herself three or four times, all on this trip, so it was clear the demographics were changing and changing rapidly. This particular woman was no beginner; she cast far and she cast fast, with nothing wasted in her motion. Stocky, she moved through the water with great delicacy and confidence, a disciplined skater in full command. With the sun behind her, the fly line decorating the sky overhead, the wind tossing back her hair, she managed in that beautiful landscape to take on a great deal of beauty herself; an old-fashioned poetical mind might have seen her as the very spirit of the river, and not be far wrong.

A few pleasantries—*How's the fishing? Fine! Three cuts!*—and then he was on his way again, climbing up onto the bank and taking off through the woods upstream. This was easier than forcing his way through the current, but not all that much easier, since blowdown pines were everywhere, and it was impossible to hike in a straight line.

Where to start? One of the conceptual tricks in fishing a big river is to try to break it up into smaller, more comprehensible channels within the expanse, not be overawed. This is hard to do on the Yellowstone—it sweeps impetuously along, with no thought for a fisherman's convenience—but not impossible. A hundred yards more of walking and the steep bank crumbled away, widening the river no more than eleven or twelve feet, and yet by this expansion making it lose several vital gallons per second of force. Some pines had fallen with the bank, and their roots were still strong enough to hold the trunks perpendicular to the current, breaking it up even more.

It wasn't long before he discovered the limits of this eddy; in tight by the bank all was fine, but eight or nine steps out it was a different story. The current was even faster and harder than it appeared from shore, so there was no going deeper than his hips without being bowled over. The bottom was tricky, too; a coating of pebbles and gravel gave good purchase, but mixed in were elliptical patches where the current had washed the gravel away, exposing the bone-white clay underneath—and to step onto one of these clay patches meant a fast ride down toward Yellowstone Falls.

Things finally settled with his feet, he began looking about for trout. They were there all right—cutthroats of seventeen and eighteen inches right in front of him, though it took a few minutes before his eyes got accustomed enough to the waters glare to penetrate it, see beneath. Back in New England, where he did most of his fishing, you could go all summer without sight-fishing to a trout, so the experience was a new one to him and exhilarating. He was fishing an attractor pattern just attractive enough to make the trout, as it floated downstream, raise their heads a fraction of an inch, quiver in interest, then— the fraud becoming apparent—relax again in boredom and sink back to their original, tail-slightly-below-head position. The same happened when he fished a nymph, though this time they were interested enough to move laterally in the current to appraise it from the side, even bluff it with a little charge, before lapsing into that same irrefutable indifference.

He'd always heard these Buffalo Ford cutthroats were picky, and it gave him an odd satisfaction to learn the stereotype was true—it was like learning that all Parisians are indeed rude. It took three hours of hard work before he caught one. Tired of fishing upstream, he climbed back out onto the bank, switched to a sink-tip line, took a long detour inland, then balanced his way out along one of the fallen trees and roll cast a weighted stonefly into the current to let it swing down.

A fish was on it right away, an important fish. The fisherman was always somewhat casual in playing trout, but there was often one during a trip that he simply *had* to land, and this was one of those—the fate of the day was resting upon this. And he did catch it, but not without making a spectacle of himself. The fish continued upstream after fastening, but then balked at too much pressure and made an abrupt U-turn, not only stripping out line to the backing, but pulling the reel off the rod, so the fisherman had to grab for it in the current, hold it in his hand, and start down the shallows in pursuit—right onto one of those treacherous clay patches. When he got up again—when with some frantic screwing he got his reel reattached—the trout was still on, though an enormous distance downstream. His fall on the clay had muddied up the river, so it seemed the trout was fleeing the milky gray cloud as much as it was the pressure of the line, and by the time he caught up with it, landed it, photographed it, let it go, he was soaked through with river, sweat, and clay, and yet happy past all description.

Clumsy, but no fool, he'd packed along some extra clothes for just such an eventuality. Dry, somewhat composed, feeling stubborn, he hooked another cutthroat from exactly the same position, walked over to the bank, sat down on a rock, and played it in comfort, refusing to engage in any more shenanigans.

He ate lunch on top of the bank in what sundial-like shade a lodgepole pine casts. A nap would have been nice, but he got caught up in watching the pelicans, a bird he had always associated with Florida, not Wyoming. Squadrons of them flew down from Yellowstone Lake, much more graceful than the comic image you get from cartoons. Their whiteness, their airiness, did a lot to cool him off.

When he got his fill of these, there were buffalo, a few of them anyway. They seemed bewildered by the fallen timber, confused that there shouldn't be an easy way down to the river; with a few bothered snorts they wheeled around again and headed back to the ford that bore their name.

The fishing was better in the afternoon—rising trout now, coming up to those tiny *Baetis* that are everywhere in a Yellowstone August. This was sight-fishing again, at least toward the end of the rise, when a yellow-brown verticality would appear underneath the fly and slowly continue upward through the surface film, remaining there for a long and very visible moment before looping back down again. Hooked upstream, these fish were easier to land, and after three or four the fisherman decided there was nothing more to ask of the day. His total wasn't high, and yet the point had been made: yes, the Yellowstone was indeed the most prolific trout river in America, the breadth of it, the very substance of the water, alive with the presence of wild and beautiful fish.

He was taking down his rod on top of the bank when an invisible and yet very real force (strong enough to be felt even with the competition of the river) made him turn around. Where the bank dipped away to let a wet spot seep into the river was what he thought at first was a coyote. A second later it saw him and stopped; it was very obviously trying to decide whether to continue past him or change direction and retreat back into the woods.

The fisherman started to reach into his vest for his camera, then thought better of it. Coyotes were nothing new. Coyotes—why, they had coyotes right at home, trotting across their meadow in the course of their daily rounds. No, he wasn't going to waste film on a mere coyote.

Like a hungry and very gaunt German shepherd—that's how he described coyotes to friends who had never seen one. But then something in the animals posture changed, some slight squaring readjustment in the way it was standing, and he realized it wasn't a gaunt German shepherd at all, but an extraordinarily healthy German shepherd, one with height and muscle, a princely attitude, and all the self-confidence in the world . . . that it wasn't a coyote at all, but the cherished object of a careful réintroduction campaign, a hero all the media was going nuts over, the subject of all those campfire talks by the rangers: a live and very real wolf.

A wolf, not ten yards away. There was no fear in this encounter, on either side. The fisherman looked at the wolf, childishly pleased that after hearing about them for so long he should actually be face to face with one; the wolf, for his part, stared into the man's expression with an alert kind of interest in which something was reciprocated, though it was impossible to say exactly what. Something mammalian at any rate; the wolf's alertness wasn't that different than the alertness of the trout, and yet that second, deeper something was much different, a consanguine kind of recognition nothing cold-blooded could ever manage.

There's no end to this encounter, not in dramatic terms. The lone wolf turned and walked unhurriedly along the riverbank; the lone fisherman turned and did the same in the opposite direction. When he entered the timber he stopped and looked back—but there they parted company, for that wolf, finding nothing remarkable in the encounter, trotted away without glancing back over his shoulder at all.

Family Trout

The conventional wisdom is that anyone who tries to combine a serious fly-fishing trip with a traditional family vacation is asking for trouble. The two simply don't mix—never have, never will. A flyfisher, reduced to essentials, is someone who's willing to travel many hundreds of miles in order to feel a tug on the end of a thin piece of line, often finding that this simple enough sensation brings with it various spiritual benefits. Of course not everyone in the family might have the same kind of yearning—there are tugs exerted by tourist attractions and art galleries, Indian reservations and historical sites, water slides and hiking trails—and so another kind of tug is created, a competitive, intramural one, the kind that when it comes to deciding how to spend the day can quite literally tear a family apart.

And yet it's so tempting—the idea of taking the family to a place where the fishing is good! The flyfisher arranges things so he has two or three days to himself, vows to be good the rest of the time, agrees the spouse can have a corresponding amount of time to do what she wants, tells himself it will be a terrific bonding experience with the kids. All this sounds great, the deposit is mailed, airline tickets reserved, junior fishing outfits purchased. So perfect are the arrangements that the flyfisher then makes a fatal mistake—he actually follows through on it—and what seems so doable in January turns out to be a fiasco in July.

For the problems are not only real, but nearly inescapable. Fly fishing is not much fun to watch if you're nine and Dad (or Mom) is the one doing it; nine is usually too young to master the intricate rhythm of casting, summon up the requisite patience; nine, especially out West, is too young to go wandering off by yourself along a precipitous and fast-moving river. Nine, in other words, is no fun at all. Of course, forty-five can be difficult, too. Here you are, in a situation where by rights you should be at your most demanding and selfish as regards *your* fun, at the very same instant your family is the most selfish and demanding about *their* fun. Both parties are right, absolutely right, and yet as anyone who's been at this game for a while knows, the arguments where both parties are right often turn out to be the most damaging, lasting, and bitter.

But it can work. With luck, with a willingness to compromise, with some imagination, the right locale, combining a family vacation with a serious fly-fishing trip can work extraordinarily well, and I would like to offer my own family as the happy, living proof. Our trip to Yellowstone was a success from start to finish, in fly-fishing terms and family-vacation terms both, and yet even while we basked in the miracle of this we didn't fully realize *how* successful until the very last moment of our very last day.

If there is one place on earth where the family versus fly fishing trick can be pulled off, it's Yellowstone. Big as the park is, it's still relatively compact, at least in the way it combines trout places and kid places. It's perfectly possible to start the day out on a trout river, be back at the lodge in time to have breakfast with the family, go hiking all day without seeing another person, do a waterfall or scenic loop on the way back, then—if you've the energy—go out again after dinner and do some more fishing while the family turns in.

This became the pattern of our days, right from the start. Driving down from the airport in Bozeman, we stopped in Livingston to stock up on picnic supplies, including flies at Dan Baileys, where the women fly tyers working by their window made a big fuss over Matthew, age five, and gave him some peacock herl as a souvenir. An hour later the kids were running up the boardwalk along Mammoth Hot Springs, marveling not only at the way the earth literally turns itself inside out, but how the elk, even on a hot August day, like to lie in the hottest, steamiest spots. Then it was time to check into our simple cabin at Roosevelt Lodge; after dinner (chicken-fried steak with all the corn muffins we could handle), it was over to the nearby Lamar, where Dad caught trout while the rest of the family had a great time exploring the banks, climbing over the boulders, taking pictures of the buffalo, cheering Dad on.

This by way of warm-up. Next morning the trip got fully in gear with a hike to a remote lake only a few hundred yards back from the east rim of the Grand Canyon of the Yellowstone. We've found over the years that kids hike best when there's a real magnet or attraction at the end, and by magnet I mean a fire tower, a cliff, or a pond. Of these, a pond works best; mountain summits, alluring enough to adults, are a bit too abstract to motivate a young child, but a *pond,* the aura of brightness it carries, the prospect of coolness, is enough to make even a reluctant hiker keep going.

We parked in the huge empty lot near the Lower Falls, hitched up our rucksacks, tied and retied all bootlaces, stuck a pack rod in Dad s pack, started out. The trail hugs the canyon's rim for the first mile, and we kept stopping to go gingerly over and peer down. Both kids remained very much in character as they did this. Erin, tall, curious, a determined thinker, took in the depth, the sheerness, the cataract of foaming whiteness an incredible distance down below, and did a little inward double-clutch with her chin—*whoa,* her expression plainly said, *what have we here?* Matthew, four years younger at five, reacted like his mother did—this great and glorious canyon made him giggle, set his glasses to jiggling on his nose, and he looked over at us, wanting us to share his fun.

It was an hour's hike to the lake—two lakes actually, one set like a transparent soup bowl inside a golden meadow that perfectly doubled it; the other smaller, cup-sized, trickling into the larger via a soft little creek. Trout were rising the moment we arrived, and I started right in on them. Celeste and Erin took their hiking boots off, waded in the cool shallows; Matthew took his boots off, too, then his pants, then his shirt, then, stripped to essentials, went after the salamanders as assiduously as he did at home.

Something for all of us here. After trying every fly I'd brought along, I found a small black nymph that took them on just about every cast—little rainbows, beautiful rainbows, waiting just beyond the fringe of weeds. I got Matthew to leave off the amphibians long enough to catch one, then it was Erin's turn, then Celeste's. When the sun got stronger the women went back under the trees for a nap, but Matthew and I kept at it, taking turns with the sunscreen, alternating slugs from the canteen, working our way around the edge of the pond to the narrow inlet where the bottom was sandy and we could wade a long way out.

Hiking back to the car, as high and happy as the canyon was deep and dark, the kids learned something else about the Yellowstone experience. The parking lot that had been empty when we started was now overflowing with tour buses and cars; the ramps and decks where you walk out to see the falls had long lines of tourists waiting their chance to snap a picture, and a great deal of shoving was going on as people tried to get at the rail.

"This is nutso!" Celeste yelled—the mob scene suggested more noise than it was actually producing.

"Bazookas!" Erin said, upping the ante.

"Crazy," I nodded. Then, "Hey, let's get a picture!"

Seeing a gap, the four of us wedged our way against the wooden rail with the white-green plunge of Lower Falls at our backs. A young hiker stood there seemingly as confused and horrified at the crowds as we were, and Celeste instantly picked him out as the one to ask.

"Sure," he said, with a big grin. Celeste handed him the camera, gave him quick instructions, stepped back. "This will be your Christmas card," he said, squinting—and he called it right. The picture came out perfect, the four of us posed there like we have the falls all to ourselves—me wearing yet another of the floppy hats that have accompanied my life like ludicrous banners; Celeste and Erin with matching grins, the bandannas pulling their hair back so their resemblance, so subtle most of the time, is obvious and striking; Matthew tucked in between us, a natural the moment a camera is near, with a forthright and charismatic grin that's enough to upstage even a higher, happier waterfall than Yellowstone's.

All this forms the first piece of advice I have for a flyfisher who has the family along—build the fishing into a hike. The second suggestion is to devote a day to having just the kids catch fish, leaving your own rod back in the car. There's a guide service based at the marina on Yellowstone Lake, small cabin cruisers that go out after cutthroats. We called ahead for reservations and our guide was waiting for us when we arrived. John was his name—a tall man with a Chicago Bulls cap on who coaches junior high basketball in the off-season in a town just outside the park. He smiled at the kids' eagerness, but it seemed a bit forced; late August now, he was getting more than a little burned out from the thousands of cuts he had caught in the course of the summer.

"Maybe we'll get a laker," he said hopefully, as he powered us out into open water.

Lake trout is what he meant, a controversial subject. Some madman had apparently dumped lake trout into the lake, thereby putting at risk the finest wild cutthroat fishery in the world. Who had done it? When? According to John there had been thirty-pound fish caught, and this would indicate the lakers had been in there a lot longer than just two summers. The Fish and Wildlife Service was trying very hard to get a handle on the situation, but they were handicapped by lack of funds; the only way they had been able to afford a simple fish finder for their runabout was when the guides chipped in to buy one for them.

"I wouldn't mind catching one," John said. "Just for the change, I mean."

I could see his point. The cutthroats in Yellowstone Lake are not hard to catch, which was fine by me, since I very much wanted the kids to have some fast and easy action. We headed into the light chop in the lake's center, then, using a distant bluff as his reference point, John got the ultralight spinning gear rigged up, explained to the kids what was required of them, flipped the bails back, let their spinners trail out in the Jacuzzi-like bubbles of our wake.

Thirty seconds after the line went out, forty at the most, Matthew had a hit. He sat bolt upright on his bench, started reeling in as if his life depended on it, and a few minutes later John landed his cutthroat, held it by Matt's shoulder for a photo, deftly removed the hook with pliers, and dropped the fish back into the lake (cuts, the big ones, have to be put back here; any laker *has* to be kept, setting up a situation where you can be fined for practicing catch and release). The moment this was accomplished Celeste had a fish on, and then a few minutes later, just when she worried she would be left out of the fun, it was Erin's turn, with the biggest one yet. Not five minutes went by without one of them catching a trout, and when once the gap went to six minutes, John (who was studying his watch) acted disgusted and instantly tried a different spot.

"Slow today," he said, without irony. "Must be those clouds moving in."

Me, I was having a great time, even though I wasn't fishing other than vicariously. Partly this was from thinking about those cutthroat—how amazing it was they would be so close to the surface in such featureless water miles from shore. Partly—and any fisherman will understand this—it was from the comfortable, reassuring sense of propinquity you get just being near any large and healthy congregation of fish. I asked John about going after them with a fly rod; he insisted I come back in July some year, when you can cruise the shallows and take trout after trout right on top.

Most of all, though, I was enjoying being out on Yellowstone Lake for the first time. All through the park you're immersed in a landscape that can feature both an exhilarating sense of expanse and, with those rivers and remote ponds, great watery beauty of much variety, and yet its only when out in the middle of this enormous lake in a boat, seeing the mountains that ring it, feeling on your face the wind that blows up from the Tetons, absorbing with your legs its swells, that you realize you still have much to learn when it comes to both water and expanse—that what you've seen in the park is only by way of a preliminary to this fluid masterpiece of water, mountain, and sky.

After an hour of this—after the kids had each caught a dozen trout—the storm that had been hovering over the mountains all morning now lashed down in magnificent violence right above our heads. We stuck it out for a few more fish, then the kids made a dive for the cabin (which looked so cozy and kid-sized they'd been eyeing it with interest ever since we came out) while Celeste and I crowded in near John at the wheel for the bouncy ride back in.

By the time we reached the dock the worst of the storm was over; a well-scrubbed sun was already streaming through the pines along shore. We thanked John, wished him well for the coming basketball season. Hope you kill one of those lakers, I told him. He smiled, bashfully, then glanced down at the notebook I only now realized he'd been scribbling in since the moment we docked.

"Two thousand three hundred and forty-six cutthroats," he said, with a perceptible sigh. "Trolling, every last one."

With our joint expeditions having gone so well, it was time for the old I'll-go-fishing-while-you-guys-go-sightseeing gambit, one I've tried before, though with mixed success. The family always has a good time without Dad, which is just the point: I get lonely without them, actually homesick, and often find the fishing can't compete with the fun of watching the kids climb a new mountain or see their very first geyser.

But this time it went well—better than well. I had a good day fishing the Yellowstone, and when I got back to the lodge at night I found the three of them already in the middle of dinner. They waved to me when I came into the dining room, glanced over at each other like conspirators who've agreed on a plan, stifled some giggles, seemed on the point of bursting with what was obviously great and important news.

The story broke upon me the moment I sat down—a collaborative effort told in the rushing kind of multi-part harmony families get so good at over time. This is what happened. After breakfast, according to plan, they had driven to Old Faithful, arriving just after one of its periodic eruptions. Old Faith has slowed down over the years due to earthquakes; for a second Celeste wondered if it was worth waiting the hour or so for the next display.

A half hour passes—the three of them wander over toward Old Faithful Lodge for a snack. Rangers all around. *Lots* of rangers. Men in suits and sunglasses, too, looking edgy. The kind of nondescript crowd that gathers in these situations, as if there are always extras stashed behind the shrubbery ready to jump out when needed. Someone pointing toward the sky—"They're here!" Helicopters appearing over the tree tops, landing in the parking lot in a huge circle made by rangers holding hands. Flashbulbs going off, video cameras, men rushing to get a better position, everyone pointing.

The president descends. As in, the President of these United States. Wife. Daughter. Walking quickly to the elevated terrace forty feet from where Celeste, Matthew, and Erin stand innocently chewing their chocolate chip cookies.

"Wave," Celeste says. Erin waves, shyly. Matthew, shy, not knowing why he has to be, waves, too. President's daughter catches his eye, waves back, shy herself. Shyness National Park.

Camera doesn't work, natch. Names and addresses exchanged with woman next to them, her promising to send picture. President in short sleeves and chinos. President's wife in floppy hat and sundress. President's daughter in jeans. Everyone pointing . . . crowd half-turns . . . Old Faithful blossoms toward the sky.

What an adventure! I'm sorry to have missed it, but not that sorry, since nothing could match the anticipation I saw in their faces when I came into the dining room, the happy eagerness with which the story came bubbling out. It wasn't until dessert that all the ramifications and little details were correctly tucked away; it was only then that Matthew remembered that someone else in the family had been out searching for stories of his own.

"Hey Dad," he said, chomping down on his seventh corn muffin. "Catch any fish?"

The next few days all had trout in them, even if it was only those small, delightful cutthroats you can catch in the tributary streams while your family enjoys a picnic in the lush undergrowth that has sprung up under the fire-blackened trees from the 1988 fires (venerable-looking now, like pillars pitted and smoothed by the forces of time). I slipped away again for a long day on Slough Creek, there were a couple of more hikes, and by our last day there was very little more to ask of our week.

It seemed greedy wanting anything more from Yellowstone, especially when we woke up to find our fine weather had moved out and it was raining heavily. We drove along the Lamar past the ranger station, the clouds hanging collapsed and crumpled on the peaks that line the road, the buffalo standing motionless, the flyfishers looking gloomily out their car windows, the entire life of the park seeming to have come to a sodden dead stop. Not immune to this mood, tired from our week, we made the mistake of driving on to Cooke City to get something to eat. I hated it from the moment we drove in, the very look of the place; it reeked of poachers and gold miners, stream rapers, "locals" who had moved there from California and were now mewing about how by rights it was *their* park. . . . Well, it was that kind of day.

Time to get going. We felt better the second we crossed back into the park, and what's more the sun was starting to come out now, and as Celeste drove westward I stared at our map searching for one last backcountry lake we could hike to before it was time to head home.

The one I picked out was just far enough back in the mountains to deter the casual; only three acres in extent, it was famous for the impressive size of its trout—and always had been. As I read later in a history of the park, the lake had been the scene of the first game bust in Yellowstone's history, when the early rangers had surprised some poachers from Cooke City who were illegally netting out the lake's enormous cutthroats. A few years later, trout were taken out of the pond to use in the park's first hatchery, since it was clear they were of a genetic strain it was worth trying to reproduce.

I didn't know this at the time—for all I knew, the lake was fishless, as so many in Yellowstone are. We parked on the pull-off, got our gear together quickly as befits old hands, then started up the trail through a delightful meadow whose late-summer wildflowers were damp enough to come alive in the sunshine like, to use my son's phrase, wet lollipops hidden in the grass.

The trail met the lake at its timbered outlet. It was a ragged kind of circle, completely open except for the patch of trees on our side, and surrounded by a steep, sandy bank that formed a kind of mezzanine looking down into the ginger-ale-colored (my daughter's simile this time) water. The alpine meadow started on the upslope edge of this bench; every way you looked, staring through the ribbony partings the sun made in the mist, your eyes ran into blue-gray mountains, the highest with snow.

Something else was needed before the scene became perfect—
and there it was. Just on the edge of the lake, slightly below a raft
of fallen branches: a quick swirl of something that immediately
disappeared. A cutthroat? Probably. It's often all we ever see of
wildlife, that quick flick of the tail that takes it from our presence,
but it was enough to make me appraise the lake differently, notice
what I should have noticed sooner: the soft dimpled rings pushed
into the surface, not by leftover raindrops, but by rising trout.

By the time we walked around to the open portion of the
lake I had my rod up, ready to cast. As usual in these circumstances, the trout were feeding about three yards past my furthest cast, and the bottom was too soft to wade out even one step
more. Celeste kept on going where the trail started to curve,
then looked back to take my picture. It's on the wall behind me
as I write, a calendar shot, me following through on a cast, my
left hand caught in a tossing motion as it releases the line, my
right shoulder curved into the plane of the cast, my rod pointing
horizontally toward a doubled loop of line caught at the very
moment of opening—all this framed and decorated by the yellow meadow grass at my waist, the pines in the background, the
mountains rising behind a decorative cliché of airy mist.

Classic form—but I couldn't quite reach those trout. Celeste
and the kids watched for a few moments, then, obviously giving
up on me, continued on around the lake and vanished over a little
ridge. About ten minutes later, while I was still fussing and fret-
ting over my impotence regarding the gulpers, Matthew ducked
back over the ridge; in his excitement, the frantic way he waved,
I thought of a cavalry scout sent to summon reinforcements.

"Over here, Dad! They're over there! Big ones!"

I quickly reeled in. "Don't scare them!" I yelled, but he was
already gone.

The first thing I saw as I hurried to catch up was that they were standing well back from the bank, in no danger of scaring them. In no danger of scaring *what* took longer to figure out. Celeste was pointing and Erin was jumping up and down and Matthew was bending forward with the rigid intentness of a pointer, and so excited were all these postures that my first reaction was that a great white shark had somehow gotten loose in the lake.

I wasn't far wrong. It was trout they were staring at, lots of trout, fat cutthroats that were almost twenty inches long. They were swimming around and around the shallows where a narrow inlet stream bubbled in—the kind of frantic behavior you would expect to see in spawning time in early July. But this was late August—what was going on? They were feeding on top, plucking midges from the surface film, and I knew in the first instant of spotting them both what was expected of me and how hard it was going to be to pull this off.

"Catch them!" Celeste commanded.

"The reddish one," Matthew added, making it sound like "radish."

"Rip their lips!" Erin yelled.

The blood lust was spreading, and why not, faced with those beautiful fish we could have reached out and touched with a stick. I put on the smallest *Baetis* I had in my box, sat down on the bank, flattened myself in the wet meadow grass, slid feet-first into the lake like a corpse being tipped down a plank.

The ripple pushed the trout back a few yards, but didn't seem to particularly bother them; in their eyes, I was merely another elk or moose come to drink. I could see now there was a pattern to their swirling; they were moving in a counterclockwise circle between a dead log to my right, the drop-off straight ahead of me, and the inlet stream to my left.

Cutthroats have the endearing habit of being difficult to frighten, but they make up for this by being inordinately fussy; these fish could get a very clear, detailed look at the insects they were feeding on, and rejected every imitation I tried. I went through pattern after pattern, trying desperately to find a winner; it was no trick at all to get a fly in place well ahead of a cruiser, but they swam right beneath it without blinking.

In the meantime the family cheering section was if anything even more involved. Up high on the bank, they could see the fish even plainer than I could, and each time one swam toward my fly they were convinced it was coming up to it, and so screamed at me to strike.

Talk about pressure! I wanted to catch one for them, wanted this very badly, and yet the more I pressed, the more indifferent those trout became, to the point where I had to forcibly stop myself from lunging forward and grabbing one by the tail. Celeste—giving up on me, but tactful enough not to admit this—called that she was going around to the other side of the lake, where we had left our packs and lunches. "Good luck, Dad," she said—then she was gone.

The kids, having more faith, squatted down on their haunches to see what would happen. I'd been fishing a 4X tippet until then, but it was obvious now that in the placid water this was far too heavy, so I switched over to the longest 6X tippet I thought I could cast. The submerged log was the favorite place for the biggest fish to linger, though if I hooked one there I would have major problems. Still, it seemed my only option. I edged around toward the inlet so I wouldn't hook the backcast on the kids, then changed flies one last time. One of my Baetis was more beat-up looking than the others, crippled and squished the way trout like, and this is what I ended up tying on.

I false cast out the right amount of line, then let the fly drop beside the submerged log, staring toward it as intently as I've ever stared toward anything in my life.

"One's coming, Daddy!" Matthew shouted from the bank.

"Oh, my gosh!" Erin yelled. "It's going to—"

Take it! The moment I realized this the fly was gone, and the moment the fly was gone my arm came up and the fish was on. It was one of the biggest trout—there was no mistaking that deep, solid kind of take. My first reaction, even before I was conscious of the kids shouting in delight behind me, was to get enough softness in my line to absorb what I knew would be that first hard double shake of his head, not be broken off right at the start.

I managed to do this, but it was hardly the end of my problems. The log stuck out of the water like a tank trap deliberately planted to vex me, and a second after getting the necessary softness in the line I was faced with the job of getting just the right amount of tightness in to turn the trout away from danger. Through some miracle I pulled this off, or perhaps it was the fish who did it to himself; faced with the choice of fleeing under the log or fleeing toward the drop-off, the fish picked the drop-off—and a moment later he was out in front of me with plenty of clear, empty water on each side.

So intent was I on keeping up with all this, so focused on the trout, it was only now that those excited shouts got through to my ears. The kids were war-dancing on the bank, jumping in ecstasy, their hands pressed down on their hats, yelling each time the trout turned. Across the lake, hidden from us by the trees, Celeste heard all the shouting, realized at once what must have happened, gathered the packs up, and came running back as fast as she could.

The longer I had the trout on the more confident I felt about him, and yet this was dangerous, too, since to take him for granted on so fine a tippet would inevitably be to lose him. Then, too, I had left my net back in the car, so there was the problem of landing him. Leading him carefully back toward the log but in closer to me than last time, I waded around so I stood between him and deeper water, then slowly closed in on him as I took back line, until finally I had him resting within inches of the steep muddy bank.

"Bring him in, Daddy! Bring him in!"

Smart up to now, steady and patient, the sight of the huge fish so close to me made me lose my composure, and I all but threw myself at him, the bow wave of my lunge making him ride up onto the grass as prettily as if I had planned it that way in the first place.

"You've got him, Daddy! Got him!"

I was sweating at this stage, exhausted, with hardly the strength to climb out next to the fish. The kids came plunging down the cliff to stare, reach out their fingers to touch him on the side, see he was real. Celeste was there now, too, panting, sweating more than I was but yelling in happiness as she fumbled in the pack for our camera.

We photographed it, the kids squatting behind me as I held him up, then—each one holding out a hand to have a part in it, count coup with the trout s strength—released him gently down the bank and watched as he swam away. It was only then that the father in me took over from the fisherman—and I could relax enough to see what I should have seen all along: my kids dancing in victory on the bank, Celeste beaming proudly . . . and not just them, but the wildflowers in the meadow grass, the pines that started behind the lake, the mountains in the distance

. . . the wide, unspoiled Yellowstone country, the warmth and majesty of which we only now fully appreciated thanks to its magic embodiment in that fish . . . how it all coalesced into a huge and comprehensible planet of brightness, me lying there on the grass with my eyes closed under the dizzying press of it, a triumphant Hercules who would gladly take ten such planets on his shoulders, my kids in my arms as we wrestled and hugged in sheer delight.

Put it down as the happiest, proudest moment in a man's fishing life? Sure, go ahead, but it was a lot more than that, too. The happiest moment in his *entire* life.

Part Five:
The Long Autumn

Private Water

I hardly knew fishing clubs existed until I was invited to fish one. Occasionally I'd come across references in a fishing book to the old "club" water, hear of such along trout streams in the Catskills or on the Restigouche, clubs that took up many thousands of Maine acres or owned the rights to an improbably high number of Quebec lakes. I always associated them with high rollers, timber barons, old money, not my kind of world at all, and I

596

was slow to pick up on the fact that fishing clubs exist on a much more humble and enjoyable scale as well, particularly in Vermont.

I'm thinking of the kind of fishing club that got its start back in the 1890s, when hill farms were being abandoned and entire mountain valleys could be bought up for a song. Shares would be issued in a corporation (doctors, lawyers, teachers, the local gentry, though a rural, likable enough one), an engineer hired, a rock and earthen dam erected across the valley's stream, a pond created, a clubhouse cobbled together, rules and regulations drawn up, an Indian name chosen to give just the right rustic flavor—and then the trout put in the pond, brookies usually, ones that were already dwelling in the stream, supplemented by larger fish taken from a nearby lake, transported by horse and wagon over rutted dirt roads in milk cans, the canoes and rowboats coming in on the next trip . . . a caretaker hired to watch over these and keep the wood box full, his wife taken on in summer to cook the meals . . . and there, Club Abenaki (Mohegan, Algonquian, Minnehaha) was in operation.

The trick was to *keep* it in operation, change it as little as possible through things like land booms, depressions, and world wars. The result is that there exists today in Vermont six or seven clubs that have changed so little since the 1890s you half expect Teddy Roosevelt to meet you at the door, or Calvin Coolidge at any rate, wearing his favorite fishing hat, and on his face the kind of thin, yet comfortable smile he let only his friends see in these precious moments at ease.

This is not just fantasy; the club I was invited to is proud of having had Silent Cal as one of its earliest members, and the very first thing I was shown when I arrived was the president's battered fishing hat hanging ready on its peg in the event his ghost should ever need it.

Catument, I'll call this; on the smaller end of the fishing-club scale, it could still stand as representative of any. Its pond is about four acres in size, stocked with brookies and rainbows that grow just big enough to be interesting. The clubhouse was constructed partly of an old schoolhouse that was pulled by wagons up from town, and it sits on a rising lawn above the water, so old, so brown and weathered, it seems not only an organic part of the slope, but the fitting centerpiece of a compact and quiet valley where the land, sky, and water seem perpetually anchored in the early autumn of 1895.

That's outside. Inside, the identifying characteristic of any good fishing club is in the furnishings, the knickknacks, the pictures that hang lopsided on the walls. They have to be old and vaguely corny (a genuine antique would look out of place) and they have to be arranged with no thought whatsoever for effect. Catument gets top marks in this respect. Fishing cartoons from the thirties and forties hang on the walls, the H. T. Webster kind that play off the old fishing widow jokes or the small boy with worms. Mixed in with these are badly focused photos taken when color film was in its infancy, handwritten lists of bird sightings, a page or two from ancient fishing logs showing enormous one-day catches . . . and then a fireplace warm with a fire that hasn't gone out in a hundred years, the kitchen with its oversize zinc sink, the cupboard full of tumblers that have the smoky patina even clear glass takes on if you pour enough bourbon into it over the years . . . and then (glass in hand now, going back out to the club's main room) the piano that hasn't been tuned in fifty years, the boxes of snelled flies resting on top (Parmachene Belles, Edson Tigers, Montreals), the playing cards, the Scrabble games, the old magazines . . . the wobbly rocker, the wobbly card tables, the dilapidated couch . . . all of these giving the kind of feel it would be impossible to duplicate without at least seventy years of happy and relaxed usage, and a place I fell in love with the moment I walked in.

Terry Boone, my friend and host, is the club's historian, guiding spirit, and very much its chief attraction, at least for this visitor. Short and trim, bearded like a sea captain, the kind of stylish dresser once described as "dapper," he's a preacher's son from West Virginia who's entirely self-taught—the kind of man who can run a radio station with one hand while inventing a best-selling board game with the other, finding time along the way to consult on political campaigns, volunteer for a dozen charities, and take on the salmon-restoration effort of one of the largest conservation organizations in the country. Catument is the only place where you have a chance of catching him motionless, at least for a few minutes; after unpacking our groceries (Catument doesn't have a cook; members bring their own food and prepare it family style in the kitchen), he had a few projects to talk over with the caretaker, so I grabbed my fly rod and headed down to the pond alone.

When the fishing is on at the club's pond you can catch dozens, without regard to flies or tactics; when it's off, the fish are extraordinarily fussy, and it's easy to get skunked. No matter how long stocked trout live in a stream, they tend to remain at the same low level of imbecility, whereas in a pond they become very smart very fast, and these Catument rainbows, get a September midge hatch going, can be inscrutable opponents for even flyfishers of long experience.

This is rowboat fishing—add that to the soothing, relaxed effect the club induces. I rowed to the east end of the pond, got a good look at the osprey that camps out there in a dead pine, then let the breeze drift me back toward the dam, picking up some nice fish on a Hare's Ear nymph twitched just below the surface.

Terry had the swordfish on the grill when I got back, but there was still time to help myself to some cheese and crackers, sip some bourbon on the porch with his other guests, who had only just arrived. One of the things you learn about fishing clubs is that though the ostensible reason for their existence is fishing, *talking* is of even more importance—the kind of relaxed medium-small talk that can only be done in a setting of rocking chairs, wood fires, and porches. The subject is often fishing, sure, but it's never limited to this, and usually has a way of coming around to subjects freely suggested by what can be seen off the porch: osprey and deer, sunsets and foliage, the natural small talk a Vermont valley tends to provide in autumn without any prompting.

This was my first experience of Catument. The second was when Terry got married there—a bright October afternoon of such perfection that tears came to your eyes well before the actual ceremony to see how rich and sweet the autumnal note could be played. Chairs had been set up on the lawn leading down to the pond, with an end table taken from the porch for a makeshift altar. Karen Kayen, Terry's bride, is a good friend of ours, a woman we admire hugely, so it was a perfect match in this respect as well, and just to see Terry's happy smile as she joined him by the pond was enough to get tears going in those who had successfully resisted the foliage.

Karen's father stood to the side playing a soft, lyric sonata on his violin; as the notes faded away across the pond, the minister stepped in and had them recite their vows. Many of those in attendance were dedicated flyfishers, and they all—how shall I put this?—stared with special *intentness* at the pond with its trout, so a good half of the congregation seemed to be leaning toward the water, as if caught in the breeze. None of them leaned far enough that they actually *went* fishing, but I know what they were thinking since I was thinking it myself. Anticipating this, in a very clever piece of strategy, Terry and Karen had arranged for *gravlax* to be served with champagne immediately after the ceremony was over—those rich salmon appetizers there is simply no resisting. It was the best wedding I've ever attended, hands down. The pond, the foliage, the warm October breeze; given a choice, who wouldn't wish to be wafted toward their future from a setting so fine?

If Catument is one of the smallest and simplest trout clubs in Vermont, then Lake Tanso is among the largest and plushest. With three ponds and a connecting brook trout stream, several hundred acres in one of the steepest, most remote notches in the Green Mountains, a hundred-year-old clubhouse that can accommodate seventy overnight guests, and a loyal membership devoted to keeping things the way they are always been, Tanso is one of those miraculous Shangri-Las you have no suspicion of until you're actually standing in its center, then, upon leaving, have trouble believing you were ever actually in at all.

I came to it first on a rainy September morning when the clouds hung so low over the ridges they seemed to merge into the placid water on the pond's far end. There was a fire going in the fireplace (three times bigger than Catument's, with three times as many rockers pulled up in front), but the lodge was deserted, and I had to poke around the empty rooms until I found my host, Dick Connors, sitting where I should have figured he'd be sitting—out on the porch with the geraniums, rocking contentedly with his pipe, staring out at the rings pushed into the water by rising trout.

"Good to see you!" he said, getting up to shake my hand. Then, a second later, reaching behind him to the wooden pegs that held his rod: "What are we waiting for? Let's catch some fish!"

The largest pond is over eight acres, and thick with brook trout and rainbows. They reproduce naturally here, at least the brookies, and each season fish are taken upward of three and four pounds. As at most fishing clubs, there's a continual debate in progress about whether the pond's natural food supply should be supplemented by feeding, and at Tanso those in the proactive camp win. Two coop-like contraptions are mounted on platforms on either end of the pond. Inside is fish food, and an automatic timing device that twice a day casts pellets out in a broad circle. The trout have learned to expect this, and the shark-like frenzy that erupts when the timer goes off is something to see. Visiting fishermen immediately try to catch one of these monsters, but it's impossible, even if you have a fly that resembles a food pellet; like junk-food addicts, these fish can spot the difference between a real Twinkie and a fake one in a quick supercilious glance, and the only thing to do is wait until their jag wears off, and a size 24 Gray Midge once again begins to look palatable.

Dick is a school superintendent in a midsize city that's seen better days—no more grueling a job now exists in this country. At Tanso, out in the boat, he seems like a man who has had a very heavy weight temporarily lifted from his shoulders; when it comes to the ponds, the fish, the mountains, he wears his heart on his sleeve.

"Deep spot here, might try a leech. Tommy North caught a four-pound rainbow here last week. Not a bad summer—decent hatches until August. Hey, is that a bear? Saw one yesterday when I got up to row coffee out to some of the old fellas. Whoops, rise up ahead, two o'clock. Think you can reach him if I turn us around? God, I love the look of those clouds! Smell those leaves!"

Only on Scottish lochs, fishing under a similar kind of mist, have I sensed such perfect self-containment, as if trout were the only purpose in life, water the medium in which the purpose dwells, a rowboat the magically suspended derrick by which the purpose can be mined. And, as mentioned, I love fishing in rowboats. Tanso has a whole fleet of them, docked inside a long weathered boathouse that dates from the turn of the century. Lapstreaked, the long wooden kind with two pairs of davits, they're just heavy enough to withstand some wind (any good rowboat is heavy), and just broad enough you can stand up in them to cast. There is something about the yielding sensation a rowboat creates in the water, the way it responds so fast to the slightest leverage, that makes you feel as if you're combing the water, and it's the kind of intimate gesture that makes you feel perfectly at one with it, a craft the water somehow *likes*.

The various streamers of mist eventually found one another, fell as a solid curtain of rain that drove us back to the boathouse. From the club's long porch came a deep drawn-out sound I thought at first was the call of a moose (or the mountains yawning), but which turned out to be one of the young women who worked in the kitchen blowing on a conch shell to signal it was time for lunch. And what a lunch. Homemade potpie, a huge spinach salad, Ben & Jerry's Cherry Garcia washed down by coffee laced with good Vermont cream. Tanso is the kind of club where wonderfully prepared meals are a big part of the attraction—not just the food, but the easy kind of talk that comes when the fishing is right outside the window and you know it will wait until you're done.

A few other members drifted in now, including Dick's mother and father, who live not far away. The club has members all over the country, but the ones who live within driving distance use it the most, especially in autumn. Dick's father showed me around the clubhouse. Like Catument's, it's decorated with old black-and-white photos from the club's early days, cartoons cut out of newspapers fifty years old, joke flies made of coat hangers, duck feathers, and ribbons, piles of old word games and Reader's Digest condensed books. The bedrooms are small and simply furnished—the bedsteads the old-fashioned iron kind even a hurricane couldn't shake, and on top are folded army blankets of thick green wool.

We fished again after lunch. Three or four boats were out now, but they hardly dented our sense of solitude. That's another nice thing about rowboats: so slow is their locomotion that there is a natural tendency to remain pretty much in the same spot, focus only on the water within reach . . . and Dick and I talked about whether this might be the simple low-tech solution to overcrowding on trout water everywhere—require everyone to fish in rowboats.

Still-water fishing is static enough that it bores some people, and often in springtime it bores me, but not in autumn; there's a relaxed feel that goes down well with the weather, the whole autumnal package of pleasurably sad regrets. Back in the shallows where the inlet came in I lost a nice fish, then landed one that was big enough to make up for my disappointment—a brookie dressed for autumn, with so much color and vibrancy

I was half afraid to take it in my hand, convinced that, like the bright golden leaves that clung to the trees above us, its beauty would burn. All the more reason to release it in the water; I reached my fingers down to the hook, twisted it gently, and saw the scarlet drop back into the amber-colored transparency from which it had emerged.

Every now and then I'll be asked, in what I'm sure is a deliberately offhand manner, whether or not I might be interested in applying for membership at one of these clubs. It's tempting, since the financial end of it is surprisingly reasonable. At Catument, you pay for an initial share plus yearly dues; at Tanso, you also pay each time you come, at least for room and board; in this respect, it functions like a small private hotel, so there's an economic incentive to have as members' young families who will use the lodge often.

So far I've always turned down these invites with thanks. We have many of these kinds of delights very close to home free of charge, and the prospect of being on a waiting list for five years or more, *any* waiting list, is more than my patience can handle. I'm not a particularly clubbable sort of guy, which is also part of it, though perhaps I'm being overly shy in this respect; sitting on those porches, sharing that bourbon, I've found the members of both clubs to be an interesting and surprisingly varied sort, and if the conversation turns momentarily to the events of the larger world, you're apt to find you're talking to as many liberal Democrats as reactionary Republicans, the one common denominator being a healthy conservatism toward any changes in the club's own domain.

There are lessons in this kind of stewardship that are applicable to public waters. The state of Vermont owns a pond over in the east-central part of the state, the site of a fishing club that couldn't pay its taxes. It's now run as a fly-fishing-only park (pay as you go, reservations required, two-fish limit), and an excellent one, combining the access of public fishing with the restricted numbers of a club. I fish there often in the fall, again using rowboats (aluminum ones, alas, a material that should be used only to wrap sandwiches), and find it has very much the same feel as Tanso, even to the clubhouse, which is not only used for conservation-related conferences and wildlife seminars, but offers simple lodgings for the night.

The great days of a state's acquiring park land through tax sales and eminent domain are over, I suppose, but it's an idea that would certainly be a good one for these overcrowded days—a state taking a few ponds or streams that are already in its possession and operating them on this controlled-access basis. I would never want to see all the fishing operated this way—our tradition of public access is too valuable and ingrained, and gives every flyfisher a stake in protecting all our water—but some such arrangement in each trout-fishing state would offer quality fishing and a club kind of feel, this time to a much wider cross-section of flyfishers. A place that is deliberately anachronistic, removed from the competitive pressure that mars so much of our current fishing? Well yes—why not? If I haven't said so already pond fishing in a rowboat for wild and catchable trout is the best way ever invented for interesting a young person in fishing, and to do this in a setting where fly fishing is honored as the simple, traditional pastime it should be makes the experience all the more vital.

Some people in Vermont find even private club waters far too public, and do most of their fishing right at home. A bulldozer is hired with a crusty old-timer who's been at this game for years, an acre-sized hole dug out where the clay lies thickest, a stream damned if there is one or an overflow pipe hooked up to a reliable artesian well, ten-inch trout ordered from one of the fish farms or feed stores, a willow or two planted on the banks, a little dock knocked together out of lumber—and there, you're in business, with your own private trout water you can stroll down to any time you want.

I'm surprised at how many of these lie scattered about these hills; driving, I'll glance through the trees and catch a quick glimpse of a compact bowl of silvery water tucked away into the landscape where it's all but invisible. Many of these contain large trout, rainbows of seven or eight pounds (my guess is the best fly fishing in New England is in private ponds), but sometimes the environment remains a little artificial and forced, so it's like you're fishing for pets in an aquarium, not catching them so much as dipping them out.

The best private ponds are the most natural—those where the water is gently borrowed from a stream and gently returned. I have a friend (let's call him, uh, Tom) who lives in a narrow valley well up in the hills. Above his property is the source of a small stream: a beaver flowage that is always marshy, even in seasons of drought. Where the flowage begins to narrow into a definite channel his property begins, and a hundred yards below this, many years ago now, a previous owner built an earthen dam housing an outflow pipe and a wooden spillway. The resulting pond isn't much over an acre, and fits into the flowage perfectly, being little more than a natural widening, the slightest pause, in the water's rush down to the valley floor three miles away.

Native brook trout live in the beaver flowage, and in times of high water will come down into the pond and do just fine; there are also brookies in the pool just below the dam, attracted by the cold and reliable spillage. Tom stocks the pond once a year with several dozen brook trout and five or six rainbows, and these grow to serious size, without his having to feed them. I've caught twenty-inch brook trout here, a twenty-four-inch rainbow, and they have the kind of thickness and strength you see on fish out in Montana.

If the pond fits perfectly into the natural order here, it also fits perfectly into the man-made one, which is what gives a private pond much of its charm. The lawn slopes down to the water from the house; a birdhouse-festooned willow overhangs the bank on which a rowboat is pulled up, waiting for guests to help themselves; the kids have left their butterfly nets about, and out in the middle of the pond floats a Wiffle ball driven there in last night's game. Tom constructed a dock near the spillway that lets you cover the deepest part of the pond with an easy cast; playing a fish here, if you give even a little yell, everyone will rush down from the house to see whether it's big enough to get excited about and stick around until it's landed.

Charming, of course—what flyfisher hasn't dreamed of having this kind of action so close at hand? And yet it's not without its worries. Careless road work will silt up the flowage, turn the pond muddy for days. Poachers will fish it when the family is gone, keep everything they catch. The dam is a constant source of worry—every now and then you read in the papers about one going out, causing a destructive flood (the great Johnstown flood, remember, was caused by the rupture of a dam at a private fishing club). Natural as the pond is, it suffers from a natural kind of predation—heron and otter can wipe out the fish in a very short time. Over the years a pond can become so precious it's hard to leave when it comes time to move on. I have friends who, faced with pressures to move to better jobs or better schools, found their pond had become so integral a part of their happiness they could not bear leaving it behind, and so took cuts in pay or accepted the fact that they would have to spend long parts of their day chauffeuring their kids to and from a distant school. Love any small portion of the landscape and an obligation falls on you to take it seriously, cherish it, protect it, and in this day and age the burden can seem exhausting.

Is it worth it? I know Tom would say yes, even though he fishes the pond only occasionally now, taking most of his pleasure from seeing his friends and his kids catch the trout he all but knows by name. He's given me a standing invite to fish it anytime I want, which usually turns out to be three or four times a year. In April, just after the ice melts, I enjoy going out with him in his canoe, to catch fish at a time when there's nowhere else to catch fish, become reacquainted with that firm tugging pressure in the arm, that dancing rod tip, the wet spring, and coil of color in my hand. In June, waiting for a windless, cloudy day, I enjoy taking fish after fish right on top with my little two-weight. A bit later in the summer I'll bring my father over, help him catch some trout his poor eyesight wouldn't allow him to catch anywhere else.

My favorite time to fish the pond is in October after a season spent chasing difficult and fussy fish. Tom will be at work, his family will be off at school, and it will just be me, the rowboat, and the trout—generous and eager fish who don't require much persuading to come leaping over to my side. Behind me the bank with the pines will be golden beneath fallen needles; by the dam the sumac and willows will have turned red and the brightest yellow; up in the shallows the brookies, the anxious ones, will be already spawning, turning in tight circles of the utmost concentration and intensity—a concentration not even a rowboat, not even the streamer that takes trout so easily just a few yards away, will manage to shake. These are gorgeous fish, the males coral and fiery, with hooked jaws that let you know what you're dealing with is passion, serious passion, that will stand no interference from the puny likes of you.

Part of my pleasure in fishing here is a selfish one, to have a trout-filled body of water all to myself, and yet it's not the snobbery, I-have-it-and-you-don't kind of selfishness, but something that carries with it gratitude and thanks. Thanks for what? For being able to concentrate so directly on the fish, know there will be no interruption in the intense and important business of trying to understand the workings of this small cup of wildness, coax it occasionally to my purpose. You realize, in the end, that even this homey body of water carries with it as much mystery as a large and untamed lake, the mystery all life seems to contain at its healthiest, something you sense very strongly, feel you can all but pull from the water with a quick dipping hand, and yet even on a perfect autumn day like this one, borne and uplifted on the backs of willing trout, will never quite be able to grasp.

All trout water is private water, seen in this light. A trout tugs us and from habit we tug back—and yet how much better to let the fish, the dweller in the mystery, pull us down into its center so we can see for ourselves what it's like to live in paradise, even the paradise that comes to us one precious acre at a time.

September 18

Perfect conditions. The sailor asks that the wind blow from just the right quarter, at just the right speed; the kayaker that the river level be propitious, neither too high nor too low; the mountaineer that the weather fronts behave themselves; the photographer, that the light be soft; the hunter, that the biological rhythm that animates the game he seeks has them fully on the move . . . and yet the flyfisher is fussier than any of these, because when he wishes for a perfect day he speaks of all these things combined, wind, water, weather, light, and instinct, so a perfect day for fishing is perhaps the rarest, most precious circumstance in any of the outdoor sports.

How rare? There's a day I look forward to all year long, yet only get perhaps one season out of five, so fussy are its requirements. It needs to be a day in the second or third week of September, when the Connecticut that runs past my home has been scoured by a long summer's flowage, so it shines brighter than it does at any other time of year, with a good three or four feet more of transparent depth. You need a frost in the early part of the week—the water must have noticeably, but not drastically cooled. It can't be past the equinox, since the storms we get then muddy things up. The wind must be from the south—from the north, you may as well stay at home. Most important of all, it must be a day when it's significantly warmer than it has been, so it feels like midsummer has been returned to you on a golden platter, with apologies for that trick of frost.

Get all these things without exception and it means the best smallmouth fishing of the year, a day when their biological clock is so exuberantly on it's as if you're fishing a solid river of bassiness, the water having by this perfect stirring of variables taken on striped bars and golden flesh and chevroned fins and glistening scales and extravagant muscle. It's something I anticipate all summer long, deliberately avoiding all engagements or appointments so I can be here at the right moment . . . and then spend September keeping track of all the various factors, trying not to get my hopes up but getting them up anyway, feeling good when that first early frost comes, feeling even better when it's followed by warmer weather, rooting for the wind to stay in the south, all but applying body English to the atmosphere, trying to bend and shape the elements to my purpose, if only for a single day.

When I woke up yesterday morning I thought I had the combination I was looking for. We'd had our frost earlier in the week, the northwest wind had swung around to the south, and there was a nostalgic stillness in the air that harkened back toward August. A heavy fog was fine with me, since one of the other ingredients in this kind of perfection is the slow warming of the shallows where the bass roam, and you get this when there's enough moisture in the air to act as a gentle scrim. By eleven, conditions would be just right, giving me time to work on my novel and thereby achieve that other cornerstone of perfection: going out to the river with a conscience that's clear.

I suppose there was some self-congratulation in my attitude—that I was clever enough not only to recognize perfection when it came, but to keep my calendar open for its arrival—and thus enough pride that it was goething for a fallething. I had the canoe up on the car, had my rod stowed, my poppers packed, a lunch ready . . . I was heading back to the house for my hat, feeling the kind of happy urgency that transforms a middle-aged man into a ten-year-old kid . . . when there was a hard, sudden tap on my shoulder, the kind that fate often likes to deliver aurally, in this case as the frantic yipping of an aging retriever who had chosen that moment to impale herself on a rusty strand of barbed wire out on the far end of our stone wall.

At thirteen, Cider is as lively as a puppy and a bit nearsighted—a bad combination when it comes to stumbling into barbed wire. She'd cut herself badly on the back of the leg, and it was obvious it was going to take stitches to close the wound. This was the kind of thing I hadn't figured into my calculations, and made me realize that my criteria for perfection, though stringent enough, were nowhere near adequate, since they hadn't taken into consideration the chances of life becoming snared in the various entanglements that seem spontaneously improvised just to ruin your day.

Our vet lives twenty miles north. Cider did fine once I got her on the back seat; her expression was a combination of guilt and embarrassment, in the usual way of goldens, and every now and then to comfort her I had to twist my head around and say something reassuring. I was vexed, of course—more than vexed. Impatient, pissed, furious. The further I drove—the greater the distance I was putting between me and the day I had planned—the angrier I became, to the point where in order not to go flying off the road altogether I had to get a moral hold on myself, start figuring out what was going on.

Part of this was easy—the normal vexation anyone feels when their plans go awry. This was multiplied (let's say doubled) by the fact that it came at a particularly bad, or rather *good* time: the perfect day I'd been waiting for all season. This is something any flyfisher will understand, something so intrinsically part of the game it's hardly worth mentioning, but after this things became a bit murkier, more personal, and it was a while before I figured them out.

My reasoning went something like this . . .

Normally I'm the luckiest of fishermen, someone who can go fishing almost any time he wants. To suddenly have this taken away from me—to discover my charmed fishing life was mortal after all, and could be lost not to a major catastrophe, but a minor one—was a hard thing to swallow, though not without its value as a kind of therapeutic lesson, a reminder of just how remarkably lucky I am most of the time. Okay, I could understand this, reason was doing its job. But not being able to go fishing, even in this one slight instance, was making me overreact in a way that went far beyond this, and I finally realized it was because it made me remember a time when I couldn't go fishing at all—the long years I was stuck in the suburbs, someone who only dreamed of fishing, but for reasons too complicated and difficult to go into here, hardly ever went out. This only changed in my thirties when I broke away from that life, moved north to the country and was, quite literally, reborn.

Thinking in these terms, it's easy to see what was at stake: even a small threat to the kind of life I'd established inflamed the old scar tissue, burned as something I had to smother immediately with all the emotion I was capable of mustering—not a small vexation in an otherwise fine day, but a threat to my very existence.

And further. Fishing, right from the start, was an expression of the rebellious half of my nature, the anti-establishment part of me, the kid who went fishing when the rest of his generation stormed ROTC buildings or did drugs—the passion in me that is partly a finger jabbed toward the conforming philistine materialistic culture I've so thoroughly despised, actively when younger, latently today. Give my new life even one small check and the old emotion comes flooding back, the fury that used to possess me in my twenties when I realized the life I imagined was passing me by.

Poor Cider! There she was bearing stoically something that must have caused considerable pain, and there her master was gripping the steering wheel like he wanted to throttle anything and everything he could get his hands around, never mind the aching dog. But I got her to the vet without ramming into anyone. I held her as Dr. Wheeler examined her, helped where I could when he sewed her up, carried her back out and laid her gently on the back seat—and like a pet-ambulance driver, raced her back home in record time.

One o'clock—only two hours lost. I got Cider settled in the mudroom, drove down River Road to the dirt launching area owned by the Nature Conservancy, loaded up the canoe with my fly rod and poppers, shoved myself off into the river. The sun had it shining in that penny brightness I had reckoned on; below the canoe, as I pried it out toward the wooded island thats my favorite spot, I could see small bass swimming over the sandy bottom, with the kind of heads-up alertness, eagerness, and hunger you see in June during spawning and then not again until a fall day like this one.

The river here is only slightly wider than where I fish for trout, and yet there's enough breadth now that it seems a much weightier proposition, something that doesn't rush and dance but sweeps and proceeds. With the breeze from the south, the surface had those little crisp folds that come at such short intervals they make the canoe seem like it's on a moving ramp, and in no time at all I was drifting past the weedbed at the island's upper edge, attached to a smallmouth that had taken the Olive Zonker I'd been trolling out the stern.

I caught six bass on the first seven casts—that's what I mean by perfection—and with everyone I felt myself relax even more. Perfection? Though from long experience I recognize the conditions that prompt this, I'm still confused as to what exactly is going on, at least as far as the bass are concerned. Yes, the water has cooled off, and their metabolism must welcome this. Yes, the water is clearer, and those crayfish become an easier target for them in the shallows. But how do they know the wind is from the south and why does this please them? How do they sense the relatively low barometric pressure, since by rising or falling a few inches in the river they can make it anything they want? How do they sense winter is coming, by what mechanism or instinct? More specifically, how come they sense winter so strongly on the most summer-like days? It's reasonable to expect a feeding binge from a creature who is faced with seven months when it hardly eats at all, but why is the frenzy so closely tied to such fussy factors? Fishing magazines have always made a great deal over this feeding binge, so its become an article of faith to most fishermen, but myself, I've rarely seen it, find fish in autumn to be at their moodiest, with this one specific exception: on the right day in September the smallmouth on the Connecticut River go absolutely wild.

As I came around the tip of the island my lee disappeared and the breeze pushed the canoe over toward the Vermont shore. This was fine with me—the bass line up there along boulders dumped down the bank when the railroad was built well over a hundred and fifty years ago. There are old telegraph wires, too, strung on sunken poles that dip right into the river, making it seem as if this whole vanished infrastructure, trains and telegraph both, have as their only function a soggy communication with sunken ghosts.

As I drifted, I cast—in autumn you can sometimes pick up a sunbathing bass right in the middle of the river—and cast standing up. This is against all the canoeing rules, of course, but we'd been using this Old Town for so many years it's become an easy and comfortable position, and there's something daring and stately about it I enjoy, like riding a surfboard towed by dolphins.

Along the bank the wild honeysuckle had turned brown; a bittern, staying just ahead of me, blended perfectly with the color, and it took the crisp rattle of leaves for me to pick him up again twenty yards downstream. Where the bank steepened into a sandy cliff I pulled the canoe in and waded the last ten feet to shore. It's a good place to relax, since the bank slopes back like a chaise lounge; as I drank my tea, ate my sandwich, my neck was tickled by sand rolling down from the holes left by nesting swallows at the top of the bank.

I was in no hurry to go back out—if anything, the perfect day was turning out to be a little too warm, and so not quite perfect after all. A temperature of seventy-three makes the bass remember winter is coming and gets them feeding; a temperature of seventy-six makes them think its August again and turns them perversely sluggish. I knew it was almost certainly the last day of bass fishing for the season. The forecast called for it to turn sharply colder, and already I could see coral-tinged thunderheads moving across the mountains to the north.

I caught more fish after lunch, though they didn't come quite so fast. On days like this one the smallmouth want a bullet-nosed popper, the slider kind with rubber legs, and they want it fished without any motion other than what the current does to those dangling legs. Casting these can be tricky. You need a mix of force and finesse to do it properly; force in ramming it sidearm under the overhanging white pine that line the shore; finesse (applied at just the last moment) in making sure the popper enters the thin window you re aiming for, the nine or ten inches between the top of the water and the bottom of the trees.

It's funny about trout and bass. As much as I love the former, I never experience anything even remotely close to a fellow feeling for them, and most of my interest revolves around finding them and getting them to strike. With smallmouth it's different. I have a very strong fellow feeling for them, and it comes primarily during the fight. Have I ever written about the glories of a smallmouth's fight? No fish, neither largemouth nor rainbow nor striper nor salmon, punches as hard as a full-bodied smallmouth. The explosive strike followed by those wild unpredictable first seconds when the fish sometimes jumps (maybe a tailwalk, maybe the classic cartwheel, maybe a wild vault back toward the bank) and sometimes dives, then the frantic second pull, followed immediately by the first seriously deep plunge, getting into your backing it dives so deep, coming back up again entirely on its own and jumping again at a distance, then plunging again *if* it's still on, plunging a third time, still reserving enough strength to jump one last time close to the canoe, and even at the very end, just when you reach down for him, retaining enough pugnacity it can flail at your hand and get away.

What is the fellow feeling in all this, the connection that makes me know exactly what the bass is experiencing? I wouldn't have known what to link it to, not until that little episode with Cider, that frantic overreaction on my part when it became likely I wouldn't be able to go fishing. Why look further? The bass fights with frantic and uncompromising purpose, and I share a portion of that frantic quality myself, at least when it comes to the passion with which I approach my time out on the water. Yes, I want a gentle, relaxed sport, one that involves myself, the river, the fish in a sometimes complicated, sometimes simple symbiosis, but how fiercely I want this, want this still. Bass and fisherman tug on opposite ends of the line, and yet on a ninety-nine and nine-tenths perfect September afternoon like this one, they end up striving toward the same kind of rebellious freedom, racing to see who gets there first.

Her Woods Still

On a late summer day in 1935, a schoolteacher from Massachusetts named Louise Dickinson neared the end of a vacation canoe trip through the Rangeley chain of lakes in western Maine. Her party was faced with a grueling portage—the five-mile length of the Rapid River, which connects Lower Richardson with Umbagog Lake at the bottom of the chain. The Rapid is said to be the most rapid river east of the Rockies, and an old dirt carry road parallels its unnavigable length; over the carry a man named Ralph Rich was picking up some extra money by ferrying canoe parties from one lake to the other with a 1924 Marmon touring car and makeshift trailer he had brought into the woods over the winter ice.

Louise and Ralph struck up a conversation, found immediately they had much in common. Ralph had sold some patent rights back in Chicago and had saved enough that he intended to spend the rest of his life in the woods; Louise's was an adventurous, nonconforming soul that until that moment had found little outlet. A few months later they were married and living along the Rapid River in an old summer house, miles from the nearest town, surrounded by thousands of acres of paper-company wilderness—a place Louise was to live for the next fifteen years, with long intervals (the longest, four years) when she never left the woods at all for "outside."

"During most of my adolescence," she begins her book, "specifically, between the time when I gave up wanting to be a brakeman on a freight train and the time when I decided to become an English teacher, I said, when asked what I was going to do with my life, that I was going to live alone in a cabin in the Maine woods and write."

Write is what she did, three books on her experiences along the Rapid River, beginning with the volume that sits beside me on the desk as I type: *We Took to the Woods*. Mine is the paperback edition of 1948, and the publishing history inside the front cover attests to the book's enormous popularity. First hardback edition from Lippincott in 1942, followed quickly by four more printings; an Atlantic Monthly condensed version published later that summer, and a Reader's Digest condensation in the fall; a Book-of-the-Month Club edition printed November 1942, with seven printings through 1944; a Liberty condensed version in 1943 and an Esquire condensed version in 1946; a Grosset and Dunlap hardback with four printings between 1946 and 1947; an Armed Services Edition in 1946; the Pocket Books paperback published in June 1948 . . . all of these, with their simple black-and-white photos (logging camp cooks, pulp-filled ponds, huge snowdrifts, craggy-looking Maine guides), their endpaper maps of the Rangeley region, the vaguely balsam, vaguely mildewed scent time has given them, being to this day the reliable staple of flea markets, library sales, and secondhand bookstores all throughout New England.

It's not hard to understand why her books were so popular. She's a good writer, with a good story to tell, Thoreau with a happy face, someone who was alive to the romance inherent in her situation, and yet managed to keep her prose and philosophy down-to-earth.

I like to think of the lakes coming down from the north of us like a gigantic staircase to the sea. Kennebago to Rangeley to Cupsuptic, down they drop, level to level, through short, snarling rivers; Mooselukmeguntic to the Richardsons to Pond-in-the-River, and through Rapid River to Umbagog, whence they empty into the Androscoggin and begin the long southeasterly curve back to the ocean. I like to say their names, and I wish I could make you see them—long, lonely stretches of water shut in by dark hills.

There are a few narrow trails, but travel through the woods is so difficult, with the swamps and blowdowns and underbrush, that the lakes have remained what they were to the Indians, the main thoroughfares.

She was lucky enough to live there when the rough exuberance of the old logging days hadn't yet been killed off by modern industrial logging, and many of her best stories revolve around the shabby, put-upon loggers who, once they were in the woods, assumed almost mythological stature. She was also lucky in her family and friends: Ralph, her cantankerous, brilliantly improvisational husband; Gerrish, the family's hired man who became much more than that; Al and Larry Parsons, who acted as winter caretakers at Coburn's, the fishing camp at the far end of the Carry Road; her son Rufus, a babe, quite literally, in the woods. She had a novelist's touch with them all. Judging by the photos of Louise herself, she was a plain but strong woman, with an open and approachable face, the kind of person who would be good in an emergency, with just enough tartness to keep you from underestimating her—and this is the quality that comes across in her books, so, reading them, you quickly become her friend.

These things help explain her popularity, but don't quite account for it all. You only have to look at the dates on the various editions, remember what was going on in the world then, to understand what underlay their extraordinary appeal. Louise Dickinson Rich lived in the woods all through the last years of the Depression and World War II, concentrating on blueberry picking and salmon fishing and sap gathering when the rest of the world was involved with something very different. It's no wonder people found solace reading her books; to someone caught up in the dislocation and chaos of war, the story of a simple, uncomplicated life miles from anywhere must have seemed an irresistible daydream. She was aware of this herself, was quick to defend her books as something more than escapist fare ("We haven't tried to escape from anything. We have only exchanged one set of problems for another"), but it's clear that for hundreds of thousands of readers it was the chance to escape to the woods for a few hours via her books that made them so compelling.

Her philosophy, too. It's simple and simply stated, yet comes across with the kind of total sincerity that seems so rare and so precious during complex times. "I am free," she says, in concluding her first book. "All ordinary people like us, everywhere, are trying to find the same things. It makes no difference whether they are New Englanders or Texans or Malaysians or Finns. They all want to be left alone to conduct their own private search for a personal peace, a reasonable security, a little love, a chance to attain happiness through achievement. It isn't much to want, but I never came anywhere near to getting most of these things until we took to the woods."

I must have been thirteen or fourteen when I first came upon her books on the dusty lower shelves of our suburban library. In a time of general prosperity her books had lost some of their popularity, and one of the first things I noticed was that none of the books had been taken out in six or seven years. I fell in love with them, of course, and how could it be otherwise, since already by that time living in the woods and writing was exactly what I wanted to do with my own life. Her books are of a type there is no shorthand name for, but which was once a flourishing genre. Henry Rowlands's account of living alone in the far north of Ontario, *Cache Lake Country*. Charlie Childs's still-readable account of building a summer home from scratch on the Maine Coast, *Roots in the Rock; The House on Nauset Marsh* by Wyman Richardson, and a dozen others, all of which seemed to be illustrated by Henry Bugbee Kane. These are not great books by any means, but they were all good books, and, like the tales

Don Quixote read of chivalry, they played havoc with the fantasy of a boy who already loved woods, water, and hills, and yet was stuck in the concrete suburbs feeling the utter impotence, when it came to dreams, of being thirteen.

I was already a passionate fisherman; one of the things I discovered, reading Rich's books, was that the fishing camp she called Coburn's (where she worked one spring to distract herself after Ralph's sudden tragic death) was now called Lakewood Camps. I sent away for their brochure—and for many years, right through my teens and twenties, I would get a postcard every May, with a picture of a pool on the Rapid River and big letters announcing *THE ICE IS OUT AT MIDDLE DAM!*

A teenager, I had no way of getting there, no one to take me, and even in my twenties I never had the chance to go, so that postcard, arriving every spring just when my hopes were at their strongest, took on a mocking quality, that grown to manhood I still should be so far from achieving even one of the smaller of my boyhood dreams: to fish the country Rich described.

And then I did move north, found myself living only a morning's drive from her part of western Maine. Now my excuse for not going was different . . . I told myself it's best to leave at least some childhood landscapes virgin and intact . . . but after a while this seemed overly refined, even silly, and when my friend Tom Ciardelli started telling me about the Rapid and its fly fishing for landlocks, I decided it was time to go, combine some fishing with some pilgrimage. One of the greatest pleasures in life is visiting a place you've fallen in love with through books, through imagination. Okay, the Rapid River isn't London or Venice or even the Allagash, but for a good many years it had teased and intrigued my wondering, and it was high time I saw it in person.

We went in late September, a week before the salmon season ended. Back along the Connecticut the leaves were just starting to turn, but once past Errol, once we crossed the Maine border and drove up the first step in the high inland plateau that dominates the state, the gold was everywhere, a wide rolling carpet spreading down toward the scraggly blue of Umbagog in the near distance to our left.

Lakewood Camps can be reached only by water; the drill is, reaching the small town of Andover, you go to the general store and call ahead so the boat can meet you at South Arm, the long southward finger of Lower Richardson Lake. There were a couple of cars parked on the gravel apron above the dock when we arrived; one of these was a state police car, the other a fish and game truck, but except for Tom making a joke about a game bust in progress we hardly gave these any thought.

Anyone who's read much Louise Dickinson Rich knows how important South Arm was to her entire way of life—virtually every trip outside went that way; most supplies, most visitors, came to the woods across the lake. On the bluff are some old weather-beaten garages that could certainly date from 1940, where those living in the woods kept their outside cars. On a late September day like this one, with no one around, a good chop cutting up the blue, Lower Richardson seemed high, wild, and lonely, little changed from how it must have looked fifty years before.

We had carried our duffle bags and rod cases down to the dock, were standing there wondering if we had missed connections, when a small cabin cruiser entered the channel, slowed, then edged sideways toward the dock.

We could see three men aboard—a man behind the wheel, a state trooper, a game warden—and it was a few more seconds before we noticed there was a fourth as well.

In the stern of the boat, riding so low we didn't at first see it, rested a tarpaulin-covered stretcher with a small pair of old-fashioned brown shoes sticking out one end. Tom and I both reached over to pull the boat in, and now, seeing this we involuntarily let go. "Give us room now," the trooper said quietly, and then without any other words being spoken, he took one end of the stretcher as the game warden took the other, and between them they carried the body up the steep ramp toward shore.

It was the Lakewood Camps boat all right; Stan Milton, the owner, helped us load our luggage, then briefly explained what had happened.

A ninety-two-year-old man had died, a longtime summer resident at one of the camps along shore. He'd come up for the salmon fishing and collapsed suddenly that morning getting into his boat. I did a quick calculation, realized he was a contemporary of Rich's, could very possibly have known her. Certainly, it was her kind of story—a bittersweet one, a fate that was tied closely to the land. As Stan steered the boat out into the open part of the lake, the engine became too noisy for us to talk about it any further, but we had agreed it wasn't a bad way to go, not at that age, not doing what he loved. His death, meeting us like that, gave a solemn quality to the landscape and seemed to place it even more solidly in times past.

Lakewood Camps sits on the edge of the lake a couple of hundred yards from Middle Dam, the old gated dam where the Rapid River spills down toward Pond-in-the-River. A weathered brown lodge with a wide veranda, brown cottages with their own porch and rockers, various outbuildings, piles of firewood lying in a ring of wood chips, a garden cart full of fresh linen, a dock with boats and canoes, everything looking as if it had been lifted from a sepia postcard circa 1888—it's all very typical of the classic Maine fishing camp, an institution I've some affectionate familiarity with and would very much like in the coming years to have more.

A Maine fishing camp! The state that's given American culture the lumberman, the lobsterman, the Maine guide, has also given it this: the camp in the woods where the trout bite even faster than the black flies, the salmon leap into your canoe of their own volition, the griddle cakes come stuffed with blueberries, the loon calls at night, the moose bellows, and you sleep soundly under thick wool blankets even in July. I've fished several over the years, and find not only do they match up remarkably well against their stereotype, not only do they offer one of the most reasonably priced fishing experiences to be found anywhere, but they seem to be the kind of places where stories happen, and there's no higher praise in my vocabulary than that.

The first one I fished was Weatherby's up on Grand Lake Stream back in the '70s. I remember one night after dinner everyone congregating on the lawn to watch a guest cast with the latest marvel: a rod made out of graphite fiber. Next day, going out with an old guide in a Grand Lake Stream canoe, I timidly mentioned I preferred fly fishing only. "Fine with me, young fella," the guide said, then promptly reached into his bait bucket and slapped a shiner on my Mickey Finn. A few years later, married now, I took my wife and baby daughter to Kidney Pond in Baxter State Park at the base of Mt. Katahdin—the old Colt family camp, operated as a modest lodge. Celeste and I spent our evenings fishing (in an Old Town wood-and-canvas canoe) a hundred yards offshore from our cabin, listening to our sleeping baby through the crib monitor we'd brought from home. On that same trip, fishing dry flies, I let my line trail out the back of the canoe as I paddled to a new spot—and was promptly arrested for trolling by a hidden game warden, despite the fact that what I was "trolling" was a size 24 Black Midge.

Maine fishing camps fell upon hard times in the '80s, partly due to changes in logging practices (more tote roads, clear-cuts, aerial spraying), and partly due to their own lack of foresight. One of the big routines at fishing camps has always been having trout for breakfast, and too many camps were too slow in getting behind catch and release. Now they are starting to see the light; Stan Milton, for example, is one of the most vocal proponents of catch and release in the state. It's paying off, with bigger fish, more fish. In our cabin at Lakewood was a creel census conducted over the course of a decade. In the first year there wasn't *one* legal salmon released by anyone; in the latest year, they *all* had been released, and the fishing had improved enormously.

The camps still have problems, including the fact that logging roads go everywhere now, and any fisherman with an ATV, a DeLorme atlas, or a Magellan navigation system can find their way to water the camps once pretty much had to themselves. You have to wonder how much longer sports will pay for ambience alone, when there is no longer this de facto kind of privacy. Against this is the fact that the fishing-camp concept is environmentally friendly, limiting the numbers of fishermen and keeping them under some kind of watchful control.

Checking in at a fishing camp is always part of the ritual. Buying a three-day license, asking about the fishing, scanning the logbook to see who's caught what, buying some locally tied streamers, adding in some postcards, getting meal times set. On the boat ride over Stan told us the fishing was slow, but Sue, his wife, assured us it was splendid, so between them they had prepared us for anything.

We picked up a picnic lunch out in the kitchen, then went back to our cabin, got our fishing duds on, headed down to the river—and right into our second fast story of the trip. The Carry Road follows the river, but we managed to take a wrong turn and before we realized it, we were pretty well lost. This was vexing, and seemed somehow part of an initiation—the land blindfolding us, spinning us three times around. Finally, after growing impatience on both our parts, we spotted Pond-in-the-River below us through the forest and sheepishly made our way down to where the river empties into the pond in what is called, none too promisingly, Chub Pool.

Whoever named Rapid River wasn't kidding . . . it really scoots along, a staircase of boisterous rapids . . . but where we intersected it the water broadens and slows. The salmon were rising when we got there and it took us a while to figure out how to connect with them, not so much the flies they were taking (small gray midges), but where to best position ourselves in the water. Unlike most salmon rivers in Maine, here the landlocks remain in the river all summer long, but they really get moving in the fall, joined by migrants up from the pond—a movement it's most enjoyable to witness, since it's seldom in New England we see the seasonal migration of fish you get in a place like the Pacific Northwest, landlocks being the closest we come to an actual bona fide run.

They're dignified-looking fish, landlocks—light silver and lightly spotted—and seemed compelled to jump primarily because they're shaped for jumping, with the muscular kind of leanness you see in world-class pole vaulters. A little one will jump five or six times before you bring it in; a thicker one, three or four times, but with a slower, more graceful kind of panache, the vaulter at the moment of releasing her pole and arcing that final millimeter over a barely trembling bar.

Sometimes in autumn spawning brook trout migrate up the Chub Pool, and for a moment I thought I had one on, but it turned out to be one of the huge and eponymous chub, just red enough around the gill area to have me fooled when I saw it deep in the water. I landed it, then waded over to the low, ragged isthmus that divides the pool in half, found a flat rock, and took a contemplative rest (reading Rich that night, I discovered this was her favorite spot to go smelting in the spring, allowing her to dip her net in either channel). Out in the deeper part of the pool, Tom, as usual, was testing the limits; he's gone as far as he can, I decided, but then, with a magician's graceful flourish, he reached into his vest for a gadget I didn't know he had; a collapsible wading staff. Extended, it gave him just enough purchase to keep going across the pool.

If you travel even a few feet into the brush here you'll come across reminders of the old logging days, thick rusty cables wound around cedars or peeling yellow birches, making it seem as if giants who had once fished here had left their set lines behind. In reality, they were cables used in getting the pulp downriver each spring; once the logs reached Pond-in-the-River they were collected in huge booms and towed across the water by ungainly vessels called Alligators.

Alligators are built like barges, flat and rectangular, but they have a huge steel cable running from a winch in the bow. The anchor is dropped, the winch unwinds as the

Alligator runs backward to the boom, and hooks on; then the winch winds up the Alligator to the anchor, trailing behind her the boomful of pulp wood which is her business to move from the Head of the Pond to Pondy dam at the foot.... The crew looked like any gang of men going about a routine job, except they were a little shabbier, a little more nondescript, a little less arresting than any bunch of road menders I ever saw. There wasn't a plaid shirt in the crew. Tied like a baby's bonnet under the chin and tucked into the shirt at the back of the neck was a bandanna handkerchief, or, failing that, just an old piece of flour sacking. On top of that was the hat proper, which might be a cheap felt, a visored cap, or a battered derby.

They didn't even do the job with dash. They just walked apathetically up and down the logs, boring holes, driving pegs and fastening ropes. People who do things well almost always do them without flourish.

A tough, backbreaking job, pulp driving was, and though Rich could romanticize it at times, her eye was too honest not to see it plain.

I thought about this as I sat there watching Tom catch salmon. I thought post-industrial kinds of thoughts, trying to imagine how all this had looked during those years, finding, surprisingly, that I could do this without much trouble. It can be one of the characteristic notes when you fly fish New England in autumn—that between old stone walls and collapsed mills and washed-out dams you feel like you're fishing over the ruins of Rome. Thats a comforting feeling in this day and age, thinking the dreck we ourselves pile skyward might, in time, come to have the same kind of wistful burnish those rusty cables have taken on, our own era, like the eras before it, tucked to sleep beneath the trees.

Would Louise Dickinson Rich recognize her woods if she came back today, fifty years after she last lived here? On the surface, yes. Her house, Forest Lodge ("From the outside it's not a bad little house—a low building with a porch and an ell, set on a knoll with a view up the river toward Pond-in-the-River") still sits above the boulders and rapids of a river she would have no trouble recognizing. Middle Dam is much the same, with its proud white caretaker's house set beside the lake, its garden with a tall fence around it to keep out deer and bears. Lakewood Camps is much the same. The Carry Road looks the same, though it's not old jalopies that bounce along it now, but mountain bikes and ATVs. The salmon and trout fishing is probably almost as good as it was then, and may very well soon be better, *if* the fish and game department stays the course with catch and release. The ridges, the views of distant mountains, the look and feel of the forest, the autumn foliage—on the surface, much remains just the same.

It's on the deeper level that things have changed here. The pulp operation of the '40s was a brutal enough process, but not terribly efficient, not when compared with modern industrial logging, with its clear-cuts and aerial spraying, its reliance on bulldozed roads, not free-flowing rivers. You have to wonder how long it will be before someone decides to play around with the dams; originally intended to provide heads of water for the log drives, they have served the Rangeleys well over the years, but in the future, who knows? Already plans have been floated to bury an enormous pipe along the Rapid River as part of a massive hydroelectric project. Second homes go up on Umbagog and the other Rangeleys as woodland is "harvested" and "liquidated." Powerful forces would like to make money out of the region, big money, and care not a whit for anything but making it pay.

What's changed the most, though, is the sense people bring to this place—the baggage we all carry now of knowing too much. Too much about what? About the threats that the last beautiful places in the world are subject to even in the best of circumstances, when their rareness and isolation alone are enough to make them targets. Fifty years ago this was a truly forgotten corner of the world; now, even on a casual visit like ours, you get the sense a garish spotlight is shining on the woods from the distance—not constantly, not even deliberately, but including it on each slow, inescapable sweep. Anyone who loves this kind of place, anyone who sought to make a life here, rather than feeling the sense of freedom that Rich felt, would inevitably feel threatened and somehow trapped. There are no malls here, of course. But in a mall kind of culture, the microbes are carried on the wind.

Gloomy thoughts? Yes, but I was trying to see things as Rich would, understand the differences of a half century measured by her own honest standards. She was quick to defend herself against charges of escapism, maybe too quick, since in a world gone mad escapism of her sort, a basic physical escape, is not necessarily such a bad thing. But this is much harder now, if not downright impossible. You duck your head, arrange your life quietly, and just because of this, the world seems to mark you out for extinction. "Happy the land that has no history," she wrote, quoting the old classic tag; perhaps, coming back now, she would find to her dismay that history has these last lonely places and the people who live there square in its sights.

For my own part, I had come to her woods to see if the land was worthy of being the stuff of boyhood dreams, and the answer to that is yes, even if some of the dream was now in the process of vanishing before my middle-aged and far-too-cynical eyes.

That night Tom and I walked over to the lodge before dinner, and, while we waited, browsed among the various announcements and articles tacked to the walls. One of these, from a newspaper only a few years old, was Louise Dickinson Richs obituary. She died in her eighties, having moved to the Maine coast after her years in the woods and written about her new life there in another round of books. Whoever had done the obituary had done some research, found men and women who had known her in the Rangeleys, including Al Parsons, the woman who was the caretaker at the fishing camp, her neighbor and friend. Mrs. Parsons allowed as to how Louise was a remarkable woman, though too prone, in her view, to swallow the stories the lumbermen told her as the gospel truth. As the obituary writer hinted at but didn't quite say, hers had been a remarkably successful career, measured in her own terms—a writer who had not only captured the spirit of a unique place, but had managed to color that place with her own spirit so the two were forever twined.

Like any good writer, Rich wrote her own epitaph without meaning to:

It seems to be that the thing you spend your life trying to build, if you would be whole, is not a bank account, or an unimpeachable social position, or success in any one of a thousand lines of endeavor; it seems to me that the only thing worth having is a certainty of yourself, a complete confidence in how you will act under any circumstance, a knowledge of yourself. People who have this knowledge are people who've kept their edges intact, people with what I can only call *core*. . . . Here in this country I found the circumstance and conditions that will make a woman of me, if anything will.

In the center of this is her elegy: Louise Dickinson Rich, taken on her own humble terms, was a writer with core.

After dinner, Tom wanted to pay homage to a local heroine of his own: Carrie Stevens, the famous fly tyer, inventor of the Gray Ghost, who had lived at Upper Dam on the north end of the Richardsons. He'd bought his tying supplies along; what better way to honor her than by tying up some of her famous patterns? Me, I strolled down to the lake, stared out across the water toward the slopes of Metallak Mountain, which still held enough red and gold in its foliage that it glowed like an eastern sunset mimicking in muted terms the one just finishing in the west.

Surely this hadn't changed—the lap of waves on the rocks, the early stars, Cassiopeia and the Dipper. I walked to the water's edge, picked up a stone, skimmed it toward what was left of the color, listened as the last faint skips faded into blackness . . . then turned and walked back to the soft yellow light of our cabin, where, silhouetted in the window, Tom bent his head down over his fly vise, getting us ready for morning.

Last Time Out

A certain Autumn light, a particular October color, can be seen on the upper reaches of the Connecticut River in its purest form—a light it's difficult to find exact words for, but that it might be possible to roughly surround. There's amber in the base of it, a watery brown-gold that widens from the streaks left in the river by a weakened and softened sun. Amber, the preservative kind, as in amber wax, so the light has an everlasting quality, making the rocks, the banks, the trees glow with the kind of burnish things take on in their final moments, fooling you into thinking they're eternal the moment before they disappear.

On a dry, crisp kind of day, there's still a humid quality to it all—you might be submerged in the shallows looking up. The gray element comes from the upper slopes of the surrounding hills, a stain leaking down from an ancient tin bucket. The tinge of copper involves the sumac, the last maple leaves just barely clinging to their branches. Blue comes in, too, but a distant, remote blue, up high in the sky on the other side of the amber, so it seems to box in and emphasize this self-contained, timeless quality all the more. It's the kind of light that might bring you intoxicating happiness or unbearable sadness, depending on your mood, your age, the circumstances of your life. It's a light, a color, that a week earlier in the season is camouflaged by the brilliant foliage, and only becomes predominate when the leaves have fallen; it is *past* the peak of foliage, and yet represents in secret, with hardly anyone noticing, the very height of the autumnal tint, the moment when the season crests and nothing will ever be quite so beautiful again.

A light that seems to carry with it a message, a simple and important lesson, yet one that comes in a code so complex you could spend your life trying to decipher it and never even find the first letter. Certainly, he'd been staring at it long enough as it was—the whole morning practically, time when he should have been fishing. Working upstream of the island he had picked up a few small trout, and had every expectation of catching something larger in the pool that turned itself around in a lazy semicircle, then widened out toward New Hampshire—and yet, seeing this color, feeling it, there was no other response possible but to wade over to the island, find a flat spot in the sandy marge, lie back with his head on a driftwood stump, and try to come to terms with what the light was telling him, even if it spoke in tongues.

The correct light of solitude. A phrase came to him after all—he always felt much better with things named. What the phrase actually meant he wasn't sure, but there was a nice lyric ring to it, and he had learned a long time ago that words with a compelling rhythm could sometimes form a working substitute for truth. He felt his own solitude with more than usual strength today; happy with friends, with children, he didn't go fishing alone as much as he had when he was younger, and something nostalgic in the sensation went down well with the amber light. His was by no means of a gloomy disposition, but it was undoubtedly a pensive one, and he had a tendency to see things with an October coloration even in July.

No one else was fishing this stretch of river. Driving north he hadn't seen any cars parked along the railroad stretch or the Trophy Pool, and even below the bridge to Colebrook, where there was almost always a spin fisherman, the river ran uninterrupted by anyones hips. The island itself was a popular enough spot, at least during summer. The river rolled past a beautifully dark bank of pine, then hooked left in some shallow, ferocious-looking rapids that divided themselves around the prow of a steep island, with deep holding pockets along both sides. With the water at its lowest level of the season, the island wore a collar of very fine sand, just wet and yielding enough to record the hops, skips, and plunges of raccoons, muskrats, and deer.

The maples on the crest of the island were already leafless; after a summer of green, an autumn of yellow, the branches seemed sharp and startling, studs without sheetrock, a scraggly grid. Toward the Vermont shore the bankside trees gave way in a narrow portal . . . there was an old town hall, a field behind it of stubbled corn, a rusty tractor, a shallow tributary stream . . . and it was through this gap that the amber color poured in at maximum strength.

But he was drifting now, so lost in looking he'd neglected his theme. The solitude part. Well, there was the solitude of the writer, which was no cliché. The solitude of the flyfisher wandering through rivers in search of trout. The solitude of a puny mortal face to face with one of nature's big deals. Here the Connecticut was the longest river in New England, some four hundred miles of beauty free for the taking, and yet on a weekday on the far side of foliage season how many people were doing what he was doing— sitting there, watching it, trying to figure out one of its tricks. To him the river wasn't something glanced at in the course of the day, not a flat, boring gray interval crossed on a concrete bridge or an opaque haze seen from an office tower, but something he must sit down and stare at and consider as the biggest, most important fact in the small corner of universe he found himself occupying.

And he felt he was getting somewhere now. Not arrived, not on the verge of anything major, but making progress, with the solitude stuff and the color both. Fishing with one of his partners he may have seen the color, but not recognized it; alone, the color merged with something inside him and so became even more noticeable, until the amber lightened toward yellow and grew even softer, more diffuse, and yet with a subtle grain (it could have been that of well-sanded maple) that connected everything to everything else. It was the light the Connecticut wore when no one was watching, and it was precisely this feat, to see a river clear, free momentarily of any human tint, that was what he had been after all along.

Closing day. It's never become the distinct ritual opening day is, and yet to many flyfishers it's a much more significant event. Opening day in northern New England is a cold and inevitably empty experience, redeemed hardly at all by the fact it's your first time out. Elsewhere in the country, fishing seasons have become so flexible, with so many special exceptions, that opening day has lost its position on the calendar as a distinctly April kind of event. Opening day is supposed to bring thoughts of rebirth and regeneration, a renewal of vows, a fresh start, but the fishing is so poor then, the climate so wretched, that the mood of nature contrasts too ironically with the mood of the fisherman for any kind of harmony to take place.

It's different in the autumn—in autumn, the flyfisher's mood and nature's mood are inevitably in sync, and even more so if the fisherman is starting to get up there in years, so any autumnal note in the river finds its immediate echo in an outlook that's taken on the same kind of gentle bittersweetness. A good year, a season full of fish, friends, and stories, and yet it's almost over now, with only one last chance to make the connections that have become so precious—and how sweet everything becomes when seen with this realization.

The only analogy is to a love affair. The beginning can be lost in obscurity, a matter of glances and idle chitchat, hardly remembered, and yet the ending—well, the ending can be remembered for a very long time. To enter upon one of these affairs each year, the kind that takes up a good deal of your being, occupies many of your waking hours, puzzles you, confuses you, fills you suddenly with delight . . . to enter upon one of these knowing in advance it will all end at sundown on October 15 with no extensions makes you pay very close attention as the days dwindle down, so those last weeks are often the sweetest, the saddest, the most intense.

Almost everyone feels something of this in autumn, or how else could it have become such a metaphor, life simultaneously at its richest and most heartbreaking. The flyfisher feels this intensely, and this particular fly fisherman, the one still sitting there on the sandbar staring out at the river, his thermos of tea sending up wispy, hookah-like clouds of steam past his head, felt it with an extra, very personal intensity and had for many years.

When he was a boy his parents owned a summer house on a lake in what was then still country. They would go there October weekends, rake leaves, take walks, go fishing, and then on Sunday it always came time to leave. The boy never accepted this—that they had to abandon what was already most precious in his life, the shining water, the fragrant woods, the sky with its wind-driven clouds, the ready supply of exhilaration. As they drove down the lake road there would come a final moment when the lake was still in sight; sitting in the back seat, craning his neck, he would steal one last glance at the full expanse of water shining golden under the afternoon sun—and often see there, in the one small wedge of blue still visible through the window, a boat with a fisherman just going out.

Never had he wanted anything so badly—the freedom to do just that, go fishing in October on a late Sunday afternoon when the rest of the world was going back to the dreary suburbs. So intense was this moment that it became one of those you hear about and seldom actually experience: a defining moment, an instant when everything he wanted in life became peculiarly concentrated and clear. A life where he could somehow marry nature, be free of the barriers that walled him off—a life, to put it in simplest terms, where autumn was perpetual and he could go fishing forever.

He was up against that right now—the moment it became clear every year that, fish as much as he wanted to, it would never be forever. This saddened him, but he had been saddened many times before, and so it had become part of the cycle—a pleasant sadness now, without the torment he knew as a boy. All those years of fishing. All those trout and bass. The stories, the friends, the adventures. Minor victories and shattering defeats. The rivers, ponds, streams. The books he had written about them. All flowed from that moment in the car, that brief glance of longing back over his shoulder as his future receded into the distance and disappeared.

But that was the good news—that he could still wish for anything as passionately at fifty as he had at fifteen. It came over him in a wave, between one moment and the next, so he jumped up from the sandbar (anyone watching would have thought he'd been stung) and waded back out into the current, high stepping through the rapids, false casting furiously even before he decided where to aim. It often happened like that in October. The introspection leading toward boyhood, hitting a memory there, rebounding back again, springing him into instant life.

Against the island the rapids ran choppy and deep, but over toward Vermont the river widened over a sandy bottom into a good-sized bay. Not a spot he would have tried ordinarily, but it was autumn, and almost any odd corner was worth a shot. The browns moved a lot in autumn—they were spawning, or soon would be, and the same was true of brookies. October 15 was a bit early for spawners (which is why it was closing day in the first place), but it had been a cold month, and the slow sandy backwater was definitely worth a few casts.

If his fly ever had a name he'd long since forgotten it—a foil-wrapped streamer with a long black shock of hackle guaranteed to make any spawner mad. He fished it near the seam that divided fast water from slow, still not convinced there could be anything in the backwater proper, and only after a half hour went by without a hit did he start casting closer to the bank. Hardly more than a foot of water covered the sandy bottom here, and it was littered with the kinds of things that regularly find their way to shallow backwaters: waterlogged branches, a scum of old leaves, broken corn stalks, a sunken tire. For one impressionistic moment it reminded him of those old Walt Kelly drawings of Okefenokee Swamp, and it was only the bright clattery rush of water to his left that reminded him he was fishing for trout and not largemouth bass.

Three casts, four casts. He took a few steps downstream, aimed for where the Vermont bank jutted out just far enough to add some vivacity to the sluggish flow. In the current, trout hit hard and fast, and so he wasn't quite prepared for a softer kind of take; the streamer was swimming sideways when something picked it up and carried it on back toward him, as if wanting to save him some stripping, help him out.

The lifting motion brought the trout's snout and gills clear of the surface. A *huge* fish—a brown trout judging by its color— and the split seconds that followed this realization were taken up by all the usual clichés. Surprise, shock, the frantic tightening—and then the sudden overwhelming disappointment as the trout, wearying instantly of the game, dropped the package and swam free.

A five- or six-pound trout by the look of it—easily the biggest fish he'd ever seen in the river. That his hunch had been correct didn't do much to assuage the pain; that the fish had simply let go, through no fault of his own, didn't help much either. He'd lost the kind of trout that comes only once a decade, the clock was reset again, and it would undoubtedly be another ten years before he had a similar chance.

What to do with this kind of disappointment? Check your barb, check your tippet, blow on the streamer for good luck, send it back out searching once again. For he had another hunch: if there was a big brown male cruising the shallows, then it was reasonable to expect an equally big female. And this is exactly what he found, sort of. A few casts later another trout took hold, and this time, rather than swimming straight for him like the first fish, it turned downstream and hooked itself firmly in the jaw.

A brook trout this time, a female about fourteen inches long, with a color not much different from the muted gray-green of the bankside shrubs. A few casts later he hooked another brookie in exactly the same spot, a male, about the same size, and yet a dozen times more fiery, with the kind of flaring redness you see in tanagers and maple leaves and hardly anything else, at least here in the north.

Between them, the three fish gave him a lot to think about. They were obviously fall spawners, ready to strike at whatever came along, so there was very little skill involved with their capture. If anything, he felt more than a little abashed. This sandy backwater formed the trout's bridal suite, the honeymoon cottage, the inner seraglio—the sanctuary an October 15 closing date was meant to ensure. Here, in all innocence (well, semi innocence; he'd cast there in the first place prospecting for spawners) he'd stumbled into it, and rather than continue any further he turned now and, all but blushing, tiptoed back toward the Vermont shore.

The trout had taught him something, no doubt about that. Here between the light and his memories he'd been indulging himself in a *temps perdu* kind of mood, seeing everything as mellow and finished, with a patina of regret that went down well with October. But this was entirely too anthropocentric of him, too narrow, because not ten yards from the island on which he lay daydreaming, rebirth and regeneration and renewals were all going on in full force, so it was spring there, and not just metaphorically—those fish weren't hanging around to give him a frisson of guilt, but planning their species' continuance, actively working at it, swimming around and around and around as if to spin the water to their genetic purpose.

It took a while before the heavy sense of intrusion left him and he began to see the backwater in a different light. That trout could still teach him things, shake up his humanity, point him where to look for the new lessons anyone his age needed if they were to continue growing was very good news indeed. The great cycle of life—there it was in action; he needed to keep a closer eye on it, factor it more into his autumnal mood, realize nature's clock didn't stop sweeping just because the small hand was brushing past the ten. He'd been looking at October 15 all wrong; if it was closing day for the fishermen, it was opening day for the trout. He'd imagined an October composed of wistful sadness; he'd neglected the October composed of exuberant lust.

Time, as a philosopher would put it, for lunch. He walked back through the empty cornfield to his car, folded his waders down around his waist, shook himself like a wet retriever, spread his anorak on the seat, got in. Colebrook in New Hampshire was the closest town, but small as it was it seemed too much like a metropolis, and so he drove the extra few miles to Bloomfield in Vermont, which hadn't been a metropolis or anything like it since the log drives at the turn of the century.

A pleasant enough drive. He had thought perhaps the amber color was entirely confined to the river, but he could see now it was much wider and more diffuse, and rather than holding over a definite channel it colored barns and farmhouses and meadows all the way up the first range of hills. He also realized he had seen this tint before, in the work of English watercolorists of late Victorian times, those who often set their landscapes in November, seeing as they did with the haze of knowing that the pastoral life, their subject, was coming to an end. It wasn't November yet, but no matter—the same mood was in the air.

A few miles north up this road a sign announced that you had crossed the 45th parallel—a sign that always seemed to him of a remarkable double significance. First, to think that northern Vermont was just as close to the equator as it was to the North Pole; second, that already, at 45 degrees one split second north, there was not only a definite northern flavor to everything, but a *high* northern flavor, at least late in fall. The Connecticut ran south, while its valley seemed like a gap up which everything poured toward the arctic, so the river alone escaped the latitude and its implications, but nothing else in the land could.

DeBannvilles sits on the highway just back from where the Nulhegan enters the Connecticut. It's typical of what country stores have become, here and elsewhere—outlets for lottery tickets, sugar, fat, salty things, and six-packs—and yet with enough chain-saw oil, fishing lures, and axes that it still retains something of the old kind of flavor. Attached on its ell is a small restaurant that serves burgers and fries; a greasy spoon, strictly speaking, but it has one feature that places it in the very forefront of American restaurants: no one cares when patrons come in wearing muddy waders.

Midafternoon now, he had the place to himself. The waitress doubled as short-order chef—an older woman, French, the *memere* kind that looked as if she would be good at a motherly kind of clucking. She grilled up his hamburger, brought it over with a tall glass of ice water, then stood there staring at the sunshine that streamed through the screen door.

"Slow day," the fisherman said.

And yes, she did cluck—and followed it up with a phrase in French that was so soft he couldn't catch it.

He took a swallow of the water. "Looks like winter is coming."

She faced the door. Oblivious to him now, griddled in sunshine by the screen, she ran her hand back through the gray of her hair, and said something so odd, so off the turn of their small talk, he ended up thinking about it the rest of the day

"Winter? Oh no," she said, again with the same softness. "It *mustn't* come, not this year."

"I'm sorry?" he said, obtuse.

She turned, blinked to see him, smiled at him like he was a little boy. "We have a very nice maple pie."

He thought about it on the way back to the river—how much force she put into the simple phrase, how odd the construction was with that prim, old-fashioned *mustn't*. May as well insist the earth stop spinning, poor woman. The sky remained soft in the east, swollen with autumnal haze, and yet to the west the clouds seemed hard and suspiciously silver, as if they had already been rolled and coated in December.

Time enough for one last pool. He parked at the airstrip, then pushed and swatted his way down through the briars until he was abreast the sandbar that formed one side of the pool. Up high on the New Hampshire bank the small brown cabin was all shuttered and closed; there was no sign of his friend who, in springtime, would stand there pointing out the trout.

He waded through the easy, slack water until he came to the tail of the pool, then veered out gradually into the heavier current, letting the force of it slide on past his hip. Halfway to the river's center he heard a sound that lay between a flute's airy whistle and a whirligig's frantic click, turned his head around and quickly ducked as two mergansers came racing downstream, their red heads extended as if each were trying to beat the other across an invisible line.

A good hatch of olives was in progress at the tail of the pool, just as he had hoped (olives being the most reliable insect emergence of the year). Little wispy things, olives, more like miniature stick figures than full-bodied bugs, dabbed together with the minimum amount of gluten; easy to imitate if you're comfortable fishing minutiae. The smaller the fly, the less there is for a trout to dislike—a theory he had always found to be true.

There were lessons here, just as there had been further upstream—the same lesson, only compressed into a tighter cycle. Fall, winter, spring, summer. The olives packed all these into the course of a single day, and this was the spring part, the miraculous regeneration going on in airy swarmings right before his eyes.

The trout rose like it was June, too—busy little sips, as if someone underwater was sticking up a thumb and stirring the surface in quick clockwise swirls. He aligned himself with the current, fussed out some line, then let the fly drop just to the inside of the closest trout. It came up for the midge and missed . . . the fisherman, in striking, skipped the fly backward . . . and a trout he hadn't seen darted out from behind a rock, curled his flank around the fly in that endearingly protective gesture trout can make, then plunged toward the bottom with the midge firmly centered in the small bull's-eye pocket of its upper lip.

And as the trout (a rainbow, a rare one so late in the fall) gambols and prances around the high maypole of the uplifted rod, perhaps it's time to discard the transparent pronoun that has just barely divided this flyfisherman from me. It's a rhetorical trick, after all—borrowing the kind of distance grammar can sometimes lend—but not a shabby one. I was trying to see things with particular clearness this last time out, and for a while this kind of transference can help.

But not now. Here at the end of a season and a book it's as good an occasion as any to explicitly link what at times have seemed separate entities: the writer and the fisherman. "Yield who will to their separation," Frost puts it, "my object in living is to unite my avocation and vocation as my two eyes make one in sight." And these two halves *are* here, or should be, as soon as I pull the knot tight with a few brief words.

Why would a novelist bother to write about fishing? Chekhov in *The Seagull* has Nina marvel that the famous Trigorin would spend so much time along the river. "And is it not wonderful that a famous writer, the darling of the public, mentioned daily in the papers, with his photograph in all the shop windows, his books translated into foreign languages, should spend his whole day fishing and be delighted because he has caught two chub." Yes, wonderful indeed, not just for celebrities, but for those humbler, more obscure writers (though I bet I could outfish the vain and cynical Trigorin any day of the week) who find almost as much solace in fishing moving waters as they do in trying to capture moving character, or pinning down, if even for a moment, a secret or two about fate.

Fly fishing for me, as for most everyone who does it, is a welcome break from the daily grind. A baker, a master, someone who loves his craft, still knows moments when the hot oven, the demands of his customers, the very texture of flour and salt become unbearable irritants against his overworked nerves; he finds, in fleeing to the river, relief in facing nothing more vexatious than the vagaries of trout. So, too, with the writer of fiction. After a while he's had enough with words, enough with plot, enough with the long hours sitting bewitched, bothered, and bewildered at his desk, and it becomes of the utmost importance to concentrate on another matter entirely. Fly fishing, in this respect, is my booze, my womanizing—my strong avocational defense of my weak vocational flank. And it s exactly this transference that accounts for the intensity with which I pursue my sport; to balance the prolonged kind of concentration writing demands, you have to place something of comparable demand on the opposite side of the scale. Tolstoy pursued peasant girls, Nabokov chased butterflies—a writer's passion, off duty, can be an odd and terrible thing.

An understandable enough motive, fishing to get away from it all, known not only by writers and pastry chefs but garage mechanics and insurance executives, history teachers and nurses.

But what gives it an added twist is that in my case when I'm out on the river I'm not only a novelist at leisure, but an essayist who sometimes writes about fly fishing, and this brings a portion of my vocation with me, so often I'm looking as hard for the right words on a river as I am back at home.

I've always thought the reasons for this are fairly straightforward, so much so that perhaps I've never bothered to spell them out. I write about fly fishing because I enjoy writing about delight; because in this day and age, when the worth of a novelist is still measured by how well he or she catches our despair, a fiction writer is not often called upon to write about simple happiness, and I'm determined to seize the chance when it comes. I enjoy writing lyrically, the old way, where the rhythm of words seeks to capture the rhythm of what they describe, and rivers lend themselves perfectly to this kind of treatment. I enjoy writing, not specifically of nature (for I find my eyes are too large and greedy to do this with any patience) but the stage nature performs on—of landscape, moving water, weather, sky, hills, and terrain.

And it's an odd thing. To the rest of the world writing fiction and writing about fishing seem totally opposite endeavors. "You write about *fishing*?" someone will say, in praising a collection of short stories. "You write *novels*?" someone will say, in praising your fishing essays. After a while you come to anticipate the little sneer that decorates the question mark, the upturned eyebrow, the slow confused shake of the head, as the person pigeonholes you as, in the first case, a redneck hick, or, in the second, a highfalutin intellectual.

Yes, I do both, find the rivers I fish in fact merge with the rivers I fish in imagination; watery metaphors are all-inclusive—they flow back around on themselves and merge.

For when you think about it, writing fiction and fly fishing for trout have much in common. Both are difficult (done right), both require long apprenticeships, both involve much patience, the capacity to withstand disappointment and failure, a healthy dose of skepticism, a certain daring, a sense of being part of a long and continuous tradition. Both, most of all, are honest and sincere attempts to come to terms with the world, make sense of it, if only for the length of a paragraph or one heartbreakingly golden yet all too perishable afternoon.

This is my third book on fly fishing—I don't think there will be a fourth. What they make up, taken together, is a record of three fishing seasons over the course of fifteen years, or rather *one* season in the life of man—a long one, extending from late youth to late middle age, the vital years of a person's prime. Together, they form a history of passionate involvement, an autobiography of small delights, and it seems to me in finishing this third book that I've gone as far with this theme as I should.

This realization has something to do with the autumnal mood I tried so hard to re-create earlier, the light that, as I fished those olives, remained so pronounced. As a man nears fifty he can become too conscious of that light. Everything takes on a burnish, a retrospective glow, and it becomes harder to find that vernal kind of brightness that makes you want to throw your hands up and shout in sheer delight. Your eyes begin noticing how the pines all seem to be dying from roadside salt or acid rain; you see the houses going up too close to the river, the wanton disregard for all you hold dear; the fishing doesn't seem quite so good anymore; rapids you would have pushed aside in disdain only a few years ago now seem dangerous; the river, in little ways, seems out to get you. If you're lucky, there's still enough boy in you to bull past this sunset kind of vision, but it takes effort now; it's not something your genes do instinctively on their own.

October 15 is an appropriate date against which to cease and desist, not only to protect the river and its young, but to protect the youthful vision these books have tried to reflect. Yes, maybe someday it will be good to write of late season in a flyfishers life, link it naturally to what's come before, but somehow I don't think so—what I have to say about rivers is largely finished. I say this in full and guilty consciousness of all those subjects I've never had time to write about at length. Swallows, for instance, the flyfishers bird. Smallmouth versus rainbow, which fights harder. How wonderful food tastes when eaten beside moving water—the delights of a fishing lunch. Casting for gulpers in our local pond. My heretical theories on rods and tackle. My first striper. Which fishing writers have meant the most to me and why. Fishing with worms. All these and more I could have some fun with, and yet that October 15 date looms in finality and I realize there's no time.

This brings it back to what any flyfisher feels as the season runs down. So many stories yet to tell! And so many places left to fish! I'd like to go back to the Yellowstone again, early in the season when you can expect a good cutthroat on every cast. I'd like to fish the coastal rivers of British Columbia and then continue on up to Alaska, preferably on float trips, so the fishing is right there every moment of a long northern day. Explore alpine lakes up and down the Rockies. The smallmouth waters of Quetico-Superior, a canoe trip with my family. A week or two on the classic English chalkstreams, especially the Kennet, since it's along its banks where my parents first met each other in World War II. I'd like to go to Argentina and Chile, dust off my high school Spanish, catch trout under volcanoes. And Labrador, since I'm being ambitious—those landlocked salmon and brook trout rivers of the true north. Given time, I'd like to return to the lochs of the Scottish highlands, with my kids this time, show them that high lonely country that speaks to something in my imagination in an intense way no other landscape can match.

Thus, my wish list. Probably most of these places will always remain there, rivers to daydream about and keep alive in the wanting, even if my bank account, my health, or the vicissitudes of fate keep me from ever visiting them in person. There are places close to home I would like to fish, too. In Vermont, I'd like to think I could return someday to a revitalized Battenkill, or a Waits that was treated as the treasure it once was and could be again. In Massachusetts are those stripers that run off the Merrimack—why have I waited so long to find out what *that's* all about? In Maine, I'd like to visit more of the old-time fishing camps, get a better sense of the vast northern forest. And, for that matter, there are mountain ponds and upland streams right here in the hills that surround my home I've always wondered about but not yet explored.

But most of all, forming the dependable foundation on which these fancies soar, I would like to think I have many seasons left on my beloved Connecticut, running purer now than it has in a hundred years. Days like this one, for instance, when its beauty manifests itself in a guise I've never seen before, so it could be an entirely new river superimposed over my familiar one, needing this trick of light for me to see it clear. Watching it, very conscious of every surge and ripple, I caught four more trout at the tail of the pool, and the fish were still rising when I decided it was time to quit. The amber remained as pronounced as it had been in the morning, and I wanted to leave while it was still in place, take away with me the illusion that the river would run beneath the color all winter, preserved and protected by that pure crystal palace of autumnal light.

Facing a long drive home, tired, saddened, but no more than I should be, I reeled in my line, carefully distributing it with my finger so it lay even on the spool, knowing it would rest undisturbed there until spring. I was reaching to take down my rod when a fish rose ten yards in front of me—a good one judging by the thick way the ring crested, much better than the little brookies I'd been playing with downstream. I looked at my watch, then up at the sun, which was still ten degrees above the horizon, stalled in the wide bar of its own yellow warmth . . . took light and fish and mileage into consideration, decided it really was time to quit, started toward the bank, then quickly turned and shoved myself back into the current for one last cast.

One last cast! That's the fly you should use if you want to catch the spirit of this sport—the fly called hope. It filled me now, just as completely, with just as much exhilaration, as if the river had lifted me up on its back and transformed me into the same surging mix of hydrogen and oxygen it consisted of itself. I felt a gratitude so strong it all but made me sob . . . that so deep in autumn I could still feel the gift of such joyous exuberance . . . and at the same time a whole list of demands raced through my wanting—not the greedy kind, but the kind that are part vow, part prayer, part command, part supplication, and together make up a man's undiminished, unquenchable appetite for life.

One more time into the current, the force of it on my waist. Once more the feel of spray kicking up off my waders, flying in my face, making me laugh. Once more the magic bend and flex of a well-designed rod. One more sunset, slow and soft there in the west. Once more that precious hour before the light disappears. One more rise, slow and dimpled. One rainbow more, leaping wildly. One brown more, pensively gorgeous. One brookie more, skittering about. One hatch more one strike more one surprise more one victory more and below and through and around all these the most vital thing enduring thing now and yesterday and tomorrow and forever one river more one river more one river more *one river more.*